Acclaim for Richard Pipes*'s* Property and Freedom

"A meditation on the close connection between property rights and the development of law and individual liberty throughout the history of civilization. . . . Pipes is massively erudite."
—*The New York Times*

"[Pipes] has made a valuable contribution to our understanding of the relationship between property rights and other rights . . . one glimmer of hope."
—*The Washington Times*

"A surprising and splendid book . . . so packed with historical meat and potatoes that it will be used as a sourcebook for years to come."
—*National Review*

"*Property and Freedom* is a work of vast scholarship and daunting erudition."
—*The Boston Globe*

"A most stimulating and original book, shedding light wherever the author ventures."
—*The American Spectator*

"A powerfully argued coda to the Cold War triumph of capitalism."
—*Publishers Weekly*

Richard Pipes
Property and Freedom

Richard Pipes, Baird Research Professor of History at Harvard University, is the author of numerous books and essays, including *A Concise History of the Russian Revolution* (1995) and *Russia Under the Bolshevik Regime* (1994). In 1981–82 he served as President Reagan's National Security Council adviser on Soviet and East European affairs. He has twice received a Guggenheim Fellowship. He lives in Cambridge, Massachusetts and Chesham, New Hampshire.

ALSO BY RICHARD PIPES

The Formation of the Soviet Union: Communism and Nationalism 1917–23 (1964)

Struve: Liberal on the Left, 1870–1905 (1970)

Russia Under the Old Regime (1974)

Struve: Liberal on the Right, 1905–1944 (1980)

Survival Is Not Enough (1984)

Russia Observed (1989)

The Russian Revolution (1990)

Communism: The Vanished Specter (1994)

Russia Under the Bolshevik Regime (1994)

A Concise History of the Russian Revolution (1995)

Three Whys of the Russian Revolution (1995)

The Unknown Lenin (1996)

PROPERTY and FREEDOM

PROPERTY and FREEDOM

Richard Pipes

VINTAGE BOOKS
A Division of Random House, Inc.
New York

FIRST VINTAGE BOOKS EDITION, JUNE 2000

Published in the United States by Vintage Books, a division of Random House, Inc., New York, and simultaneously in Canada by Random House of Canada Limited, Toronto. Originally published in hardcover in the United States by Alfred A. Knopf, a division of Random House, Inc., New York, in 1999.

Grateful acknowledgment is made to the following for permission to reprint previously published material:
American Economic Association: Excerpt from an article by Harold Demsetz (*The American Economic Review*, Vol. LVII, No. 2, May 1967, pp. 354–356). Reprinted by permission of the American Economic Association.
The Yale Law Journal Company and *Fred B. Rothman & Company*: Excerpt from "The New Property" by Charles A. Reich (*The Yale Law Journal*, Vol. 73, pp. 773–787). Reprinted by permission of
The Yale Law Journal Company and Fred B. Rothman & Company.

The Library of Congress has cataloged the Knopf edition as follows:
Pipes, Richard.
Property and freedom / Richard Pipes. —1st ed.
p. cm.
Includes bibliographical references and index.
1. Right of property—History. 2. Property—History.
3. Liberty—History. I. Title.
JC605.P56 1999
323.4'6—dc21 98-41728 CIP

Vintage ISBN: 0-375-70447-7

Author photograph © Tania D'Avignon
Book design by Anthea Lingeman

www.vintagebooks.com

Printed in the United States of America
10 9 8 7

I dedicate this book to my wife, Irene, who for over fifty years has created for me ideal conditions to pursue scholarship

CONTENTS

ACKNOWLEDGMENTS

I should like to express my appreciation to several colleagues who have taken the time to read parts of this book and offered me critical advice: Thomas Bisson (Harvard), Richard Epstein (Chicago), Nathan Glazer and Mark Kishlansky (Harvard), and Douglass North (Washington University). They bear no responsibility for any mistakes that may have crept into this book.

My editor at Knopf, Ashbel Green, has, as always, proved a most helpful counselor.

The John M. Olin Foundation has generously subsidized this work. I owe it and its executive director, James Piereson, a great debt of gratitude.

I would also like to express appreciation to the Mark DeWolfe Howe Fund of the Harvard Law School for supporting the editorial work on this book.

INTRODUCTION

> There is nothing which so generally strikes the imagination, and engages the affections of mankind, as the right of property. . . .
>
> —Blackstone, *Commentaries*[1]

> Property never has been abolished and never will be abolished. It is simply a question of who has it. And the fairest system ever devised is one by which all, rather than none, [are] property owners.
>
> —A. N. Wilson[2]

The subject of this book differs from that of every book I have ever written, all of which (apart from a college textbook on modern Europe) have dealt with Russia, past and present. And yet it grows naturally out of my previous work. From the time I interested myself seriously in Russia, I became aware that one of the fundamental differences between her history and that of the other European countries lay in the weak development of property. Western historians (unlike Western philosophers and political theorists) take property for granted: they rarely pay it much attention, despite its intimate link with every aspect of Western life and its immense role in the history of Western thought:

> [I]f you look for the word *property* in the index of books dealing with the evolution of American attitudes you will tend to find nothing there. Run your eyes down the list: *progress, prohibition* . . ., then a gap where you might expect to see *property*. The series passes straight on to, say, *prostitution*.[3]

In the case of Russia, it is not the presence but the absence of property that is taken for granted. One of the major themes of Western political theory during the past 2,500 years has been controversy over the benefits and drawbacks of private ownership; in Russian intellectual history, this topic is hardly mentioned because of the virtual unanimity that it is an unmitigated evil.

The word "property" evokes in our minds the idea of physical objects: real estate, bank accounts, stocks and bonds. But in fact, it has a much broader meaning, for increasingly in the modern world it has come to apply to incorporeal assets such as credit, patents, and copyrights. Furthermore, as we shall point out in due course, in Western thought during the seventeenth and eighteenth centuries it acquired a still more comprehensive meaning to include everything that one can claim as one's own, beginning with life and liberty. The whole complex of modern ideas connected with human rights has its source in such an extensive definition of property. This was noted two hundred years ago by James Madison:

> Property . . . in its particular application means "that domination which one man claims and exercises over the external things of the world, in exclusion of every other individual." In its larger and juster meaning, it embraces everything to which a man may attach a value and have a right; and *which leaves to everyone else a like advantage*. In the former sense, a man's land, or merchandise, or money is called his property. In the latter sense, a man has property in his opinions and the free communication of them. He has a property of peculiar value in his religious opinions, and in the profession and practice dictated by them. He has property very dear to him in the safety and liberty of his person. He has an equal property in the free use of his faculties and free choice of the objects on which to employ them. In a word, as a man is said to have a right to his property, he may be equally said to have a property in his rights.[4]

The idea occurred to me some forty years ago that property, in both the narrow and broad senses of the word, provides the key to the emergence of political and legal institutions that guarantee liberty. This idea served as the premise of the survey of Russia's political history which I published in 1974 under the title *Russia Under the Old Regime*. Here I argued that totalitarianism, which reached its consummation in the Soviet Union, had its roots in the "patrimonial" system of government that had prevailed through much of Russian history, a system which recognized no distinction between sovereignty and property, allowing the tsar to act as both the ruler and the owner of his realm.

The idea that liberty and property are connected is hardly new—it emerged in the seventeenth century and became commonplace in the eighteenth—but to the best of my knowledge no one has as yet attempted to demonstrate this connection on the basis of historical evidence. The literature on each of these subjects is immense: there are hundreds if not thousands of works on property and as many on liberty. They proceed, however, on separate tracks. Books on freedom concentrate on the evolution of the concept of freedom and the political institutions that guarantee it, all but ignoring its economic foundations. The typical economic treatise on the history of property will ignore its political and cultural aspects. Legal treatises on the subject, as a rule, ignore alike its philosophical, economic, and political dimensions. As a result, we lack an explanation, based on concrete historical material, of just how property gives rise to freedom and how its absence makes possible arbitrary authority.

It is this gap that I thought of filling. My starting hypothesis held that there is an intimate connection between public guarantees of ownership and individual liberty: that while property in some form is possible without liberty, the contrary is inconceivable.

To test this hypothesis, I began to survey the relationship between property and political systems since the dawn of recorded history. When I first ventured on this endeavor, I had no inkling how difficult it would turn out to be. I realized, of course, the immense variety of forms that ownership has assumed in various societies at different times, but I did not anticipate that so much that goes under this name finds no reflection in documents and that so much that theoretically is merely possessed, i.e., physically held, is in fact owned. Nor did I foresee the difficulties of relating property in its various guises to politics, particularly in non-Western countries where the sources remain unpublished and the secondary literature on the subject is virtually nonexistent. It soon became apparent, therefore, that such an enterprise exceeds the capacities of any one individual. To study the economics of ancient China and classical Greece, Mesopotamia and Mexico, medieval France and modern England, as they bore on the political evolution of each of these countries would require teams of historians. Rather than abandon the project as unrealistic, I decided to write something more modest—an essay which would treat the subject selectively, sacrificing breadth for depth. I disclaim any pretense at systematic or comprehensive coverage, content to demonstrate through a few historical examples the relationship between economic and political power.

The first two chapters deal with the historical evolution of both the idea and the institution of property. The middle part of this book—Chapters 3 and 4—analyzes the relationship between property relationships and politics in England and Russia, two extreme cases which convey forcefully the point I am trying to make. The concluding chapter concentrates on the twentieth century, with emphasis on the United States, and stresses the threats to liberty implicit in the welfare state's striving for social and economic equality.

Even in its more limited scope, this book covers so much outside the field of my academic specialty that I offer it with some trepidation. With the exception of the chapter on Russia and parts of the chapter on the history of the idea of property, my information comes mainly from secondary sources, which often disagree among themselves. Undoubtedly, therefore, experts will find cause to criticize me on this or that fact or one or another interpretation. I trust, however, that they will bear in mind that if the purpose of history is understanding, the historian must once in a while venture outside his field of expertise into fields of which his knowledge is derivative. In defense of this proposition, I can cite the authority of Jacob Burckhardt, who wrote that dilettantism

> owes its bad reputation to the arts, where, of course, one is either nothing or a master who devotes his entire life to them, because the arts demand perfection.
>
> In learning, by contrast, one can attain mastery only of a limited field, namely as a specialist, and this mastery one should attain. But if one does not wish to forfeit the ability to form a general overview—indeed, to have respect for such an overview—then one should be a dilettante in as many fields as possible—at any rate, privately—in order to enhance one's own knowledge and enrichment of diverse historical viewpoints. Otherwise one remains an ignoramus in all that lies beyond one's specialty, and, under the circumstances, on the whole, a barbarous fellow.[5]

Richard Pipes

Cambridge, Massachusetts
October 1998

DEFINITIONS

Possession refers to the physical control of assets, material or incorporeal, without formal title to them: it is ownership *de facto,* not *de jure*. It is customarily justified by prolonged use and/or inheritance from one's progenitors, what in English law is called "prescription," and asserted by physical force and tacit community support. Although objects possessed cannot be disposed of by sale, in practice they almost always entitle the possessor to bequeath it to his offspring and in this manner tend to turn into property. Through most of history and in many parts of the world today, assets are held in this form.

Property refers to the right of the owner or owners, formally acknowledged by public authority, both to exploit assets to the exclusion of everyone else and to dispose of them by sale or otherwise. "What distinguishes property from mere momentary possession is that property is a claim that will be enforced by society or the state, by customs or convention or law."[6] In practice, it postulates public authority of some kind. The concept originated in ancient Rome, whose jurists designated what we understand as "property" by the term *dominium.**

Property is of two kinds: productive, i.e., the kind that can create more property (e.g., land, capital), and personal, which serves exclusively for use (e.g., housing, clothing, weapons, jewelry). Such is the customary usage. But more broadly, in the terminology of Western theory since the late Middle Ages, "property" has come to encompass everything that properly belongs to a person (*suum* in Latin), including his life and liberty. It is this broad definition of property or "propriety," as it came to be known in seventeenth-century England and hence was transplanted to colonial America, that provides the philosophical link between ownership and freedom.

Under the influence of Marx, some modern theorists prefer to define "property" (in the narrow, conventional sense) not as the right over

*Etymologically, "property" derives from the Latin *proprius,* meaning particular to, or appropriate to, an individual person. From it Byzantine jurisprudence evolved the term *proprietas,* or "ownership."

"things" but as "relations among persons in respect to things."[7] "Property right is not to be identified with the fact of physical possession. . . . property right is a relation not between an owner and a thing, but between the owner and other individuals in reference to things."[8] But such a definition is hardly satisfactory, inasmuch as "property" involves a great deal more than the right over "things."

Property can be held in two ways: (1) communally, and (2) privately. Title to communal property is vested jointly in all its members, but the community does not dispose of it; neither does it have any collective rights to it (e.g., a modern cooperative apartment). Private property belongs to an individual, a kinship group, or an association of individuals. "Communist property" is a contradiction in terms, inasmuch as "property" belongs to the realm of private law, whereas under communism the state, a public institution, is the exclusive owner of all productive assets in its capacity as sovereign authority.

In everyday usage, the reader should be warned, it is very difficult to maintain the legal distinction between possession and property. In the body of the book, therefore, except where specifically noted, "possession" and "property" may be used interchangeably.

The term *freedom* as used in this study covers four subjects: (1) *political freedom,* i.e., the right of the individual to participate in the choice of officials of the government under which he lives; (2) *legal freedom,* i.e., the right in relations with other individuals and the state to be judged by third parties in accord with the law; (3) *economic freedom,* i.e., the right freely to use and dispose of one's assets; and (4) *personal rights,* i.e., the claim of the individual to his life and liberty and the license to do whatever he wishes as long as he does not infringe on the liberties and rights of others: in other words, absence of coercion. Freedom and personal rights are not necessarily included in political democracy: "there is no necessary connection between individual liberty and democratic rule."[9] Thus the citizens of ancient Athens enjoyed political but not civil rights, whereas privileged subjects of some enlightened despots had civil but not political rights.

Freedom does *not* include the so-called "right" to public security and support (such as implied in the slogan phrases "freedom from want" and "the right to housing") which infringe on the rights of others since it is they who have to pay for them. Such "rights" are at best a moral claim, and at worst, if enforced by public authority, an unearned privilege.

PROPERTY
and FREEDOM

1

THE IDEA OF PROPERTY

Property can be studied from two distinct points of view: as a concept and as an institution. The two approaches yield very different results. Throughout the history of thought, property has enjoyed a mixed reputation, being identified sometimes with prosperity and freedom, sometimes with moral corruption, social injustice, and war. Utopian fantasies, as a rule, place the abolition of the distinction between "mine" and "thine" at the center of their vision. Even many thinkers favoring property view it as, at best, an unavoidable evil. The history of all societies, on the other hand, from the most primitive to the most advanced, reveals the universality of property claims and the failure of every attempt to found a propertyless community, whether voluntarily or by force. In this instance, therefore, there is an unusually wide disparity between what mankind thinks it wants and what, judging by its actions, it really prefers. Lewis Mumford explained this disparity by suggesting that man lives in two worlds—the world within and the world without, the first being the realm of ideas, wishes, and images, the latter that of harsh, inescapable reality. "If the physical environment is the earth, the world of ideas corresponds to the heavens."[1]

We shall, accordingly, divide our discussion into two parts. The present chapter will deal with the attitudes toward property of Western philosophers, theologians, and political theorists.* The chapter that follows will be devoted to the institution of property as revealed by history, psychology, anthropology, and sociobiology. The distinction, of course, is artificial and is introduced only for the sake of clarity of exposition; in actuality, ideas and events have constantly interacted. As we shall point out, every change in attitude toward property can be explained by political or economic developments.

Discussions of property from the time of Plato and Aristotle to the present have revolved around four principal themes: its relation to politics, ethics, economics, and psychology.

1. The political argument in favor of property holds that (unless distributed in a grossly unfair manner) it promotes stability and constrains the power of government. Against property it is claimed that the inequality which necessarily accompanies it generates social unrest.

2. From the moral point of view, it is said that property is legitimate because everyone is entitled to the fruits of his labor. To which critics respond that many owners exert no effort to acquire what they own and that the same logic requires everyone to have an equal opportunity to acquire property.

3. The economic line of reasoning for property holds that it is the most efficient means of producing wealth, whereas opponents hold that economic activity driven by the pursuit of private gain leads to wasteful competition.

4. The psychological defense of property maintains that it enhances the individual's sense of identity and self-esteem. Others assert that it corrupts the personality by infecting it with greed.

These four approaches fairly exhaust the range of arguments for and against property articulated during the past three thousand years. At its most fundamental, the controversy pits the moral approach against the pragmatic.[2]

*I limit my discussion to the West in part because the existing secondary literature confines itself almost exclusively to this region of the world and in part because I do not feel competent to deal with other civilizations. The subject, however, has a history in Chinese thought, and in other non-European civilizations: see Arnold Künzli, *Mein und Dein: Zur Idee der Eigentumsfeindschaft* (Köln,1986), 43–60. Its reflection mainly in classical Western but also Iranian, Babylonian, and Indian as well as Chinese mythology is traced in Bodo Gatz, *Weltalter, goldene Zeit und sinnverwandte Vorstellungen* (Hildesheim, 1967). On property in contemporary Islamic legal thought see Sohrab Behdad in *Review of Social Economy* 47, No. 2 (1989), 185–211. The most comprehensive treatment of Western attitudes is Richard Schlatter's *Private Property: The History of an Idea* (New Brunswick, N.J.,1951). Also instructive is Alexander Gray's *The Socialist Tradition: From Moses to Lenin* (London etc., 1947), which traces the attitude to property of socialist writers and their precursors.

I. Classical antiquity

The ethical treatment of property, which has dominated the discussion until modern times, has evolved against the background of a pervasive belief in the existence of a "Golden Age." In its most familiar guise, the Golden Age is the Jewish, Christian, and Islamic Paradise (Garden of Eden), but in one form or another it is common to all civilizations. The outstanding quality of this mythical past is the absence of private ownership: in the Golden Age everything is said to have been held in common and the words "mine" and "thine" were unknown. Since, as we shall show in the chapter that follows, no society has ever existed without some kind of property, the vision of an ideal propertyless world must be grounded not in collective memory but in collective longing. It is inspired by the belief that inequalities of status and wealth are "unnatural." They have to be man-made, not God-made: for are not all beings born equal and, upon death, do they not turn alike to dust?

The earliest known depiction of the Golden Age occurs in a work by Hesiod, a contemporary of Homer, called *Works and Days*. The Greek poet of the early seventh century B.C.E.* speaks of four "metallic" ages of mankind—the Golden, Silver, Bronze, and Iron, each latter age marked by progressive moral decline. In the earliest, Golden age, when the world was ruled by the Titan Cronus, all goods were available in abundance and peace prevailed. But in his own time, which he labeled the Age of Iron, Hesiod saw violence and the "shameful lust for gain" prevail over justice.[3] This image of the blissful infancy of humanity entered the mainstream of Greek and Roman literature. As we shall see, the idea of the Golden Age exerted great influence on European thought of the Renaissance period, stimulating the voyages of discovery and influencing how the discoveries were perceived.

The earliest theoretical assault on property is to be found in Plato's *Republic,* a work which has exerted influence on all subsequent utopias. The *Republic* and its successor, the *Laws,* were not the first works to seek ways of eliminating property as the cause of social strife, but the writings of Plato's predecessors have not survived and are known only from hearsay. Plato wrote at a time when Greece was in turmoil from social conflicts within the city-states and wars among them. He is said to have been inspired by the example of Sparta, a highly centralized

*B.C.E. = Before the Common Era; C.E. = Common Era.

state in which the government prevented the concentration of wealth in the hands of the elite, and which in the drawn-out Peloponnesian war ultimately defeated and subjugated Athens. Sparta's triumph was widely attributed to her constitution, said to have been drawn up by Lycurgus, her legendary founder, which outlawed trade and industry in order to free the citizens for war. Spartans were forbidden to own not only material goods but even their wives and children: wives they were expected to share with other men, likely to breed healthier and stronger offspring, and children they had to turn over to the state at the age of seven for martial training. Plutarch, who summarized the views of Greek historians on the subject, wrote that Lycurgus had ordered the notables of Sparta to renounce their properties. He also commanded all gold and silver to be surrendered and replaced with iron coinage. As a result, luxury, theft, bribery, and lawsuits disappeared. Disparities of wealth and poverty gave way to equality. An egalitarian society devoted entirely to the needs of the state must have seemed highly attractive to an Athenian who witnessed his own city-state destroyed by ambition and greed. As we shall note in the following chapter, Athens had a highly developed system of private property, which explains the attention paid to it by her philosophers.

Plato outlined his utopian communism through the mouth of Socrates in Books 5–7 of the *Republic*. His objective was to devise a social order in which the ruling elite would not be driven by selfishness but dedicate itself wholly to the public good. To this end, it was divested of belongings. Referring to contemporary political upheavals, Socrates says:

> Such differences commonly originate in a disagreement about the use of the terms "mine" and "not mine," "his" and "not his." . . And is not that the best-ordered State in which the greatest number of persons apply the terms "mine" and "not mine" in the same way to the same thing?[4]

The ideal Platonic state consisted of two castes: the rulers, called "Guardians," made up of the oldest and wisest members of the community, and the rest. The Guardians, who ran the state, acquired their status after passing rigorous tests. They owned no property—neither houses nor land—so that they would not "tear the city in pieces by differing about 'mine' and 'not mine.' "[5] Plato saw property and virtue as incompatible: "For are not money and virtue like the two scales of a balance:

as one goes up the other goes down?"[6] The Guardians lived communally, like the Spartans, holding wives and children in common; their basic material needs were provided for by the commoners, whose status Plato left vague, but who seem to have been allowed to have families and to own property. As a consequence, rivalries within the ruling class ceased: there was no more cause for violence, quarrels, or flattery. This ideal of a selfless caste of the select, totally devoted to the state, would be realized (in theory, at any rate) 2,500 years later in the Communist and Nazi parties.

In the *Laws,* a later work, Plato attempted to design a state that would conform more closely to reality, and hence he abandoned the insistence on abolishing the family and having the state assume responsibility for the education of children. But his earlier egalitarian utopianism survived. He now allowed private property but wanted the state to ensure that it did not lead to extremes of wealth and poverty, especially in the distribution of land. The ideal of a propertyless world remained:

> The first and highest form of the State and of the government and of the law is that in which there prevails most widely the ancient saying, that "Friends have all things in common." Whether there is anywhere now, or will ever be, this communion of women and children and of property, in which the private and individual is altogether banished from life, and things which are by nature private, such as eyes and ears and hands, have become common, and in some way see and hear and act in common, and all men express praise and blame and feel joy and sorrow on the same occasions, and whatever laws there are unite the city to the utmost—whether this is possible or not, I say that no man, acting upon any other principle, will ever constitute a state which will be truer or better or more exalted in virtue.[7]

Plato's vision of the ideal society was challenged by Aristotle in the *Politics.* Aristotle shared his teacher's belief that extreme inequalities in the distribution of wealth lead to social strife.[8] But he regarded the institution of property as indestructible and ultimately a positive force. Plato, in Aristotle's judgment, confused and treated as one the diverse elements that make up the body politic—household, community (village), and state. His error lay in treating the state as if it were a household and hence assigning it control of wealth.[9] Property, in fact, is an attribute of the household and not of the community or the state: "states require property, but property . . . is no part of a state."[10]

Aristotle based his opposition to common ownership not only on logical but also, and principally, on utilitarian grounds. It is impractical because no one takes proper care of objects that are not his: "How immeasurably greater is the pleasure, when a man feels a thing to be his own; for surely the love of self is a feeling implanted by nature. . . ."[11] Gratification of self-love is thus the basis of a good society. Aristotle rejects Plato's argument that common ownership does away with social discord, arguing that, on the contrary, people who hold things in common tend to quarrel more than those who own them personally. He sees the cause of social discord not in the striving for property but in human nature—"it is not possessions but the desires of mankind which require to be equalized"[12]—from which it follows that dissension is best eliminated by enlightenment rather than the abolition of private ownership. Furthermore, Aristotle argues, possessions enable men to rise to a higher ethical level by giving them the opportunity to be generous: "liberality consists in the use which is made of property"[13]—an argument which would greatly appeal to Christian theologians of the Middle Ages. Aristotle's preferred regime was one founded on a middle class, with an equitable distribution of assets.[14]

The differences between the two Athenian philosophers foreshadow the course of thought on the subject for the next 2,500 years: the continuing controversy between ethical idealism and utilitarian realism. Throughout the history of Western thought, writers on property will align themselves, broadly speaking, either with Plato or with Aristotle, stressing either the potential benefits of its abolition or the tangible rewards of its acceptance.

In the fourth century B.C.E., after the death of Plato and Aristotle, the discussion of property was raised to a higher, more abstract level through the introduction of the Stoic principle of Natural Law. Stoicism's contribution to the shaping of the Western intellectual tradition is probably second only to that of Jewish monotheism. If monotheism advanced the revolutionary concept of an all-powerful and all-pervasive but non-material God ruling the universe, the theory of Natural Law posited that God's universe was rational and capable of being grasped by human intelligence. Although, like so much else, the concept of the Law of Nature was already incipient in Aristotle, it matured only after he had passed from the scene, first in Greece under Macedonian rule and then in Rome.

Plato and Aristotle thought exclusively in terms of city-states, small communities of citizens of the same ethnic origin, religion, and culture. Politics was for them largely a matter of custom, not of laws—hence for Plato the ideal society had no statutes. (According to Plutarch, Lycurgus would not permit the rules he had laid down for Sparta to be committed to writing.) But the problem of laws arose in an acute form in the fourth century when Philip of Macedon and his son, Alexander the Great, liquidated the *polis* in favor first of the national state and then of the multinational empire. The Macedonian Empire at its height extended from the Aegean Sea to the Indus River and the Arabian peninsula. Subject to Macedonian authority, in addition to the Greeks, were Armenians, Bactrians, Jews, Egyptians, Indians, Parthians, Sogdians, and a host of other nationalities speaking different languages and professing different faiths. And applying different laws. These legal disparities the Macedonian statesmen had somehow to reconcile for the sake of imperial unity and administrative efficiency. But their existence also raised a fundamental philosophical question: were there as many conceptions of justice as there were nations—in other words, was there no universal standard of right and wrong—or were the diverse legal canons and procedures merely adaptations of the same universal law to local conditions?

The answer was supplied by the Stoic school, which emerged concurrently with the Macedonian Empire. Its central notion of a rational world order was already incipient in early Greek science, which differentiated between the infinite variety of discrete natural phenomena and the underlying unity of the laws governing Nature. This idea was in time applied to human affairs. It can be discerned in casual passages of Aristotle's *Nicomachean Ethics* which speak of justice as existing in two forms: "legal" (conventional) and "natural."[15] The former finds expression in positive law, adapted to the particular needs of a given society, and hence differing from nation to nation, whereas the latter is uniform for all mankind.

Aristotle had no need to develop this idea further, since he dealt with homogeneous societies. This was done by Zeno, the founder of the Stoic school: "The fundamental principle of the Stoic ethics and politics is the existence of a universal and world-wide law, which is one with reason both in nature and in human nature. . . ."[16] Just as the physical world has its universal and eternal laws, so does humanity. The revolutionary element implicit in Stoic philosophy was the contention that the fundamental principles of the social order are not subject to change because they are embedded in the natural order. At the core of this order is the equality of men and women, freemen and slaves. Freedom consists of living according to the laws of nature.

During the three centuries that separated Aristotle from Cicero the idea of the Law of Nature gained wide acceptance in the Mediterranean world, although its apogee lay still far ahead, in sixteenth- and seventeenth-century Europe, where it would help jurists and political theorists emancipate their disciplines from theology. It has been said that since Plato and Aristotle no one has been able to write about private property without asking whether or not it is "natural."[17] Indeed, until the late eighteenth century, and in some respects until today, the discussion about property has revolved around the question whether it belongs to the "natural" or the "conventional" order of things. This issue lies at the heart of the dispute between the moral and pragmatic approaches: for if property is a matter of convention it can be done away with, but if it belongs to the realm of nature, it is an unalterable fact of life.

Stoic philosophy and the concept of Natural Law had greater influence in Rome than in Greece, its country of origin. The ancient Romans were not given to abstract speculation, and they neither debated the advantages and drawbacks of private ownership nor thought up imaginary ideal communities. But men who take pride in their pragmatism often follow trails cleared by idealists. Roman poets adopted the Greek notion of the Golden Age when all goods were held in common and which came to an end with the triumph of avarice and the resultant reign of injustice and strife. Virgil wrote of the Golden Age as a time when

> no tenants mastered holdings,
> Even to mark the land with private bounds
> Was wrong: men worked for the common store, and earth
> Herself, unbidden, yielded all more fully.[18]

Ovid portrayed the Iron Age as one in which

> The earth itself, which before had been, like air and sunshine,
> A treasure for all to share, was now crisscrossed with lines
> men measured and marked with boundary posts and fences.[19]

Seneca, the leading Stoic in Rome, who has been called "a millionaire with a guilty conscience," never tired of extolling poverty.* "He

*Künzli, *Mein und Dein*, 134. Although Stoicism exercised great influence on early Christianity, the Stoic philosophers belonged to the upper class, and unlike the early

who has made a fair compact with poverty is rich," he taught his friend Lucilius.[20]

> The social virtues had remained pure and inviolate before covetousness distracted society and introduced poverty, for men ceased to possess all things when they began to call anything their own. . . . How happy was the primitive age when the bounties of nature lay in common and were used promiscuously [indiscriminately]; nor had avarice and luxury disunited mortals and made them prey upon one another. They enjoyed all nature in common, which thus gave them secure possession of the public wealth. Why should I not think them the richest of all people, among whom there was not to be found one poor man?[21]

This praise of social equality in Stoicism made it a kind of religion and enabled it to exert influence on Christianity in its formative phase.

The main Roman contribution to the idea of property lay in the realm of law. Roman jurists were the first to formulate the concept of absolute private ownership, which they called *dominium* and applied to real estate and slaves—a concept lacking in the Greek vocabulary. For an object to qualify as *dominium,* it had to satisfy four criteria: it had to be lawfully obtained, exclusive, absolute, and permanent.[22] The best-known Roman law definition described *dominium* as "the right to use and consume one's thing as allowed by law" (*jus utendi et abutendi re sua quatenus iuris ratio patitur*).* Roman jurisprudence went to great lengths to stipulate every conceivable nuance of property rights: how acquired and how lost, how transferred, how sold.[23] The rights implicit in *dominium* were so absolute that ancient Rome knew nothing of eminent domain.†

Christians did not look forward, to the Kingdom of God, but back, to the lost Golden Age.

**Utendi* meant the right to use, and *abutendi* to consume, i.e., dispose of at will (rather than "abuse" as the term is sometimes mistranslated). According to modern scholarship, this famous definition of property is not of Roman origin but dates to the sixteenth century, although the concept was familiar to ancient Romans: Vittorio Scialoja, *Teoria della proprietà nel diritto romano*, I (Rome, 1928), 262. It has been said that "no ancient legal text contains a Roman definition of ownership": Alan Rodger, *Owners and Neighbours in Roman Law* (Oxford, 1972), 1.

†C. Reinold Noyes, *The Institution of Property* (New York, 1936), 84. Roman law, however, did recognize other forms of ownership, such as *possessio* (precarious tenure), and *usufructus* (lifetime tenure), later adopted by feudal Europe.

For all their pragmatism, Roman jurists were compelled to seek a philosophic basis to law because, like the Macedonians, as their domain expanded from a city-state first into a nation-state and then into an empire, they confronted a bewildering variety of legal norms and procedures that differed from their own as well as from each other. The problem arose even before Rome had become mistress of the Italian peninsula, for from early on Roman courts had to deal with foreigners who came on business or who married Romans. The local law, *jus civile,* did not apply to them, as it was restricted to Roman citizens. Roman jurists had to seek, therefore, common principles underlying the diverse legal systems with which they came in contact. As Rome's territory expanded around the Mediterranean basin, they formulated a Law of Nations (*jus gentium*) which synthesized the rules shared by all nations known to them. Under the influence of Stoic philosophy, the Law of Nations gradually fused with the Law of Nature (*jus naturale*); the process was completed in the early third century C.E., when Roman citizenship was extended to all the subjects of the empire.[24] Thus came into being a fundamental postulate of Western thought: that right and wrong are not arbitrary concepts but norms rooted in nature and therefore binding on all mankind; ethical problems are to be solved with reference to the Law of Nature, which is rational and supersedes the positive law (*jus civile*) of individual societies. An essential element of the Law of Nature is the equality of man, specifically, equality before the law, and the principle of human rights, including the rights to property, which antedate the state, and thus are independent of it.* Fifteen hundred years later these ideas would furnish the philosophical cornerstone of Western democracy.

Initially, Roman philosophers and jurists treated private property as part not of the Law of Nature but of the Law of Nations. In time, however, as the two concepts fused, they came to view it as grounded in Natural Law.[25] A theoretical defense of private property as a feature of Natural Law, however, was not fully made until the sixteenth and seventeenth centuries, the age of Jean Bodin and Hugo Grotius. But that the idea occurred to Romans is evident from Cicero's argument that gov-

*Schlatter, *Private Property*, 23. An unresolved problem was slavery, which, although universal in the ancient world, was widely recognized as contrary to nature. James Bryce, *Studies in History and Jurisprudence*, II (New York, 1901), 583. One way out of the difficulty was suggested by the Roman jurist Ulpian, who relegated slavery to civil law, which deprived slaves of all rights, in contradistinction to the Law of Nature, under which all human beings were equal. John Hine Mundy in R. W. Davis, ed., *The Origins of Modern Freedom in the West* (Stanford, Calif., 1995), 120.

ernment could not interfere with private property because it had been created in order to protect it.[26]

2. *The Middle Ages*

The church fathers faced serious difficulty in confronting the subject of private property. According to the Gospels, Jesus urged the rich to turn their belongings over to the poor because wealth was an obstacle to salvation. He rejected possessions for himself and his disciples. The Gospels and other parts of the Christian Bible are filled with censure of riches and exhortations to renounce them, as in the familiar aphorism "It is easier for a camel to go through the eye of a needle than for a rich man to enter the kingdom of God."[27] At the same time, in his personal life Jesus was not an ascetic: he did not spurn property or even wealth but visited the houses of the rich and allowed himself to be entertained by them.[28] Because of the expectation of the imminence of the Kingdom of God, the Christian Bible "does not seem to contain any definite theory of property."[29]

Some historians question whether Jesus really propounded a program of social reform: according to a leading specialist on the subject, his was rather "the summons to prepare for the coming of the Kingdom of God" to take place "within the framework of the present world order."* In any event, the early Christians applied the teachings of Jesus to themselves only:

> The new social order . . . was confined to the Christian community; it was not a popular program of social reform in general. Within the Church itself . . . the only communism which was possible was one which differed from all other forms of communism and can only be described as the religious Communism of Love. That is to say, it was a communism which regarded the pooling of possession as a proof of love and of the religious spirit of sacrifice. It was a communism composed solely of consumers, a communism based on the assumption that its members will continue to earn their living by private

*Ernst Troeltsch, *The Social Teaching of the Christian Churches*, I (Chicago and London, 1976), 61. Referring to Nietzsche, Havelock Ellis writes: Jesus "never denied the world, the state, culture, work; he simply never knew or realized their existence. . . . The only realities to him were inner realities, so living that they make one feel 'in Heaven' and 'eternal'; this it was to be 'saved.'" *Affirmations* (Boston and New York, 1915), 49.

> enterprise, in order to be able to practice generosity and sacrifice. Above all, it had no theory of equality at all, whether it be the absolute equality of sharing possessions, or the relative equality of the contribution of the various members to the life of the whole according to merit and service. . . . Finally . . . there was no hostility to that which forms the real hindrance to a true communism—opposition to the institution of the family, which is so closely connected with private enterprise.[30]

The early Christian church accepted private property as a fact of life and concentrated on exhorting the faithful to engage to the maximum extent possible in charity. Belongings were considered evil only if selfishly used.*

Yet a church based on the advocacy of self-denial grew before long into a huge temporal power with vast landed possessions and other forms of wealth which it needed to carry out its religious and secular responsibilities. It also faced the reality, tacitly assumed by Jesus but often misunderstood by more devout Christians, that for the millions of its adherents material goods were a necessity: clearly, not everyone could take the vows of poverty and devote his or her entire life to Christian piety as a priest, monk, or nun, any more than everyone could practice celibacy.

A compromise thus had to be found between the Christian ideal and the mundane reality.

It was found, and proved eminently satisfactory. The basic premise of Christian theologians held that property derived not from the Law of Nature but from conventional (positive) law and as such had to be respected. It was *potentially* an evil capable of corrupting the soul and leading to sin. But, in the words of Augustine, a propertyless society was possible only in Paradise, because it demanded perfection[31]—the kind of perfection that since the Fall was beyond the reach of

*"The frequent exhortations to regard property as nothing, and all the talk about community of possessions . . . were . . . only a challenge to energetic charitable activity. In all these discussions the possession of private property itself was always assumed." Troeltsch, *Social Teaching*, I, 115–16. In this connection it must be noted that the oft-cited passage from one of Paul's Epistles (1 Timothy 6:10) concerning money is almost always misquoted: Paul did not say that money is "the root of all evil" but the "*love* of money," i.e., avarice. The saying was commonplace in antiquity and can be found in Thucydides, Democritus, Propertius, Plutarch, and other classical authors. See C. Spicq, *Saint Paul: Les épitres pastorales*, 4th ed., I (Paris, 1969), 563–65.

most of humanity.* Furthermore, possessions were ethically neutral and became evil only if they gave rise to avarice. Augustine wrote that a thing ought not to be condemned because it lent itself to abuse: "Is gold not good?" he asked, responding: "Yes, it is good. But the evil use good gold for evil, and the good use good gold for good."[32] According to Augustine, Jesus' admonitions to give up one's fortune were counsel, not command.[33] In the world as we know it, it could be followed only by a chosen few. Augustine viewed property as a responsibility rather than a warrant for license—a kind of "trust" held by individuals for the public good.

In support of their tolerance of property, Christian theologians could point to passages in the Hebrew Bible that indicated it enjoyed divine sanction. The Eighth Commandment, prohibiting theft, clearly implies the sanctity of property; the same holds true of the Tenth Commandment, which proscribes coveting "anything that is your neighbor's." Then there is the story of Abraham and Lot, who separated their pastures in order to put an end to disputes among their herdsmen and in this manner established their respective claims to a share of the land (Genesis 13). Reference was made also to the story of King Ahab (1 Kings 21), who coveted a vineyard of one Naboth and offered either to exchange it for another vineyard or to buy it. When Naboth refused to part with his land, Jezebel, Ahab's wife, concocted against him false accusations of blasphemy, which led to Naboth's being stoned to death, following which Ahab took possession of the vineyard. For this crime, God through the Prophet Elijah, threatened him and his wife with an ignominious death. The story provided an example of greed leading to sin, but it also affirmed the inviolability of property.

In the Jewish legal tradition, wealth honestly acquired was considered a blessing: the rabbis forbade people to give away their wealth, or to engage in excessive alms-giving, so as not to become themselves a burden to the community.[34] In contrast to the Christian Gospels, the Hebrew Bible extols neither poverty nor the poor.[35] At the same time, it is filled with condemnations of injustice by the rich and injunctions of charity and assistance not only to those of one's own community but also to strangers and even animals.† In fulfillment of these injunctions,

*According to Matthew 19:16–21, when someone asked Jesus how to attain eternal life, Jesus told him to obey the Commandments, adding that if he wished to be "perfect" he should sell his possessions and give the proceeds to the poor.

†The Torah, however, does have certain provisions limiting excessive accumulation of wealth, especially as concerns land. Theoretically, all the land belongs to the Lord and

Jewish communities developed a system of welfare that was probably unique in antiquity: its basis was the tithe for "the stranger, the fatherless, and the widow" as called for in the Hebrew Bible.[36]

The Catholic view of property was codified by Thomas Aquinas in the *Summa Theologica.* Aquinas approached the subject in the context of justice, which he defined as the "perpetual and constant will to render to each one that which is his."[37] He conceded that in a certain sense it was "not natural for man to possess external things," because all goods belong to God and are the common property of God's children.[38] However, drawing on Aristotle's *Politics,* he argued that common ownership promoted neither efficiency nor harmony but discord. To perfect himself spiritually, man had to have the kind of security that only ownership provided. Aquinas also adopted from Aristotle the idea that possessions enabled a person to engage in charity, a Christian obligation: almsgiving was an essential corollary of ownership, and the rich were morally bound to give to the poor all their superfluous wealth.[39] Any excesses to which wealth gives rise have to be restrained by society.

The general view of the patristic writers on this subject has been summarized as follows. The early church theoreticians recognized

> that human life, as it actually is, needs discipline, needs an order enforced by coercion. And thus they came to make a distinction between an ideal, which they think of as also the primitive condition of man, and the actual. Ideally, man, following his truest nature, obeying the laws of reason and justice . . . would have needed no such coercive discipline. But, being what he is, a creature whose true instincts and nature are constantly overpowered by his lower nature, it is only by means of hard discipline that he can be kept from anarchy and disorder. . . . Private property . . . with its enormous inequalities, they could not accept as a primitive and natural institution. In a primitive or natural state the rights of property could have been nothing more than the right to use that which a man required. But again, in face of the actual condition of human nature as it actually is, they found that a formal regulation of the exercise of the right to use was necessary. Private property is really

hence it cannot be bought in perpetuity, but only for a maximum of forty-nine years, at the end of which time (during the so-called Jubilee Year) all the land that the original owner had sold, presumably because of extreme need, is to revert to him (Leviticus 25:10, 23–28). This injunction apparently was never enforced. Max Weber, *Gesammelte Aufsätze zur Religionssoziologie,* III (Tübingen, 1921), 77.

another disciplinary institution intended to check and counteract the vicious disposition of men.[40]

Contrary to a widely held misconception, the church did not condone, let alone propagate, communism, for which reason the church fathers cannot be cited as authorities for it.[41] As the Russian philosopher Vladimir Soloviev observed a century ago, Christians exhort their followers to give away their own wealth, whereas socialists call for the seizure and distribution of the wealth of others. The economic doctrines of the Christian churches did not go beyond the voluntary renunciation of one's own wealth. It was, therefore, not inconsistent that the church treated as heretics those groups, such as the twelfth-century Waldensians, who preached poverty and, later, the Anabaptists, who sought to impose communism. Generally speaking, "veneration of poverty" was one of the hallmarks of heretical movements, not of the established church.[42] In the late thirteenth and early fourteenth centuries a fierce controversy broke out in the Franciscan Order between the "Spirituals," who advocated the renunciation of all possessions, and the "Conventuals," who wished to hold on to the sizable properties that the order had acquired. During the papacy of John XXII, the church crushed the Spirituals, over one hundred of whom it condemned to be burned at the stake. In a bull issued in 1323, this pope declared it a heresy to deny that Christ and the Apostles had had possessions.[43] Six years later, in another bull, John XXII asserted that the property (*dominium*) of man over his possessions does not differ from the property asserted by God over the universe, which He bestowed on man created in His image. It is therefore a natural right which predates human law.[44]

The founders of Protestantism went beyond the Catholic Church's tolerance of property: both Luther and Calvin emphatically endorsed it, linking it with labor, which they regarded as a Christian duty. Luther condemned the rebellious peasants of Germany as "mad dogs" for seizing estates, saying that the Gospels did not call for making the goods of others common property and holding on to one's own but urged Christians of their free will to give up what they had.[45] The Calvinists held even more positive views of property. Calvin wrote approvingly of industry and trade and the great profits they brought to some, rejecting the medieval prohibitions on usury and acknowledging the benefits of money and credit.[46] It is widely recognized by historians that Calvinism did a great deal to foster the capitalist spirit.

In the later Middle Ages the Catholic Church turned from defending property as a regrettable but unavoidable reality to defending it on principle. The shift occurred in reaction to assaults on the church's wealth by the secular authorities. The issue arose in an acute form at the beginning of the fourteenth century when Philip IV (Philip the Fair) of France, in need of money to finance his war with England, imposed a tax on the clergy and forbade the export of precious metals, including papal revenues. To protect clerical holdings from seizures by the crown, theologians now referred to property as an inalienable right—primarily church property, but by inference property in general. In the course of this polemic, clerical theorists formulated the doctrine, later adopted by such prominent secular writers as Bodin and Grotius, that the authority of the state, however absolute in other respects, did not extend to the property of its subjects. The argument was buttressed with references to Roman law, which was rediscovered and taught in Italian universities beginning in the early twelfth century.

A prominent exponent of this new clerical theory of property was Aegidius Romanus (Colonna), a pupil of Thomas Aquinas, who argued that Philip IV did not have it in his power to appropriate the church's possessions because the rights of property antedated and transcended those of the state. The church and the supreme pontiff had lordship over all temporal things and were the ultimate owner of the world's assets. Employing feudal terminology, he asserted that kings had "superior dominion" but not the ownership of their vassals' holdings.[47]

Aegidius Romanus's opponent John of Paris maintained in defense of Philip IV that private property derived from princely grants and that the church, too, held its estates by virtue of these grants. But he concurred that property rights could not be violated, whether by the king or the pope.[48] In these debates the influence of Roman law was clearly evident. John of Paris held that

> individual persons, in their individual capacities, have in themselves the right, power, and true lordship, and anyone can order, dispose, dispense, retain, alienate his property at pleasure without injury to another, since he is lord. . . . And, therefore, neither prince nor pope has lordship or dispensation in such things. . . .[49]

The dispute between the papacy and secular authorities of the late Middle Ages had the effect of firming the status of private property in that both parties to the controversy, while tracing the legal justification of ownership to different sources, agreed that it was sacrosanct, protected from the encroachments alike of the Holy See and the royal court.*

3. *The discovery of the "noble savage"*

Throughout the Middle Ages, Europeans kept alive the myth of the Golden Age when man had been innocent and property unknown. Some believed that even in their own time there existed remote regions, often pictured as islands on the edge of the world, where people continued to live in such bliss. Because of Original Sin, most humanity was excluded from these realms, but they were accessible to heroes and saints able to surmount great perils.[50] The church fathers debated for centuries whether an earthly paradise still existed.[51] This myth may have been one of the factors that inspired Columbus to undertake his voyage of discovery: some historians believe that before venturing on his first expedition, he had read Pierre d'Ailly's *Imago mundi*, which depicted the happy land of Hyperboreans living in a state of virtual immortality.†

When Columbus first encountered the Caribbean natives, what struck him and his ludicrously overdressed companions most forcibly was their nudity, for it immediately brought to mind Adam and Eve before the Fall.‡ He was further impressed by the fact that they were "guileless" and "never refuse[d] anything which they possess, if it be asked of them; on the contrary, they invite anyone to share it. . . ."[52] He could not, Columbus conceded, learn whether the natives held private property, but he carried away the impression that "in that which one

*"Rival claims to supreme jurisdiction, urged with abundance of plausible authority on behalf of potentates who owned no common earthly superior, furnished exactly the field in which the Law of Nature might be used with brilliant dialectic effect as a *deus ex machina*. . . . On all hands it was admitted, even by extreme partisans, that both pope and emperor were subject to the Law of Nature. . . ." F. Pollock, *Essays in the Law* (London, 1922), 45–46.

†Gilbert Chinard, *L'exotisme américain dans la littérature française au XVIe siècle* (Paris, 1911), xii–xv. But Cecil Jane (*Select Documents Illustrating the Four Voyages of Columbus*, I [London, 1930], lxxxix–xl) doubts Ailly's influence, since it is impossible to determine when this work was written: it may have appeared only after Columbus had returned from his first voyage.

‡A literary historian who has studied hundreds of travel accounts of America, Africa, and some islands of the East Indies published in France before 1610 found nudity to be the most prevalent theme. Geoffroy Atkinson, *Les nouveaux horizons de la Renaissance française* (Paris, 1935), 63–73.

had, all took a share, especially of eatable things."[53] In the fragmentary account of Columbus's voyages from his own pen, in America

> it is perpetual spring, the nightingale sings, the flowers bloom, the trees are green, the rivers wind, the mountains are high, and the inhabitants are innocent and happy.*

These first impressions set the tone for the entire utopian literature of the next five hundred years, providing seeming proof that imperfect man could attain perfection if he adopted the ways of the "noble savages."† And the most outstanding quality of the savages' life, besides ignorance of shame, was ignorance of property. One French literary historian perceives a direct line of descent from the First Letter of Columbus relating his discoveries to Rousseau's *Discourse on Inequality,* written two and a half centuries later, in which property was declared the source of every social evil.[54]

Impressions similar to Columbus's were conveyed to the European reading public by two early-fifteenth-century travel accounts which exerted great influence in shaping images of the noble savage.

Amerigo Vespucci, the Italian geographer and explorer after whom America is named, painted in his *Voyages,* published in 1505–6, an enchanting picture of the New World's Indians. According to him, they had no "captains" over them but lived in liberty. If they went to war it was to avenge the death of their kin, not for loot or dominion. They knew neither religion (for which he berated them), nor law, nor marriage. They did not engage in commerce, and attached no value to gold or precious stones.[55] They lived in a terrestrial paradise.

Peter Martyr d'Anghiera, an Italian active in Spain, published in 1516

*Howard Mumford Jones, *O Strange New World* (New York, 1964), 14. Repeated contact with the fierce Caribs, who raised captive children for consumption, as if they were piglets, did not disturb this idyllic picture; even the wise Montaigne, in his essay "The Cannibals," halfheartedly defended them as being no worse than Europeans.

†The earliest use of this term is believed to occur in Dryden's drama *The Conquest of Granada* (1670): "I am as free as nature first made man,/Ere the base laws of servitude began/When wild in woods the noble savage ran." Karl-Heinz Kohl, *Entzauberter Blick* (Berlin, 1981), 34. But the idea, if not the term, has classical antecedents: the Greek geographer Strabo (c. 63 B.C.E.–c. 24 C.E.) depicted the Scythians as barbarians who devoured the flesh of their defeated enemies and yet, because they knew no property and held all things in common, including wives and children, were "the most straightforward of men and least prone to mischief." *The Geography of Strabo,* trans. H. L. Jones, III (Cambridge, Mass., and London, 1961), Book VII, 3, 7–9, pp. 195–209.

a description of the New World (*De Orbe Novo*). There he reconstructed as follows what Columbus had seen:

> [A]mong them, the land is as common as the sun and water: And . . . Mine and Thine (the seeds of all mischief) have no place with them. They are content with so little, that in so large a country, they have rather superfluity than scarceness. So that . . . they seem to live in the golden world, without toil, living in open gardens, not entrenched with dikes, divided with hedges, or defended with walls. They deal truly with one another, without laws, without books, and without judges.[56]

It was not long before Europeans who came to the Americas as traders or settlers arrived at a very different view of native Indians. Those who came into prolonged contact with them tended to depict them as contemptible barbarians fit only to be slaves. Ignorance of private property was now taken as proof of their inferiority.[57] As early as 1525 a Dominican friar wrote that

> on the mainland they eat human flesh. They are more given to sodomy than any other nation. There is no justice among them. They go naked. They have no respect either for love or for virginity. . . . they are more stupid than asses and refuse to improve in anything.[58]

Samuel Purchas, the English publisher of travel literature, writing in 1625, referred to the American Indians as inhuman, more animal than wild animals.[59] Some French writers also gave, from firsthand experience, highly unflattering portrayals of Indians, depicting them as brutes.[60] Disenchantment spread as eyewitnesses related such odious practices as human sacrifices and torture. Before long, the "noble savage" of America turned into Satan.[61] But the original image left its traces, since many Europeans and some Americans to this day retain the romanticized view of the American Indian projected by the earliest explorers.

With the image of the Indian tainted, the attention of Europeans in quest of a terrestrial paradise shifted to the South Pacific: in the eighteenth century, the American utopia yielded to the Australian utopia. The chosen land was Tahiti. Sighted by the Portuguese in the early seventeenth century, it was forgotten until "rediscovered" by the English and French a century and a half later. Tahiti owed its reputation as an earthly

Eden to the description of a 1768 voyage by Louis de Bougainville. The French traveler did not give a uniformly favorable picture of the natives, stressing their cruelty in war and incurable habit of robbing strangers. (Stealing from their own people, he noted, was punished by hanging.) He highly praised, however, their indifference to material goods:

> Whether they be at home or no, by day or by night, their houses are always open. Everyone gathers fruits from the first tree he meets with, or takes some in any house into which he enters. It should seem as if, in regard to things absolutely necessary for the maintenance of life, there was no personal property amongst them, and that they all had an equal right to those articles.[62]

The communality of ownership extended to women. Bougainville and his companions were astounded by the casual ease with which Tahitian women gave themselves to any man who struck their fancy and even more by the fact that copulation sometimes occurred in public view. Hence he labeled Tahiti the "New Cythera," after the island in Greek mythology dedicated to the cult of Aphrodite (Venus). When Diderot wrote his comments on Bougainville's journey, he emphasized the sexual licentiousness of Tahitians, ignoring Bougainville's disparaging observations.[63] Thus there occurred the "erotization" of the noble savage, which probably played its part in the loosening of sexual mores in the closing years of the French *ancien régime*.

When in 1769 Philibert Commerson brought out another account of the enchanted isle of Tahiti, he viewed it through Rousseau's rosy spectacles, justifying the thievery of which his predecessor had complained as proving conclusively the absence among its inhabitants of a sense of property.[64]

We tend to think of the effect of the voyages of discovery mainly in political and economic terms. But it had no less bearing on Western social theories. For the discovery of America and the South Pacific islands encouraged a utopian idealism that clashed with the pragmatic idealism of Christian theology and new currents of thought associated with the revival of Natural Law theories.

The prototype of such utopian idealism was Thomas More's *Utopia*. The influence on More of the literature on the voyages of discovery was so strong that some contemporaries viewed his book, published in 1516, as a true representation of the New World.[65] Although modern scholars prefer to stress the influence on More of Plato and Erasmus of Rotterdam, it is certain that More had read the accounts of the discoveries and came under their spell. In his vision of a terrestrial paradise, however, a curious metamorphosis occurred. A common theme of travelers' accounts was that the "noble savages" lived an unconstrained life, ignorant alike of government and law. In More's *Utopia,* as in virtually all imaginary commonwealths written subsequently, the dominant theme is harsh discipline.* Like medieval theologians, utopian writers conceive man to be corrupt, but unlike them, they believe it possible to make him perfect by subjecting him, forcibly if necessary, to the rule of reason. And by a life of reason they usually mean a life of exemplary equality: for utopian writers, equality displaces freedom as the supreme good.[66] Since in his present state man is prey to passions, driven by selfishness rather than reason, he requires for his own good to be placed under an iron regimen. This notion, common to utopian writers—that man is corrupt but basically good and capable of being made virtuous by the combined influence of laws and education—makes for a very reactionary doctrine. Utopians devise make-believe communities to bridle human passions and ambitions, projecting a life that is diametrically opposed to that of the (imaginary) cheerful natives of America or Tahiti and rather resembles that of somber Sparta.

More's imaginary island is a dismal place where all the cities are built on the same plan and all the inhabitants dress alike. The residential houses are open to everyone and are exchanged, by lot, every ten years. Privacy has no place. The denizens consume in communal facilities food served by slaves. No one can travel without permission; a second violation of this rule leads to enslavement. Women must not marry before the age of eighteen; men, before twenty-two. Premarital sex is severely punished, and adultery incurs penal servitude. Citizens must not meddle in the affairs of government: they are subject to the death penalty if they "take counsel on matters of common interest" in private. They can spend the time free from work as they please, provided it is not in "revelry or idleness." And, of course, they know nothing of private property—money does not circulate, being used only for purposes of commerce with outsiders—for More believed that the abolition of money would cause all evils afflicting mankind to vanish:

> In Utopia all greed for money was entirely removed with the use of money. What a mass of troubles was then cut away! What a crop of crimes was then pulled up by the roots! Who does not know that fraud, theft, rapine, quarrels, disorders,

*Thomas More, it may be noted, practiced what he preached by wearing a hair shirt next to his skin and carrying a whip for self-flagellation.

> brawls, seditions, murders, treasons, poisonings, which are avenged rather than restrained by daily executions, die out with the destruction of money? Who does not know that fear, anxiety, worries, toils, and sleepless nights will also perish at the same time as money? What is more, poverty, which money alone seemed to make poor, forthwith would itself dwindle and disappear if money were entirely done away with everywhere.[67]

Gold and silver are used to make chamber pots and the chains with which the slaves are fettered.* The result is peace of mind and the opportunity to dedicate oneself to intellectual pursuits.

R. W. Chambers has rightly observed that "few books have been more misunderstood than *Utopia*":

> It has given the English language a word "Utopian" to signify something visionary and unpractical. Yet the remarkable thing about *Utopia* is the extent to which it adumbrates social and political reforms which have either been actually carried into practice, or which have come to be regarded as very practical politics. *Utopia* is depicted as a sternly righteous and puritanical State, where few of us would feel quite happy; yet we go on using the word "Utopia" to signify an easy-going paradise, whose only fault is that it is too happy and ideal to be realized.†

Much the same may be said of another early utopia, Tommaso Campanella's *City of the Sun,* written in 1602 (but published only thirty-five years later).[68] Campanella, a Dominican friar and religious fanatic whom the Inquisition kept twenty-seven years in prison for heresy, envisaged a society in which everything would be held in common, including the products of the intellect. The City of the Sun is surrounded by a wall and ruled by a priest called Hoh ("Metaphysic") along with three princes, one of whom is "Love." "Love" regulates sexual relations, pairing men and women so as to produce the healthiest possible offspring. The city also governs the children's education. The

*Four hundred years later, echoing More, Lenin promised that once Communism triumphed globally, gold would be used exclusively for the construction of lavatories on the streets of some of the largest cities in the world. V. I. Lenin, *Polnoe sobranie sochinenii*, Vol. 44 (Moscow, 1964), 225.

†R. W. Chambers, in Robert B. Adams, ed., Sir Thomas More, *Utopia* (London, 1935), 125. Gray goes further, saying that "no utopia has ever been described in which any sane man would on any conditions consent to live." *Socialist Tradition*, 62.

family is abolished because Campanella views it as the reason people lust for goods. So, of course, is private property: "All things are common with them," even arts, honors, and pleasures. This removes self-love and leaves only love of the state. Sedition is punished with death. The denizens of the City of the Sun live communally. Unlike in More's Utopia, there are in it no slaves, because all work ennobles. The people are strangers to gluttony and drunkenness, as well as such ailments as gout and colds. Campanella's communistic fantasy, along with More's, exerted influence on Lenin.[69]

These two early utopias had this in common, that they were written by churchmen whose ideal was the monastery. But whereas monastic establishments were peopled by individuals who had voluntarily given up secular life, the utopian communities were meant to be imposed on all inhabitants by the state. The ideal world of unconstrained natural men is thus transformed into a controlled enterprise in which there is no place for individualism and draconian punishments follow violations of all-pervasive rules. Individual property and family disappear. To promote virtue, all utopias eliminate choice. As we shall show later by citing Frederick Hayek, this is bound to happen because individuals can agree on very little and any attempt to have them agree on more than the minimum requires coercion.

The utopian mindset, gloomy and harsh, ran contrary to the ebullient spirit of individualism and entrepreneurship which emerged concurrently in Western Europe.

4. Early modern times

Sometime during the period in European history vaguely labeled "early modern," there occurred a major break in the attitude toward property. It was the consequence of a remarkable expansion of commerce which began in the late Middle Ages and accelerated following the discovery of the New World. Prior to that time, "property" essentially meant land; and since land was inextricably bound up with the powers of sovereignty, discussions of property raised questions of royal (or papal) authority. With the surge of commerce, however, property in some parts of Europe came also to mean capital; and capital was free of association with politics, being treated as a personal asset and, as such, owned without qualifications. A change of attitude followed: whereas in theoretical discussions of the preceding millennium property had been treated as an unavoidable evil, it now could be regarded as a positive good. This attitude prevailed until the second half of the eighteenth century, when egalitarian sentiments led to a renewed assault on the institution of property, this time in an uncompromising manner for which there was no precedent.

Two further factors contributed to the ascendancy of property.

One was the rise of individualism. Increasingly the community came to be viewed as an abstraction made up of individuals, and communal well-being as the sum total of individual prosperity. Individual prosperity, in turn, came to be seen as the reward of a rational life. The early Florentine humanist Leonardo Bruni (c. 1370–1444) praised riches as indispensable to an active public life, which alone deserved to be called "virtuous." "All in all," he wrote, "we need many material goods in order to accomplish deeds, and the greater and more excellent our acts of virtue, the more we depend on those means."[70] Leon Battista Alberti (1404–1472), an even more prominent Italian humanist of the Renaissance, preached a "bourgeois" morality very much like the one that would be propounded by Benjamin Franklin three hundred years later:

> Be virtuous and you will be happy: that is the chief idea of [the two men's] lives. Virtue is economic efficiency: to live virtuously means to husband body and soul. This is the reason for sobriety: the highest virtue for Alberti is "*sobrietà*," for Franklin it is "frugality."... The goal of the wise is thus the complete rationalization and economization of life's conduct.[71]

Sixteenth- and seventeenth-century literature provides many examples of unqualified approval of the pursuit of private interest which it would be difficult to find in earlier ages. We have noted them in Calvin. We find them also in Spinoza, who wrote in *Ethics:*

> The more each person strives and is able to seek what is of use to him, that is to say, to preserve his own being, the more virtue does he possess; on the contrary, insofar as each person neglects what is of use to him . . . he is wanting in power.[72]

And finally mention must be made of the reemergence of the Stoic idea of the Law of Nature. The concept was never wholly abandoned in the Middle Ages, but then it was identified with the will of God as revealed in the Holy Scriptures.[73] Seeking a more rational justification of worldly authority than that provided by the Scriptures, Renaissance theorists turned to Roman literary and legal texts.[74] They revived the idea, pregnant with revolutionary potential, that the Law of Nature antedated positive laws, and that all humans possessed innate rights which governments could not violate because states had been set up for the express purpose of protecting them.

Although the surge of commercial activity began in Italy, the Italian city-states did not produce an economic doctrine to justify capitalism. We find, however, evidence of the change in attitude which it brought about in Alberti's remarkable treatise on the family. Proud of having been born to a prosperous family, this archetypal Renaissance man felt no qualms in extolling wealth. His treatise, written in the form of a dialogue, equated material prosperity (honestly attained) with virtue. An interlocutor named Giannozzo (Werner Sombart saw in him one of the earliest representatives of the "spirit of capitalism") praises the rewards of profitable manufacture and trade such as a solid house in the city and a villa in the country.[75] Wealth properly managed—that is, managed prudently, not greedily or wastefully—is essential to family happiness, bringing fame and enabling a person to aid his country. Indeed, it is a precondition of personal freedom and dignity:

> It is, perhaps, a kind of slavery to be forced to plead and beg from other men in order to satisfy our necessity. That is why we do not scorn riches, but learn to govern ourselves and to subdue our desires while we live free and happy in the midst of affluence and abundance.[76]

Although not uncontested, this positive view of property and wealth came to dominate Western thought in the seventeenth and eighteenth centuries.

An early resort to the theory of Natural Law to justify ownership can be found in Jean Bodin's *Six Books of the Commonwealth* (1576), the first systematic political treatise of modern times.[77] Bodin's purpose was to justify royal prerogative, which he proceeded to do by formulating a novel definition of sovereignty as authority "not limited either in power, charge, or time."[78] By not being limited in "power," Bodin meant unrestrained by human will or man-made laws (Aristotle's "conventional law"). The sovereign, however, is always and everywhere subject to Divine and Natural Law, which require that he honor agreements and respect the property of his subjects on the grounds (previously stated by Thomas Aquinas) that "every man shall have his due." The government owes its origin to the fact that people, in the state of nature, feeling the need for protection of their belongings, entered into a political compact. The foundation of the state is the property-owning household. The authority of the sovereign stops at the boundary of the household: *imperium* or *potestas* is never to be confused with *dominium* or *proprietas*. Bodin cites Seneca to the effect that "to kings appertains the power over all, but property belongs to individuals."[79] Plato's ideal state which knows no distinction between "mine" and "thine" appears to him a contradiction in terms inasmuch as "nothing can be public, where nothing is private," any more than there can be a king where all are kings.[80] From which it follows that the sovereign, all-powerful as he is, cannot appropriate the belongings of his subjects. He must neither confiscate his subjects' assets nor tax them without their assent (arbitrary taxation being tantamount to confiscation), because divine law lays it down that "no one may plunder that which is the property of another."[81] Nor can he alienate any part of the royal domain, since it is given to him only for use, not in ownership.[82]

Bodin's treatise formulated the fundamental principle of Western political theory and practice, incipient already in late medieval discussions of royal claims to church assets, that government has no claim on private property.

The next influential theorist to insist on the sanctity of property with arguments drawn from the Law of Nature was the Dutch jurist Hugo Grotius. Grotius's pioneering treatise, *On the Law of War and Peace* (1625), widely acknowledged to have laid the foundations of international law, deals mainly with relations among sovereign states, but in the process discusses civil rights as well.[83] Grotius also devotes to property the lion's share of another book which deals with Dutch law.[84] His major premise holds that men are under the obligation "to preserve social peace" and that "the principal condition for a peaceful community is respect for one another's rights,"[85] prominent among which are the rights of ownership.

Grotius addresses the subject of property in the opening chapters of Book 2 of *On the Law of War and Peace*, in which he seeks to ascertain the lawful causes of war. Among these he lists, first and foremost, the defense and recovery of one's belongings: "for the preservation of our goods it is lawful, if there is a necessity for it, to kill him that would seize upon them."[86] This statement leads him to discuss the origins and legal bases of property. Originally, he asserts, all things were held in common, as was still the case among American Indians. But the bounty of nature is not inexhaustible:

> Almighty God has created all visible and sensible things for the good of the human race in general.... But of created things some are of such a nature that they are sufficient for the use of all men, as sun, moon, stars and sky, and to some extent also air and sea; others are not sufficient, namely such things as cannot be enjoyed equally by all. Of these... some are such that they are immediately or in process of time consumed by use: immediately, as meat and drink: the very nature of these things does not admit of their continuing to be enjoyed in common; for as soon as any one consumes for his own account any part of the common provision, this is applied to the sustenance of that person and no one else; and here we see already something like ownership, springing from an act which accords with the law of nature.[87]

The increase in population and the influence of ambition and avarice induced people to claim ownership of their flocks, pastures, and arable lands, by the "Right of First Occupancy." This occurred before there were states.

Like Bodin, Grotius cites Seneca to the effect that sovereignty and property are distinct. And like him, even while defining sovereign authority as subject to no external controls, he sees it as subordinate to the Law of Nature: that Law is "so unalterable that God Himself cannot change it."[88]

Thus, in the course of the seventeenth century, it became widely accepted in Western Europe that there exists a Law of Nature which is rational, unchanging and unchangeable, and transcends human (positive) laws; that one facet of the Law of Nature is the inviolability of private property; and that sovereigns are bound to respect their subjects' belongings, even as they deny them the right to participate in affairs of state. Indeed, the acknowledgment of the subjects' right to the undisturbed enjoyment of their properties justified denying them political rights, on the grounds that reciprocity demanded the subjects leave the sovereign the full power to run the affairs of state. Which is what Charles I seems to have had in mind when, standing on the scaffold, he said that the people's

> liberty and freedom consist in having of Government, those laws by which their life and goods may be most their own. It is not for having share in Government, Sirs; that is nothing pertaining to them.[89]

5. *Seventeenth-century England: property sanctified*

In the seventeenth century, the whole complex of ideas associated with Natural Law would find practical application in the Cromwellian and "Glorious" revolutions in England. Although this subject properly belongs to Chapter 3, a few words need to be said here about the politics of seventeenth-century England, because they provide the background for the novel ideas on property and its relationship to political power formulated by English theorists of that age.

In the first half of the seventeenth century, England underwent a succession of conflicts between the crown and parliament over their respective powers and, specifically, over the right of the king to tax without parliamentary consent—a conflict which culminated in 1649 in the execution of Charles I. Under the Commonwealth which succeeded the monarchy, the royal estates, which had always provided the crown with revenues, were confiscated. The result was a novel situation: the country had no king and all the landed wealth of the crown passed into the hands of the state, which sold a good part of it to private persons. This singular circumstance inspired novel political ideas in which the relationship between property and freedom was examined for the first time.

During this turbulent time, the term "property" underwent a metamorphosis, revolutionary in its implications, by being broadened to mean not only material objects but everything which the individual had a natural right to claim as his own. This notion was prefigured in medieval thought, which defined the concept of *suum* as including everything belonging to man by virtue of his inherent or "natural" right, and that embraced, along with his worldly goods, also his life and freedom.[90] The Latin formula *suum cuique tribuere,* translated into Latin from Plato and popularized by Cicero, was cited by Thomas Aquinas to define justice ("the perpetual and constant will to render to each one what is his").[91] Thomas Hobbes in the middle of the seventeenth century translated the phrase "giving to every man his own" or *suum* by "propriety."[92]

There were hints of this concept in Grotius's writings. He divided "things belonging to individuals" into "alienable" and "inalienable." The former applied to "things which by their nature can belong to one person as well as to another." "Inalienable things are things which belong so essentially to one man that they could not belong to another, as a man's life, body, freedom, honor"—attributes of the personality, sanctified by the Law of Nature. The distinction allowed Grotius to deny people the right to give up their liberty by placing themselves in bondage.[93] These passages, which Grotius wrote between 1618 and 1621 while in prison for political dissidence, may well be the earliest articulation in intellectual history of the theory that liberty is "inalienable" property, thereby laying the foundation of the concept of inalienable rights.

In seventeenth-century England these ideas acquired direct political relevance. From the onset of the conflict between crown and Commons, references were made to the "birthright" of Englishmen. This term first appeared in the sixteenth century, but at that time it referred to one's patrimony, i.e., that which one could claim by virtue of being born into a family that had specified rights, such as the right to inherit the crown. Now it acquired a much broader meaning to include such prerogatives as every human being, no matter how humble, enjoyed simply by virtue of being human. As early as 1621, the House of Commons asserted that the privileges of parliament were "the ancient and undoubted birthright and inheritance of the subjects of England."[94] In 1640, in the course of debates over the king's imposition of "ship money," widely considered an unlawful tax, one member of parliament asserted that the king's subjects "have a birthright in the laws of the kingdom."[95] Six years later, a radical Leveller insisted that "by natural birth all men are equally and alike born to like propriety, liberty, and freedom."[96] The notion of "inalienable rights," popularized by English radicals in the seventeenth century, has been said to cover "anything which it was reasonable to want," including one's religion and even proprietary rights over one's wife.[97] Together with the notion of *suum,* it formed the basis of the modern concept of human rights, a concept unknown anywhere outside the range of Western civilization.

The prerogatives of the crown were defended by several theorists, of whom Thomas Hobbes is the best known. Hobbes's principal writings appeared between 1640 and 1651—that is, during and immediately following the reign of Charles I. In his own words, Hobbes began his studies of "natural justice" by asking himself on what grounds anyone could claim something to be his. He decided that ownership derived not from nature but from consent, inasmuch as the state of nature, which he, as most everyone else at the time, envisioned as a condition in which goods belonged to no one, competition for them produced a "war of all against all."[98] Driven by the instinct of self-preservation, eager to escape endless strife, men surrendered their natural right to govern themselves by transferring it to the state. Thus the state precedes society and does not (as Bodin and Grotius would have it) issue from it: before it came into being, there were only warring individuals. Hobbes derided the idea that liberty was a "private inheritance" or "birth right": in his view, liberty was bestowed by the sovereign authority.[99] Private property is the creation of the state which protects the owners from encroachments by fellowmen. The sovereign's authority is absolute—the only alternative to it is anarchy, the reversion to mankind's original condition of perpetual conflict. Since it is the king who has made property possible, he has a legitimate claim on it: he can tax and confiscate without his subjects' consent.

Hobbes's doctrinaire pronouncements ignored developments in property relations that had occurred in England since the accession of the Tudors. A far more realistic account of the crown's prerogatives vis-à-vis its subjects and their properties was provided by Hobbes's contemporary James Harrington in his *Oceana* (1656).* A pioneering work of political sociology, *Oceana* sought to explain the reasons for the breakdown of the English monarchy in realistic rather than metaphysical or moralistic terms. In his methodology Harrington resembled Machiavelli in that he insisted on depicting things not as they should be but as they actually are. Harrington interpreted political developments as determined by the distribution not of power but of property, by which he meant land. His basic assumption held that "[a]ll Government is interest, and the predominant interest gives the matter or foundation of government."[100] He was the first political theorist to view political power as a by-product of economics, or, more specifically, of the distribution of property between the state and the population. He talked of an "equilibrium" of property rights between crown and subjects, a notion which had great appeal in the age of mechanistic science. His thesis was as simple as it was innovative: he who controls the country's wealth controls its politics, in large measure because political power rests on military might and the armed forces must be paid. From the point of view of political and social stability—a consideration uppermost in his mind following the upheavals of the 1640s—the worst arrangement is one under which the crown and the nobles have one half and the commoners the other half of the nation's assets, for such a distribution leads to permanent unrest and even civil war as the former seek unlimited

*James Harrington, *The Commonwealth of Oceana; and A System of Politics*, ed. J. G. A. Pocock (Cambridge, 1992). It is an unusual utopia in that it upholds private property.

authority and the latter liberty.[101] Stability obtains when one of the three social groups acquires a "predominant interest." Absolute monarchy results when the crown owns all or at least two-thirds of the landed wealth; aristocracy, when the nobles own a similar share. When the people possess two-thirds or more, the result is democracy.[102] The locus of sovereignty must, sooner or later, follow the distribution of wealth.* Harrington saw the root cause of the monarchy's collapse in 1649 in the land policies of the early Tudors, which benefited the yeomanry at the expense of the crown and nobility. Henry VII divided large estates among small owners, a practice Henry VIII continued by turning over to them the land confiscated from the clergy. According to Harrington, by the reign of Elizabeth, the balance of property in England shifted decisively from the crown and the nobility to the commoners, by whom he meant the gentry and yeomanry.[103] These new proprietors could raise a larger army than the crown and hence prevailed in the Civil War. They also demanded and ultimately obtained a voice in government. Modern scholars concur with Harrington's estimate that in his time the majority of Englishmen were, in some measure, property owners.[104]

Harrington's successor was Henry Neville, whose *Plato Redivivus* appeared in 1681.[105] But as early as 1658, two years after the publication of Harrington's *Oceana,* addressing the House of Commons, Neville called attention to a dramatic shift in property relations that had occurred in England:

> The Commons, till Henry VII, never exercised a negative voice. All depended on the Lords. In that time it would have been hard to have found in this house so many gentlemen of estates. The gentry do not now depend on the peerage. The balance is in the gentry. They have all the lands.[106]

Neville accepted Harrington's premise that everywhere and at all times "dominion is founded in property" and government is determined by the distribution of property between ruler and subjects.[107] In contrast to such Asian monarchies as the Persian, Assyrian, and Ottoman (and, he

*This contention does not mean, however, that Harrington "anticipated" Marx, as some historians have claimed. For Marx, ownership of property (in the means of production) determined the nature and the actions of government, which is a helpless instrument of the owners. For Harrington, as later for Marx, the distribution of property determined the nature of government and its policies, but government was a self-sufficient entity. For Marx, the state was a tool of private interests; for Harrington, it was their competitor.

might have added, had he known about it, the Russian), where the monarch is the "absolute proprietor of all the lands," in England the monarch owns very little: in Neville's estimate, after the Restoration the king held but one-tenth of the land, the remaining nine-tenths having passed into the hands of his subjects.

> The consequence is: that the natural part of our government, which is power, is by means of property in the hands of the people; while the artificial part, or the parchment in which the form of government is written, remains the frame.

Because the princes had "alienated their own inheritance,"

> the king must have a precarious revenue out of the peoples' purses; and to be beholden to parliament for his bread in time of peace. . . . And this alone . . . is enough to make the king depend upon his people. . . .[108]

The arrangement assures that the people of England "have entire freedom of their lives, properties, and their persons."[109] By contrast, in France, the king, being financially independent of his subjects, can act despotically.

Harrington, and to a lesser extent Neville, exerted great influence both in England and in the United States,* although not quite in the sense in which they might have intended or even anticipated, as practicing politicians invoked their theories to justify property qualifications for both voters and legislators.[110]

From the point of view of the evolution of the idea of property, the immensely influential work of John Locke, *Two Treatises of Government,* marked a regression because it rested on the metaphysical concept of Natural Law rather than on political sociology. Locke set himself the task of refuting Robert Filmer's royalist tract, *De Patriarcha,* written in the early part of the century but first published in 1680, which advanced an argument similar to Hobbes's. *Two Treatises* was published anonymously in 1690, two years after the exile of James II and the accession of William and Mary, and was long believed, incor-

*John Adams praised Harrington for his discovery of the political "balance" and compared him to William Harvey, the discoverer of the circulation of blood. *The Works of John Adams*, ed. Charles Francis Adams, IV (Boston, 1851), 428. "Harrington," he wrote, "has shown that power always follows property." Ibid., IX (Boston, 1854), 376.

rectly, to have been intended as a justification of the Glorious Revolution: in fact, the treatises were written before it occurred.*

Locke's book focuses on property as the source and *raison d'être* of all government. Many commentators see Locke as using "property" in two senses: sometimes in the narrow sense of material assets ("estate"), and at other times in the broader one of general rights as grounded in the Law of Nature. However, closer scrutiny reveals that he consistently uses the concept in the latter, i.e., broad, sense. As he says on one occasion: "By *Property* I must be understood here, as in other places, to mean that Property which men have in their Persons as well as Goods," that is, "life, liberties and estates"[111]—the sphere, called in Latin *suum* and in English "propriety," in which each human being is sovereign.† Like Bodin, Grotius, and Harrington and unlike Hobbes and Filmer, Locke considered property to predate sovereignty. The state of nature was not, as Hobbes thought, a ferocious jungle, but a happy condition of freedom and equality.

This being the case, why did mankind forsake its blissful state to enter into a social and political compact? Locke's answer: for the sake of property (always understood in the broad sense).[112] With the development of trade and the invention of money came greed and discord. People then surrendered their unbridled freedom and equality for the sake of security of their persons and possessions: thus the state came into being. And this remains its primary function: "*Political Power* . . . [is] a *Right* of making laws . . . for the Regulating and preserving of Property. . . ."[113] from which it necessarily follows that "[t]he great and *chief end* . . . of Mens uniting into Commonwealths, and putting themselves under Government, *is the Preservation of their Property.*"[114] Given its origin, the state stands or falls on its ability to fulfill this supreme responsibility. Locke asserts the right of the people to rebel against a monarch who fails to carry it out.

Locke introduced the notion that the origin of material property lies in labor, a notion that greatly appealed to a country the large proportion of whose inhabitants consisted of independent farmers, artisans, and shopkeepers. According to Locke, property comes into existence when

*Modern researches have shown that *Two Treatises* was composed in 1679–80, i.e., a decade before the Glorious Revolution. Peter Laslett in John Locke, *Two Treatises of Government,* ed. Peter Laslett (Cambridge, 1960), 35.

†This concept was adopted in the Fifth Amendment to the U.S. Constitution, which forbids the government to deprive its citizens of "life, liberty, and property" without due process.

an individual applies labor to objects belonging to no one. And this is the case because we indisputably "own" ourselves and, by extension, everything that we produce:

> Though the Earth and all inferior Creatures be common to all Men, yet every Man has a *Property* in his own *Person*. This no Body has any Right to but himself. The *Labour* of his Body, and the *Work* of his Hands, we may say, are properly his. Whatsoever, then, he removes out of the State that Nature hath provided, and left it in, he hath mixed his *Labour* with, and joyned to it something that is his own, and thereby makes it his *Property*. It being by him removed from the common state Nature hath placed it in, it hath by this *labour* something annexed to it, that excludes the common right of other Men. For this *Labour* being the unquestionable Property of the Labourer, no Man but he can have a right to what that is once joyned to, at least where there is enough, and as good left in common for others.*

To Descartes's "I think, therefore I am," Locke, as it were, added "I am, therefore I own": I own myself, that is, and all that I create. More than that: the notion that our elemental property is ourselves, i.e., our persons and bodies, means that property necessarily entails liberty. Because to say that we "own ourselves," that is, are our own "property," is tantamount to saying that we are free to dispose of ourselves, which is the meaning of freedom.

Attractive and even self-evident as it may appear, the labor theory of property is a two-edged sword, for it can also be used to assail property. How is one to justify inherited wealth which requires no personal effort, or the fact that farm laborers and factory workers do not own what they produce? As we shall see, the radical, antiproprietary implications of Locke's theory would be exploited by nineteenth-century socialists and anarchists to argue that under the "capitalist" mode of production, the mass of workers do not earn the fruits of their labor and hence productive assets should be nationalized.[115]

*Locke, *Two Treatises*, 305–6. This argument was not original with Locke, having been made half a century earlier by the Leveller Richard Overton. Schlatter, *Property*, 132–33. And much earlier still, two thousand years before, Pericles spoke of every Athenian's being "in his own person . . . self-sufficient" (see below, p. 119). It has been adopted in recent times by Robert Nozick in *Anarchy, State and Utopia* (New York, 1974), 171ff.

The political message of Locke, however, is clear and unambiguous: the king must not violate any of his subjects' property rights; if he does, he is "at war" with them and may be disobeyed.[116]

For all the acceptance in seventeenth-century England and her possessions of the principle that private property is sacrosanct, there were also dissenting voices. The most radical objections came from the so-called "Diggers." The founder and leader of the movement, Gerrard Winstanley, active in the years 1648–52, exhorted the small band of his followers to "dig up" the commons, which at the time made up a sizable portion of England's land surface. This they proceeded to do until stopped and evicted by the joint efforts of the government and farmers. Winstanley, however, went beyond such unlawful actions to develop a communistic theory. One of its principles held that neither land nor its fruits should be marketable commodities.[117] Especially interesting is his hostility to intellectual property: he claimed that academic savants who monopolized learning were as evil as landlords who monopolized the soil. His ideal was a harsh tyranny where everyone worked and shirking was punished by whipping and beheading.[118]

Notions of the sanctity of property and its political corollary, which in the seventeenth century carried a revolutionary message, acquired in the eighteenth century, at any rate in England, a conservative connotation. It now came to be widely believed that inasmuch as politics were a function of property, only owners of property had a legitimate right to participate in politics. Arguing against the clamor of the radical Levellers for universal suffrage, Henry Ireton, Oliver Cromwell's son-in-law, asserted, in a breathtaking non sequitur:

> I wish we may all consider of what right you challenge that all the people should have right to Elections. Is it by the right of nature? If you will hold forth that as your ground, then I thinke you must deny property too. . . . By the same right of nature . . . by which you can say one man hath an equall right with another to the chusing of him that shall governe him, by the same right of nature hee has an equal right in any goods he sees, meate, drinke, clothes, to take and use them for his sustenance.[119]

A Whig publicist formulated the argument more reasonably:

> It is owned, that all governments are made by man, and ought to be made by those men who are owners of the territory over

> which the government extends. It must likewise be confessed, that the FREEHOLDERS of England are the owners of the English territory, and therefore have a natural right to erect what government they please.[120]

Such arguments had two corollaries. First, they made political authority dependent on the landowners. Second (on the Athenian model), they excluded from political participation anyone who owned no land. In England, where land was scarce, the application of this principle restricted the franchise rather severely. In the North American colonies, where a number of states, following the English example, adopted landownership as a prerequisite of franchise but where land was abundant, it had a much less restrictive effect.[121]

In the closing years of the eighteenth century a fresh approach to property emerged. English liberals, who had had recourse to the theory of Natural Law against royal authority, became frightened by the uses which the radicals among French *philosophes* had made of this theory. As a result, some of them now preferred to justify property by the utilitarian argument that whatever its moral drawbacks, it was preferable to any alternative, because it was most conducive to general prosperity. The pioneer of this approach was David Hume, who depicted property as a mere "convention" that people respected because it was advantageous to them. "What is a man's property?" he asked, answering:

> Any thing, which it is lawful for him, and for him alone, to use. But what rule have we, by which we can distinguish these objects? Here we must have recourse to statutes, customs, precedents, analogies, and a hundred other circumstances; some of which are constant and inflexible, some variable and arbitrary. But the ultimate point, in which they all professedly terminate, is, the interest and happiness of human society.[122]

Just what this "interest and happiness" consisted of was spelled out by the most influential economist of the age, Adam Smith. For Smith, private property proved its worth by enhancing productivity. It is on these grounds that he argued slave labor was prohibitively expensive, inasmuch as "[a] person who can acquire no property, can have no other interest but to eat as much, and to labor as little as possible."[123] As we shall see, two centuries later, because of the insoluble difficulties of justifying property on moral grounds, the utilitarian argument would largely displace rival theories.

6. *Eighteenth-century France: the assault on property begins in earnest*

If the glorification of private property reached its apogee in England, where it enjoyed the support of a large body of private owners, it first came under frontal onslaught in *ancien régime* France.* The leading lights of this movement were intellectuals who, inspired by ancient authors and by modern travelers' descriptions of faraway places, sought to draw the blueprint of a terrestrial paradise. The endeavor gave rise to a whole literature of *exotisme,* which idealized the life of non-Europeans.[124] Its outstanding feature was the alleged absence of "mine" and "thine" among the carefree savages.[125] The implication was that contemporary mankind, depraved by the institution of ownership, could attain happiness as soon as it rid itself of its corrupting influence.

Whereas in England the impetus to deliberations on the origins and nature of property stemmed from strictly pragmatic considerations—the desire to rein in the arbitrary power of the crown, especially in matters of taxation—in France it was inspired by a philosophical revulsion from the world as constituted. The French *philosophes* viewed the actual world as a perversion of the true or ideal world, of the world as it should and could be. When James Boswell visited Rousseau, who more than any Frenchman of his time influenced public opinion against property, his host told him: "Sir, I have no liking for the world. I live here in a world of fantasies, and I cannot tolerate the world as it is. . . . Mankind disgusts me."[126] Ill-tempered but honest: utopias have always served as an outlet for misanthropic emotions.

Tempting as it may be to seek social and economic causes for every political and social idea, it is difficult to find in eighteenth-century France such grounds for her intellectuals' animus against property. To the extent that the population at large was dissatisfied with social and economic conditions it was not because it disapproved of property but because it wanted more of it. Philosophic socialism was a pure intellectual movement led by "those men who," in Trollope's words, "if they had hitherto established little, had at any rate achieved the doubting of

*"The egalitarian doctrines were concentrated in France, without [a] significant echo in eighteenth century England or elsewhere on the continent, where outright attacks on the private ownership of property were virtually nonexistent before 1789." Frank E. Manuel and Fritzie P. Manuel, *Utopian Thought in the Western World* (Cambridge, Mass., 1979), 357.

much." In their thinking, the materialistic conception of man played a central part. Locke's theory of knowledge, expounded in *The Essay on Human Understanding* (1690), which claimed that human beings have no "innate" ideas but form ideas exclusively from sensory perceptions, remained in England an abstruse epistemological doctrine, devoid of political significance. In France, however, it was applied to politics, providing a theoretical basis for the conviction that by properly shaping the human environment—the exclusive source of all ideas—it was possible so to mold human behavior as to create an ideal society. And the ideal society, much as Plato had envisioned it, was characterized by equality.

The onset of the eighteenth century thus marked a radical break with traditional concepts of human nature. Since the triumph of Christianity thirteen hundred years earlier, man was believed to have lost in the Fall his capacity for perfection and turned into a corrupt being who required discipline to keep him from straying onto the path of depravity. The Christian view was conservative in that it saw human nature as immutable. But now another view emerged and in time came to dominate Western thought: it entailed the outright rejection of the doctrine of Original Sin. It held that there was no such thing as human nature: there was only human conduct, and that was shaped by the social and intellectual environment. The philosopher's task was to design a social system that would make it virtually impossible for humans to be depraved. Once this outlook was accepted—and it became conventional wisdom among both socialists and liberals a century later—there was no theoretical limit to the manipulation of the social and intellectual environment in the quest for human perfectibility.

Beginning with Helvétius, French *philosophes* maintained that the decisive factor in shaping human attitudes and conduct was "education," by which they meant, in addition to formal schooling, man's social milieu and laws. Private property they saw as the principal obstacle to a virtuous life, because it corrupted the personality and produced intolerable social inequalities.

A representative example of eighteenth-century French antiproprietary literature is *Code de la Nature*, published anonymously in 1755 by an author who used the pen name Morelly and whose identity remains a mystery to this day. Morelly rejected the argument that people had to be accepted as they were, because he believed that they had been perverted by their past: their true nature had been depraved by social institutions, especially private property. "Natural" human beings were still to be found among American Indians, who hunted and fished in common and knew nothing of personal belongings. Modern man was thoroughly warped by his craving for belongings:

> The only vice which I know in the universe is *avarice;* all the others, whatever name one gives them, are merely forms, degrees of it: it is the Proteus, the Mercury, the base, the vehicle of all the other vices. Analyze vanity, conceit, pride, ambition, deceitfulness, hypocrisy, villainy; break down the majority of our sophisticated virtues themselves, all dissolve in this subtle and pernicious element, *the desire to possess*. . . .[127]

Morelly outlined a kind of constitution to instruct mankind how to live according to "nature." Its opening article reads: "Nothing in society belongs uniquely or in property to anyone."[128] By abolishing ownership, Morelly expected to create "a situation in which it is virtually impossible for man to be depraved or wicked."[129] Morelly's society of the future, as is true of other utopian visions, enforces a grim and regimented life.

The work that did most to spur antiproprietary sentiments in France, however, was not Morelly's turgid treatise, but Jean-Jacques Rousseau's *Discourse on the Origin of Inequality* (1755), submitted to a contest of the Academy of Dijon for the best response to the question "What is the source of inequality among men and is it sanctioned by Natural Law?" Rousseau's work, which the academy rejected because it exceeded its length limitations, opened with a passage that has acquired fame by virtue of frequent citation, although it is by no means original, echoing the sentiments of writers of classical antiquity:

> The first person who, having enclosed a plot of land, took it into his head to say *this is mine* and found people simple enough to believe him, was the true founder of civil society. What crimes, wars, murders, what miseries and horrors would the human race have been spared, had someone pulled up the stakes or filled in the ditch and cried out to his fellow men: "Do not listen to this impostor. You are lost if you forget that the fruits of this earth belong to all and the earth to no one!"*

*Jean-Jacques Rousseau, *Discourse on the Origin of Inequality* (Indianapolis, 1992), 44. Morelly's *Code de la Nature* (Paris, 1910), which came out the same year, made a similar claim but in less florid language, p. 34. The reader will recall that both Virgil and Ovid talked of the Golden Age as one which knew no property boundaries.

This rhetorical outburst, based on no historical evidence, expressed Rousseau's idiosyncratic methodology, which held that the more we know the less we understand. To study man in his original condition, Rousseau argued, we must set aside all facts and resort to "hypothetical" or "conditional" reasoning.[130] In his *Discourse* Rousseau provided a rambling account of how, out of original equality, there developed private property, and how it led to jealousy and envy, slavery and wars. He described the existing inequalities of wealth as evil but, surprisingly, did not propose that property be abolished. The implication of his argument was that the harm derived not from property as such but from its unequal distribution: he fully favored property acquired through honest labor.

A notoriously inconsistent writer, in *The Discourse on Political Economy,* published the same year, Rousseau called the right to property "the most sacred of all the citizens' rights, and more important in certain respects than liberty itself." It was "the true foundation of civil society."[131] But then again, in his most famous book, *The Social Contract* (1762), he implied that inasmuch as it was society that sanctioned property, "each individual's right to his very own store is always subordinate to the community's right to all."[132] It is his antiproprietary views, however—the notion that property is "artificial" and communism "natural," and that the state has a legitimate right to regulate the uses to which property is put—that have exerted the greatest influence on Western thought.* They displayed just the right mixture of noble sentiment, lofty rhetoric, muddled thinking, and disregard for reality to attract those intellectuals who, like him, refused to "tolerate the world as it is." Robespierre is said to have reread *The Social Contract* every day.[133]

"After the middle of the eighteenth century," writes Franco Venturi, "the idea that the abolition of property might change the very basis of human society, might abolish all traditional morality and every political form of the past, was never again to disappear." Communism was born "halfway through the eighteenth century"[134]—before the emergence of industrial capitalism and the glaring social inequalities to which it

*Two centuries later, the English social historian R. H. Tawney virtually echoed Rousseau when he asserted: "The individual has no absolute rights. . . . all rights . . . are conditional and derivative. . . . they are derived from the end or purpose of the society in which they exist. They are conditional on being used to contribute to the attainment of that end, not to thwart it. And this means in practice that, if society is to be healthy, men must regard themselves not as the owners of rights, but as trustees for the discharge of functions and the instruments of a social purpose." *The Acquisitive Society* (New York, 1920), 51. Hitler held the same view of rights, including property rights; see below, pp. 221–22.

would give rise. It was a pure intellectual construct, conceived in the imagination of thinkers who looked backward to a Golden Age. It held an irresistible attraction for those intellectuals who liked to blame their personal problems on the society in which they happened to live. For in a world in which material assets were perfectly equalized, superior social status and the power that goes with it would derive from intellectual capabilities, with which they believed themselves uniquely endowed.

Prevalent as they were in eighteenth-century France, antiproprietary sentiments did not have the field entirely to themselves, for there were practical Frenchmen who saw the advantages of property. The most influential of them belonged to the Physiocratic school, which adhered to the idea of Natural Law and regarded property as its integral component. A leading Physiocrat, Mercier de la Rivière, repeated Locke when he wrote: "It is from nature that every man has exclusive property of his person and of all things acquired by his pursuits and labors."[135] Or: "Property may be regarded as a tree of which social institutions are as branches growing from a trunk that it puts forth."[136] According to the Physiocrats, land was the most authentic form of property because only agriculture added to existing wealth. The state should be governed by landowners, who were unique in that they alone might be said to possess a fatherland: fatherland (*patrie*) and patrimony (*patrimoine*) were identical.[137]

The Physiocrats exerted strong influence on the French revolutionaries' commitment to property as a sacrosanct institution. In May 1789 the Estates General drafted *cahiers de doléances* defining liberty along with property as sacred rights which the state was duty-bound to uphold.[138] The consecration of property rights justified the abolition of feudal rights, which the revolutionaries declared to be not property but privilege. In August of the same year, the National Assembly adopted the Declaration of Rights of Man and the Citizen, which declared property to be one of the "natural and imprescriptible rights of man."[139] The constitution adopted by the Convention in 1793 stated in Article 2 that "equality, liberty, security, and property" were among the fundamental and inalienable rights of man. Similar sentiments pervaded the Napoleonic Code (Code Civil) of 1804, which swept aside all limitations on ownership left over from feudal times and adopted virtually word for word the Roman definition of property:

> Property is the right to enjoy and dispose of objects in the most absolute manner, provided that one does not make use of it in a

> manner prohibited by laws or regulations. No one can be forced to give up his property unless it is for the public good and by means of a fair and previous indemnity.[140]

Although they resorted to the principle of private property to justify the disestablishment of the aristocracy and the abolition of its privileges, the French revolutionaries did not consistently observe it in their legislative practice. They sequestered the belongings of the church and émigrés without compensation; they also subjected inheritance to state regulation. They justified such measures with the argument that since property had been created by the state, the state had the right to regulate it in the public interest. Thus in the debate in the National Assembly in 1791 concerning citizens' freedom to dispose of their estates by testament, Mirabeau declared that the right of property was a social creation and hence society, through its laws, not only protected it but also could determine its uses. This echoed the reactionary doctrines of Hobbes and Filmer, a fact camouflaged by the substitution of "society" for "state." The Jacobins, followed by even more radical communists, would frontally attack private ownership.

These trends foreshadowed the future treatment of property. The notion of the inalienability of private property would soon be forced into retreat under the onslaught of antiproprietary passions that would come to dominate thought from the middle of the nineteenth century to the end of the twentieth.

7. *Socialism, communism, and anarchism*

The nineteenth century witnessed a widening discrepancy between prevailing attitudes toward property and the reality of proprietary relationships. It marked the apogee of ownership in Europe, as immense quantities of newly generated capital were concentrated in private hands. Property acquired the status of an inviolate institution, protected from encroachments of the state by constitutions and from fellowmen by civil laws. At the same time, the public turned increasingly hostile to it: for the first time in history, a sizable body of opinion called for state regulation and even the abolition of property. Previously, apart from occasional dissident voices, such as Thomas More's, Campanella's, or Winstanley's, critics of property concentrated on its excesses—the inequities of its distribution and the avarice to which it gave rise. Now, however, the very institution of property came under assault on the grounds that it was inherently immoral. Its traditional justification, that it was grounded in the Law of Nature, came under critical scrutiny:

> [F]rom the conception of property as a natural right follow certain unexpected consequences, which undermine the foundations of that conception. If property is essential to the development of man's natural liberty, it ought not to be enjoyed exclusively by a few, as an odious privilege; all ought to be owners of property. The same theory of natural rights which consecrated individual property, and for its sake demolished the castle of feudalism, issued in the opposite conception, namely communism. . . . Thus the utter negation of individualism proceeds by a logical development from the conception of individuality.[141]

In the words of Pierre-Joseph Proudhon, one of the founders of anarchism:

> [I]f the liberty of man is sacred, it is equally sacred in all individuals. . . if it needs property for its objective action, that is, for its life, [then] the appropriation of material is equally necessary for all. . .[142]

The spread of democracy obviously had something to do with this shift in opinion. For as the franchise was broadened and ultimately made universal, governments came to depend on the mass of voters who, owning little if anything, demanded from the state that it ensure a fairer distribution of the country's resources. This demand was eventually satisfied in democratic countries through such devices as death duties and the graduated income tax, the proceeds of which went to finance social welfare programs. In totalitarian regimes, it led either to wholesale expropriations or to government regulation of productive assets which transformed them into conditional ownership; in both cases, the violations of property rights served to solidify the power of the rulers at the expense of private owners.

Another factor conducive to antiproprietary sentiments was changes in the nature of property. Although trade and manufacture, and the moneyed wealth to which they give rise, had existed from the earliest periods of recorded history, and although moneyed wealth had been a significant element of the Western economy since the late Middle Ages, still, until the nineteenth century, for all practical purposes, "property" meant land. Even in eighteenth- and early-nineteenth-century England, when the country was in the throes of the Industrial Revolution, debates about property centered on real estate: until the 1867 Reform Act in England, the franchise was restricted to persons holding or renting rural or urban real estate worth a specified amount of money or bringing specified income. In the novels of Trollope, written at the zenith of the Victorian era in a nation that was well on its way to relegating agriculture to a side occupation, property (along with love) stands at the center of the plot, and property means, first and foremost, landed estates and the revenues they provide. It took time for public opinion to become aware that capital was displacing real estate as the principal form of wealth.

Now the relationship between a landowner and his tenants or farm hands is very different from that linking an industrialist with his employees. In the former case, physical proximity and exposure to the same vagaries of nature create a bond that is quasi-political in character. There are personal links, sometimes going back for generations. All of this has the effect of making disparities of wealth more "natural" and therefore less rankling. In the latter case, the relationship is impersonal: the employee performs the work, the employer compensates him with wages, and there the connection ends. If no longer needed, the employee is let go. Although in the early phases of industrialization there were instances of patriarchal relations between employer and employee modeled on rural conditions, in a fully matured capitalist economy the employer bears neither a moral nor a social responsibility for his workers. Such responsibility, insofar as it is acknowledged, is assumed by the state. It is certainly more troublesome to evict a tenant farmer than to lay off a factory worker. The disparities of wealth become accordingly more perceptible and less tolerable.

The first half of the nineteenth century witnessed the unbridled expansion of capitalist fortunes and a rising tide of hostility to it. At first, as had been the case in the past, this hostility focused on inequalities. In the second half of the century, however, it turned into a general assault on the very institution of property. Except for classical liberalism, which found itself increasingly on the defensive, most political movements and ideologies of the second half of the nineteenth century—from extreme radical ones like anarchism and communism to liberalism and even nationalism—assumed, in varying degrees, a critical attitude toward private ownership.

In retrospect it is apparent that the fury of the assault was due to the conviction that capitalism and industrialism were destroying what there was of social equality and security, launching mankind on an inevitable course of ever-growing discrepancies of wealth. This conviction found fullest expression in the Marxist theory of "pauperization," according to which capitalism would remorselessly impoverish the working class until it was left no alternative but to revolt and abolish property. In so arguing, the theorists of socialism overlooked two factors. One is that even in the initial, most brutal phase of industrialization in the late eighteenth and early nineteenth centuries, the situation of the lower classes in Great Britain, the country which pioneered capitalist industrialization, was far from hopeless, as demonstrated by declining mortality rates and steady population growth.[143] Second, they ignored that the wealth generated by the new economy would, in time, filter down and benefit the population as a whole—a development that by the end of the century would make a mockery of the notion of "pauperization" and the alleged inevitability of social revolution in the advanced industrial countries. In the twentieth century, social revolutions would in fact occur exclusively in preindustrial and precapitalist agrarian countries with weakly developed property rights and correspondingly low rates of economic growth.

As might be expected from what we know of the attitudes of the *philosophes*, the theoretical assault on property in the name of communism occurred first in France, and this at the very time when property was celebrating there its greatest legislative triumphs as the foundation of freedom. In the 1790s several French revolutionaries, led by Jacques-Pierre Brissot, defying prevailing opinion, denounced property as "theft."[144] The Jacobins, in the final phase of their dictatorship, contemplated legislation (the so-called Laws of Ventôse) that came close to communism.[145] Robespierre's associate Louis de Saint-Just outlined a program of massive expropriations of large properties: the Laws of Ventôse declared also the properties of "recognized enemies of the revolution" subject to expropriation. The Jacobins never realized this radical program—in fact, their advocacy of it contributed greatly to their fall from power, for it frightened small property owners who had benefited from the revolution and now made common cause with the well-to-do. But it was a harbinger of things to come.

The progenitor of modern communism was the Frenchman François-Noël ("Gracchus") Babeuf, a follower of Morelly. His historical importance derives from two facts: one, that he demanded common ownership of all economic resources rather than their equal distribution among individual proprietors, as customarily demanded by critics of property;[146] and two, that in him the animus against property, articulated a century and half earlier by Winstanley, proceeded from thought to action. Babeuf organized a plot to overthrow the Directory which ruled France following the fall of the Jacobins, but he was discovered before he could carry it out, and executed. In 1828, his associate Filippo Buonarroti published the program of the group, called "Conspiracy for Equality," which is the original communist manifesto.[147] As would Lenin a century later, Babeuf and his followers revived an idea popular among the Jacobins that the French Revolution had stopped halfway:[148] limited to politics, it had to be followed by a social revolution, which would supplement liberty with equality. Babeuf saw the world as a living hell, lorded over by unscrupulous crooks. It had to be destroyed and replaced with a communist commonwealth:

> We aim at . . . *common property,* or the *community of goods!* . . . No more individual property in lands. *The earth belongs to no one . . . the fruits belong to all.*[149]

Equality is "the first vow of nature" and "the first want of man," but so far it has been only an empty slogan. "We desire real equality or death" and "we shall have this real equality, no matter at what price": by "real" equality he meant that which rested on communal property. "Woe to him who will offer resistance to so determined a resolve!" Let all the arts perish, if necessary. According to Babeuf, the establishment of such a regime would require a long period of dictatorship. Babeuf's ideal was an ascetic community which severely punished shirkers.

In the plans of the Babeuvists, "equality" acquired a new sense. For Locke and the ideologists of the French Revolution it meant equality of opportunity. Locke regarded it as an aspect of liberty, defining it to mean "the *equal Right* that every man hath, to his *Natural Freedom,* without being subjected to the Will or Authority of any other Man."[150] With Babeuf and the communists, it signified equality of reward, which became the usage of twentieth-century welfare philosophies.

Babeuf had a counterpart in England in the person of William Godwin. The husband of the early feminist Mary Wollstonecraft and the father of Mary Shelley, Godwin introduced to England the ideas of French radicalism. His writings display little originality and at times verge on the bizarre. The most important of them is *An Enquiry Concerning Political Justice,*[151] written in response to Burke's *Reflections on the French Revolution* and published in 1793, at the height of the French Revolution, to the great acclaim of the intellectual elite: it so turned the heads of Wordsworth, Coleridge, and Southey that they wanted to proceed at once with the creation of a communistic society. Godwin restated the criticisms of private property familiar from French radical literature, to conclude that property and family were the source of every evil that befell mankind. Justice required the resources of this world to be equally distributed: inequality corrupted the rich and diverted the poor from the higher things of life.* Once property had been done away with, humanity would experience an unprecedented flowering of genius. Crime would disappear, and so would wars. Mind would triumph over matter and willpower over necessity. Man would become immortal, inasmuch as "we are sick and we die, generally speaking, because we consent to suffer these accidents[!]."[152] To counter anticipated objections to his theory, Godwin disarmingly admitted that his propositions were a matter of "probable conjecture" and that the "grand argument of this division of the work is altogether independent of its truth or falsehood."†

It would be redundant to recapitulate the views on property of prominent socialists of the first half of the nineteenth century—Saint-Simon, Fourier, Robert Owen, and Louis Blanc—because they essentially restate the arguments already made familiar by Helvétius and Rousseau, Morelly and Mably, Babeuf and Godwin.[153] All called for restrictions on private property, if not its outright elimination.

Less conventional speculations on the subject can be found in the writings of Proudhon. Proudhon's fame rests on the declaration "What is property? It is theft"[154]—a *bon mot* of which he was so proud that he never tired of repeating it. The Bolsheviks exploited it in 1917–18 to incite Russian peasants and workers to seize private belongings under the slogan "Loot the loot." Proudhon pointed out with considerable persuasiveness that every argument in favor of property is also an argument against it. If, as is maintained, first occupancy of no one's land provides the basis of property claims, then what are latecomers to do? And if property is a fundamental right, then all should have equal access to it:

*It was to rebut Godwin that Malthus in 1798 published *The Essay on the Principle of Population*, in which he argued the practical impossibility of egalitarianism because of the insufficient quantity of food to sustain a growing population.

†William Godwin, *Political and Philosophical Writings*, III (London, 1993), 465. Max Beer explains this otherwise incomprehensible statement by saying that Godwin was at heart a Calvinist preacher, who "held the historical view of society as of little use compared with the philosophical view, which he considered to be 'of a higher order and more essential importance.'" *A History of British Socialism*, I (London, 1919), 115. In fact, Godwin had been trained as a Calvinist minister.

but equality is the negation of property. Labor applied to objects that have no owner, Locke's justification of ownership, has little meaning in a world in which all the productive resources have been preempted. Proudhon was not against private property as such, only against its abuses under capitalism which enabled the capitalist to appropriate by means of rents, interest, etc., assets to which he had no moral right. Proudhon despised authority even more than inequality, however, and late in life, in his posthumously published *Theory of Property,* he depicted property and the family as the only effective bulwarks against tyranny.

Until the 1840s, arguments against property were essentially of a moral nature. Now, however, a new line of argument emerged which held property to be an historic aberration, a transient phenomenon connected with one particular organization of economic life, namely "capitalism." Karl Marx and Friedrich Engels, the founders of what they labeled "scientific socialism," in dealing with property set aside ethical criteria and dealt with it on what they claimed to be strictly scientific, that is, "value-free," grounds.

They proceeded on the assumption that mankind in its original condition had known no private property in land: it was a modern phenomenon, the by-product of the capitalist mode of production.[155] This belief initially rested on the metaphysical construct called the "dialectic," but after the middle of the century it drew on evidence supplied by contemporary agrarian historians. One of them, Georg Hanssen, in essays published in 1835–37, claimed that in the agrarian settlements of ancient Germany land had been collectively owned.[156] These findings seemed confirmed by the researches carried out in Russia in the1840s by the Prussian agrarian expert August von Haxthausen, who alerted the world to the existence of the *mir,* or repartitional commune, under which Russian peasants held land in common and redistributed it among themselves periodically to allow for changes in the size of households. Haxthausen assumed the *mir* to be of ancient origin, a living relic of an institution that had once prevailed throughout the world.[157] The following decade saw the appearance of two books by the jurist and historian Georg von Maurer, which contended that early Germanic tribes had known no property in land and first developed it under Roman influence.[158] Maurer's views gained wide acceptance because they pleased alike German nationalists and socialists. The notion of primitive communism received powerful reinforcement from the English legal historian Sumner Maine, who found evidence of it in India. In 1875, Maine generalized his findings to assert that in all primitive societies land was held collectively:

> The collective ownership of the soil by groups of men either in fact united by blood-relationship, or believing or assuming that they are so united, is now entitled to take rank as an ascertained primitive phenomenon, once universally characterizing those communities of mankind between whose civilization and our own there is any distinct connection or analogy.[159]

Thus it came to be believed that between nomadic existence, when private property was unknown, and fully settled agricultural life, based on individual or family ownership, there intervened a transitional stage of collective landownership or primitive communism.[160]

But those who shared this conviction still had to show why and how collective ownership had turned into private property. This was the contribution of the American anthropologist Lewis Morgan, on the basis of his studies of American Indians. Morgan's *Ancient Society,* brought out in 1877, acquired historical importance because of the uses made of it by Engels. According to Morgan, in conditions of "savagery," the lowest stage of human evolution, mankind knew no private property except in personal belongings (weapons, utensils, clothing). It also knew as yet nothing of the passion for possessions and the "greed for gain." Land was held in common by the tribe, habitations by their occupants. It was only gradually that the notion of ownership developed: land belonging to the tribe was first subdivided among the clans and then turned over to individuals. The reason for this evolution lay in objective factors, notably increase in population and technological innovation. Morgan felt that in his own time property had created social divisions of such magnitude that it threatened humanity with self-destruction. The only alternative was a return to ancient conditions of economic equality, i.e., to a propertyless world.

In the doctrines of the founders of "scientific socialism," private property occupies a central place. Suffice it to say that in the *Communist Manifesto* of 1848, Marx and Engels asserted that "the theory of the Communists may be summed up in a single sentence: Abolition of private property."[161] And yet they contributed very little to the understanding of the origins of private property. For all their claims to scientific methodology, they dealt with the problem much as their like-minded forerunners had done: that is, they constructed a theoretical model of society before the emergence of property and then described—with minimal recourse to either anthropology or history, of which they were largely ignorant—how property might have evolved.* The scheme was abstract ("metaphysical"), although the injection of a vocabulary drawn from economics, sociology, and psychology gave it the appearance of being more scientific than previous theories. Their view was rooted not in empirical evidence but in the Romantic vision of the "brotherhood" of mankind: its pathos was that of Schiller's "Ode to Joy."

Their chief objection to property was that it dehumanized people, "alienating" man from himself by making him submerge his identity in money (a concept borrowed from Ludwig Feuerbach and Moses Hess). Unlike Hegel, for whom ownership was "human freedom realizing itself in the world of phenomena," Marx and Engels saw it as having the very opposite effect: "property is not the realization of personality but its negation."[162]

How did property emerge?

Marx and Engels from their earliest writings assumed that originally all property had been held collectively: this assumption they made even before the writings of Haxthausen, Maurer, Maine, and Morgan had become available. To the extent that families organized in tribes disposed of movable and immovable assets, they were subordinated to the community at large and hence they did not suffer from the "alienation" that would characterize mature capitalism. It is only later that Marx and Engels found support for this *a priori* belief in the writings of Maurer and Morgan.

According to Marx, even in the more advanced economy of the ancient Greek *polis* the community prevailed: private property existed but it was "an abnormal form subordinate to communal ownership," in good measure because society enforced slavery, an institution critical to the ancient social and economic order.[163] Feudal property "like tribal and communal ownership [was] based again on a community," the binding factor being the exploitation of serf labor.[164]

The emergence of private property Engels explained with arguments drawn from Morgan. In *The Origin of the Family, Private Property and the State* (1884) he attempted to show how families emerged from orig-

*E. J. Hobsbawm, an admirer of Marx and Engels, concedes that their historical knowledge "was thin on pre-history, on primitive communal societies and on pre-Colombian America, and virtually non-existent on Africa. It was not impressive on the ancient or medieval Middle East, but markedly better on certain parts of Asia, notably India, but not on Japan." Introduction to Marx's *Pre-Capitalist Economic Formations* (London, 1964), 26.

inal bands of hunter-gatherers and how, concurrently, there appeared property. He explained the latter by the division of labor:

> [Private property] developed [in the ancient primitive communes] at first through barter with strangers, till it reached the form of commodities. The more the products of the commune assumed the commodity form, that is, the less they were produced for their producers' own use, and the more for the purpose of exchange, the more the original primitive natural division of labor was replaced by exchange also within the commune, the more did inequality develop in the property of the individual members of the commune, the more deeply was the ancient common ownership of land undermined. . . . Everywhere where private property developed, this took place as the result of altered relations of production and exchange, in the interests of increased production and in furtherance of intercourse—that is to say, as a result of economic causes. Force plays no part in this at all.*

This is a remarkably wrongheaded view of the origins of private property in that it ignores the elementary fact that until very recent times—Engels's own, in fact—the principal form of property had been land, which for most of history was not a "commodity" in the ordinary sense of the word and which never had any connection with the division of labor.

Genuine private property—that is, property entirely divorced from any social controls, according to Marx and Engels—first emerged under capitalism. The capitalist, however, for all the ostensible freedom his wealth affords him, is in fact as much enslaved as is the proletarian whom he exploits. The key concept is "alienation." The capitalist must accumulate wealth and therefore deny himself gratification, which is as much as to say that he deprives himself of the enjoyment of his riches. In his *Economical-Philosophical Manuscripts,* written in 1844, Marx

*Frederick Engels, *Herr Eugen Dühring's Revolution in Science* (New York, 1939), 179–80 (Part II, Section ii). The division of labor as the source of private property is mentioned already in *The German Ideology*, written in 1845–46 (pp. 52–53). In an early essay, Engels described trade as an activity in which the participants are not partners pursuing mutual profit but natural enemies, because what one gains the other loses: "In a word, trade is legalized swindle." *Marx-Engels Gesamtausgabe*, Part I, Vol. 3 (Berlin, 1985), 473. Such puerile blather the Communists solemnly reproduced in their scholarly editions of Marx and Engels.

spoke of money as alienated self, the quest for which compels the owner to behave "ascetically":

> Since money saved is deferred consumption, the values inherent in money have been preserved in it because they have not been realized by man: "the less you eat, drink, buy books, go to the theater or balls, or to the public house, and the less you think, love, theorize, sing, paint, fence etc. the more you will be able to save and the greater will become your treasure which neither moth nor rust will corrupt—your capital. The less you are, the less you express your life, the more you have, the greater is your alienated life and the greater is the saving of your alienated being."*

The capitalist's "practical asceticism" has its counterpart in the worker's unavoidable self-denial, caused by his separation from the means of production, controlled by the capitalist. Its consequence is both destitution and dehumanization.

The two hostile classes thus find themselves locked in a "dialectical" relationship:

> Proletariat and wealth are opposites; as such they form a single whole. They are both forms of the world of private property. . . . Private property as private property, as wealth, is compelled to maintain *itself* and thereby its opposite, the proletariat, in *existence*. . . . The proletariat, on the other hand, is compelled, as proletariat, to abolish itself and thereby its opposite, the condition for its existence, what makes it the proletariat, i.e. private property.[165]

Ultimately, the propertyless will overthrow the propertied, and in the process abolish property altogether. Economic assets will first be nationalized and then become common good, with the result that everyone will contribute according to his abilities and receive according to his needs, which is the ultimate goal of communism.

*Shlomo Avineri, *The Social and Political Thought of Karl Marx* (Cambridge, 1968), 110. Some contemporary economic historians arrive at a judgment diametrically opposite to Marx's in the above passage; with reference to the disastrous experience of Communist Bloc countries, they conclude that "too much capital accumulation, with too little output in consumption goods, may *reduce* the rate of economic growth." Nathan Rosenberg and L. E. Birdzell, Jr., *How the West Grew Rich* (New York, 1986), 168. Emphasis added.

As envisaged by Marx and Engels, the new communist order would combine the original communality of property with the greatly heightened productivity achieved by capitalism. Marx was convinced that industrial machinery simplified work to the point where it would require of workers no special skills and no repetitive motions: "Modern industry, by its very nature . . . necessitates variation of labor, fluency of function, universal mobility of the laborer. . . ."[166]

> In communist society . . . society regulates the general production and thus makes it possible for me to do one thing to-day and another to-morrow, to hunt in the morning, fish in the afternoon, rear cattle in the evening, criticize after dinner, just as I have in mind, without ever becoming hunter, fisherman, shepherd or critic.[167]

The society of the future will realize the anarchist ideal of a free and equal association of the producers, without a state to supervise it, in which individuals will find complete fulfillment.[168] The individual will no longer be "atomized" by being isolated from the community.

This Romantic theory, based on the thinnest evidence, most of it subsequently discredited, became henceforth mandatory in the socialist literature and in much general literature. But it met with resistance even in its own time. The criticism of the doctrine of primitive communism, the central postulate of the antiproprietary literature, was undermined by theoretical writings of contemporary writers and demolished by anthropology in the twentieth century.

Writing in the 1850s, the Russian scholar Boris Chicherin challenged the interpretation of the *mir* formulated by Russian Romantic nationalists known as Slavophiles and brought to the attention of the West by Haxthausen. Chicherin argued that far from being an ancient institution embodying a precapitalist, nonacquisitive, communal spirit, the *mir* was the product of the tsarist state, created in connection with the imposition of serfdom in the late sixteenth century to ensure, through the device of collective responsibility, that the peasants stayed put and paid their taxes.[169]

Next came von Maurer's turn. In 1883 the American Denman W. Ross demonstrated that theories of primitive communism among Germanic tribes rested on a misreading of Tacitus and Caesar, the principal sources of information on the subject. The absence of boundaries among early German cultivators (as reported by Caesar) meant that the land was undivided rather than jointly owned: "Holding in common and communistic holding must be carefully distinguished. They are very different things. We have plenty of holding in common described in the early records, but no communistic holding."[170] According to Ross, none of the existing records indicates that the early Germanic community enjoyed rights over the land of its members: "The community did not exist as a landowning corporation," for which reason conflicts over land were settled not by the community but by the individual parties to the dispute, with resort to duels.

The main onslaught on the theory of ancient communism came from the pen of the celebrated French historian Fustel de Coulanges, author of *The Ancient City,* a work which depicted the emergence of private property in classical antiquity as a corollary of religious cults centered on the family and its hearth. In 1889, Fustel de Coulanges published a lengthy article, later brought out as a book, in which he rejected the theory of primitive communism on the same grounds as Ross, namely that it misinterpreted the sources, but he went further than Ross in denying even common ownership of land among the ancient Germans.[171] His principal target was von Maurer. Tacitus and Caesar gave no warrant for Maurer's theories: "The whole body of German law is, in fact, a law in which property reigns supreme."[172] Common ownership of land would require periodic redistribution of the soil, of which there is no evidence among early Germans. He found the widespread belief in primitive communism to derive not from historical evidence but from the climate of opinion prevalent in late-nineteenth-century Europe:

> Among the current ideas which take possession of the imagination of men is one they have learnt from Rousseau. It is that property is contrary to nature and that communism is natural; and this idea has power even over writers who yield to it without being aware that they do so.[173]

Such arguments did not sway public opinion at the time, not only because of prejudice in favor of "natural communism" but also because from the middle of the nineteenth century onward even liberals came to be troubled by the growing disparities in the distribution of wealth. Typical was the case of John Stuart Mill, who in his widely read *Principles of Political Economy* (1848), moved liberal ideology closer to socialism.[174] Mill believed communism to be just, workable, and probably congruous with liberty: "[T]he laws of property," he wrote, "have never yet conformed to the principles on which the justification of private property rests."[175] He favored private ownership because it raised the productivity of labor rather than because it served the cause of freedom:

in his best-known work, *On Liberty* (1859), he hardly mentions property. Mill departed in two respects from the traditional liberal view of the subject. He questioned whether heirs of property owners should have unlimited rights to their legacy. Ideally he would "restrict not what anyone may bequeath, but what anyone should be permitted to acquire, by bequest or inheritance," with some kind of maximum norms.[176] Secondly, he questioned whether land should be treated as merely one particular form of property, on the grounds, first, that no one had made it, and second, that whereas in creating movable wealth one did not deprive one's fellowmen of an opportunity to do likewise, in appropriating land one excluded others.[177] The claims of landlords, therefore, ought to be subordinate to those of the state, which should have the right of confiscating (with due compensation) properties which the owners failed to improve: "In the case of land, no exclusive right should be permitted in any individual, which cannot be shown to be productive of positive good."*

Mill was one of the early liberals who infused liberalism with socialist ideas, stressing the overriding importance of an equitable distribution of productive wealth. His ideas encouraged the rise of a "New Liberalism" in England, which occurred in part from fear of socialism, and in part from the realization that under modern conditions poverty was not eliminated by hard work and sobriety alone, as had once been generally believed. Philosophical currents emerged around the turn of the century which maintained that poverty, alcoholism, and theft were the fault not of their victims but of capitalism, which forced them to act as they did.[178] It was embedded in the "system." Without explaining why unsocial and destructive behavior had existed long before capitalism appeared on the scene and persisted in noncapitalist societies, the advocates of this theory demanded that the state intervene to protect its less fortunate citizens. Such ideas provided the theoretical justification of the social reforms that in the twentieth century would lead to the emergence of the welfare state.

Thus on the eve of the twentieth century, liberals began to accept restraints on private property. They did so by subjecting the claims of property to the test of social justice and investing the state with the

*John Stuart Mill, *Principles of Political Economy* (London, 1909), 235. In this, Mill had been anticipated by Thomas Jefferson, who, having spent some time in France on the eve of the French Revolution, concluded that it was immoral to allow land to lie fallow, although he seemed unable to reconcile this concern with his commitment to the sanctity of property. William B. Scott, *In Pursuit of Happiness* (Bloomington, Ind., 1977), 42–43.

moral authority to curtail the right of absolute ownership for the sake of the common good. Ownership was perceived not only as a private right but also as a social function: if the owner met his obligation, society protected his possessions; if not, society could legitimately intervene to ensure that property performed its proper role.[179] And of this matter, the state was the sole judge.

8. *The twentieth century*

Antiproprietary sentiments inspired by social concerns were bolstered by new trends in the discipline of psychology. In the second half of the nineteenth century, under the influence of Darwin, who had maintained that human beings, like animals, were driven by instincts, William James developed a psychological theory in which instinct rather than cultural conditioning determined human behavior. For James, "acquisitiveness" was one such instinct.[180] The most influential champion of this approach was William McDougall, a British-born professor at Harvard and Duke universities, who in his widely used manual *Introduction to Social Psychology* (1908) provided a veritable catalog of what he called "the principal instincts and emotions of man," such as the instincts of flight, repulsion, curiosity, pugnacity, and, of course, acquisition. The French anthropologist Charles Letourneau, in a pioneering attempt at evolutionary sociology, classified acquisitiveness as a manifestation of the instinct of self-preservation.[181]

In the early years of the twentieth century, however, the concepts of "instinct" and its foundation, "human nature," ran into resistance; by the1920s, they were totally driven from the field. The reasons for this reversal included the obvious absurdity of tracing all behavior to instincts and the emotions that accompany them, as McDougall had done, as well as objections to its political implications. The biological explanation of human behavior could be, and indeed was, exploited for purposes of racial discrimination and persecution, first of blacks and then of Jews. Franz Boas, the founder of cultural anthropology in the United States, led the charge against it. An immigrant from Germany, where he had been raised in a liberal Jewish family, he made it his life's task to demolish theories that justified racism. To this end, he ejected from anthropology everything that resembled biological determinism, replacing it with cultural conditioning. His strongest argument was evidence that children of immigrants to the United States from diverse ethnic and racial stocks acquired in their adopted homeland common physical characteristics, which suggested that they also acquired the same intellectual and psychological traits. In *The Mind of Primitive Man* (1911), Boas argued that so-called "savages" did not differ in mental capacity from civilized people. He and his disciples decoupled sociology from biology, banishing "instinct" and "human nature" from the academic vocabulary. Boas acknowledged no such thing as human nature: there was only human behavior as shaped by culture. In the words of Margaret Mead, Boas and his followers saw humans as "dependent neither on instinct nor on genetically transmitted specific capabilities but on learned ways of life that accumulated slowly through endless borrowing, readaptation and innovation."[182]

In the 1920s, Boas's anthropological views received support from the "behaviorist" school of psychology founded by the American John B. Watson, which also banished biological factors from human conduct, reducing it to responses to external stimuli. Aggressiveness, dominance, and possessiveness were accordingly treated as cultural rather than biological phenomena.

After World War II the pendulum swung back once again, though not the whole way. Cultural anthropology and its ally behaviorist psychology, which had acquired near-monopoly status in academic circles during the interwar period, suffered from a striking contradiction. Their adherents accepted as conclusively proven Darwin's thesis of a continuum in the evolution of living creatures, according to which humans, even if the most highly evolved of all animal species, were in no respect unique. The evolutionary theory implied that animal behavior was relevant to the understanding of human behavior. However, Boas, Watson, and their followers denied that biology had any bearing on human conduct. So while biologically related to animals, psychologically (behaviorally) man was *sui generis*. The same people who would be appalled at the suggestion that man was a singular creature rather than a species of animal saw no incongruity in arguing that in terms of intelligence and conduct he was indeed unique because, lacking "instincts," he and he alone was conditioned by his cultural milieu.[183] But as the geneticist Theodosius Dobzhansky has observed, it is inconsistent to treat biological and cultural evolution as independent of each other. The unwillingness of modern cultural anthropologists to admit behavioral links between humans and animals replicates the refusal of Darwin's adversaries to concede biological links between humans and animals.[184] In the words of A. Irving Hallowell:

> Whereas opponents of human evolution in the nineteenth century were those who naturally stressed evidence that implied discontinuity between man and his primate precursors, anthropologists of the twentieth century, while giving lip service to morphological evolution, have by the special emphasis laid upon culture as the prime human differential, implied what is, in effect, an unbridged behavioral gap between ourselves and our closest relatives.[185]

This inconsistency was the target of a new school of ethologists and sociobiologists which emerged in the 1930s and reasserted the primacy of instincts. This subject will be treated in the chapter that follows.

As had been the case since classical antiquity, dominant views of property since the end of World War II have been largely shaped by contemporary events. Still, some works appeared in the old tradition which treated property exclusively in moral terms. The most influential of these was John Rawls's utopian treatise *A Theory of Justice.*[186] This book, which endeavors to delineate the principles of a "well-ordered society" based on "fairness," all but ignores psychological, political, and economic realities, as well as the record of history and the findings of anthropology.* It nowhere so much as hints how its principles are to be realized. In this respect it is still more abstract than the works of the church fathers, since they at least accepted man as he actually is. In his quest for perfect justice, Rawls proposes to reform or abolish "laws and institutions, no matter how efficient and well arranged . . . if they are unjust."[187] And the essence of injustice is inequality. Rawls's ideal, as is true of all social utopias, is perfect egalitarianism: income and wealth are to be apportioned evenly, although there is a rather perplexing qualifier, "unless unequal distribution . . . is to everyone's advantage."[188] Rawls cites with approval the communist maxim that society should rest on the principle "from each according to his ability, to each according to his needs."[189]

The relative novelty of the book lies in its insistence on applying the principle of equality not only to material goods but also to intelligence and inborn skills. These advantages gained, as it were, in nature's "lottery" ought not to bring the fortunate possessor any special benefits, because they are unearned. According to Rawls, the allocation of talents and abilities must be regarded "as arbitrary from a moral perspective."

*The reader will recall that the notion of a "well-ordered" society (or state) goes back to Plato's *Republic* (above, p. 6).

He objects to "the distribution of wealth and income [being] determined by the natural distribution of abilities and talents."[190] Talents should be viewed as "a common asset" and their possessors should profit from them "only on terms that improve the situation of those who have lost out."* If need be, efficiency must be sacrificed in order to attain perfect equality.[191] Rawls thus goes beyond the most radical communist theorists in wishing to socialize natural talents, that is, to deny more talented individuals the benefits which their talents bring them. "Equality of opportunity" is rejected as inherently unfair, since it "means an equal chance to leave the less fortunate behind in the personal quest for influence and social position."[192] The abilities of the more talented have to be used for common advantage: they become a "common asset." In this manner, not only inequality will be eliminated but also envy.[193]

Such ideas, which make minimal reference to either history or economics but a great deal to the ideal of justice, are especially popular among professional philosophers and psychologists.[194] A good example of moralizing on the subject of property can be found in the works of the psychiatrist Erich Fromm, the author of numerous books on what he perceives to be the predicament of modern man, one of which bears the title *To Have or to Be?*[195] Realization of the alleged dichotomy in the book's title is said by Fromm to be the result of his experience as a psychoanalyst, which convinced him that "having and being are two fundamental modes of experience."[196] The emergence of the "New Man" appears to him essential because the physical survival of the human race will require people to "give up all forms of having in order to fully *be*."[197] Such dicta are devoid of any realism, given that human beings must have in order to be.

The most influential changes in the theory of property which have occurred in the latter decades of the twentieth century have had less to do with ethics than with economics. In the past, professional economists have paid little attention to property rights, being principally concerned with material factors making for economic growth, such as capital formation and technological innovation. But a new generation of economic historians have turned their attention to the legal infrastructure of the economy, notably the institution of private property. Developing the utilitarian theme first articulated by David Hume, they have brushed aside arguments advocating property on grounds of Natural

*John Rawls, *A Theory of Justice* (Cambridge, Mass., 1971), 101–2. This proposal revives the long-forgotten argument of Campanella and Godwin that an individual's intellectual attainments belong to society at large.

Law or speculations about the origin of the state, to assert that its justification lies in its contribution to prosperity. In the words of Alfred Marshall, which can be found restated in many academic manuals published after World War I,

> the tendency of careful economic study is to base the rights of property, not on any abstract principle, but on the observation that in the past they have been inseparable from solid progress; and that therefore it is the part of responsible men to proceed cautiously and tentatively in abrogating or modifying even such rights as may seem inappropriate to the ideal conditions of social life.[198]

This approach, as it were, skirted the traditional arguments against property on the grounds that it fostered inequalities in wealth and, through inheritance, promoted injustice: it countered directly the contention of the eighteenth-century French *philosophe* Condorcet that equality was the quintessence of progress.[199]

The new trend gained momentum after World War II against the background of an open contest between communism and the market economies. The victory of the Allies over the Axis powers created an unprecedented situation: for the first time in history two opposed economic regimes—one based on an economic monopoly by the state (or, more accurately, the Communist Party), the other on private enterprise—confronted each other head-on, and they did so in an atmosphere of keen political rivalry.* This confrontation pitted the principles of public property and private property, heretofore compared theoretically, in direct competition. And there can be no question that as the twentieth century drew to a close, the principle of private property has triumphed all along the line. The contrasts between East Germany (DDR) and the Federal Republic, or between North Korea and South Korea, or between Taiwan and mainland China, grew more apparent with each year: contrasts alike in prosperity and the personal security of their citizens. The collapse of the Soviet Union and its empire in the years 1989–91 and the commit-

*The two blocs were not wholly polarized. Communist countries tolerated a small private sector in agriculture (in Poland, it was larger than the state sector) and the so-called "second economy," an euphemism for the black market. The industrial democracies, for their part, through various devices, mainly taxation, but also antitrust legislation and other regulatory means, prevented extreme disparities in the distribution of wealth as well as the development of unbridled private enterprise. Even so, the two blocs operated on fundamentally different principles.

ment by the Communist successor governments to private enterprise sealed the contest, whose origins date back to ancient Greece.

As the scales were tipping in favor of private enterprise, some economists turned their attention to its foundation, private property, traditionally the province of philosophers and political theorists. They formulated a novel theory of "economics of property rights" which treats property as a critical factor in economic growth. In the view of one member of this school, private property comes into existence "under the impulse of pressures towards efficiency through a process parallel to that of natural selection."[200]

The economic historians Douglass North and R. P. Thomas have applied this thesis to the past to argue that societies which provide firm guarantees of property rights are the most likely to experience economic development. In their view, the determinant of economic growth lies in the legal institutions which ensure to enterprising individuals the fruits of their labors.

> Efficient economic organization is the key to growth; the development of efficient economic organization in Western Europe accounts for the rise of the West.
>
> Efficient organization entails the establishment of institutional arrangements and property rights that create an incentive to channel individual economic effort into activities that bring the private rate of return close to the social rate of return.[201]

Property guarantees are thus of critical importance: "Economic growth will occur if property rights make it worthwhile to undertake socially productive activity."[202] North has demonstrated in particular how the introduction in England of patent rights encouraged inventors to make public their inventions and in this manner stimulated the Industrial Revolution.[203]

As the twentieth century draws to a close, the benefits of private ownership for both liberty and prosperity are acknowledged as they had not been in nearly two hundred years. Except for a few isolated oases of self-perpetuating poverty, such as North Korea and Cuba, where Communists manage to hang on to power, and except for the minds of a still sizable but dwindling number of academics, the ideal of common ownership is everywhere in retreat. Since the 1980s, "privatization" has been sweeping the world at an ever-accelerating pace. Thus Aristotle has triumphed over Plato.

2

THE INSTITUTION OF PROPERTY

The question which has stood at the center of discussion of property throughout the history of Western philosophy and political theory—whether property is "natural" or the product of convention—obviously cannot be answered with reference either to Rousseau's "fantasy," which deliberately ignores facts and resorts to "hypothetical" or "conditional" reasoning, or to William Godwin's "conjectural" thinking, whose argument, according to Godwin, is "altogether independent of its truth or falsehood." The answer must rest on evidence. Those who assert that property is merely a social custom characteristic of a certain period in human evolution must be able to demonstrate that children lack acquisitive impulses and indicate societies unacquainted with property. Those who claim acquisitiveness is embedded in human nature must produce data showing its universality.

The subject presents formidable difficulties, because of the immense variety of forms which property can take. It is simply impossible to trace throughout the world the emergence of private property in land—the principal form of property until recent times. Attempts at such a study were made in the late nineteenth century (e.g., by Émile de Laveleye),[1] but, being based on impressionistic accounts of travelers and early anthropologists, they are today mainly historical curiosities.[2] The greatest obstacle confronting the student of the subject is the absence of records: for in most countries property took the form of possession, claims to which rested not on documented legal title but on prolonged tenure, which custom acknowledged as proof of ownership. The English historian L. T. Hobhouse despaired of the possibility of writing a general history of property—even for a country with such excellent records as Britain—because of the paucity of data and the difficulty of distinguishing law from reality.[3]

In this chapter, we shall uphold the thesis that acquisitiveness is universal among humans as well as animals, and that it involves a great deal more than the desire to control physical objects, being intimately connected with the human personality by promoting a sense of identity and competence. Images of a propertyless world of "natural man" are a mirage, Lewis Mumford's visions of "heaven."

1. *Possessiveness among animals*

The principal objects of the acquisitive behavior of animals are territory and space, the subject of new academic disciplines with such awkward names as "territorology" and "proxemics."*

"Ethology," the study of animals in the wild, is a young science. Its origins date to the end of the nineteenth century, but intensive fieldwork, pioneered by Konrad Lorenz and Nikolaas Tinbergen, first got underway in the interwar period. After World War II, ethological studies made rapid strides, giving rise to sociobiology, which seeks to explain animal and, by inference, human behavior in biological terms closely related to the theory of evolution. The findings of these disciplines have cast serious doubts on the psychological and sociological doctrines dominant in the first third of this century—theories which had posited a sharp distinction between human and animal behavior on the grounds that while animals act instinctively, human behavior is primarily or even exclusively conditioned by culture. They revealed that acquisitiveness, previously regarded as a specific human trait and attributed to cultural influences, is common to all living creatures.

Animals in the wild are entirely dependent for survival on their phys-

*"Proxemics," a term coined by Edward T. Hall, deals, among other things, with the distances which humans—and, by extension, animals—observe in regard to other individuals of the same and different species. Edward T. Hall, *The Hidden Dimension* (Garden City, N.Y., 1966).

ical environment: since they neither cultivate nor manufacture, they subsist on the bounty of nature. For this reason they require undisturbed access to a defined territory where they can draw nourishment and breed; its size depends on the species' particular needs. Property among animals applies, therefore, first and foremost, to territory. The concept of the "territorial imperative" is by now well established, even if some sociologists and psychologists still have difficulty acknowledging it because of its political implications (of which more later).[4]

> Animals in what is known as their "natural state of freedom" never, as far as we yet know, enjoy the unconstrained and carefree freedom which a sentimental view of nature ascribes to them. No free-ranging animal, whether it belongs to a species living gregariously or spends the greater part of its life in solitude, has freedom of movement, i.e., moves as it pleases and at random. Already through its organization it is bound to a limited living space which offers it the conditions necessary for life. Even where this area is fairly large and provides these conditions uniformly well throughout, the animal is still not independent in its movement. Instead it limits itself to one or more small areas, known as its range; this it does not normally leave except under dire necessity. Within this range, too, the animal does not move at random, but only along particular paths and according to a fairly fixed schedule.[5]

In addition to asserting access to and control over territory, animals also maintain two kinds of distances: from other species and from individuals of their own species. These spatial "bubbles" have been quite precisely determined for the different breeds, the general rule being that the larger the animal, the greater the distance it requires to feel secure. When that critical distance is crossed by another creature, the animal either flees or attacks. Some species, however, prefer to live in close proximity to their kind.[6] As a rule, animals that dwell near bodies of water and feed on fish and other products of lakes, rivers, and seas tolerate crowding far better than those that are landlocked. Thus puffins, guillemots, penguins, and other birds which inhabit riverbanks and seashores and have small distances to travel to reach their source of food live in remarkably crowded colonies.

Pioneering work on animal territoriality was carried out during World War I by the English amateur ornithologist H. Eliot Howard. Howard found among birds no proprietary instinct independent of specific need: their claims to territory appeared to him directly connected with mating. He noted that during the winter, finches, the object of his investigations, lived side by side in harmony. But with the advent of spring their behavior underwent striking change. At issue was competition for females and breeding grounds:

> Observe . . . one of the numerous flocks of Finches that roam about the fields throughout the winter. Though it may be composed of large numbers of individuals of different kinds, yet the various units form an amicable society actuated by one motive—the procuring of food. . . . In response, however, to some internal organic change, which occurs early in the season, individuality emerges as a factor in the developing situation, and one by one the males betake themselves to secluded positions, where each one, occupying a limited area, isolates itself from companions. Thereafter we no longer find that certain fields are tenanted by flocks of greater or less dimensions, while acres of land are uninhabited, but we observe that the hedgerows and thickets are divided up into so many territories, each of which contains its owner. . . . [S]uch a radical departure from the normal routine of behavior could scarcely appear generation after generation in so many widely divergent forms, and still be so uniform in occurrence each returning season, if it were not founded upon some congenital basis . . . undertaken in response to some inherited disposition. . . .*

Howard explained this territorial possessiveness by the fact that birds nesting too close to one another would have to fly long distances to procure nourishment, endangering their brood, which is extremely sensitive to cold.[7] For this reason, birds aggressively defend their range: songs are one of the ways male birds proclaim title to territory and warn other males to stay away. Howard concluded that the territorial behavior of birds was "instinctive," i.e., "dependent upon purely biological conditions, nowise guided by conscious experience."[8]

Subsequent researches confirmed Howard's findings. It was discovered that territorial possessiveness was nearly universal among animals

*H. Eliot Howard, *Territory in Bird Life* (London, 1920), 4–5. Since these words were written it has been found that some species of birds, notably nonmigratory ones, defend their habitat also in the winter. Torsten Malmberg, *Human Territoriality* (The Hague etc., 1980), 33.

from the most primitive protozoa to the most advanced primates.[9] Ernest Beaglehole, in a study of property, devoted a lengthy chapter to possessive behavior among insects.[10] Thus, for example, dragonflies attack other dragonflies that approach the areas where they have laid their eggs.[11] Similar conduct was observed among marine life: a fish called the three-spined stickleback defends fiercely its breeding territory.[12] Such examples can be multiplied *ad infinitum*. Animals often mark areas over which they claim control with optical, acoustical, and olfactory devices, alone or in combination, and shield them from interlopers, sometimes jointly, sometimes individually. Unlike humans, however, when challenged they defend them with resort not to life-threatening violence but to bodily signals and other demonstrative actions, including contests which rarely draw blood—a fact which makes one wonder why vicious behavior among humans is called "bestial."

An important corollary of these findings is that animals require a territory of their own not only to escape predators and feed themselves and their offspring, but to engage in the very act of breeding:

> In most but not all territorial species . . . the female is sexually unresponsive to an unpropertied male. As a general pattern of behavior, in territorial species the competition between males which we formerly believed was one for the possession of females is in truth for the possession of property.[13]

An Irish observer explained as early as 1903 the constant number of birds of the same species in any given area by the fact that only those birds procreate which manage to acquire a territory on which to breed and raise progeny.[14] In other words, territorial constraints act as an efficient means of population control.

Some primates assert exclusive claims to land by physically occupying or "sitting" on it.[15] This behavior is not so different from that of humans, as indicated by the etymology of words denoting possession in many languages. Thus, the German verb for "to own," *besitzen,* and the noun for "possession," *Besitz*, literally reflect the idea of sitting on or, figuratively, settling upon. The Polish verb *posiadać*, "to own," as the noun *posiadłość,* "property," have an identical origin. The same root underpins the Latin *possidere,* namely *sedere,* "to sit," from which derive the French *posséder* and the English "to possess."[16] The word "nest" derives from a root (*nisad* or *nizdo*) signifying "to sit."[17] The monarch occupying the throne has been described as engaging in "nothing else but the symbolic act of sitting on the realm."[18]

Ethological researches have revealed that in addition to enabling them to obtain food and to breed, possession of territory and the resultant familiarity with its features is of critical importance to animals' physical survival:

> Occupation of a particular territory enables an animal to develop a detailed knowledge of its environment and at the same time to construct an inventory of reflex responses to landscape features and environmental cues—vantage points, hiding places, etc.—which facilitate quick and effective responses to danger and attack. Combined with what may be psychological advantages, this produces the familiar "home base" effect in which weaker animals are able to defend themselves against stronger opponents when they are in their home territory.[19]

In many cases it has proved possible to establish quite precisely the area which a given species requires for survival and procreation. As a rough rule, animals whose diet consists of meat need ten times as much territory as herbivorous animals.[20] As may be expected, animals defend their territory more fiercely as it shrinks.[21] Overcrowding causes them to behave in an abnormally aggressive and even neurotic manner. Even when adequate food is available, overcrowding induces physiological changes which can lead to wholesale deaths.[22]

One of the founders of sociobiology, Edward O. Wilson, asserts that nearly all vertebrates and most of the advanced invertebrates "conduct their lives according to precise rules of land tenure, spacing, and dominance," observing characteristic and precise distances from each other.[23] Social animals, like ants, are especially protective of their territory, the anthill, and have been said to live in a state of permanent war.[24] Other animals aggressively protect their core territory but tolerate interlopers in a vaguely defined zone surrounding it.

Lorenz, Tinbergen, and some other ethologists trace the roots of animal and human aggressiveness to a "territorial instinct." This contention has caused acrimonious debates, for it implies that aggressiveness is genetic in origin and hence ineradicable.[25] The opponents of this view sometimes go to extreme lengths in the effort to discredit it. While some concede that human behavior is a mixture of instinct and learning, others reject the biological factor altogether: thus in rejecting the theories of Lorenz and Ardrey concerning inherent aggressiveness in humans, the cultural anthropologist Ashley Montagu has pronounced them to be without any merit whatsoever:

> [M]an is man because he has no instincts, because *everything* he is and has become he has learned, acquired, from his culture, from the man-made part of the environment, from other human beings.[26]

Tinbergen has cautioned against a mechanical transfer of lessons learned from animal behavior to the behavior of humans because human beings possess superior intelligence as manifested in the ability to control their environment and to pass on knowledge. Disregarding this caution, an astonishingly large number of psychologists and anthropologists refuse to make any concession to ethology and sociobiology. At their most tolerant, they shrug off the findings of these new disciplines as "oversimplifications"; at their most bigoted, they subject their authors to ostracism and abuse. Edward Wilson was not only verbally reviled but physically assaulted for having the temerity to argue that sociobiology sheds light on human behavior.[27] Stephen Jay Gould in *The Mismeasure of Man* has challenged "biological determinism" on the political grounds that it must be wrong because it is "in its essence, *a theory of limits*"[28]—as if one's vision of what man can and should (by the standards of the observer) be or do determined what, in fact, he is and does. Gould concentrates on the uses made of biological determinism to promote racism, "fascism," and even genocide.[29] Resorting to such logic, sociobiologists could accuse proponents of cultural conditioning of advocating ideas that promote social engineering and hence lead to communism and Stalin's Gulag. To someone not personally involved in these controversies, the question is not whether biology can be exploited for political ends (as it undoubtedly can be and has been) but what observations of animals tell us about human beings.

As we have noted before in connection with the theories of Franz Boas, the reason a sizable segment of the scholarly community refuses to acknowledge the evidence supplied by sociobiology has, ultimately, to do with politics. Thus one critic of sociobiology says that the views of Lorenz on the sources of human aggression must be rejected not only because they are scientifically unsound but also because of their "policy implications."[30] It is a cardinal tenet of liberalism, socialism, and communism that human beings are infinitely malleable creatures who, through legislation and education (and indoctrination), can be purged of their socially undesirable attributes—acquisitiveness and aggressiveness, above all—and transformed into congenial beings happy to live among equals. The "perfectibility" of man has been declared by a prominent American liberal to be a prerequisite of democracy;[31] the premise is even more essential to the ambitions of socialists and communists. This vision is tenable only if human behavior is interpreted to be exclusively or almost exclusively conditioned by the environment ("culture"). If it is rooted in biology, then the possibilities of altering it are necessarily limited. The most that one can expect, under these circumstances, is that training, punishments, social disapproval, and similar devices will restrain undesirable forms of social behavior, with the risk that man's inborn acquisitiveness and aggressiveness will reassert themselves the instant these restraints are relaxed. The issue thus is of paramount importance to all who aspire fundamentally to remake society. It explains the emotions which the controversy between "nature and nurture" arouses and the reason why people, otherwise perfectly capable of observing and analyzing dispassionately scientific evidence, become highly agitated when the subject of human nature comes up. This experience confirms that humans can study every conceivable object with scientific detachment except themselves. No matter how hard they try to be disinterested, when it comes to analyzing human behavior the question creeps in how to direct it into constructive channels. And one's conception of "constructive channels" invariably affects how one views human motivation. For all the determination to address the subject as if it were value-free by means of scientific terminology and even mathematical formulae, in practice the method proves ultimately to be deductive and guided by political preferences.

2. *Possessiveness in children*

To prove that acquisitiveness is the product of cultural conditioning, one would need to demonstrate that children are strangers to possessive behavior and learn it only as they grow older under the influence of adults. In fact, evidence gathered by child psychologists indicates the very opposite to be the case, namely that toddlers are exceedingly possessive and learn to share as they grow up because they are taught to do so.

As in the case of animals, the leading causes of human acquisitiveness are economic and biological: the need of territory and of objects with which to sustain oneself and to procreate. All human activity "takes place at particular locations or within particular geographic contexts," for which reason "localization" is "one of the most basic aspects of human society."[32] But there is also a subtle psychological aspect to property-owning which causes objects owned to be treated as an extension of oneself. Hegel already stressed the positive psychological effects of ownership, in his own, Hegelian language: "[I]t is only through owning and controlling property that he [man] can embody his will in external objects and begin to transcend the subjectivity of his immediate existence."[33] Highly perceptive remarks on this subject come from the pen of William James:

> The Empirical Self of each of us is all that he is tempted to call by the name of *me*. But it is clear that between what a man calls *me* and what he simply calls *mine* the line is difficult to draw. We feel and act about certain things that are ours very much as we feel and act about ourselves. Our fame, our children, the work of our hands, may be as dear to us as our bodies are, and arouse the same feelings and the same acts of reprisal if attacked. . . . *In its widest possible sense . . . a man's Self is the sum total of all that he CAN call his*, not only his body and his psychic powers, but his clothes and his house, his wife and children, his ancestors and friends, his reputation and works, his lands and horses, and yacht and bank-account. All these things give him the same emotions. If they wax and prosper, he feels triumphant; if they dwindle and die away, he feels cast down. . . .
>
> An . . . instinctive impulse drives us to collect property; and the collections thus made become, with different degrees of intimacy, parts of our empirical selves. . . . [I]n every case [of the loss of possessions] there remains . . . a sense of the shrinkage of our personality, a partial conversion of ourselves to nothingness. . . . *

It has been observed that in all the major European languages—Greek, Latin, German, English, Italian, and French—"property" is used in two related senses: that which is an attribute of someone or something and that which belongs to someone.[34] "Proper" and "appropriate" have the same etymology. In other words, the vocabulary treats belongings as defining qualities. This is the reason why all communistic schemes, from Plato's *Republic* to the radical kibbutzim in Israel, strive

*William James, *The Principles of Psychology*, I (New York, 1890), Chapter x, 291, 293. Although usually ignored, the contrary is also true: inherited, i.e., unearned, wealth, causes insecurity and guilt. The problem is evidently serious and widespread since it has given rise to the profession of "wealth counselors and therapists." A list of such specialists can be found in Barbara Blouin, ed., *The Legacy of Inherited Wealth* (Halifax, N.S., 1995), 179–80.

to eradicate the individual personality, seeing in it an obstacle to the attainment of perfect equality. In the early Soviet Union this obsession went so far that some ideologues seriously proposed replacing the proper names of citizens with ciphers or numbers.[35]

The psychological dimension of ownership requires emphasis because the opponents of property rights invariably ignore it. Thus the English historian and socialist Richard Tawney attempted to explain the willingness of ordinary people to tolerate the inequalities and exploitation associated with capitalism by the fear of losing the savings they have managed to accumulate for their security in illness and old age. They were misguided, in his view: "Property is the instrument, security is the object, and when some alternative way is forthcoming of providing the latter, it does not appear in practice that any loss of confidence, or freedom or independence is caused by the absence of the former."[36] But as experience demonstrates, attachment to property is not only a negative but also a positive force: its motive is not merely fear of loss but also hope of gain. It is the failure to recognize this fact that accounts for the dismal economic performance of societies that have abolished private property.

James's insight has been vindicated by clinical studies of children. The English child psychologist D. W. Winnicott has labeled as "transitional objects" the blankets and teddy bears to which an infant clings, explaining that they serve, at one and the same time, as mother surrogates and objects that enable a child to wean itself from dependence on its mother and to establish a personal identity by recognizing things which are external to itself, i.e., "not me."[37] Studies of child development have made it possible to chart the evolution of acquisitive impulses. Two psychologists have observed something parents are well aware of, namely that infants of eighteen months have difficulty falling asleep without a special toy, blanket, or other familiar object, and are clearly aware what belongs to whom. At two years, a child "possesses as many things as possible" and displays a "strong feeling of ownership, especially in toys. 'It's mine' is a constant refrain." As they grow older, children learn to share, but the spirit of ownership remains strong, as does the desire to accumulate. By the age of nine there is a pronounced interest in money and the urge to acquire as much of it as possible.[38] This evidence supports James's view that ownership promotes the development of human personality. The "this is mine" of a two-year-old implies "this is not yours," and so conveys that "I am I" and "you are you."

Researches conducted in the United States in the early 1930s revealed the degree to which preschool children display aggressiveness in regard to possessions. One psychologist studied forty nursery children aged eighteen months to sixty months during playtime. As soon as a quarrel in some part of the nursery broke out, she or one of her associates moved in, "armed with stopwatches, notebooks, and other paraphernalia," to record the nature and duration of the dissension. The team logged some two hundred quarrels. It found that in all age groups, disagreements over possessions were the leading cause of conflict. They were the most frequent, however, in the youngest category (eighteen to twenty-nine months) where they accounted for 73.5 percent of the squabbles.[39] These results suggest that rather than being culturally inspired, acquisitive behavior is instinctive and attenuates under cultural influence.

Now it is conceivable that children raised in societies which place a premium on material goods learn possessive behavior from their elders. However, studies of children reared in communistic communities reveal identical patterns. In his pioneering work on communistic kibbutzim in Israel, Melford Spiro found the same acquisitive impulses and envy of possession among kibbutz children as among those living under capitalism. Brought up in communal nurseries, they would claim as property such objects as paints and towels and know precisely what it meant to say "It's mine." "[T]here is abundant evidence, in all but the very youngest children, that the preschool children [aged two to four] do perceive certain objects as belonging to them." In grade school "they are strongly assertive of their property rights. . . . Some are envious of another's possessions. . . ." It is only as they grow up that, under the influence of the communal ideology, they come to deny the need for private possessions. From which evidence the author concluded that

> the child is no *tabula rasa,* who, depending on his cultural environment, is equally amenable to private or collective property arrangements. On the contrary, the data suggest that the child's early motivations are strongly directed toward private ownership, an orientation from which he is only gradually weaned by effective cultural techniques.[40]

Lita Furby, who has also studied children in communistic kibbutzim, found lurking underneath the indifference to private property among adults raised in them a strong acquisitive spirit which was socially suppressed. Her study was inspired by the feeling that as late as the 1970s "[t]here has been almost no empirical work, and no systematic theoretical work, on the psychology of possession—on the origins and development of individual possessiveness."[41] Seeking to fill the gap, she discovered that the acquisitive spirit (or instinct) emerged at a very young age even in a milieu uncompromisingly hostile to it: children reared in communistic kibbutzim display the same acquisitiveness as American ones raised in a culture that encourages materialism. Her researches corroborated William James's stress on a close association between possession and the sense of self, as well as the effect possessions have on enhancing the feeling of competence: "The first notions of possession revolve around what *I* control and what responds to *my* actions."[42] Children use the pronoun "mine" very early, and when they are ready to form two-word phrases, one of the first concepts they articulate relates to possession (e.g., "daddy chair").[43]

Bruno Bettelheim learned to his surprise that while it was possible, over time, to inculcate in kibbutz children indifference to private belongings, this exacted a heavy price. Israelis brought up in such a Spartan environment showed exceptional group loyalty and grew up to become excellent soldiers, but they experienced great difficulty making an emotional commitment to any one individual, whether by forming a friendship or falling in love:

> Emotion shared with only one other person is a sign of selfishness no less than other private possessions. Nowhere more than in the kibbutz did I realize the degree to which private property, in the deep layers of the mind, relates to private emotions. If one is absent, the other tends to be absent as well.*

Kibbutz youths admitted to being inhibited about writing poetry or painting, because such activities were considered "selfish" and brought the opprobrium of the group.[44]

Empirical studies have further demonstrated that in order to develop normally, children, like animals, require a certain amount of private space. "[T]erritorial demarcation is necessary for [their] full psychic health"; "Lack of territory in children is followed by regression."[45] Like animals, too, children observe precise distances from friends, acquaintances, and strangers, the intervals being somewhat different for boys and girls.[46] They similarly surround themselves with invisible spatial "bubbles" to which they assert exclusive property. When they grow up,

*Bruno Bettelheim, *The Children of the Dream* (London, 1969), 261. This observation confirmed the finding of Spiro that children raised under such conditions "seldom form emotional attachments or intimate friendships." Melford E. Spiro, *Children of the Kibbutz* (Cambridge, Mass., 1958), 424.

humans of various cultures maintain habitual distances from one another and react strongly when their personal space is invaded.* The whole concept of privacy derives from the knowledge that we can withdraw, partly or wholly, into our own space: the ability to isolate oneself is an important aspect of property rights. Where property does not exist, privacy is not respected.† We have noted the insistence of utopian writers beginning with Thomas More that members of their fictitious communities mingle and act in concert. The Nazis and Communists did all in their power to destroy the privacy of the home and bring people into constant social contact. In dealing with political outcasts, they went to extreme lengths to deprive them of privacy. In their determination utterly to dehumanize their victims, the Nazis robbed them also of personal space, crowding inmates of concentration camps in such a way that they could not avoid touching each other when sleeping in packed bunks. Similar deliberate overcrowding prevailed in Stalin's prisons and camps.

3. *Possession among primitive peoples*

As we have noted in the preceding chapter, the belief in the Golden Age when mankind held all goods in common is as old as recorded history. It has provided the psychological support to the theoretical argument that property is "unnatural." And yet this is an article of faith to which modern anthropology gives no warrant. On the contrary: anthropologists have concluded that there never was a society so primitive as not to acknowledge some forms of ownership.[47]

> Property is a universal feature of human culture. The land upon which the social group is located, from which it draws its sustenance, the beasts that rove upon it wild, the animals that graze upon it tame, the trees and the crops, the houses that men erect, the clothes they wear, the songs they sing, the dances they execute, the chants they incant, these and many more are objects of property. Whatever men rely upon for the maintenance of life,

*Among adult Americans, the "personal distance" which separates "intimate distance" from "social distance" seems to fluctuate between eighteen and thirty inches. Hall, *Hidden Dimension*, 112–14.

†Which helps explain why the Russian language—the language of a people who through most of their history knew no private property in the means of production—has no word for "privacy."

> or value, they tend to bring within the scope of property. So it is that property is as ubiquitous as man, a part of the basic fabric of all society.[48]

The fact that all societies condemn and punish theft, at any rate within their own community, testifies to their respect for property.* Indeed, the surviving ancient legal codes, next to bodily injuries, concern themselves mainly with ownership and ownership violations. This holds true of the Code of Hammurabi (c. 1750 B.C.E.), many articles of which relate to the theft of goods and slaves, the possession of land, cattle and sheep, investments, and debts. Two of the three surviving tablets of the Assyrian law code, dating from c. 1100 B.C.E., deal with land law and other forms of possession: much of the tablet devoted to women also concerns ownership rights and claims. The Roman code of Twelve Tables (fifth century B.C.E.) treats of such matters as debts, thefts, and inheritance: the owner's right to dispose of his property is firmly guaranteed. "Primitive communism" turns out to be as much of a myth as the notion that possessiveness is socially inculcated. And still, most manuals of anthropology make no mention of property or, at best, do so only in passing.†

The belief in primitive communism which persists in much of the scholarly literature rests not on concrete evidence from history or anthropology, but on a logical deduction from evolutionary sociology, a theory now generally discredited which emerged in the middle of the nineteenth century under the influence of Darwin's *Origin of Species*. Darwin depicted biological phenomena as undergoing constant flux, "evolving" from lower to higher, more complex forms according to ascertainable principles of progression and regulated by the principle of natural selection. This theory was promptly applied to sociology. The evolutionary school of sociology assumed that just like living creatures,

*Edward Westermarck, *The Origin and Development of Moral Ideas,* II (Freeport, N.Y., 1971), I, 20. In his *Primitive Law* (London etc., 1935), which deals not with tribal societies but with ancient legal codes, A. S. Diamond asserts that "primitive law has no such conception as 'ownership'" (p. 261). Yet not many pages later he enumerates the punishments which primitive law (in his definition) inflicts for robbery (pp. 299, 328–29).

†Thus Carleton Coon, in his *Hunting Peoples* (London, 1972), finds space to condemn modern man's alleged exhaustion of the earth's oxygen and his (allegedly useless) journey to the moon, but none to discuss either territorial claims or property holdings among primitive hunters, the subject of his book. It is surprising to read in a work published by Cambridge University Press as recently as 1990 a defense of "primitive communism": Richard B. Lee in Steadman Upham, ed., *The Evolution of Political Systems* (Cambridge, 1990), 225–46.

institutions undergo development from more primitive to more advanced forms: nothing, therefore, could ever be said "to be" because everything was always becoming. Thus it was postulated that the history of mankind reflected a pattern of evolution from hunting and gathering to cattle grazing, followed by agriculture, and culminating in industry.

> The far-reaching significance of different modes of life was already recognized in classical times, and they were soon endowed with a developmental value as "economic stages." In the nineteenth century, when attention was first seriously devoted to the economies of primitive peoples, these hoary economic stages met with little criticism from the ideas of unilinear evolution, themselves transferred uncritically from biology to human culture. Man had begun everywhere, it was suggested, as a hunter, had later learned to domesticate some of his game animals and so became a pastoralist, and finally rose to the stage of agriculture. Little distinction was drawn between the very different kinds of food gathering, or between the rudimentary digging of planted roots and advanced cereal agriculture with the plough. Nor were any valid reasons adduced for supposing that pastoralism everywhere preceded cultivation. Finally, the concept of cultural diffusion and the recognition of the part it played in affecting the economic pattern over vast areas was almost entirely neglected. The ideas of evolution and progress that dominated scientific and social thought produced a vague and abstract "man" living nowhere in particular, who was always tending to struggle up to a higher stage. . . . People do not live at economic stages. They possess economies; and again we do not find single and exclusive economies but combinations of them.[49]

Anthropological and historical evidence indicates that various economies can and do coexist, even as one or another prevails. Thus, among ancient Germanic tribes, cattle grazing was the primary occupation, with agriculture pursued as an auxiliary enterprise, entrusted mainly to women. Men began to take over cultivation only when the plow, which required greater physical strength, replaced the traditional hoe.[50] Medieval Russians relied principally on agriculture, but they also fished, hunted, and trapped; later on, they supplemented agriculture with cottage industries.

The imaginary evolutionary progression from one to another economic "stage" was said to be accompanied by the emergence of property, allegedly unknown in mankind's most primitive phase of "savagery" when all things were held in common. In the pithy phrase of Robert Lowie, since the influence of property "in modern industrial civilization was potent . . . the evolutionary schematist naturally assumed that in the earliest phase of culture it had been nil."[51] The prevalent opinion today holds

> that the so-called collective land system in almost all early stages has been merely a family system, no more collective or socialistic than undivided family property at the present; that no definite and universal sequence in the change in the forms of land possession has existed; that from the earliest stages at least of agricultural man there have been different land systems with individual, family or tribe ownership; and that if any, family possession has predominated.[52]

As best as it is possible to determine, in primitive societies claims to territory derive from occupation of *res nullius* and to movable goods from the application of labor: rather the way classical theorists like Locke imagined private property to have come into being.[53]

Ownership among primitive peoples takes two forms: kinship (tribal or family) and individual. Kinship groups commonly control the land on which their members gather, hunt, fish, or, more rarely, cultivate, to the exclusion of nonmembers. Individual property consists of personal effects—clothes, weapons, tools—as well as incorporeal assets such as songs, myths, prayers, incantations, etc.

To begin with personal effects. There is universal agreement among anthropologists that people everywhere regard clothing, ornaments, weapons, etc. as absolute private property which the possessor can dispose of at will.[54] This happens because such belongings, usually handmade by the owner, are treated as extensions of his person: "personal property is, by the native, believed to be part of the self, somehow attached, assimilated to or set apart from the self . . . something of the individual's own life spirit is integrated with that which he has taken up and handled."[55] Among the Maoris of New Zealand, for example, it was customary for the owners of personal property to place a religious injunction upon it in the form of a "taboo" (*tapu*) which rendered it immune to encroachments by others. In Melanesia, the owner would protect his property by casting magic spells on the potential thief which would cause him to fall ill.[56] Such personal belongings were customarily either burned or interred with the deceased. In many primitive societies, housing is also regarded as absolute private property, usually allocated to the female heirs, because it is they who are likely to have built it.

As concerns the status of wives in primitive societies, some anthropologists regard them as the personal property of their husbands, because they can be sold or used as collateral.[57] Female premarital chastity and a wife's fidelity, where insisted upon, have also been interpreted as expressions of the "property taboo."* But there is also a phenomenon known as "wife hospitality," the practice of primitive men sharing their spouses with visitors without the woman's personal wishes being taken into account, which is another manifestation of ownership.† Widows are generally regarded as part of the deceased man's estate;[58] hence in some societies, they are killed and buried or cremated with him.

Primitive people assert personal ownership claims not only to material objects but also to what we would consider intellectual property, namely songs, legends, designs, and magic incantations, which are believed to lose their effectiveness if learned by others, unless properly transferred to them by gift or sale.‡ Such incorporeal assets are protected by elaborate social conventions.[59] Robert Lowie attributes to primitive peoples practices akin to modern copyright and patent laws.[60] An example of the latter is the knowledge of ironworking once jealously guarded by certain East African families.[61]

When we turn to nonpersonal objects, notably land, it is far easier to describe what people think of such property than how they deal with it. In a modern Western society, for such reasons as taxation and a highly developed commercial culture, nearly everything has an owner, be it government, corporation, partnership, or an individual; in other words,

*Ernest Beaglehole, *Property: A Study in Social Psychology* (London, 1931), 158–63. This principle was not confined to primitive societies. In seventeenth-century England, a married woman was "for particular purposes . . . regarded as her husband's possession," and at least one English writer of the time argued that a wife's infidelity was an infringement of her husband's property rights. Howard Nenner in J. R. Jones, ed., *Liberty Secured? Britain Before and After 1688* (Stanford, Calif., 1992), 95.

†This was also the custom among early Germanic tribes. C. Reinold Noyes, *The Institution of Property* (New York, 1936), 65.

‡Robert H. Lowie in *Yale Law Journal* 37 (March 1928), 551–63. "No Greenlander or Andaman Islander ventures to sing the song of another without his permission." Robert H. Lowie, *An Introduction to Cultural Anthropology* (New York, 1940), 282.

nearly everything, except for life itself, is a commodity. But this is not the case in premodern societies. For property to arise, two conditions have to be met: an object has to be desirable and available in limited quantities. Obviously, people will not bother to claim and defend objects which no one wants and/or which exist in inexhaustible profusion. When the world's population was but a small fraction of what it is today and widely dispersed, land and its products were tacitly assumed to be the possession of those living on it, and possession was enforced only when physically challenged. (And just how sparsely humans were distributed in prehistoric times may be gathered from the fact that the total population of England during the early Paleolithic era—from c. 750,000 B.C.E. on—is estimated at some 250 persons, and that of France at 10,000.)[62] Neither the concept of "possession" nor that of "property" was articulated, because there was no need to do so, inasmuch as an essential feature of either claim—the right to *exclude* others—becomes operative only when there is crowding and a resultant competition for scarce resources. This, in the case of predominantly agricultural economies, is believed to occur when rural population densities attain the figure of 150 to 250 persons per square mile, which indicates intense cultivation.[63]

The practice of staking property claims to assets is reversible if they cease to be either scarce or desirable. Thus the post–World War I mechanization of farming and the decision of the U.S. Cavalry to suspend purchases led to a precipitous fall in the price of horses and made it uneconomical in the Great Plains to enforce property claims to them, with the result that many horses were set loose, becoming ownerless.[64] Waters bereft of fish may lose value; the same holds true of cultivated land that turns to desert.

The more that is known of the practices of primitive societies, the more evident appears their tenacity in enforcing exclusive claims to whatever it is that their subsistence depends on. They "almost never go out of their regions because in strange places they cannot depend on food reciprocity and either do not know where wild foods grow or might not be allowed to gather them."[65] Which brings to mind the advantages animals derive from staying close to familiar territory.

Economic benefit is not the only reason why primitive people defend their home grounds and hesitate to venture outside it. Their attachment has roots also in religious belief as well as psychology.

Primitive peoples maintain a totemic bond with their ancestors and believe that abandoning the land where these had once lived will cut them off from communication with them.[66] In many societies, such as those of the ancient Greeks and the Chinese, the deceased were buried not in cemeteries but in the soil they had once tilled, which established a mystic bond between the ancestors and their descendants. Fustel de Coulanges attached such importance to this bond that he saw in it the original source of property claims. Speaking of the emergence of landed property in ancient Greece, his disciple, Paul Guiraud, wrote:

> If the Greeks dreamt of appropriating land, it was because they had to eat and clothe themselves; if they succeeded in appropriating it, it was because they were strong enough to take possession; if they made of it a patrimonial and hereditary asset, it was because the household ancestors required near the dwelling of their descendants a permanent place from which the family would never be dispossessed, where they could repose for all eternity, certain to receive always its veneration and to be always one with them.[67]

The emotional attachment to one's birthplace, manifested in "homesickness," is not an acquired characteristic, not something learned.[68] Jomo Kenyatta, the first president of independent Kenya, who happened to have been trained as an anthropologist, recalling his youth in the Gikuyu (Kikuyu) tribe, indirectly confirms Fustel de Coulanges's view of the ancient Greeks by depicting the attitude of his people to the land:

> In studying the Gikuyu tribal organization it is necessary to take into consideration land tenure as the most important factor in the social, political, religious, and economic life of the tribe. . . . Communion with the ancestral spirits is perpetuated through contact with the soil in which the ancestors of the tribe lie buried. The Gikuyu consider the earth as the "mother" of the tribe, for the reason that the mother bears her burden for about eight or nine moons while the child is in her womb, and then for a short period of suckling. But it is the soil that feeds the child through his lifetime; and again after death it is the soil that nurses the spirits of the dead for eternity. Thus the earth is the most sacred thing above all that dwell in or on it.[69]

Such emotional bonds explain why primitive people do not view land as a commodity, that is, as something that can be alienated. A Canadian geographer, referring to the difficulties Westerners have in comprehending the attitude to land of the Inuits (Eskimos), writes:

> To the extent that [these] people articulated their relationship to the land, they saw themselves as belonging to it rather than it to them. Traditional cosmology did not share with Western thought the clear subject-object distinction between man and nature, the idea that nature is but insentient matter for man to dominate or master. The land was home and sustenance but could not be reduced to individual possession and could not be alienated.[70]

For these reasons, primitive people do not trade in land: the African Bantu, to cite but one example of many, never sell it.* Since the right freely to alienate belongings is to modern Westerners one of the primary attributes of ownership, this may be another reason why they have difficulty recognizing the existence of private property in land among non-Europeans.† The latter's property claims are negative rather than positive: the stress is on excluding others rather than on asserting one's

*Herskovitz, *Economic Anthropology*, 365; Armand Cuvillier, *Manuel de sociologie*, II (Paris, 1956), 505–6. According to M. I. Finley, *Economy and Society in Ancient Greece* (London, 1981), 71, this also held true of ancient Athens, where there was property in land but very little trade in land: land was not a commodity in the true sense of the word. The well-known case of Indians "selling" Manhattan to the Dutch for sixty guilders rests on a typical misunderstanding. "The redskins had no conception of individual or tribal ownership of land . . . none lived on Manhattan; they merely hunted and fished there. The Indians understood that they would yield from time to time such portions of the island as the palefaces might need. They never expected to be driven completely off it." Edward Robb Ellis, *The Epic of New York City* (New York, 1966), 25–26. Apart from the author's erroneous assertions that the Indians knew nothing of landownership—since if that were the case they could not have granted the Dutch access—the statement is substantially correct. "The Dutch never boasted of having duped the Algonquins," writes another historian, "they simply sought a way of conciliating the natives and securing the right of living alongside them. Moreover the Indians did not abandon the island: they continued to penetrate freely the villages and had no sense of a transfer of powers." Anka Muhlstein, *Manhattan* (Paris, 1986), 23–24. Similar arrangements were observed among the Eskimos of Canada, who would allow outsiders occasional access to their land. Peter J. Usher in Terry L. Anderson, ed., *Property Rights and Indian Economies* (Lanham, Md., 1992), 47.

†A frequently used Western argument to justify the expropriation of Indian land held that the natives, who were nomadic hunters, had done nothing to improve the land and hence had no claim on it. This argument was heard already in colonial North America. See Wilcomb E. Washburn in James Morton Smith, ed., *Seventeenth Century America* (Chapel Hill, N.C., 1959), 22–23. In an 1823 Supreme Court case concerning a suit brought by Indian tribes against white settlers, the latter claimed that the Indians had not improved the land to establish their property claim and, being constantly on the move,

own right of full disposal. Whereas for the modern man owning land, following Roman law, entails the freedom to sell it to others, for primitive man it means mainly the right to keep others out. Primitive man's situation in this respect is not different from that of animals: "The fundamental importance of territory [for birds] lies not in the mechanism (overt defense or any other action) by which the territory becomes identified with its occupant, but in the degree to which it is in fact used exclusively by its occupant."[71]

The emotional attachment to the homeland is strong also among modern people. Its most dramatic manifestation was the return, after two thousand years of diaspora, of the Jewish people to their ancestral homeland in Israel, a unique instance in world history. Another example is the return to their native lands of the several small nations deported by Stalin in 1944 for alleged collaboration with the German invaders (the Chechens, Ingush, Balkar, Kalmycks, and Crimean Tatars).[72]

Throughout history, peoples lacking a homeland of their own have been held in contempt. The best illustration of this fact is the traditional attitude of Christians toward the Jews. When, following the adoption of Christianity by the rulers of the Roman Empire in the fourth century, a substantial part of the Jewish population refused to convert to the new faith, they found themselves the object of the same persecution by Christians that the latter had previously suffered at the hands of the Romans. From the fourth century on, Christian theologians depicted Jews as an accursed people, condemned to eternal grief. As "proof" of God's disfavor and punishment for their alleged responsibility for the crucifixion of Jesus, they pointed out that the Jews had had no home of their own since their Temple had been destroyed by the Romans and they themselves scattered:

> Almost all the Church Fathers of the fourth century speak with the same voice, from Saint Ephrem to Saint Jerome, from Saint John Chrysostom to Saint Augustine. In the great Augustinian treatise *The City of God* we read: "But the Jews who rejected him . . . after that were miserably spoiled by the Romans . . . and dispersed over the face of the whole earth."[73]

This myth—and it is nothing but a myth, for the dispersal of Jews from Palestine had begun centuries before the birth of Jesus[74]—sank deep

left "few traces" to prove the validity of their claim. Carol M. Rose in *University of Chicago Law Review* 52, No. 1 (1985), 85–86.

roots in the Christian consciousness, to emerge time and again as allegedly conclusive proof that Jews were a pariah nation doomed to eternal suffering.

The following is an example of this mentality. It is drawn from the Russian chronicle's explanation of why the Kievan Great Prince Vladimir, in search of a religion for his people, rejected Judaism as proffered by Khazar converts to that faith:

> The Prince then asked [the Jewish Khazars] where their native land was and they replied that it was in Jerusalem. When Vladimir inquired where that was, they made answer, "God was angry at our forefathers, and scattered us among the gentiles on account of our sins. Our land was then given to the Christians." The Prince then demanded, "How can you hope to teach others while you yourselves are cast out and scattered abroad by the hand of God? If God loved you and your faith, you would not be thus dispersed in foreign lands."[75]

This notion continues to play a significant role in the hostility toward the state of Israel of many Christians, a hostility so puzzling to Jews, for the Jews' return to their homeland can be interpreted to mean that they have been absolved of guilt for the martyrdom of Jesus.

And, finally, there is the psychological dimension of ownership. Primitive people seem to derive from possession the same sense of well-being and enhanced competence as Western man. Studies of the very primitive Negrito people of Southeast Asia have shown that they not only have a highly developed sense of ownership but receive from the objects they own psychic gratification: "The psychological bases of private property" among these people "derive from a clearly developed consciousness of individuality which is linked with the consciousness of personal achievement."[76]

It has been suggested that the deterritorializing of much of modern humanity is responsible for many social problems, inasmuch as the absence of a bond with the land lowers a people's sense of dignity and responsibility.[77] The nineteenth-century Russian novelist Gleb Uspenskii has written eloquently about the devastating effect on the Russian peasant of losing contact with the soil.[78] The wholesale and violent uprooting of peasants from their land by Stalin may well have been the single most traumatic experience in the history of the Russian people, the disastrous effects of which are likely to be felt for generations to come.

4. *Societies of hunters and gatherers*

Hunting-and-gathering is a mode of subsistence that has characterized perhaps as much as 99 percent of humanity's past. A more conservative estimate holds that of the eighty billion people, all told, who have inhabited the earth down to the present, more than 90 percent have maintained themselves by hunting-and-gathering, that is, a manner of sustenance no different from that of animals in the wild ("For some fifteen million years members of the family of man foraged as animals among animals").[79] Only 6 percent are said to have engaged in agriculture, and the remaining 4 percent in industrial occupations.[80]

Unless they have far more space than they need, hunters and gatherers jealously guard their territories, because they are completely dependent on them for survival. It is customary for such groups, usually organized into extended families, to limit to their kin the exploitation of the area where they forage. Although permission may occasionally be granted to outsiders, trespassers are likely to be ambushed and killed.[81] The ferocity with which primitive tribes defend their territory has been likened to that of other mammals.[82] A study by Frank G. Speck, published during World War I, of Indian groups inhabiting northern and northeastern United States and Canada has disproved the contention of Lewis Morgan and his followers that Indian hunters did not assert exclusive rights to their areas. Speck found that

> [t]he whole territory claimed by each tribe was subdivided into tracts owned from time immemorial by the same families and handed down from generation to generation. The almost exact bounds of these territories were known and recognized, and trespass, which indeed was a rare occurrence, was summarily punishable.*

*University of Pennsylvania, *University Bulletin,* 15th Series, No. 4, Pt. ii, *University Lectures* (Philadelphia, 1915), 183. Yet such evidence did not inhibit the late professor of social anthropology at the University of Cambridge from insisting, "No human society, ancient or modern, primitive or civilized, has ever developed customs which correspond at all closely to [the] stereotype of 'territorial behavior.'" Edmund Leach in *New York Review of Books* 11, No. 6 (October 10, 1968), 26. Ignoring the record of cruelty and incessant warfare among primitive societies, Leach attributed aggressiveness exclusively to "Western industrial man who has been culturally conditioned to act with brutality in a ruthlessly competitive society." Ibid., 28. A corrective to such fatuous assertions is a recent study by Lawrence H. Keeley, *War Before Civilization* (New York,

Subsequent researches have revealed an interesting fact about the Indians of northeastern America, namely that their territorial claims received added impetus from the arrival of Europeans in quest of beaver furs. Until then, beavers had been so abundant that they were, for all practical purposes, worthless and hence not an object of ownership claims. As soon as white traders appeared willing to pay for beaver skins, the Indians drew up boundary lines delineating their separate claims.[83] The Caribou Eskimos, by contrast, stake out no territorial claims for the caribou, their staple food, because these animals graze over too vast expanses to permit the drawing up of boundaries.[84] The Indians of the southwestern plains also pressed no territorial claims, in part because the animals they hunted had no commercial value and in part because they grazed too extensively to permit enforcing such claims.[85]

Hunters and gatherers, along with pastoral people, often display interest not in the land but in objects growing on it, such as fruit trees or trees that furnish poison for arrows or provide a home for honey bees.[86] Thus, primitive tribes regard a tree and its product (e.g., olive or cacao bean) as belonging to him who plants and cultivates it, regardless of who farms the land on which it stands.* Among the Sierra Popoluca people of Mexico, for example, trees were traditionally owned but not the land on which they grew. Landownership began only with the introduction of coffee culture, which required intensive cultivation.†

A visitor to Central Asia before the 1930s, when its nomadic population was forcibly settled, might have concluded that these nomads recognized no property in pasture because during the summer months they grazed their flocks without regard to boundaries. Closer investigation,

---

1996), which demonstrates the savage brutality of primitive warfare that anthropologists have traditionally preferred to ignore. Its victims outnumber many times those inflicted by modern warfare (p. ix): "the proportion of war casualties in primitive societies almost always exceeds that suffered by even the most bellicose or war-torn modern states" (88–89). Keeley assails the persistent myth that primitive people show no interest in territory: in fact, armed conflicts among them very often break out over territory (108–9).

*This fact, learned from personal observations in Asia Minor, was reported with great surprise a century ago by Hyde Clark in *Journal of the Anthropological Institute of Great Britain and Ireland* 19, No. 2 (November 1890), 199–211. Cf. Melville J. Herskovits, *Man and His Works* (New York, 1952), 283.

†René F. Millon in *American Anthropologist* 57 (1955), 698–712. It is striking proof of the universality of human behavior that medieval German law similarly acknowledged that "buildings, like meadows and forest as well as fruit-bearing plants need not be part (*Bestandteile*) of the ground on which they stand but represent independent objects that can have their own legal existence." Rudolf Hübner, *Grundzüge des deutschen Privatrechts*, 2nd ed. (Leipzig, 1913), 384.

however, would reveal that once they moved to winter pastures, Central Asian clans enforced strict proprietary claims: because of their scarcity, "the winter quarters alone [were] thought of as territorial possessions."[87] Similarly, the Bushmen hunter-gatherers of Africa do not press claims to territory in general but only to certain precious landmarks, such as water holes.[88]

Very likely it is this selective exercise of exclusive claims, as determined by desirability and scarcity, along with the unwillingness to sell land, that misled early Western travelers and anthropologists, accustomed to everything having either a sovereign or an owner, into concluding that primitive peoples regarded land as common property. It still confuses some modern anthropologists who, noting that primitive peoples are often interested only in the product of the land and not in the land itself, deny them knowledge of true ownership.[89] The modern dichotomy ownership/usufruct is not applicable to premodern conditions. Neither is the antithesis communism/private ownership, because a primitive people may share some objects and yet insist on exclusive ownership of others.[90] Thus it is customary for primitive hunters to share their quarry, because hunting is usually done collectively and because they do not know what to do with the surplus; most primitive societies have precise rules on how to split the kill.* Vegetables and small game, however, garnered mostly by the women, are family property and not shared, except in emergencies.[91]

5. *The emergence of property in land*

We have established the universality of property relations throughout history in all societies, including the most primitive. To this generalization, however, we have made one major exception: land. Until very recently, land and its products were mankind's most important source of livelihood. Even in the West, where trade has come to play an increasing economic role since the late Middle Ages and manufacture from the eighteenth century onward, land was the basis of wealth. But, as pointed out above, in all primitive societies and most

*Helmut Schoeck in *Envy* (New York, 1970), 30–1, makes the interesting suggestion that the main reason for sharing animal kills is the need to propitiate the feeling of envy, which is very strongly developed among many primitive tribes. This explanation is supported by an anthropologist who had studied intensively one Mexican village and found envy to be very prevalent. In Italy and India it has been found to be "a dominant note in people's character." George M. Foster, *Tzintzuntzan* (Boston, 1967), 153.

non-Western societies in general, land was not treated as a commodity and hence was not truly property, which, by definition, entails the right of disposal. Land was universally considered a resource that one could exploit exclusively but not own and sell.

The question then arises: when and why did land become a commodity? It is an important question to answer, for it is with land that the modern concept of property in productive assets comes into existence.

The most persuasive answer is economic. The transformation of land into tribal, family, or individual ownership seems to occur, first and foremost, in consequence of population pressures which call for a more rational method of exploitation, and it does so because the unregulated exploitation of natural resources leads to their depletion.

> Economists have long been familiar with the proposition that unconstrained nonpriced access to any common-property resource such as a fishing or hunting ground . . . leads to the inefficient use of such resources.[92]

> Suppose that land is communally owned. Every person has the right to hunt, till, or mine the land. This form of ownership fails to concentrate the cost associated with any person's exercise of his communal right on that person. If a person seeks to maximize the value of his communal rights, he will tend to overhunt and overwork the land because some of the costs of his doing so are borne by others. The stock of game and the richness of the soil will be diminished too quickly. . . . If a single person owns land, he will attempt to maximize its present value by taking into account alternative future time streams of benefits and costs and selecting that one which he believes will maximize the present value of his privately-owned land rights. . . . In effect, an owner of a private right to use land acts as a broker whose wealth depends on how well he takes into account the competing claims of the present and the future. But with communal rights there is no broker, and the claims of the present generation will be given an uneconomically large weight in determining the intensity with which the land is worked. . . . [P]rivate ownership of land will internalize many of the external costs associated with communal ownership, for now an owner, by virtue of his power to exclude others, can generally count on realizing the rewards associated with husbanding the

game and increasing the fertility of his land. The concentration of benefits and costs on owners creates incentives to utilize resources more efficiently.*

The inefficiency of common ownership is aggravated by the phenomenon of the "free rider" who claims his share of the fruits of common labor but shirks his obligations—a phenomenon which sooner or later leads to the collapse of the nonprivate enterprise. This occurred in North America in the course of the seventeenth century, when attempts at joint cultivation failed and, except in the slave-owning states, yielded to freehold farming.

A striking illustration of this fact is provided by the history of the Virginia Company's Jamestown, the first permanent British settlement in North America. The company initially adopted the communistic principle that each member of the community would contribute what he could to the common store and receive, in return, whatever he needed. Since this policy brought the colony to the brink of starvation, the Virginia Company gave it up and awarded each member a three-acre plot from which to support himself and his family. The result was a tenfold increase in productivity. In the words of a contemporary:

> [F]ormerly, when our people were fedde out of the common store and laboured jointly in the manuring of the ground, and planting corne, glad was that man that could slippe from his labour, nay, the most honest of them in a general businesse, would not take so much faithfull and true paines, in a weeke, as now he will doe in a day, neither cared they for the increase, presuming that howsoever their harvest prospered, the generall store must maintain them, by which meanes we reaped not so much corne from the labours of 30 men, as three men have done for themselves [since]. . . .†

*Demsetz in *American Economic Review* 57, No. 2 (May 1967), 354–56. On this, see further Garrett Hardin in *Science* 162 (December 13, 1968), 1,243–48. Hardin gives credit for this explanation to William Forster Lloyd, the author of *Two Lectures on the Checks to Population* (1833). It has been challenged, however, on the grounds that it fails to distinguish between *common* and *communal* usage and therefore ignores communal checks on individual exploitation of common resources such as are observed among many primitive peoples. Peter J. Usher in Terry L. Anderson, ed., *Property Rights and Indian Economies* (Lanham, Md., 1992), 50–1.

†Ralph Hamor, *A True Discourse of the Present State of Virginia* (London, 1615; repr. Richmond, Va., 1957), 17. The experience was replicated in contemporary Plymouth: William B. Scott, *In Pursuit of Happiness* (Bloomington, Ind., 1977), 12.

Even in our own time, people who depend for their livelihood on resources that have not been made subject to property claims or that by their very nature cannot be thus treated (as, for example, large bodies of water) have been known to enter into agreements that maximize their profits by establishing informal property rights.[93] We have noted such arrangements among Indian beaver trappers in seventeenth-century North America. Nineteenth-century whalers established rules regulating the ownership of whales that broke loose of the harpoon.[94] More recently, lobster fishermen on the Maine coast have "virtually created extralegal property rights for themselves in the midst of the oceanic common property" by agreeing to exclude outsiders.[95]

The same principle can also operate on land, as demonstrated by an interesting account of the emergence of property claims in the American west following the discovery of gold.[96] When gold was first found in California (January 1848), the area was about to come under United States jurisdiction by virtue of a treaty with Mexico. During the transition period, all of California was the property of the federal government. No rules existed concerning the exploitation of mineral resources on public lands. As hundreds of prospectors converged on the gold-bearing regions, California had neither government, nor courts, nor procedures for establishing property claims. Nevertheless, there was little contention, because the territory was vast and the number of claimants small. But in 1849 and 1850, as tens of thousands of prospectors descended on California, the situation changed:

> In 1848 the ratio of land to miners was large enough that mining rights had relatively little value. If one area got too crowded, the miners just moved upstream to a new gold field. However, as the new wave of miners entered California in 1849, gold land became scarcer and scarcer.[97]

It now became common practice for the miners to convene meetings at which, by majority vote, the right of claimants to exploit a fixed number of square feet was formally recognized. The right was tantamount to a property title, because it could be sold. This incident provides a classic example of how private property comes into existence by common consent as desired objects become scarce.

Evidence of this sort casts doubt on the accepted wisdom that all property claims derive from forcible appropriation. In fact, rational economic self-interest often intervenes to transform common into private property: "the market tends to be an under-appreciated and misunderstood mechanism for generating cooperative behavior."[98] Hence it is reasonable to assume that in prehistoric times, too, considerations of economic efficiency played their part in imposing property boundaries on land and fishing grounds that previously had been open to all comers.

6. *Agricultural societies*

The transition from primary reliance on hunting-and-gathering to agriculture in Europe, the Middle East, and the Americas is believed to have occurred sometime around 10,000 to 8000 B.C.E. Jericho, founded between 7000 and 9000 B.C.E., is the earliest known agricultural settlement in the world. Egypt is said to have practiced regular agriculture by 4500 B.C.E.

This transition was an involved process which is only dimly understood. It certainly was not an "event," as perceived by evolutionary anthropologists of the nineteenth century who thought in terms of regular progressions from lower to higher stages: as pointed out above, different economies can and usually do coexist. Nevertheless, there are occurrences which cause one or another economic pursuit to become dominant, usually either as a result of overpopulation, which demands more intense forms of land use, or because of the exhaustion of the previous source of sustenance.*

Hunting-and-gathering, though involving relatively little effort, is exceedingly wasteful of land. Some estimates—and they vary considerably—hold that a typical band of hunters-and-gatherers numbering twenty-five individuals requires for its survival between one thousand and three thousand square kilometers.[99] In Tasmania, as late as 1770, between two thousand and four thousand people hunted over an area of 25,000 square miles.[100] Settled land cultivation can support a much larger population than an economy based primarily or exclusively on hunting-and-gathering. Pre-agricultural man required ten or more square kilometers per person; with the introduction of agriculture, this requirement shrank to between one and five square kilometers, and with

*"[T]he predominant historical motivation for agriculture has been growth of population." Mark N. Cohen in Steven Polgar, ed., *Population, Ecology, and Social Evolution* (The Hague and Paris, 1975), 86. Cohen supports this statement with evidence gathered from the archaeology of the coast of Peru. On this subject, see further Ester Boserup, *The Conditions of Agricultural Growth* (Chicago, 1965).

the domestication of animals it declined to 0.5 square kilometer or less per person.[101]

One theory accounting for the abandonment of hunting-and-gathering in favor of settled agriculture attributes it to Paleolithic man's overhunting.[102] The extinction of large, gregarious herbivores, closely associated with the geographic spread of humans, is attributed to the ease with which these animals could be hunted down. Thus by about 10,000 B.C.E., the approximate end of the Paleolithic era and the dawn of settled agriculture, the nomads who had moved into America from Asia some two millennia earlier had managed to exterminate mammoths and certain species of bison. When this wildlife was gone, the big-game hunters turned to smaller animals and then increasingly to agriculture (corn, beans, squash) supplemented by small-game hunting. Recent researches have revealed the notion of pre-Columbian North America teeming with wildlife to be a myth. Native Indians slaughtered moose, elk, deer, and other wildlife at such a rate that early-nineteenth-century white travelers in the west rarely sighted any of these animals. There are said to be more bison today in Yellowstone National Park than there were before 1500.[103] Much the same holds true of other parts of the world. Primitive people are prone mindlessly to exterminate animals and destroy forests, to the extent they are physically able, without any thought of the future.[104]

Reliance on agriculture enhances the sense of property.

The reasons why agricultural people hold on even more tenaciously to their land than hunters-and-gatherers are not far to seek. For one, cultivation of the soil is a drawn-out process: cereals and vegetables require months to mature, while olive trees and vines—the principal crops of the Mediterranean, where the systematic pursuit of agriculture is believed to have originated—take years. They demand, therefore, constant attention: the labor that goes into cultivation transforms crops into personal belongings with all the attendant psychological side effects. Secondly, people engaged in this kind of work settle on the land they cultivate to be able to give it the attention it requires.* Thus it is customary for agricultural peoples to mark off their area with natural objects (rivers, trees, rocks, etc.), which is less often done in the case of hunting grounds or grazing lands, of which the boundaries are generally

*An exception is nomadic agriculture, known as slash-and-burn (see below, p. 161). In this case, title was claimed not to the land but only to the crops. But this inefficient form of cultivation was practiced only in the early stages of agriculture and disappeared with the shortage of land brought about by population growth.

known and, in any event, less precise.[105] A constant companion of agriculture—as well as the institution of property in land—is the practice of surveying. Evidence exists that land surveys were carried out in ancient Egypt as well as Sumer, Greece, and Rome. It is not surprising, therefore, that studies of the economies of primitive peoples show that those among them who rely primarily on agriculture develop an enhanced sense of private ownership.[106] According to Jomo Kenyatta, Gikuyu (Kikuyu) customary law provided that every family had a right to the land: "While the whole tribe defended collectively the boundary of their territory, every inch of land within it had its owner."*

Ownership of agricultural land among primitive people, as a rule, is vested in kinship groups: "[T]here is no communism in land so far as the territorial body goes but only within a strictly limited body of actual kindred." There is no evidence of the soil being held in common, and joint holding never goes beyond a "certain limit of blood kinship."[107]

7. *The emergence of political organization*

Although the shift from primitive social organization to statehood is of transcendent importance, it is very poorly understood. The historical sources are too meager to shed unambiguous light on the issue. Anthropologists for a long time found the subject to hold little professional interest, preferring to concentrate on societies in the pre-

*Jomo Kenyatta, *Facing Mount Kenya* (London, 1953), 21, 25. In ch. 2 the author shows what complex forms landownership in such a society could assume. The same held true of the Maoris in New Zealand. Raymond Firth, *Primitive Economics of the New Zealand Maori* (New York, 1929), 360–75. One of the complicating factors in tracing the emergence of property in agriculture derives from the fact that under primitive methods of cultivation, arable land is left fallow for long periods, confusing the issue of ownership: "Under the system of forest fallow, all the members of a tribe dominating a given territory have a general right to cultivate plots of land within the territory. . . . This general right . . . can never be lost for any member of the cultivator families. . . . Under all systems of fallow a family will retain the exclusive right to the plot it has cleared and cultivated until the harvest has been reaped but it seems to depend upon the pattern of land use in the particular territory for how long a time after the harvesting this exclusive right can still be claimed. Usually, a family can retain its right to cultivate a given plot throughout the period of fallow, unless this is so long that all traces of previous cultivation [are] lost. But if, after the lapse of the normal period of fallow, the family does not re-cultivate a given plot, it may lose its right to this particular plot while retaining, of course, the general right to clear a plot within the tribal territory." Boserup, *The Conditions of Agricultural Growth*, 79–80. This book is based on extensive study of contemporary African and Asian societies.

political stage of development.* To the historian of private property, however, the matter is critical, because it helps clarify the ancient debate whether it was property that gave rise to the state or, on the contrary, the state that created property.

Such anthropological evidence as is available suggests that in societies of hunters and gatherers as well as among primarily pastoral people, public authority, as distinct from the authority of the kinship group, either does not exist or is negligible. These societies commonly choose headmen (chieftains) because of their military skills and force of personality. Their authority is purely personal and not precisely defined; they are readily displaced. The typical headman is "first among equals." Coercive instruments are absent, and order is maintained by social pressure. Such procedures suffice in hunting bands which typically number between twenty-five and one hundred individuals. Pastoral societies may occasionally vest considerable authority in one of their members during movement to summer pasture, which requires precise regulation of traffic among the tribes, but such authority is vested only in this respect and only for a limited time.[108]

The question emerges why and how such informal arrangements give rise to political institutions endowed with formal coercive powers.† In one of the earliest anthropological studies devoted to this subject, Robert H. Lowie's *The Origin of the State*,[109] the following answer was suggested: the transition from "social" or "tribal" organization to political organization occurs when authority becomes territorialized, that is, when it comes to extend over all the inhabitants of a given area rather than exclusively over those linked by ties of kinship. This theory rests on the findings of Sir Henry Maine, who in his *Ancient Law* (1861) first suggested that a critical watershed in the evolution of humanity occurred when bonds based on consanguinity yielded to those resting on territorial contiguity:

*Until recently, at any rate. The new discipline of "political anthropology," born in the 1950s, has sought to fill the gap. See, e.g., Morton H. Fried, *The Evolution of Political Society* (New York, 1967), and Georges Balandier, *Political Anthropology* (London, 1970). Unfortunately, like many other works in the "social sciences" published in the past fifty years or so, the authors of such publications are verbose, scholastic in their methodology, and given to quibbling over the validity of common words, and to endlessly quoting each other without arriving at clear conclusions.

†An account of the various theories concerning the emergence of the state can be found in Elman R. Service, *Origins of the State and Civilization* (New York, 1975). The author shows no preference for any of them. See also Henri J. M. Claessen and Peter Skalnik, eds., *The Early State* (The Hague, 1978), especially pp. 533–96.

> The history of political ideas begins, in fact, with the assumption that kinship in blood is the sole possible ground of community in political functions; nor is there any of those subversions of feeling, which we term emphatically revolutions, so startling and so complete as the change which is accomplished when some other principle—such as that, for instance, of *local contiguity*—establishes itself for the first time as the basis of common political action. . . . [T]he idea that a number of persons should exercise political rights in common simply because they happened to live within the same topographical limits was utterly strange and monstrous to primitive antiquity.[110]

Lewis Morgan, who adopted Maine's thesis, defined the transition as one from *societas,* in which the bonds were personal, to *civitas,* in which they were territorial.[111] As a result of this evolution, the informal practices of kindred groups, based on private law, gave way to formal public law. The right to participation and consultation in decision-making, previously restricted to free members of the tribe or clan, came to be extended to all the free inhabitants of the given area; and over time, when the population of that area grew too large for all those eligible to participate personally in the political process, to their elected representatives. The political history of the modern world has been characterized by a steady shift from informal authority, extended over kinship groups, to public authority, exercised over all inhabitants of a given territory. One of its first manifestations is that a third party—the state—does away with private vendettas by assuming responsibility for punishing crime. This occurred in Babylon as early as 1750 B.C.E. in the Code of Hammurabi. In Anglo-Saxon England, the practice was established about 900 C.E.[112]

Some contemporary anthropologists, while accepting Maine's thesis in general, question whether the kinship/territorial distinction was ever as stark as he assumed. There is evidence that even primitive societies organized along bloodlines recognize some territorial bonds. In seventh-century England, when kinship bonds predominated, people living side by side regarded themselves as kin whether or not they were actually related.[113] The transition, therefore, may be marked not so much by the replacement of one system by another as by the emergence of the territorial principle from a subordinate to a dominant position.

Two factors seem to account for it. One is warfare. Primitive people tend to respect the territorial rights of others: if they conquer, they usually do not dispossess the losers, but subjugate them.[114] This procedure automatically introduces a nonkinship—i.e., territorial—basis of authority. Secondly, the growth of population and the pressures on limited land resources lead to a commingling of tribes and clans, which has the effect of making the territorial principle prevail over kinship ties.

A number of anthropologists still adhere to a Marxist explanation according to which political authority emerges as a means of regulating class tensions in tribal society and, in consequence of the emergence of private property, enabling the class of owners to safeguard its possessions and the authority flowing from them. But like other Marxist schemes, this one constructs a Procrustean bed which known facts do not fit.[115]

A more persuasive economic explanation than the Marxist of the origin of political organization has been suggested by Douglass North. In his view, the state is an organization which, in return for the revenues (taxes) it collects, defends the properties and rights of its citizens. "The state trades a group of services, which we shall call protection and justice, for revenue."[116]

> Economic growth occurs if output grows faster than the population. . . . [E]conomic growth will occur if property rights make it worthwhile to undertake socially productive activity. The creating, specifying and enacting such property rights are costly. . . . As the potential grows for private gains to exceed transaction costs, efforts will be made to establish such property rights. Governments take over the protection and enforcement of property rights because they can do so at a lower cost than private volunteer groups.[117]

Such juridical and economic theories provide the best explanations of the emergence of statehood presently available.*

8. *Private property in antiquity*

Private property in the legal sense of the word comes into existence with the emergence of the state, that is, public authority. Until

*Marx, followed a century later by Karl Wittfogel (*Oriental Despotism* [New Haven, Conn., 1957]), spoke occasionally of an "Asiatic mode of production." Wittfogel developed the notion of "Oriental despotism" connected with the need to regulate large bodies of water (the Nile, the Euphrates, etc.) for purposes of irrigation and flood prevention. However correct this explanation may be, it holds only for certain regions at certain times in history.

then, it is possession protected by physical force and/or customary law and legitimized by inheritance and/or prolonged usage. Primitive societies recognize the right to occupy and cultivate fallow land as well as to hold on to land inherited from one's father. This practice was known in Europe during the Middle Ages. In feudal France it was unusual for anyone to speak of ownership, of either an estate or an office; much rarer still to engage in lawsuits over belongings. Instead, the parties to a dispute would claim "prescription" or *seizin* (*seisin*), that is, "possession made venerable by the lapse of time." In such litigations, victory went to him who could prove that he had occupied and tilled the soil longer than any other claimant, or, better still, that his ancestors had done so.[118]

Claims of ownership based on the collective memory of a community left few traces on paper. Thus, although there is overwhelming evidence that agriculture has been pursued from the earliest times by clans, families, or even individuals, and that custom acknowledged the land as theirs, documentation of this fact is not available because it was not needed. This greatly hinders historical inquiry. It explains why, in the words of Douglass North, "there is very little serious historical study of the evolution of property rights."[119]

In the ancient Middle East (Mesopotamia and pharaonic Egypt), the prevalent form of government was the "patrimonial" regime, under which the monarch owned as well as ruled the land and its inhabitants, treating his realm as a gigantic royal estate.* Ownership meant the absence of outside interference: to use Weber's term, the patrimonial ruler was *regelfrei,* that is, free of rules or restraints.[120] This fusion of sovereignty and ownership was quite common outside Europe until modern times, especially in the Middle East. Until recently, it was believed that in ancient Mesopotamia and Egypt all the land belonged either to palaces or to temples. This view has been somewhat modified in view of researches carried out in the past several decades which have established that both these regions knew private property in land.[121] Still, such properties constituted but a small part of the arable land surface, the bulk of which was under state or temple control. Furthermore, they belonged to extended families which very rarely resorted to sales. The leading Russian authority on the subject, conceding that there were exceptions to the royal or clerical monopoly on land, concluded that

*The classic exposition of patrimonialism is by Max Weber, in his *Grundriss der Sozialökonomik: III Abt., Wirtschaft und Gesellschaft*, 3rd ed., II (Tübingen, 1947), 679–723. Weber included under this category the Inca Empire and the Jesuit state of seventeenth-century Paraguay. To this list may be added Muscovite Russia.

"private property in land in the modern sense of the word was not known in any of the ancient societies, whether in Europe or in Asia, at least up to the latest period of antiquity."* The king's subjects consisted of officials, priests, and serfs. The absence of political and civil rights as well as the scant and marginal presence of private property in land is the distinguishing feature of Oriental Despotisms.

The situation was quite different in ancient Greece and Rome, where property rights in the modern sense first made their appearance.

Ancient Greece occupies a unique place in the history of institutions on at least two counts. It was the world's first democracy—indeed, the very concept of "politics" originated there, the word deriving from the Greek word for city, *polis*: it meant "that which concerns everyone" or "that which is public," in contrast to "private," "personal," and "self-interested."[122] (One of the original Greek meanings of "idiot" was a private person, one who did not participate in public life.) It was in Greece that there emerged, for the first time in history, the phenomenon of citizenship with its fusion of rights and obligations. It is in ancient Greece, too, that we find the earliest evidence of agriculture pursued largely by independent, landowning farmers, forerunners of the English yeomanry. The concurrence was anything but fortuitous: both citizenship and landownership entailed the exclusion of outsiders, forging bonds of interdependence among property-owning citizens.

To begin with landed property.

Ancient Greece was overwhelmingly an agricultural society, with as much as 90 percent of the population living off the land. Because of the scarcity of water in Attica, the rural population lived not in scattered farmsteads but in compact settlements grouped near the water sources. It was made up of small farmers who, according to scholarly estimates, owned, on the average, four hectares (less than ten acres); large estates were an exception. These farmers cultivated grapes, olives, figs, and cereals (barley and wheat). Farmland (*kleros*), the main source of the nation's wealth, was not treated as a commodity. It was bequeathed but it was rarely traded (although it could be), because its possession was linked to personal freedom and the rights of citizenship: a Greek (as

*I. M. Diakonoff, in *Acta Antiqua Academiae Scientiarum Hungaricae*, XXII, Fasc. 1–4 (1974), 51. A dissenting opinion on the subject is presented by Robert C. Ellickson and Charles DiA. Thorland in *The Chicago-Kent Law Review* 71, No. 1 (1995), 321–411. The authors assert that "Four millennia ago, ancient peoples conferred land entitlements in bundles much like our fee simple, and engaged in transactions . . . that a modern-day real-estate lawyer can readily recognize" (p. 410). This extreme position is not widely shared.

well as a Roman) who lost his land turned into a proletarian.[123] Ever since the days of Solon, these independent farmers were considered freemen (*eleutheroi*), exempt from the duty of paying tribute or providing services to the aristocrats. They labored for themselves, and this economic independence became a hallmark of freedom. It is they who manned the phalanx, columns of heavily armed infantry who marched to battle to defend their city and their fields.

Nineteenth-century historians, committed to the theory of primitive communism, assumed, without examining the data or else misinterpreting them to suit their preconceptions, that ancient Greece knew only communal property in land.[124] This theory was challenged by Fustel de Coulanges in his *Ancient City.* Modern scholars agree with Fustel de Coulanges that already in the eighth and seventh centuries B.C.E, the age of Homer and Hesiod, land in Greece was held in private ownership, that is, by individuals and families. In the words of Jules Toutain, "If we adhere to Homer and Hesiod, we find that all ownership is private, so far as arable land is concerned. . . . [N]owhere is there any mention of cultivated land owned collectively."[125] The Anglo-American historian of antiquity Sir Moses Finley concurs:

> In the Homeric poems, the property regime, in particular, was already fully established. . . . The regime that we see in the poems was, above all, one of private ownership. . . . [T]here was free, untrammeled right to dispose of all movable wealth. . . . [T]he transmission of a man's estate by inheritance, the movables and immovables together, was taken for granted as the normal procedure upon his death.[126]

According to Finley, the Homeric world knew "no feudal, or comparably conditional, tenures."[127] In ancient Greece "private property [was] recognized and protected by the State as the basis of society" and the state very rarely interfered with the "free play of economic forces and economic initiative."[128] It is precisely because private property was prevalent in classical Greece that Plato and Aristotle devoted so much attention to it.

The *polis* or city-state has been described as a "system of government in which citizens had rights as well as duties under the rule of law, a system hitherto unknown in human history."[129] It prevailed in much of Greece by the end of the sixth century B.C.E. Following the reforms of Cleisthenes of that time, the Athenian population was divided into territorial units (replacing the previous divisions based on kinship), each of which sent representatives to the Athenian Council. The purpose of these reforms was to break the power of the clans: they laid the basis of Athenian democracy. The *polis* had a regular state structure, with permanent public authority, consisting of magistrates elected annually and usually drawn from aristocratic families; a Council of Four Hundred which prepared the agenda for the Assembly; and an Assembly of all the citizens (*ecclesia*), which had the ultimate legislative and judiciary authority. The *polis,* encompassing a definite territory, usually surrounded by a wall and centered on a temple, governed itself, passing its own laws and administering its own justice; being dependent on no outside authority, it was sovereign.

One historian of antiquity perceives a direct link between the sovereign city-state and the sovereign owner and cultivator of land. In his view it was the emergence in ancient Greece of private property in land, free of any outside obligations, that gave birth to the world's first democracy:

> The rise of independent farmers who owned and worked without encumbrance their small plots at the end of the Greek Dark Ages [c. 750 B.C.E.] was an entirely new phenomenon in history. . . . Their efforts to create a greater community of agrarian equals resulted, I believe, in the system of independent but interconnected Greek city-states (*poleis*) which characterized Western culture.[130]

In ancient Athens landownership and citizenship were indissolubly linked, in that only citizens could own land and only landowners could be citizens: noncitizens could pursue finance and commerce, they could lease land and mines, but they could not own real estate. Since Solon's time, there were property qualifications for high office. Thus, in effect, a property census was established for political participation, not unlike that which would prevail in England, the United States, and a number of other Western countries in the eighteenth and nineteenth centuries.

If we add to this information the fact that Athenian citizens were not taxed, considering taxation a hallmark of lower status,* the correlation between landownership, citizenship, and democratic participation is striking.

*There are indications that the Greek term for "freemen," *eleutheroi,* originally had a fiscal meaning, being applied to people exempt from the payment of tribute. Ellen M. Wood, *Peasant-Citizen and Slave* (London and New York, 1988), 130.

It is apparent that the wide distribution of property in land and the prevalence of economic laissez-faire played a critical role in the evolution of Athenian democracy. Furthermore, whereas in the Middle East artisans worked for the kings, in the Greek city-states they were independent entrepreneurs. Altogether, the majority of the people, notably in Athens, whether residing on the land or in the city, were self-employed.[131]

In Sparta, by contrast, where private property in land was marginal, personal freedom was absent. Adult males, all enrolled as soldiers, received from the state land allotments of fairly uniform size cultivated by bondsmen (helots). Their property rights were tenuous, for they held the soil conditionally: if they failed to exploit it efficiently, the state took it back and gave it to someone more capable. Soldiers and officers, who made up the bulk of the male citizens, were forbidden to engage in commerce or to practice crafts.[132] Their economic security was fully assured by the state.

This prevalent view of Spartan conditions, based largely on information supplied by ancient historians, has been challenged by a revisionist school which maintains that the Spartan land-tenure system was "pre-eminently one of private estates transmitted by partible inheritance and diverging devolution and open to alienation through lifetime gifts, testamentary bequests and betrothal of heiresses."[133] But this opinion seems to be held only by a minority of classical scholars, the majority of whom adhere to the traditional view. Even the revisionists do not claim that land in Sparta could be sold, a right which to Aristotle was, along with that of disposing by gift, the criterion of ownership.*

An outstanding feature of ancient Greece was the close correlation between ownership and political as well as civil liberty. The wide distribution of property, especially in land, the main source of productive wealth, made possible in Athens the emergence of the first democratic regime in history. Elsewhere in the ancient world, it was the state that owned the economic resources, with the result that the population served the state, which imposed on it numerous duties but accorded it no rights.

When the Macedonians conquered most of the Middle East, they adopted the Oriental rather than the Athenian model. The Hellenistic successors to Alexander the Great's empire retained the patrimonial regimes under which the land belonged to the ruler. Their economies

*An object is "'our own' if it is in our own power to dispose of it or keep it. By 'disposing of it' I mean giving it away or selling it." Aristotle, *Rhetoric*, 1361a-21-23.

were strictly regimented. In Egypt, the best-known of the Hellenistic states, the Ptolemies built some cities on the Greek model, giving them land as endowment. They also made lavish land grants to temples. Here and there, private property in land established itself. But ultimately the realm was the patrimony of the king-god: "the whole of the land of Egypt belonged to Ptolemy as it had once belonged to Pharaoh."[134] The sovereign "owned the goods of his subjects as he did their persons. . . . From the theoretical point of view, entire Egypt was royal domain, populated by serfs who labored for the king. . . ."[135] The king exploited part of his domain directly and leased the rest, but he owned it all. In particular, the vast domains turned over to the clergy belonged to him by virtue of the fact that he was the representative of the gods on earth, and these domains served the gods. The priests merely exploited them to the extent permitted by the crown.[136] In Ptolemaic Egypt, artisans worked not for themselves but for the court: they were members of an extensive network of royal monopolies which embraced both the production and the sale of goods.[137]

The evolution of the concept and institution of property in ancient Rome is the subject of interminable scholarly discussion.[138] A leading authority on Roman economic history asserts that

> the laws of private property had developed long and far before the fifth century [B.C.E.] when the twelve tables were drawn up. . . . [T]he ancestors of the Romans were orderly agriculturists more than a millennium before these laws were written, [hence] it is highly probable that the Latin people respected property rights before they settled the plains about Rome.[139]

It is reasonably certain that in Rome property, concentrated in the hands of the head of the household or *pater familias,* predated the polity. The head enjoyed unlimited authority over both the persons (wife and children along with the slaves) and the goods of the household. Gradually a differentiation occurred under which the free members of the household emancipated themselves from total subservience to the *pater familias,* while slaves, cattle, and other material objects continued to be treated as his outright property. The latter were held by virtue of *dominium,*[140] and as such were subject to alienation.

Rome was the earliest state in history to evolve complete legal rules and procedures regulating both civil and public life, rules and procedures known to the public and enforced by professional jurists. In this respect it went far beyond Athens. In its statutes, laws dealing with property achieved their fullest development. This historic fact confirms Jeremy Bentham's dictum "Property and law are born and must die together. Before the laws there was no property; take away the laws, all property ceases."* The reason for this connection is that property represents an asset to which the owner claims exclusive title, a claim which requires enforcement not by physical power or social custom, as is the case with mere possession, but by law. Hence, "it is almost impossible to conceive of a society in which private property is recognized and permitted, but is not protected by the law."[141]

In ancient Rome, only land located on the Italian peninsula, the so-called *ager Romanus,* could be held as absolute property (known as quiritarian ownership), and only by Roman citizens. It was not taxed. Land which Rome conquered became *ager publicus* and as such was subject to tax (a form of tribute): it was either leased or colonized but, being state property, it could not be fully owned. Outside Italy, even Roman citizens could not hold outright title to the land and had to pay tax or *tributum* (both on land and a capitation tax) as a reminder that the state had the ultimate claim on conquered territories.[142] Although in Italy large expanses of cultivated soil belonged to the emperor and to nobles, the prevalent form of ownership, as in Greece, was small property, held by yeomen who tilled the land personally or with the aid of slaves.† In the conquered territories, it was common for rich Romans to cultivate large latifundia employing slave labor.

Quiritarian property, which covered only a small part of the land of the Roman Empire, corresponded closely to property in the modern meaning of the word: it belonged personally to the head of the family, who could sell it or bequeath it.[143] In that sense it was the direct precursor of modern property concepts and laws, a fact of great historic importance:

> The law of contract and property . . . bore a deep impress of Roman influence even in those regions of Europe that never

*Jeremy Bentham, *Principles of the Civil Code*, in *Works*, I (Edinburgh, 1843), 309. Bentham argued this point in support of his contention that the rights of property derived from state authority rather than the Law of Nature, but the principle he enunciated is valid regardless of one's view of how property originates. Heinrich Altrichter, *Wandlungen des Eigentumsbegriffs und neuere Ausgestaltung des Eigentumsrechts* (Marburg-Lahn, 1930), 16.

†Rostovtseff, *A History of the Ancient World*, II (Oxford, 1927), 47. Such is the prevalent view. Moses Finley, however, challenges it, asserting that we do not possess even an approximate idea of how land was distributed in Italy and the rest of the Roman Empire. M. I. Finley, ed., *Studies in Roman Property* (Cambridge, 1976), 3.

formally "received" the full body of Roman law. These concepts . . . with the ethical concepts of Christianity . . . are the underlying factors of continuity and unification in the history of our culture.[144]

9. *Feudal Europe*

Roman laws pertaining to private property were largely lost sight of in Western Europe during the so-called Dark Ages, the six or seven hundred years that followed the collapse of the Roman Empire. The Germanic tribes that invaded and ultimately conquered the European parts of the empire initially enforced their own, "barbarian," codes, but as they settled down and mingled with the local population, they replaced personal jurisdiction with the territorial and adopted certain features of Roman law. The result was a synthesis of Roman and Germanic codes. At first the newcomers evinced little interest in laws pertaining to private property in land, because they were primarily pastoralists organized into clans. But as they went over to agriculture they adopted Roman legal practices based on private property.[145]

The systems of lordship and subjection which prevailed in Western Europe between approximately 900 and 1250 C.E. were characterized by a unique fusion of sovereignty and ownership, of the public and private spheres.* It was unique in the sense that while a similar fusion had prevailed among the patrimonial monarchies of the ancient Middle East, in Europe it was moderated by the principle of mutual obligation that had been entirely unknown—indeed, inconceivable—in Oriental despotisms.† The feudal lord was both sovereign and landlord to his vassal but he also assumed obligations toward him. In the symbolic ceremony of homage the vassal pledged to serve faithfully his lord, and the lord vowed, in return, to protect him. It was, in the words of Marc Bloch, a "reciprocity in unequal obligations," but the element of mutuality was always present: it was a genuine contract.[146] The failure of the lord to fulfill his part of the bargain released the vassal from his duties. Disputes concerning fulfillment of pledges by either party were settled

*"Just in so far as the ideal of feudalism is perfectly realized, all that we call public law is merged in private law: jurisdiction is property, office is property, the kingship itself is property; the same word *dominium* has to stand now for *ownership* and now for *lordship*." Frederick Pollock and Frederick William Maitland, *The History of English Law*, 2nd ed., I (Cambridge, 1923), 230.

†It was unknown also to Japan, which developed a regime that bore some resemblance to European feudalism.

sometimes by royal courts, sometimes by courts made up of vassals, and sometimes by a trial of arms. The reciprocal obligation between private parties acquired in time a public dimension and provided the foundation of constitutional government in Europe and countries colonized by Europeans, since a constitution, too, is a contract that spells out the mutual rights and duties of the government and the citizens. The Magna Carta is interpreted by one historian as "applying the feudal principle of contract, exacted by vassals from a lord who had failed to fulfil his duty to them."[147]

In theory, under the regime of lordship and vassalage, all land belonged to the sovereign and everyone else held it conditionally. Estates were typically held by a vassal as a fief, title to which stayed with the lord. However, over time, conditional tenure evolved by an irresistible momentum into outright property. According to feudal practice, the lord was under no obligation to continue the arrangement he had made with a vassal with that vassal's offspring. Still, he had every inducement to do so. From the lord's point of view, the sons of a vassal, provided they seemed able conscientiously to fulfill their father's obligations to him, were the preferred successors, inasmuch as they were a familiar quantity and likely to know their responsibilities better than a newcomer.[148] For the same reason, feudal offices, originally granted conditionally and temporarily, over time became the hereditary property of their holders. As early as the tenth and eleventh centuries, it was customary in France, England, Italy, and Germany for the vassals to inherit fiefs.[149] In Norman England, whose conquerors imported customs from Normandy, land was heritable from the beginning, and by women as well as men: in the opinion of Maitland, the Domesday Book, the cadastre of English landed properties compiled under William the Conqueror, probably used the terms "feodum" (conditional tenure) and "alodium" (outright property) as equivalents to mean "a heritable estate, as absolute an ownership of land as is conceivable."* This fact is confirmed by the practice of the king's tenants in chief (his direct vassals) of deriving their family names from the locations of their estates. Although formally such hereditary fiefs could not be alienated, in fact by the twelfth century alienation had become a common occur-

*F. W. Maitland, *Domesday Book and Beyond* (Cambridge, 1921), 154, n. 1. Citing this passage, J. C. Holt adds: "The very language of feudalism, from its inception in Norman England, implied inheritance. A non-hereditary fief was a contradiction in terms. . . ." In *Past and Present*, No. 57 (1972), 7. Cf. Theodore F. T. Plucknett, *A Concise History of the Common Law*, 5th ed. (Boston, 1956), 524.

rence.[150] In this manner, fiefs imperceptibly evolved into private property. The rediscovery in the eleventh century of Roman law with its unambiguous definitions of private ownership provided this process with legal sanction.

A similar process occurred among the villeins, who also gradually acquired hereditary rights to the land they were cultivating.

The Scandinavian Vikings knew private property for both men and women. This can be established from the fact that the majority of the surviving runic stones were raised to serve as deeds of property claims and inheritance rights of individuals and families.[151]

10. *Medieval cities*

Nothing contributed more to the emergence of private property in the West and the rights associated with ownership than the appearance in the late Middle Ages of urban communities. For what happened on the land quietly and informally in the cities assumed distinct legal forms.

Private property gains importance in a commercial economy, the sinews of urban life, because while it is possible to possess and exploit land without holding clear title to it or having the right to sell it, this is not the case with commodities or money, which make economic sense only if traded or invested, and they can be traded and invested only if incontestably owned.

> Since trade presupposes ownership by the traders of whatever they are trading, and since trades based on future delivery or payment are a central subject of contracts, urban life almost inevitably gives much the same place to property and contract that they occupy among capitalist institutions.*

Thus, if the spread of agriculture made it possible to enforce property claims more strictly than under hunting and gathering, in a commercial

*Nathan Rosenberg and L. E. Birdzell, Jr., *How the West Grew Rich* (New York, 1986), 50. Cf. Max Weber: "[T]here is no object with the character of money which does not have that of individual ownership." *General Economic History* (New Brunswick, N.J., 1981), 236.

(and manufacturing) economy property came fairly to dominate men's relations to assets and each other.

During the second half of the millennium after Christ the once flourishing European cities went into a severe decline. Its causes are in dispute, even if the fact itself is not. The Belgian medievalist Henri Pirenne argued that it was due not to the barbarian invasions, as commonly believed, but to the Muslim conquest of the Mediterranean in the seventh and eighth centuries, which disrupted Europe's trade with the Near East. Some historians reject this explanation, preferring to find the reasons for urban decay in internal European developments. Whatever the cause, it is not disputed that in the five or six centuries that followed the fall of Rome, European cities turned into fortresses, which protected their residents from physical harm but performed few if any economic functions. Residence in them bestowed neither status nor rights.

Cities began to revive in the tenth century, and by the eleventh they had turned into thriving commercial centers. Venice and Genoa profited from renewed trade with the Near East, while Flemish cities grew rich from the export of textiles. Commercial prosperity led to the emergence of a new urban class. Previously composed of itinerant peddlers and other lower-class elements without a place in a countryside structured along feudal lines and centered on agriculture, the new burghers were people of means whose wealth consisted of commodities, real estate, and capital. The first urban middle class in history,[152] they were an anomaly in a world in which everyone else was beholden to a superior and rooted in the soil.

It is precisely the fact that their lifestyle did not fit into the feudal mold that enabled—indeed, compelled—the burghers to aspire to self-government. Because it was not part of feudal society, which provided its members with a modicum of security in a turbulent age, the bourgeoisie had a vital interest in procuring privileges from the princes, nobles, and clerics on whose land they lived—notably, guarantees of person and property. These privileges entailed the right of burghers to govern themselves and to administer their own justice, very much as had been the case with the citizens of the ancient Greek *polis*. Self-administered justice was especially important to the burghers because as commercial people they frequently entered into private contracts which neither royal nor feudal courts would enforce. In time, other rights were added. If the feudal contract is the basis of modern constitutionalism, the charters gained by the medieval burghers from the region's lords may be said to provide the foundation of modern civil rights.* Their greatest triumphs occurred in countries that did not have national monarchies: Italy, the Low Countries, and Germany. In England, France, and Spain, they were less successful.

The cities gained their freedoms sometimes by rebelling, sometimes by coming to terms with the local ruler. Throughout the eleventh century in Western Europe, there flared up urban revolts in the course of which the burghers, often with royal backing, won concessions from regional feudal lords. Such cities became self-governing and self-judging communes. One of the earliest towns (late tenth century) to secure the right to govern itself was the Saxon city of Magdeburg; its law books, compiled at the end of the thirteenth century, defined freedom as "the natural liberty of a man to do what he wants, unless prohibited by force or law."[153] Magdeburg law served as a model for many urban communities of Eastern Europe. In the early eleventh century a number of cities won similar rights in southern Italy, and somewhat later in Lombardy.

All male residents of such urban communes enjoyed equal status and the right to participate in communal assemblies—an enormously important innovation, in that it established the principle of territorial rights in place of rights derived from social status. Residents of such cities, regardless of their social origin, were free men: a runaway serf who had managed to reside in them for a year and a day gained his freedom. Officials were elected for limited terms. Thus the notion of common citizenship, first forged in ancient Athens, reemerged in the urban enclaves located within a highly stratified feudal society. The principle *Stadtluft macht frei*—"City air makes free"—which the Nazis obscenely mimicked at the entrance to their mass murder camp at Auschwitz to lull the victims about to be gassed (*Arbeit macht frei*)—marks the onset of modern citizenship. (As its etymology indicates, the word "citizen" derives from the French *cité* and originally applied only to urban inhabitants.) It has been said that if by the early twelfth century in countries on the periphery of Europe "burgher" signified someone

*The Magna Carta of 1215, which is generally regarded as the cornerstone of modern liberty, some modern scholars view as a replica of the rights first acquired by urban inhabitants. Indeed, at the insistence of the barons the king affirmed in the Magna Carta the liberties of London and other towns of the realm. The urban model of medieval liberties is also discernible in the Golden Bull of Hungary (1222), in which the impoverished king pledged to convene the Diet annually, not to imprison nobles arbitrarily, not to tax either secular or clerical vassals, and to respect the ownership of landed estates. Robert von Keller, *Freiheitsgarantien für Person und Eigentum im Mittelalter* (Heidelberg, 1933), 76–77, 82.

residing on the territory of a city, in its heartland it referred to the member of a commune.*

Gradually, the townspeople evolved into a "Third Estate" alongside the clergy and nobility. And because of their wealth they were increasingly called upon by monarchs, ever short of money to wage war, to participate in legislation: around 1300 in both England and France, burghers were for the first time invited to take part in parliamentary sessions convened to vote taxes.

It is in the medieval cities that real estate first assumed the aspect of a completely unencumbered commodity. Proprietors of urban dwellings, which usually served as both residences and places of business, owned outright the land on which their houses stood and were free to dispose of it at will.

The freedoms which the burghers ultimately gained make a formidable list. They can be tabulated under four headings: political, personal, economic, and legal.[154]

Political freedoms

The right to self-government

Personal freedoms

1. The freedom to marry without permission
2. Exemption from feudal obligations
3. Freedom of testation
4. Freedom of movement
5. Emancipation from servile status after urban residence of a year and a day
6. Freedom of alienation (i.e., the transfer of property to another person)
7. Exemption from military service

Economic freedoms

1. Freedom from billeting: if required to accommodate the king and his retainers, proper compensation to be paid
2. Exemption from external taxes
3. The right to tax fellow citizens
4. Exemption from tolls
5. The right to hold markets

*Ernst Pitz, *Europäisches Städtewesen und Bürgertum* (Darmstadt, 1991), 392. However, as we shall note in Chapter 4, the northern Russian city-state of Novgorod during the Middle Ages and before its conquest by Moscow, although on the periphery of Europe, closely resembled in its internal organization West European communes.

Legal freedoms

1. The right of citizens to be judged by urban magistrates
2. The right to due process
3. Protection from arbitrary arrests and searches
4. Freedom from compulsory services

Thus, trade, along with manufacture and the capital to which both gave rise, created in the midst of an agrarian society, based on duties and privileges, oases of liberty based on rights. It is difficult, therefore, to disagree with the contention that modern democracy originated in the medieval towns and that free enterprise, which begot these towns, is the "principal or sole means for the advancement of human liberty."[155] These institutions were unique to Europe: "[O]utside the occident there have not been cities in the sense of a unitary community."[156]

In the course of the fourteenth and fifteenth centuries, as a result of the rise of the national state, urban social conflicts, and other factors (such as the introduction of gunpowder, which rendered useless the cities' protective walls), most of the European cities lost their autonomy. The sixteenth and seventeenth centuries were an era of absolutism which had no tolerance for urban self-rule. But the ideals the cities had fostered and the institutions they had created became an intrinsic part of the Western political tradition.

11. Early modern Europe

By the sixteenth century, it was axiomatic in Western Europe that the king ruled but that his subjects owned, and that royal authority stopped where private property began. "Property belongs to the family, sovereignty to the prince and his magistrates," the consensus held.[157] Seneca's dictum that "unto kings belongs the power of all things, and under particular men the property," came to be regarded as a truism. It was also convention that the king did not own the realm and could not dispose of any part of it. A fifteenth-century Spanish jurist declared: "To the king is confided solely the administration of the kingdom, and not dominion over things, for the property and rights of the State are public, and cannot be the private patrimony of anyone."[158] Jean Bodin, who in the sixteenth century formulated the modern concept of sovereignty, laid it down that sovereignty is not ownership and that the prince's revenues were inalienable.[159] These conceptions became a foundation of European freedom, especially as in the seventeenth century the term "property" came to embrace not only physical possessions of persons but also their life and liberty. As such, it automatically fell outside the scope of state authority.

The sanctity of property was occasionally violated. Jews, who lived under the protection of secular powers and therefore at their mercy, were fleeced with impunity to fill the coffers of kings as well as those of princes, barons, and cities. The laws of the English king Edward the Confessor stated that "the Jews and their possessions belong to the king."[160] The same principle held in Germany: Rudolf von Hapsburg declared in 1286 that the Jews along with their goods belonged personally to him.[161] Jews were banished from England in 1290 after the king seized their belongings, and from France in 1306 under similar circumstances. In 1307, the French king confiscated the assets of the Order of the Knights Templar, a prosperous international banking syndicate. In 1492, Jews were despoiled and expelled from Spain, and four years later from Portugal. In 1502, the Moors suffered the same fate in Castile. In all these cases, however, the victims were foreigners or transnational organizations, usually professing a different religion.

An unusual (for Europe) violation of private property rights occurred in Sweden in the late seventeenth century. In the preceding hundred years, the Swedish crown, in perpetual financial distress, had sold off to the nobles large portions of the royal domain. By 1650, the king and individual farmers owned only 28 percent of Sweden's agricultural land, the rest being in the hands of nobles.[162] In 1680, Charles XI, with the support of small landlords and taxpayers, had the Rigsdag pass a law providing for the "Reduction" of noble holdings, which led to the confiscation of large landed estates. As a result, the crown acquired about one-third of the country's land. This new wealth laid the basis for royal absolutism, but for a brief time only. After the disastrous war against Russia in the early 1700s, the "Reductions" were repealed and the crown had to submit to severe limitations on its authority. Much of the property which it had sequestered passed subsequently into peasant hands, and the power of the Swedish monarchy was cut down to virtually nothing.

European monarchs and some ideologists of royal absolutism in the seventeenth and eighteenth centuries liked to claim for the crown unlimited authority, which, on occasion, extended to their subjects' belongings: both James I and Charles I of England believed that the properties of their subjects were theirs to dispose of if, in their judgment, the interests of the nation required it.[163] In 1666, Louis XIV, in an instruction to the Dauphin, his eldest son, proffered the following wrongheaded advice:

> Thus you must first of all be convinced that kings are absolute seigneurs, and have by nature the clear and free right to dispose of all the goods possessed alike by the clergy and laymen, to use them at any time in the manner of prudent stewards, that is to say, in accord with the general requirements of the state.[164]

But such claims were meaningless. Whatever absolutist theory may have held, even monarchs as powerful as the Bourbons did not dare to encroach on the property of their subjects, because the principle of private property was so firmly entrenched that any assault on it was certain to precipitate a violent reaction if not a revolution. The best illustration of this fact is the fate of Charles I, who lost his throne and his head in a staunchly monarchical country because he persisted in what his subjects perceived to be arbitrary taxation.

By the eighteenth century, it became commonplace to see in property, especially land, the chief sanction of citizenship; and to the extent that citizens were given the vote, it was restricted to persons who held real estate or other tangible assets. The discrimination was justified with the argument that individuals lacking income-producing property were not independent agents and hence were open to manipulation. Blackstone in his *Commentaries on the Laws of England*, highly influential in both Britain and her American colonies, asserted that

> The true reason of requiring any qualification, with regard to property, in voters, is to exclude such persons as are in so mean a situation that they are esteemed to have no will of their own. If these persons had votes, they would be tempted to dispose of them under some undue influence or other.[165]

People who owned no property were further regarded as "shiftless" and lacking a genuine stake in the country and its government. In early colonial North America, which generally emulated British practices, the right to vote was predicated on ownership of land: it "was claimed in very much the same way that one would claim a right to vote as a stockholder in a corporation."[166] The suffrage was thus treated as another property right and as such restricted to proprietors.*

*"I have failed in the past," writes Jacob Viner, "after some effort, to find a single substantial affirmation of belief, before the 1770s, in the desirability of immediate or

England, which had the oldest continuous record of parliamentary elections, maintained since the Middle Ages a complicated system of suffrage, different for the towns (boroughs) and counties (shires). After 1430, the franchise in the shires was restricted to adult males in possession of freehold property yielding at least 40 shillings a year, which was regarded as the minimum required for financial independence. In 1710, parliament introduced property qualifications for members of the House of Commons; they were abolished only in 1858. The 1832 parliamentary reform bill extended the vote in the boroughs to all male inhabitants who owned or rented real estate worth £10 a year, and in the shires to tenants at will of land worth £50 a year and copyholders or leaseholders of land worth a minimum of £10 a year. The 1867 reform bill broadened the suffrage in the cities, and that of 1884 extended it to most agricultural laborers, but only the 1918 bill abolished all property qualifications for voters, replacing them with simple residential requirements.[167]

In the American colonies, as in England, voting rights were confined to property owners. Most of the rebellious colonies maintained property qualifications for voters, usually in the form of real estate, although several allowed the substitution of personal assets. Some of those which extended the franchise to all taxpayers established property qualification for officeholding. After gaining independence, all thirteen colonies imposed property prerequisites for the suffrage.[168] The logic behind these requirements was that "those who pay for supporting the government should have the exclusive right to control it."[169] But there were also weightier reasons for restricting the suffrage to persons of property. These were voiced by James Madison: the fear that under "universal and equal suffrage" the rights of property would not be as effectively guarded as the rights of persons, whereas freehold suffrage was likely to assure both.[170] The suffrage standards in the United States, however, were not as restrictive as those in Great Britain, because land in America was much easier to obtain and, indeed, was often given away, so that by 1750 most white males owned land.[171] Gradually even these moderate preconditions were relaxed. By the middle of the nineteenth century, they disappeared altogether: North Carolina in 1856 was the last state to do away with them.

France during its revolution introduced voting qualifications based on tax payments. They were not onerous: of the 24–27 million citizens

---

early universal or near-universal (male) adult suffrage." *Canadian Journal of Economics and Political Science*, 29, No. 4 (1963), 549.

of all ages and both sexes, 4 million enjoyed the franchise, which, given that France at the time had six million adult males, meant that two out of three of them had the vote. Even so, the provision violated the spirit of equality proclaimed by the revolutionaries. After the Restoration, under Louis XVIII, the franchise was considerably narrowed, so that only some 100,000 citizens enjoyed voting rights, and fewer than one-fifth of that number were qualified to hold office. Under Louis Philippe, the list of eligible voters was increased to a quarter of a million.[172] Marx with some justification described the regime of Louis Philippe as "nothing other than a joint-stock company for the exploitation of France's national wealth," of which the king was the director and whose dividends were distributed among the ministers, deputies, and 240,000 voters.[173] It was the dictator Napoleon III who abolished all franchise restrictions based on property: the constitution of 1852 extended the franchise to every male citizen.

Imperial Germany maintained from 1871 until 1914 a peculiar suffrage system. The national parliament, the Reichstag, was chosen by all male citizens age twenty-five and over. However, the Reichstag essentially disposed only of the defense budget, which accounted for 90 percent of its budgetary allocations. On the principle that indirect taxes went to the national government and direct ones to the states and local communities, the latter received the bulk of the country's revenues: it was they who made appropriations for education, welfare, and other public services. Local governments, however, did not adopt the principle of universal male franchise, restricting the right to vote according to their own criteria, in which property qualifications played an important role. In Prussia, for example, the richest citizens enjoyed a triple vote and those from the middle class a double vote, while the poorest had only a single vote.[174]

Other European countries—Italy, Denmark, Sweden, Belgium—also enforced property qualifications, in some instances into the twentieth century.

These restrictions, antithetical as they may have been to the spirit of democracy, must be judged in the light of past experience which indicates that propertied interests constituted the earliest effective barrier to absolutism and its arbitrary powers. Just as the liberties gained by the feudal nobility and medieval communes were originally exclusive privileges that, in time, turned into common rights, so too the franchise, first restricted to property owners, became, in time, universal. Indeed, only countries which initially limited the franchise developed into genuine democracies: governments that bestowed the right to vote on all citizens outright more often than not used the universal franchise to maintain themselves in power. A recent book on the history of suffrage in America is subtitled *From Property to Democracy*. In light of the historical record, it should read *Through Property to Democracy*.

12. *Summing up*

The overview of the emergence and evolution of the idea and institution of private property has sought to establish the following propositions:

Acquisitiveness is a universal phenomenon, among animals as well as human beings, children as well as adults, primitive peoples as well as those culturally advanced. It is rooted in the instinct of self-preservation, but it also has an important psychological dimension in that it enhances feelings of self-assurance and competence. Its objects are, in the first place, material goods, but it has also an incorporeal aspect, embracing ideas, artistic creations, inventions, and even the very space that surrounds us. Claims to exclusive use are especially emphatic in respect to land with which humans are linked by mystic bonds. The notion of primitive communism has no basis in fact: it is simply the ancient—and, apparently, indestructible—myth of the Golden Age dressed up in modern pseudo-scientific language. Anthropology has no knowledge of societies ignorant of property rights: in the words of E. A. Hoebel cited above, "property is as ubiquitous as man, a part of the basic fabric of all society." Which means, to employ Aristotelian terminology, that it is not merely a "legal" or "conventional" but a "natural" institution. As such it is no more a subject of moralizing (unless it be for its excesses) than mortality or any other aspect of existence over which humans have at best minimal control.

Through 90 percent or more of human history when hunting and gathering were the principal forms of economic activity, claims of ownership centered on tribal control of territory, which was jealously defended from interlopers; individual property claims focused on weapons, tools, and other personal effects. Livestock was always treated as property, usually tribal. With the gradual shift to settled life centered on agriculture, property rights devolved on households. Public authority—the state—was one of the by-products of these changes. Although the origins of the state are obscure and subject to much controversy, it seems that the decisive cause of its emergence was the transition from social organization based on kinship and a pre-agrarian economy to one based on territory and soil cultivation, largely forced by the pressure of population growth and the resultant increase in competition for natural resources. In settled, politically organized societies, private property gained in importance, because cultivated soil requires intense and continuous care. The movement toward exclusive control of land is well-nigh irresistible for both economic and psychological reasons: it occurred even in feudal Europe when, in theory, most land was held conditionally. One of the prime functions of the state is to guarantee the security of ownership. Before the state there is only possession, title to which the owner asserts by claiming long tenure and which enjoys the backing of custom, and, ultimately, force; in political organization, this responsibility is assumed by public authority. The transformation of possession into ownership proceeds everywhere with an inexorable force, owing mainly to the institution of inheritance, which suits both owner and possessor but works to the advantage of the latter because he is in uninterrupted physical control of the objects at stake.

The next phase in the development of private property is the product of commerce and urbanization. Land can be owned in a great variety of ways which restrict the duration of tenure or impose various other limitations on it. Commodities used in trade, however, and the money they bring are always and everywhere private property. As the importance of agriculture declines relative to that of trade and manufacture, money assumes an ever greater economic role, and so does property. The elevation of private property in Europe of the eighteenth and nineteenth centuries to the status of a sacrosanct institution was a direct result of economic developments promoting trade and industry.

The relationship of private property to civil and political liberty is the principal theme of our inquiry. Liberty and the rights that flow from it come into existence only with the emergence of public authority, that is, the state. In social organization based on kinship, human relations are informal and the individual is not able to advance legal claims on his behalf. Once the state comes into being, with its authority extending over a definite territory and all its inhabitants, such claims become possible. A "right" has been aptly defined as "one man's capacity of influencing the acts of another, by means, not of his own strength, but of the opinion or the force of society."[175] Under these conditions, property—where it is allowed to emerge—is protected by the state as a "right," but the same right also protects the individual *from* the state: along with law, its by-product, it becomes the most efficacious means of limiting the state's power. Where the state claims ownership of all productive resources, as in the case of the ancient Oriental monarchies, individuals or families have no means of asserting their freedom because economically they are entirely dependent on the sovereign power. It is certainly no coincidence that private property in land as well as democracy first came into existence in ancient Hellas, notably in Athens, a city-state founded and governed by independent farmers, the backbone of its economy and armed forces. Nor was it fortuitous that many of the major institutions of modern democracy trace their descent directly from the medieval urban community, in which trade and manufacture produced a powerful moneyed class that treated its possessions as an aspect of its liberty.

Out of these experiences evolved the modern notion of freedom and rights. In medieval Europe, and especially in the seventeenth century, when the modern ideas of liberty were born, "property" came to be conceived as "propriety," the sum total of rights to possessions as well as personal rights with which man is endowed by nature and of which he cannot be deprived except with his consent and not even always then (as, for instance, in the denial of the "right" to sell oneself into slavery). The notion of "inalienable rights," which has played an increasing role in the political thought and practice of the West since the seventeenth century, grows out of the right to property, the most elementary of rights. One of its aspects is the principle that the sovereign rules but does not own and hence must not appropriate the belongings of his subjects or violate their persons—a principle that erected a powerful barrier to political authority and permitted the evolution first of civil and then of political rights.

The historian of classical antiquity Moses Finley notes that "it is impossible to translate the word 'freedom,' *eleutheria* in Greek, *libertas* in Latin, or 'free man,' into any ancient Near Eastern language, including Hebrew, or into any Far Eastern language either, for that matter."* Why should this be the case? What did ancient Greece and ancient

*M. I. Finley, *The Ancient Economy* (Berkeley and Los Angeles, 1973), 28. The Japanese, when first exposed to Western influences in the nineteenth century, had great difficulty translating "freedom"; they finally settled on *jiyu*, which means "licentiousness." The same held true of China and Korea. Orlando Patterson, *Freedom* (New York, 1991), p. x. Muslim writers faced a similar difficulty: "The first examples in Islamic lands of the use of the term freedom in a clearly defined political sense come from the Ottoman Empire in the late 18th and early 19th centuries, and are patently due to European influence, sometimes to direct translations from European texts. . . . Early references to freedom in works of Muslim authorship are hostile, and equate it with libertinism, licentiousness, and anarchy." Bernard Lewis, *Islam in History* (New York, 1973), 267, 269.

Rome have in common that the empires of the Middle East or Far East lacked? One answer is the idea of freedom. But then the question arises: what was it in the culture of these two countries that gave rise to such a novel idea? For ideas do not form in a vacuum: like words which articulate them, they refer to things that matter sufficiently to require a name in order to make it possible to communicate about them.

It has been suggested that the idea of freedom springs from the consciousness of slavery and the contrast which it creates between free and unfree: the nonslave is said to become aware of his status as freeman by contrasting himself with the slave. In the words of one proponent of this explanation, "The origins of Western culture and its most cherished ideal, freedom, were founded . . . not upon a rock of human virtue but upon the degraded time fill of man's vilest inhumanity to man."[176] But this explanation is unconvincing. Although slavery was universal, and widely practiced even by "noble savages" like the American Indians, the concept of personal freedom did not arise in any slave-owning society outside the West. In Russia, for instance, where the vast majority of the population had been bonded since the late sixteenth century, no one seemed to conceive of personal freedom in contrast to serfdom or view serfdom as unnatural until abolitionist sentiments were imported from the West under the German-born empress Catherine the Great.

It is the sense of economic independence and that of personal worth which it generates that give rise to the idea of freedom. That the ancient Greeks realized this is suggested by a passage in the *History* of Herodotus which attributes the valor of the Athenians in the war against the Persians to the fact that they no longer "worked for a master."[177] Herodotus meant specifically that they had liberated themselves from the whims of tyrants. But the concept had broader implications than the political one, defining also the person who worked for himself, who was economically independent. The theme resounds in the funeral oration of Pericles, in which every individual Athenian is declared to be "in his own person . . . self-sufficient in the most varied forms of activity."[178]

And such self-sufficiency is possible only in societies that recognize private ownership. It is much more likely, therefore, that the idea of freedom arose from the contrast between owner and nonowner (which category in ancient Athens included all noncitizens) than from that between freeman and slave, because an insuperable psychological barrier separates the latter two which makes comparisons between them hard to conceive. The original source of economic self-reliance was privately cultivated land, and that made its earliest appearance in ancient

Israel, Greece, and Rome. Finley clearly points to this solution to the question of the Western origins of freedom even if he does not spell it out:

> The Near Eastern economies [of antiquity] were dominated by large palace- or temple-complexes, [which] owned the greater part of the arable, virtually monopolized anything that can be called "industrial production" as well as foreign trade . . . and organized the economic, military, political and religious life of the society through a single complicated, bureaucratic, record-keeping operation for which the word "rationing," taken very broadly, is as good a one-word description as I can think of. None of this is relevant to the Graeco-Roman world until the conquests of Alexander the Great and later of the Romans [after they had] incorporated large Near Eastern territories. . . .
>
> I do not wish to over-simplify. There were private holdings of land in the Near East, privately worked; there were "independent" craftsmen and peddlers in the towns. Our evidence does not permit quantification, but I do not believe it possible to elevate these people to the prevailing pattern of economy, whereas the Graeco-Roman world was *essentially and precisely one of private ownership,* whether of a few acres or of the enormous domains of Roman senators and emperors, a world of private trade, private manufacture.[179]

The contrast between the Graeco-Roman world of antiquity and the Middle Eastern monarchies was replicated, *mutatis mutandis,* in modern Europe, in the divergent development of both property and freedom in the westernmost and easternmost halves of the continent, epitomized by England and Russia. The former developed private property early and provided the model of political democracy to the rest of the world, while the other, having become acquainted with property late in its history, and even then only fitfully, failed to create institutions capable of protecting its people from the despotic authority of Leviathan.

3

ENGLAND AND THE BIRTH OF PARLIAMENTARY DEMOCRACY

> Liberty inheres in some sensible object; and every nation has formed to itself some favourite point, which by way of eminence becomes the criterion of their happiness. It happened, you know, sir, that the great contests for freedom in this country were from the earliest times chiefly upon the question of taxing.
>
> —Edmund Burke[1]

England is the home of parliamentary democracy, and hence the history of her political evolution holds universal interest: the constitutional historian A. F. Pollard called parliament England's greatest contribution to civilization.[2] Her records are abundant and the literature on her constitutional evolution of the highest quality. England is by no means typical: indeed, in many respects she is unique, and was long recognized as such by Englishmen as well as foreigners. Sir John Fortescue, writing in the fifteenth century, and Sir Thomas Smith, writing a century later, were already quite conscious of the difference between England and contemporary continental states. Lest such views be attributed to chauvinism, it must be noted that many visitors from abroad shared this view. Montesquieu called the English the freest people in the world because they limited the power of the king by law.[3] Voltaire was similarly impressed, describing the English as "the only people upon earth who have been able to prescribe limits to the power of Kings by resisting them; and who, by a series of struggles, have at last established that wise Government, where the Prince is all-powerful to do good, and at the same time is restrained from doing evil. . . ."[4]

England was the first country in the world to form a national state;

she also institutionalized earlier than other nations the primitive democratic practices of Germanic tribes. She thus constitutes a laboratory which reveals the conditions under which political freedom and civil rights have the best opportunity to develop.

Why and how did parliament, as the representative of the population at large, triumph over the crown and secure for the people the rights and liberties that aroused the admiration of the rest of Europe? British constitutional history records the advance of parliament from being a servant of the crown (eleventh to fifteenth century) to being its partner (sixteenth to early seventeenth century) and, finally, its master (from the 1640s on).* In this evolution, the distribution of wealth between the crown and its subjects played a decisive role, inasmuch as the decline of royal power accompanied the shrinkage of royal estates and the revenues derived from them. The wealth of the English crown dwindled because its expenditures exceeded its income as a result of wars, court extravagance, poor management of the royal domain, and inflation. The decrease of its private income forced the crown to rely ever more on revenues from customs and taxation.

This impoverishment had momentous political consequences, for customs duties and most taxes required parliamentary sanction. "The Crown became poorer and poorer, and when compelled to resort to Parliament, had to surrender constitutional rights in return for funds."[5] "The threshold over which the kings repeatedly stumbled was money. They demanded from the people hard cash, the people demanded from them freedoms and reforms. This is the red thread, if there is one, that

*I am well aware that it has been fashionable among some English historians, since the appearance in 1931 of H. Butterfield's *The Whig Interpretation of History*, to dismiss the theory of the relentless progress of parliamentary power as partisan and flawed. This book was a brilliant example of scholarly revisionism, but it does not hold up. On rereading it half a century later, G. R. Elton found it "perilously thin": "truly an essay, lacking in substance and in particular lacking in history." *Studies in Tudor and Stuart Politics and Government*, IV (Cambridge, 1992), 273. Granted that many of the traditional historians overstated their case, depicting parliamentary history as concerned exclusively with power contests with the crown, and seeing all the virtue concentrated in parliament. Still, a nonspecialist looking at England's constitutional evolution from the outside, say the perspective of Russia, finds this traditional interpretation compelling. The trouble with most "revisionism" is that it treats deviations and exceptions not as shadings of phenomena but as their essence: hence it produces mainly caveats rather than alternative interpretations. J. P. Kenyon, who subscribes to the revisionist school, concedes that the "Whig interpretation" has not been replaced by a "plausible" alternative. *Stuart England* (London, 1978), 9. The same holds true of the revisionist representation of the English Civil War. Richard Cust and Ann Hughes, eds., *Conflict in Early Stuart England* (London and New York, 1989), 11. The editors' introduction to the latter work provides a good critique of English historical revisionism.

runs through English parliamentary history."[6] Indeed, as James Harrington wisely observed three and a half centuries ago, it was the people's growing wealth and the king's increasing dependence on it that compelled the crown to grant its subjects rights and freedoms. England's constitutional evolution may thus be said to march to the drumbeat of her financial history. It provides a classic illustration of how private wealth restrains public authority.

1. *Pre-Norman England*

As in other parts of the Roman Empire outside the Italian peninsula, under Roman rule all the land in England was ultimately the property of the emperor: the inhabitants cultivated the soil as imperial tenants.[7] For this right, they paid rents to Roman officials.

After the Romans withdrew from Britain in the middle of the fifth century, the island was subjected to repeated invasions by bands of Anglo-Saxon barbarians from Schleswig-Holstein and Jutland. The invaders' basic social unit was the clan; they settled by clans made up of freemen and large contingents of slaves. The land was divided into royal, private, and public; the public portion steadily decreased and eventually disappeared, being absorbed into the royal demesne.[8] Private land was held in outright ownership.

Although the six-hundred-year interlude between the Roman withdrawal from Britain and the Norman Conquest is commonly viewed as one long interval of anarchy, it was during the latter part of this period that the foundations of many future British institutions were laid. In the two centuries preceding the Norman Conquest, when England was unified under a single monarch, following traditions deeply embedded in barbarian societies (see below), kings were expected not to legislate but to maintain custom—a principle that severely circumscribed their authority, because it meant that they could introduce no changes without the explicit approval of the community.* Anglo-Saxon kings, like other Germanic rulers, administered the country with the assistance of a council of the wise (*witena gemot* or *witan*), composed of leading nobles and churchmen.† It occasionally elected kings, legislated when

*This principle corresponded to the practices of primitive communities in other parts of the world, of which an anthropologist says that "the business of such governmental machinery as exists is rather to exact obedience to traditional usage than to create new precedents." Robert H. Lowie, *Primitive Society* (New York, 1920), 358–59.

†*Wita* (plural *witan*) means "sage"; *gemot* means "assembly."

absolutely necessary, and levied taxes.[9] Major decisions were submitted for popular approval of the "folkmoot," which met twice a year to serve as a court of justice and to consider such public matters as came up. Attendance was open to all freemen. Maitland calls attention to the fact that such practices were identical with those which Tacitus had described as prevalent among the Germanic tribes of his time and which we know from anthropology to be also common among primitive peoples today.* Even prior to the Norman Conquest, English kings could neither legislate nor tax without the consent of the "great" of the realm and the folkmoot.[10] This principle certainly derived from the convention of Germanic tribes that "the law remains the domain of the community" and the king rules not as the sovereign of his people but as their representative.†

The most likely reason that these Germanic traditions survived better in England than on the continent is that England, being an island, was inhabited by a compact population and physically separated from the non-Germanic peoples of the European continent among whom the other Germanic tribes had settled and under whose influence they soon fell.

Government by consent can emerge under various conditions as long as the politically active population is economically independent and thus, in a sense, co-sovereign. We have seen it appear in ancient Greece among small, self-sufficient farmers. It is common among nomadic societies which support themselves by hunting and livestock breeding, because such societies, structured along kinship lines, treat all adult male members as equal and equally entitled to participate in decisions affecting the group. This is a characteristic feature of all kinship groups, whether the Germanic tribes as described by Tacitus, American Indians, or African peoples.[11] Although tyranny is not unknown among primitive kinship societies, their political life is typically participatory.[12]

The basic unit of organization of the Germanic peoples who conquered Europe was the clan composed of kinfolk claiming descent from a common ancestor. The supreme authority was vested in the assembly

*F. W. Maitland, *The Constitutional History of England* (Cambridge, 1946), 55–56; J.E.A. Jolliffe, *The Constitutional History of Medieval England,* 4th ed. (London, 1961), 25–29; Helen Cam, *England Before Elizabeth* (New York, 1952), 48. The reader must bear in mind that "Germanic" does not mean "German." It is a generic term covering the various ethnic groups which conquered the Roman Empire, and from whom descended, in addition to the modern Germans, the English, French, Scandinavians, etc.

†Jolliffe, *Constitutional History,* 23–24, 41–42. Herbert Butterfield in his *Whig Interpretation,* 32, however, dismisses this idea as a "myth" concocted by the seventeenth-century jurist Sir Edward Coke.

of warriors, presided over by a leader who was powerless to overrule its decisions. The assembly decided on war and peace and it allotted land.[13]

Such was the situation as long as the tribes and clans pursued a nomadic or seminomadic existence. But when these groups adopted agriculture as their main occupation and abandoned nomadism, democratic procedures practiced within the kinship group acquired a territorial dimension. This did not happen suddenly: the Germanic invaders of England, having settled down in kinship clusters, initially followed their kinship laws.[14] The same held true of the barbarian conquerors of continental Europe, who, as we have noted previously, applied not the Roman law prevalent on the territories which they occupied but their own "barbarian" codes. Gradually, however, the territorial principle triumphed and the law of the dominant group became the law of the land.[15] It is only in this manner that one can explain how such savages as the Jutes, Angles, and Saxons laid the foundations of representative government in conquered England.

This transition—from kinship to territorial organization—occurred in England in the late ninth century, during the reign of Alfred the Great, with the introduction of a method of taxation based on shires (counties) rather than on tribal units.* The constitutional historian J.E.A. Jolliffe called it the most profound formative change in the entire course of English history because it made possible the amalgamation of diverse communities into a nation and a national state.[16] It is at this point that the modern state was born—an institution that lays claim to public authority over all the inhabitants of a given territory. In the case of England the state grew out of the community of free men, and it never lost this character.

A great deal of public activity during the Anglo-Saxon period concerned property. There is evidence that in pre-Norman Britain, private property in land was the rule and the owners enjoyed the full right of alienation.[17] According to Maitland, the earliest document of English law, dating to King Ethelbert (c. 600), dealt with this subject.[18] The folkmoots were much concerned with it as well, settling ownership disputes as well as combatting crime, including theft.[19]

As concerned taxation, the principle was—and it remained in force,

*Keith Feiling, *A History of England* (New York etc., 1950), 67–68. This replicated a process that had occurred in Sparta in the seventh century B.C.E. Chester G. Starr, *Individual and Community* (New York and Oxford, 1986), 55–56. It also paralleled the reforms of Cleisthenes in Athens (570–508 B.C.E.), which based the responsibilities of citizenship on residence in a locality rather than membership in a clan.

at least in theory, until the mid-seventeenth century—that English kings covered normal expenditures, both private and public, from the revenues of their private domains and the dispensation of justice. It is believed that when they needed to raise additional income by means of taxes, they had to obtain the *witena gemot*'s consent. But such levies were so rare that next to nothing is known of them.[20]

2. *Norman rule*

At the time of the Norman Conquest the landed estates of English royalty stood at their zenith.[21] The conquerors abolished allodial holdings: previous owners, if permitted to keep their estates, became royal tenants in chief. Norman royalty not only inherited the holdings of the deposed Anglo-Saxon kings but also confiscated properties from the lords who had offered them resistance, much of which they distributed among their tenants.[22] The tenants in chief were required to provide the king with fixed quotas of cavalry. To ensure that they had the required number of horsemen, they, in turn, granted estates to knights. Thus the feudal chain was forged. But William the Conqueror assumed that all the land, secular as well as clerical, belonged to him and was held by his tenants on feudal terms. A tenant in chief who failed in his duties forfeited his lands to the crown.

As had been the case with the Anglo-Saxon kings, the Norman rulers were expected to maintain their court and administer the country from private revenues.[23] During the two hundred years which followed the Norman conquest, that is, until the middle of the thirteenth century, English kings derived up to 60 percent of their income from rents furnished by the royal demesne.[24] This they augmented with the proceeds of feudal dues, mainly escheat and wardship.* The principle was affirmed in a famous declaration made by Edward IV in 1467 to the Commons long after it had become an anachronism: "I purpose to live upon my own, and not to charge my subjects but in great and urgent causes. . . ." By which he meant that apart from customs revenues, he would live off rents from crown lands and his rights as feudal suzerain, all deposited in the Exchequer.[25] Tax levies were reserved for

*H. P. R. Finberg, *The Agrarian History of England and Wales,* IV (Cambridge, 1967), 256. Escheat was the right of the sovereign or any other feudal lord to the land of subjects who died intestate or without lawful heirs, as well as properties confiscated for failure to fulfill feudal obligations, for treason, and for felony. Wardship was the royal claim to administer the estates of the minor children of tenants in chief.

emergencies: in such situations, the king had to claim urgent need to defend the realm and then obtain the consent of the people taxed. In the Magna Carta (1215), King John, having returned in defeat from France, reaffirmed that he would levy no taxes without the consent of the realm. In 1297, the Confirmation of Charters, which included the Magna Carta, restated the principle that the king had no authority to impose nonfeudal levies without a parliamentary grant.[26] These concessions have long been recognized by historians as marking fundamental guarantees of the security of private property in England. And although the crown then and later exerted much ingenuity in its efforts to subvert this principle, it remained the foundation of the English constitution: the English king "*never* had any right to take an aid or subsidy from the subject without the consent of parliament."* Which meant, in effect, that unless he had enough income of his own, he could not rule effectively without the consent of his subjects. This principle was well established before the middle of the fourteenth century.[27] It was this principle and this need that launched the House of Commons on its spectacular career.

Which brings us to the history of parliament. It has been said that it is impossible to determine when this institution came into being. The modern usage of the term—to mean an assembly of representatives empowered to legislate—seems to date to the reign of Henry III in the middle of the thirteenth century. Until then, "parliament" was applied loosely to all kinds of gatherings ("parleys"); it was only around 1250 that it came to refer specifically to a conference held by a king for state purposes.[28] In this guise, parliament emerged from the *curia regis,* or royal council, of Norman kings. The king's tenants in chief were duty-bound to attend the royal court whenever summoned. Initially, their function was not to legislate but to render opinions on customary laws and to judge. This limited scope of action was the result of the view prevalent in the Middle Ages which held laws to be eternal and immutable: they were not made but interpreted. This attitude survived surprisingly long. Before the Reform Act of 1832, law in England was not something that was "made" but that was "there," in the background, to be deduced from custom and the Law of Nature.[29] Because it consumed much time and money, attendance at such councils was consid-

*Stephen Dowell, *A History of Taxation and Taxes in England,* I (London, 1888), 211. Emphasis added. There were only two exceptions to this rule: the tenants on the royal demesne, who by virtue of their relation to the king as their landlord could be subjected to "tallage," or tax, when he was in debt; and the Jews, who were "liable to indefinite extortion at the hands of the king because they were permitted to be here solely at his will." Ibid., 210–11.

ered a burdensome duty rather than a prerogative: at any rate, no instances are known of lords demanding the right to attend.[30] Still, legislative acts of the early period, rare as they may have been, were enacted with the advice and consent of the "great." William I, the Conqueror, followed the Anglo-Saxon tradition of passing no new laws or levying taxes without the consent of the "wise" and powerful men of the realm.[31]

The critical step in the evolution of parliament occurred toward the end of the thirteenth century, when the crown, greatly in need of money and unable to procure it from its own sources, invited representatives of knights and burghers to attend special sessions of the feudal council.[32] Here lay a rich and untapped source of potential revenues. We have noted that fiefs very early became hereditary possessions (see above, p. 106), and there were numerous ways in which tenants could with or even without their lord's explicit permission alienate their land.[33] As early as the twelfth century, royal courts in England dealt with property disputes of large and small holders.[34] Alan Macfarlane has demonstrated the very early development of individual landed property in feudal England.[35] He has shown that in pre-Tudor times (thirteenth and fourteenth centuries) freehold land belonged not to families but to individuals (women included), and that its owners were free to dispose of it at will, disinheriting their children if they so chose and selling it to outsiders.* Thirteenth-century England had farmers who regarded the land they tilled as a commodity. Macfarlane concludes that

> property [in England] was highly individualized by the end of the thirteenth century, if not much earlier. It was held by individuals and not by larger groups; it could be bought and sold; children did not have automatic rights in land; there is no evidence of strong family attachment to a particular plot of land.[36]

The evolution of a market in land occurred mainly among the farmers, because for the nobles possession of land was the "hallmark" of aristocratic status, which they were unwilling to trade for money.†

The disappearance in England of serfdom (villeinage) toward the end

*Later on, English women lost to their husbands the legal right to own property. They did not recover it until 1881.

†Donald R. Denman, *Origins of Ownership* (London, 1958), 150. Donald N. McCloskey, cited in T. Eggertsson, *Economic Behavior and Institutions* (Cambridge, 1990), 285–86n, says that there is plenty of evidence of an "active market in land among [medieval] peasants."

of the Middle Ages further strengthened private property, because the ex-villeins, now freemen, could hold title. According to Tawney, in the fourteenth and fifteenth centuries manorial tenants turned into well-to-do farmers; most cultivators owned the land rather than leased it.[37]

Here was a source of potential revenues that the crown could hardly ignore, especially since it was accompanied by the growth of towns and the emergence of a merchant class.

An early instance of commoner attendance in parliament occurred in 1265 in the course of a struggle between the nobles and Henry III. Simon de Montfort, who led the resistance to the crown, had the king arrested and then invited each shire and borough to send two representatives to Westminster. Although his rebellion was crushed, a novel principle was introduced and a precedent set.[38] Henceforth, representatives of the burghers and the shires were routinely summoned to advise on legislation and to vote subsidies. As a result the role of parliament increased significantly. In 1295–96, the crown convened the first of what came to be known as "model" parliaments. (A similar event occurred at the same time in France.) The novel principle introduced here was that the participants represented not themselves but their constituencies. The Exchequer under Edward III (1327–77) refused to give money to the king unless he met certain stipulations, one of them making his ministers accountable to parliament and another requiring parliament to be informed of the uses made of its appropriations (subsidies).[39] These demands did not become constitutional practice until many centuries later, but they were indicative of parliament's growing aspirations.

Parliaments thus became an integral part of government, but they were still summoned ad hoc rather than regularly; each parliament was new and required fresh elections. Thus England had not "parliament" but only discrete "parliaments." The rule that parliaments sit continuously was not adopted until the early eighteenth century: until then, they were convened whenever the government needed money.

Beginning with the fourteenth century, parliaments demanded and were granted a voice in legislation. In the fifteenth century it came to be accepted practice that for an act to acquire the quality of a statute it had to have the assent of both the Lords and the Commons; ordinances, which had temporary force, did not.[40] After 1530 a statute became the law of the realm only if it had the concurrence of parliament.[41] For the king to revoke or alter a statute on his own was deemed an abuse of authority.

Thus came into being certain crucial attributes of modern democracy: that the government could not on its own authority abrogate a statute or impose a tax. Added to these limitations was the ban on interfering with justice.[42] An early writer on the English constitution, Sir John Fortescue, chief justice of the King's Bench, argued in the years 1469–71 that English law was fundamentally unaltered since antiquity. The purpose of government, in the past as in the present, was to protect persons and their belongings. For this reason, kings could not impose taxes without their subjects' consent. Fortescue contrasted the king of England with his French counterpart by distinguishing between a monarch who ruled only "regally" (as he did in France) and one who ruled both "regally" and "politically" (in modern language, constitutionally), as was the case in England. The difference lay in the fact that the latter "is not able himself to change the laws of his kingdom at pleasure" nor arbitrarily impose taxes, thereby allowing his subjects the undisturbed enjoyment of their properties.[43] First published in Latin in 1537 and in English in 1567, Fortescue's treatise became something of a best-seller in the reign of Queen Elizabeth. Its historical accuracy need not concern us; what matters is that it reflected an opinion widely shared in educated circles of England by the fifteenth century that good government obeyed the law.

3. *The role of common law*

Fortescue was one of several medieval jurists who profoundly affected the way Englishmen viewed their government. In no other country did legal experts exert such influence on politics as in England.[44] The profession of lay lawyers emerged in the course of the thirteenth century. By 1300, England had regular law schools ("inns of court"). Their products were not academic theoreticians—these had their base at the universities, which taught canon law and Roman civil law—but practitioners of common law who had the same professional background as the judges before whom they pleaded. Because the common law, like English politics, was rooted in historic precedent, lawyers, recognized as authorities on the past, assumed a prominent role in interpreting the constitution.[45] They are credited with helping abolish serfdom (villeinage) and establishing the principle that "no one may be imprisoned without lawful cause."[46]

The extraordinary prominence of law and lawyers in England and the entire English-speaking world is in good measure explainable by the early development of property, for inasmuch as property means ownership claims enforceable by legal means, law is its indispensable adjunct.

Common-law jurists laid great stress on private property: "the declaring of *meum* and *tuum* . . . is the very object of the laws of England," the historian William Camden wrote in the reign of James I.[47] And, indeed, this matter preoccupied English courts from the earliest times.

> [T]he common law of the twelfth and thirteenth centuries is in large part the law of land and tenures, the law of property rights and services together with rules of procedure for the administration of justice. A glance at the chapters of the Magna Carta or at any collection of common-law writs will reveal the dominant concern with rights in land: the possession, or seisin, of land, the services owed for the tenure of land, the inheritance of land, the leasing of land, the wardship of land, the profits from land, the burdens on land, and the wrongs to land.[48]

In sum, "medieval common law was principally land law."[49]

This situation did not change in the centuries that followed. Describing the situation as it was in 1770, the legal historian P. S. Atiyah writes that

> the function of the judges [in England] was, to a large degree, to protect . . . property rights, to enforce contracts arising out of property, and to punish crime most of which was seen as a threat to property rights.[50]

Under the Tudors, there were several courts that functioned independently of the royal court: the Court of Exchequer, which tried financial disputes between the king and his subjects; the King's Bench, which dealt with civil and criminal cases between king and subjects; and Common Pleas, which tried civil disputes between subjects.[51]

Fortescue was followed by Sir Edward Coke (pronounced "Cook"), one of the most influential legal minds in English history, an uncommon blend of theorist and politician. Coke played a leading role in the evolution of the doctrine of government by consent by inventing a romanticized picture of England's "ancient constitution" according to which the country's kings had always respected the country's customs. Customs were embodied in common law, which was the supreme arbiter of public life because it was created and acknowledged by the people as well as rooted in "common right and reason."[52] According to Coke, the ultimate right to interpret the laws of the realm resided neither with the king nor with parliament nor yet with both acting jointly but with the common law as interpreted by the courts.[53] No one has contributed more than Coke to the view, prevalent in British and American cultures, that law is the ultimate arbiter of right and wrong not only in civil and criminal cases but also in affairs of state.[54] There is virtual unanimity among modern scholars that Coke's insistence on the historical supremacy of law in England was wrong, but he is credited with establishing the principle (in Thomas Paine's words) that "law is king." It had far-reaching implications: it meant that jurists were the ultimate judges of what governments could or could not lawfully do. English courts came early to deal with constitutional issues, passing judgment on the respective authority of the crown and parliament—an authority which lawyers enjoyed in no other country.[55] Coke in his younger years supported royal absolutism; it was after the accession of James I, in his capacity as chief justice, that he joined the opposition, arguing that kings could not judge: judges alone could interpret the law. He lived long enough to see his principles prevail in the reign of Charles I.

The evolution of English common law proceeded in a manner that sooner or later was bound to produce a confrontation between king and Commons. The "liberties" granted by the crown were privileges, available to a select few; common law, however, protected the private property and personal liberty of all:

> It was [the] common-law concepts of personal rights, of property rights and liberty that came into conflict, in the reigns of Elizabeth and the Stuart Kings, with the prerogative of the monarch. The way was prepared for a double meaning of the word liberty. It might mean the "libertates" of Magna Carta, which were the privileges of landlords granted by the monarch, or it might mean the liberty to buy and sell, to be free from violence, theft and trespass, derived from the approved customs which constituted common law. The two were inconsistent. One was a contradiction of the other. Freedom, or liberty, in the sense of a grant out of the royal prerogative, stood for a relation of superior to inferior; freedom or liberty in the sense of the common law stood for a relation of equality between members of the same class. The first is more properly to be distinguished as "freedom," the second as "liberty." Freedom was a grant of power to participate in the privileges of those who were specially favored by a superior. Liberty was a common-law right to equality of treatment among individuals who belonged to the

same class whether privileged or unprivileged. Equal liberty was inconsistent with unequal freedom.

It was this contradiction and double meaning of liberty that characterized the long struggle of the 17th century until it was finally closed by the Act of Settlement in the year 1700.[56]

4. *Taxation*

Traditionally, Englishmen have been very lightly taxed, and in the reign of Elizabeth they were the least taxed people in Europe. Taxes of the upper class rested on self-assessment; they were assessed not by a professional bureaucracy but by the local gentry, who had a common interest with the taxpayers in keeping taxes low.[57] And, of course, parliament, which had the ultimate say in matters of taxation, made sure the crown did not gain fiscal independence.

In the 1330s, on the eve of the Hundred Years War, Edward III imposed a tax on movable (personal) property, which required annual renewal by parliament. It set a levy of one-tenth on the personal assets of urban (borough) inhabitants and one-fifteenth on those living in the countryside (shires). It was a so-called "quota" tax, which fixed the amount due from the whole country and entrusted the communities with responsibility for apportioning it among the taxpayers. It was gradually replaced by the "Subsidy," an "assessed" tax which taxed wealth.[58] The Subsidy formed the basis of the appropriations which parliament voted to the crown. In times of war, parliament would double, triple, or even quadruple it.

Another source of crown revenues, and one that grew in importance, was customs. The crown enjoyed, with parliamentary sanction, the right to tax imports of wine and exports of wool; these were known as "tonnage and poundage."* These revenues parliament first granted for life to Richard II in 1397, and then (until 1625) routinely to each successive king or queen upon his or her accession.[59] As British foreign trade expanded in the sixteenth and seventeenth centuries, income from customs increased to the point where, as we shall see, the House of Commons refused in 1625 to grant tonnage and poundage for life to Charles I, insisting on annual appropriations from fear that otherwise the king

*Tonnage was duty on wine and poundage duty on wool.

would become financially independent of it. This refusal would set off a grave constitutional crisis that would culminate in the Civil War.

5. *The Tudors*

On the accession of the Tudor dynasty in 1485, the population of England and Wales is estimated to have numbered around three million, nine-tenths of it rural. Villeinage had virtually disappeared; the population was free. By then England had a large class of independent farmers. Freeholder yeomen had no feudal obligations at all, while leaseholders were secure in the knowledge that they could not be evicted nor have their rents raised.[60]

Like their predecessors, in times of peace the Tudor kings derived the bulk of their revenues from rents furnished by royal estates and the traditional feudal fees[61] supplemented with tonnage and poundage. The proportion of the income which the crown drew from its estates had declined, however, and by 1485 amounted to barely 30 percent of its total revenues.[62] This situation changed temporarily for the better under Henry VIII, who increased the royal domain by expropriating the holdings of over eight hundred monastic and clerical establishments. The revenues of these secularized properties brought in an annual income of £140,000, a sum somewhat in excess of the normal revenues of the crown.[63] The expropriation was accomplished without arousing violent resistance because most of the monastic land had been leased, and the crown left the lessors in possession.[64] Although clearly in violation of property rights, these expropriations were not arbitrary actions, having been carried out with the consent of parliament.[65] Some of the confiscated lands were added to the royal domain and a few turned over to favorites, but most were sold to meet the expenses of war.[66] The main beneficiaries of these sales were the gentry, but not a few yeomen, merchants, and artisans also profited, joining in this manner the ranks of landed proprietors.[67] By the time Henry VIII died, only one-third of the ex-monastic land still remained in the crown's possession.[68] As a consequence, the crown's ability to live on its own did not significantly improve.

Queen Elizabeth (ruled 1558–1603) inherited much landed wealth, but even so her land revenues did not suffice for her needs, because of the corruption and poor management of royal estates.[69] In addition, the moneys obtained depreciated in value owing to the general European inflation, which increased expenditures while rents remained fixed: the inflation in sixteenth-century England is estimated to have exceeded 300 percent.[70] Just how small was the regular royal income under Elizabeth is illustrated by the fact that when Francis Drake returned from his piratical expedition to the Americas, one of his ships carried loot equivalent to at least two years' royal revenues.[71] And the crown's expenses mounted rapidly, mainly owing to the war with Spain. Between 1588 and 1601, parliament allocated some £2 million for the war, but the actual outlays were double that figure.[72] The shortfall forced the queen to sell crown lands. Because of these sales, her annual income from crown lands fell from £150,000 to £110,000.[73] Penury was one of the reasons that toward the end of her reign the queen was compelled to convene parliaments more frequently.

Under the Tudors, especially under Henry VIII, the power of parliament increased appreciably. All of Henry's major policies received parliamentary sanction. Like the other Tudor kings, Henry VIII preferred to rule with parliamentary approval rather than by ordinance.[74] Lengthy parliamentary sessions common in his reign created a body of seasoned legislators linked by an *esprit de corps*: by the end of the sixteenth century, membership in the House of Commons became a valued privilege.[75] Even so, parliament was not yet a working part of the constitution, inasmuch as there was no regular calendar of convocations, the House of Commons being summoned at the pleasure of the crown.[76] And the crown exercised this privilege mainly when it stood in need of money to pay for wars. Henry VIII summoned parliament every 4.2 years; Elizabeth, every 4.5 years.[77] Thus, as in the Middle Ages, there was as yet no concept of "parliament"[78] but only of individual "parliaments."

The notion that parliament was an essential part of the constitution, however, was in the air. It was forcefully articulated by Sir Thomas Smith in his *The Commonwealth of England* (written in 1565 but first published in 1583). According to Smith, parliament was neither an adjunct of the crown nor its counterweight but an essential element of sovereign power, which Smith defined as "King-in-Parliament." In 1610, parliament formally adopted this doctrine, declaring sovereignty to reside in "King-in-Parliament" rather than "King-in-Council."[79]

The inviolate principle that the crown could not levy new taxes without parliamentary sanction created in England a partnership under which power was not only theoretically but also effectively shared by the crown and Commons. Attempts to circumvent parliamentary authority in this matter by extorting forced loans, made both by Henry VIII and Queen Mary, met with such fierce resistance that they had to be abandoned.[80] Secondly, the crown acknowledged that it could not legislate by proclamation. And finally, there were the courts of justice whose verdicts, based on historical precedent, limited the powers of the crown to treat its subjects arbitrarily.[81] Given these restraints on royal authority, some modern historians deny that one can speak of Tudor "despotism." "The faults and lapses of Tudor governments," writes G. R. Elton, a leading authority on the period, "do not disprove the existence of the rule of law under which they governed."[82]

Thus emerged a political climate that would frustrate all attempts by the Stuart successors to the Tudors to impose on England a regime of royal absolutism, and in the end make the crown subservient to parliament.

6. *The early Stuarts*

The first king of Stuart lineage, James I, resolutely believed in the divine right of kings; he even wrote a treatise, *Trew Law of Free Monarchies* (1598), to justify it. By "free monarchy" he meant what Jean Bodin had defined twenty years earlier as "sovereignty," that is, rule exercised in a supreme and unrestrained manner: kings were "above the law," because they made the laws and were responsible for their actions only to God.[83] James was convinced that he owned his kingdom's material assets and could use them as he thought best: like fathers, kings had the power to disinherit their children-subjects. Monarchs were perhaps morally but were in no way legally bound to respect the property rights of their people. This doctrine had originated in France and was imported to England by way of Scotland, whence James had come. It ran contrary to traditions rooted in England since earliest times, and would have required a revolution to be enforced.

James inherited an empty exchequer, with a debt of £400,000, which he managed by 1608 to more than double.[84] By 1615, tradesmen refused to extend him credit.[85] He did not improve the health of his treasury by squandering fortunes on jewels and other luxuries. His financial distress was further aggravated by the general European inflation which had made itself felt in the reign of his predecessor, Elizabeth. Thus, whatever his theoretical claims on his subjects' assets, to make ends meet he had to resort to very devious practices, for their wealth was beyond his reach. He raised money by selling titles, charging, for example, £1,000 for a barony and proportionately more for higher ones.[86] Denied private credit, he resorted to forced loans. But he relied mainly on the familiar device of selling crown lands. During the first decade of his reign, the crown disposed of land valued at £655,000; in a single year (1610), such sales realized £68,000.[87] Since James also lavishly distributed estates to Scottish favorites, by 1628 crown lands had "ceased to be an important part of the royal income."[88] Funding from this source, which at the time of James's accession had brought in some £100,000 a year, shrank by 1640 to £50,000 to £55,000 a year, and possibly less.[89] As a result, James's son and successor, Charles I, was even more desperate for money—which he sought with the concurrence of parliament if possible or, if that was not forthcoming, without it.

It was during the reign of Charles I that the upheavals which would transform England into the world's first parliamentary democracy first broke out, in the years 1640–42; they were consummated almost half a century later when, following the flight of James II to France, parliament offered the crown to William and Mary on the condition that they formally acknowledged limitations on their authority.

Charles I antagonized his subjects virtually from the moment he ascended the throne in 1625. At first, hostility to him was due mainly to suspicions concerning his religious sympathies; and throughout the events leading up to the Civil War, religion, politics, and fiscal matters would be inextricably joined. The new king had married the sister of France's Louis XIII, a devout Catholic. To gain her hand, he had to promise all manner of concessions to his Catholic subjects. English Protestants, notably the powerful Puritan constituency, came to fear that he would be succeeded by a Catholic. But before long, the conflict between king and country came to center on fiscal matters: Francis Bacon, in the essay "Of Seditions and Troubles," republished the year Charles came to the throne, explained "seditions" as caused firstly by "innovation in religion" and secondly by "taxes."

The prevalent view among the English people in the early seventeenth century held property to be the essence of liberty:

> To say that something was a man's property . . . was precisely to say that the thing in question could not be taken away from him without his consent. To take property without consent was to steal, and thus to break the Eighth Commandment.[90]

From which it followed that the king could not tax his subjects or otherwise diminish their assets except with their consent given through their representatives. Thus it happened that at the center of the revolutionary crisis of England under the early Stuarts stood the question of property:

> [It] would be mistaken to suppose that principled antagonism toward the crown's financial policies was merely a negligible afterthought, developed at a late date to provide a specious excuse for opposition. From the very beginning of James I's reign two separate accounts of the relationship between royal power and the subject's property were current among Englishmen. Absolute royal power faced absolute property. The result was conflict.[91]

In other words, the political resistance to early Stuart absolutism was driven by the defense of property, which acquired a political dimension. The parliamentary opposition which emerged under James I and exploded into rebellion under his successor did not so much insist on the king's convening parliaments and honoring their authority in taxation on the grounds of historical precedent or constitutional principle, but rather invoked these precedents and this principle to ensure the inviolability of property.

But fears ran deeper still, for there was the worry that the new dynasty intended not only to circumvent parliament in pursuit of its absolutist ambitions but to abolish it altogether. The apprehension was not groundless, for several important continental monarchs of the time had allowed parliaments to lapse. In France, the last Estates General had convened in 1614; representative assemblies had also disappeared in Spain, Portugal, Naples, Denmark, and several other continental monarchies.[92] Hence "fears about the future of the English parliament were apparent in every parliamentary session."[93] The truculence of parliament under the first two Stuart kings was in good measure due to the desire to accumulate as much power as possible in order to ensure its very survival.

Charles I shared his father's exalted ideas of royal authority (although he was less eloquent in articulating them), and in this he was encouraged by his spouse, who had grown up in the absolutist atmosphere of the French court. On his accession he found himself in extreme fiscal distress. The net income from his estates was pitifully small, probably not exceeding £25,000 a year, a third of what it had been on his father's accession; by 1630 it had declined further to £10,000.[94] Charles immediately resumed sales of royal properties: in the first ten years of his reign (1625–35) he disposed of land valued at £642,000.[95] But these incomes fell quite short of his immediate needs, estimated at £1 million, forcing Charles to ask parliament for generous "subsidies" to meet his military expenses and foreign obligations. The parliament of

1625, like its immediate successors, was dominated by a new breed of gentry representatives, very conscious of being the "owners" of England and hence intolerant of absolutist claims; the voters who elected them were in their majority freeholders who thought of themselves as "the Country."[96]

> The predominant element in the opposition movement . . . was the gentry, in particular the upper gentry. The men in the House of Commons who led the struggle for parliamentary privilege, liberty of the subject, and security of property; their friends and associates outside parliament; the persons who showed themselves most refractory to forced loans, ship money, and other devices of the regime: they were almost all gentry.[97]

The "Country" in this sense included some peers and also some royal officials, along with ordinary citizens. This constituency made up a formidable force in that it owned the soil, dispensed the law, and played an important role in local government as agents of the crown.[98] How much Charles I depended on this group to administer the country is indicated by the fact that his entire professional bureaucracy numbered 1,200; his French counterpart had at his disposal a corps of 40,000 officials.[99] In contrast to continental Europe, where the struggle for political liberty had been led by burghers, in England the urban middle class was rather quiescent, and the leadership fell into the hands of landed elements.[100]

As apparent from "The Humble Answer" and "The Form of Apology and Satisfaction,"[101] documents drafted by the House of Commons as early as 1604, the parliamentary majority came to believe that its own privileges and liberties—basic to which were freedom of speech and guarantees against arbitrary arrest—were not a gift of the crown but the natural rights of every Englishman:

> [T]hese men . . . sought to defend the free choice of parliamentary representatives and the freedom of their duly chosen members from detention, arrest and imprisonment during their parliamentary service, as well as the freedom for these same members to speak their consciences in the House without threat of punishment by the Crown. . . . [B]y the beginning of the seventeenth century a significant body of politically engaged Englishmen had come to see the Privileges of Parliament simultaneously as a principal right of Englishmen and as an essential bulwark to protect all their rights and freedoms.[102]

"Our privileges and liberties," the House declared, "are our right and due inheritance, no less than our very lands and goods."[103]

Of a sudden, the concept of "rights" made its appearance and in no time came to embrace everything of value, material as well as incorporeal. The conflict over the king's forced loan of 1626–27, for instance, according to one contemporary, Sir John Eliot, involved not merely property: "Upon this dispute not alone our lands and goods are engaged, but all that we call ours."[104] This redefinition was an event of immense historical importance, inasmuch as the notion of "rights," thus defined, would constitute the cornerstone of modern notions of liberty.

The parliamentary opposition had the good fortune of being led by an exceptionally competent and self-assured body of gentry politicians, many of them connected with one another by marriage and friendship. They formed an effective parliamentary bloc which displayed some features of a political party at a time when parties did not as yet exist. Mistrusting Charles and dissatisfied with his lack of a clear course, opposed to his foreign policy, they persuaded the House to vote only a portion of the funds he had requested. To add insult to injury, they refused to grant him the lifelong right to customs duties ("tonnage and poundage") which had been the prerogative of English kings since the fifteenth century; henceforth it was to be granted (if at all) on an annual basis. This radical move was prompted by the spectacular growth in England's foreign trade, which greatly enhanced the income from customs and aroused the fear that it might make the crown independent of parliament. Customs receipts, indeed, grew at a remarkable pace: in 1590 a modest £50,000, they brought in 1613 £148,000 and in 1623 £323,000.*

Charles, in dire financial straits, for he had unwisely gone to war simultaneously against France and Spain, responded to this humiliation by dissolving parliament and proceeding to collect tonnage and poundage without parliamentary sanction, on the grounds that it was a traditional royal prerogative. Henceforth, fiscal problems, always exacerbated by religious differences, would serve as the principal source of friction between crown and country.

Charles's second parliament, which met in the first half of 1626, gave the king no greater satisfaction. It demanded that he dismiss his personal favorite and chief advisor, the first Duke of Buckingham, who combined a penchant for embezzling the nation's properties with a sin-

*Dowell, *History of Taxation,* I, 195. Not all this money ended up in the Exchequer, however, because the crown, lacking an adequate civil service to do the job, farmed out the collection of customs to merchant syndicates, which pocketed a goodly share. Barry Coward, *The Stuart Age,* 2nd ed. (London and New York, 1994), 109.

gular ineptitude in leading its armies in combat. Buckingham insisted that in his actions, which had invoked the displeasure of the parliament, he was faithfully carrying out the king's commands. Parliament's impeachment papers against him rejected this argument as an excuse for wrongdoing:

> The Laws of England teach us, That Kings cannot command ill or unlawful things, whenever they speak, though by their Letters Patents, or their Seals. If the things be evil, these Letters Patents are void, and whatsoever ill event succeeds, the execution of such commands must ever answer for them.[105]

This reasoning implied that ministers were accountable to parliament—a principle that later was to become one of the mainstays of the English constitution.[106] In retaliation, the king dissolved parliament.

Having run into a hostile and combative Commons, Charles after 1629 tried to govern without it, but his ability to do so hinged on his ability to finance his government without parliamentary subsidies. The trouble, of course, was that nonparliamentary taxation was widely perceived as violating English traditions and was bound to lead to a confrontation with the House of Commons and the people whom it represented.

The king resorted to various ruses. He continued to appropriate the proceeds of customs without parliamentary sanction. These exactions the nation tolerated. But he overstepped the bounds of popular tolerance when he demanded "loans" from affluent subjects, specifying how much each was to contribute. Hundreds refused to pay, and seventy-six Englishmen—among them a future celebrity, John Hampden—suffered arrest. The government held these "patriots," as they were popularly known, in prison "without showing cause," which raised serious doubts about the king's respect for the law and the rights of his subjects.

By such devices Charles raised his income to £600,000, but this sum still fell short of his needs. Acting on the advice of a resourceful fiscal consultant, he resorted to more subterfuges, most of them with some precedent in English history but by his time widely regarded as unlawful.

As the costs of military operations against France and Spain, one more disastrous than the next, kept on mounting, the king sought additional funding from yet another, third, parliament (1628). This body was prepared to meet his wishes but only at the price of political concessions. One of its leaders suggested that money be granted to the king on condition that he affix his seal to a bill that would formally acknowledge his obligation to respect the traditional rights and liberties of his subjects. The document, originally drafted by Sir Edward Coke, previously a judge and now a member of parliament, is known as the Petition of Right. The petition, which the House of Lords supported and Charles agreed to sign, provided that "no man hereafter [shall] be compelled to make or yield any gift, loan, benevolence, tax or such like charge, without common consent by Act of Parliament."[107] It further forbade confiscation of estates, imprisonment, or execution without "due process of law."[108] The king signed the petition in June 1628 and received from parliament the money he had requested. The incident has been called "the decisive first step in the direction of modern freedom, of liberty as we know it in our world."[109] By signing the petition, the English crown made itself formally dependent on parliamentary approval for any and all revenues except such as it could raise from its own, greatly diminished, properties, voluntary loans, and remaining feudal prerogatives. At least such was the theory—for parliament had no means of enforcing these provisions, and the king continued to collect tonnage and poundage and to imprison merchants who refused to pay them. The provisions of the petition became an intrinsic part of the constitution only sixty years later.

In 1629, having had his fill of contention, Charles dissolved parliament on the grounds that it had encroached on royal powers, and for the next eleven years ruled on his own. He filled his coffers by selling to private interests monopolies (the exclusive right to manufacture and trade in specified commodities),* and disposing of still more land from his now-minuscule domain. He felt justified in ruling without parliament because he regarded parliament as complementary to his power in regard to convocation, duration, and dissolution.[110] To alleviate his financial distress, Charles made peace with France (1629) and Spain (1630). In 1630, he revived the medieval practice of requiring owners of land that brought an annual income of £40 or more either to be knights or to accept knighthood: refusal led to fines which brought the Exche-

*In 1624 the House of Commons had closed this loophole by declaring monopolies illegal. The crown got around this ruling by selling monopolies—renamed "patents"—to persons who invented new and valuable manufacturing processes. Shortly afterward, in 1648, Massachusetts permitted monopoly grants for new inventions "that are profitable for the Countrie." James W. Ely, Jr., *The Guardian of Every Other Right,* 2nd ed. (New York and Oxford, 1998), 19. Patents for intellectual property are believed to have originated in fifteenth-century Venice.

quer over £170,000.[111] By such means he did attain virtual financial and political independence.

But in 1634 and the two years that followed, Charles once again overstepped the boundary of what his subjects considered tolerable means of extracting revenue by imposing "ship money" on inland cities and shires. Ship money was a tax which English kings had had the authority to collect since the early fourteenth century without parliamentary consent whenever, in their judgment, the country faced an external threat. Subject to it were ports and counties bordering on the sea. The funds raised from this source went to outfit the navy. The English, a large proportion of whom made their living from the sea, took great pride in their navy and paid ship money willingly. But Charles violated tradition in two ways: first by imposing ship money at a time when England faced no apparent external threat, and second by levying it on towns and counties which had no ports and never before had been asked to contribute. His action aroused instant resistance, because the levy was seen as a tax and hence unlawful without parliamentary sanction. It was the deed that did most to rally the country against the king, in good measure because it affected thousands of smallholders and householders. Charles got the courts to affirm that he had the right to impose ship money when the country was in danger,[112] the "danger" in this case being rampant piracy in the waters bordering on Britain. The crown's argument in favor of levying the tax beyond the coastal areas was that when the country was threatened, the entire country should bear the costs of defending it. But the nation was not convinced, and resistance mounted. Because of the defiance not only of taxpayers but also of tax collectors, the king obtained only one-fifth of the ship money he had demanded.[113] One member of parliament with a sense of humor argued that since by imposing ship money on inland cities and shires the king had demonstrated that his subjects owned no property, there was no point in voting the king further subsidies, on the grounds that one cannot give what one does not have.[114]

A number of Englishmen residing inland defied the demand for ship money. One of them courted a trial and likely prison sentence. He was John Hampden, a well-educated and affluent Puritan landlord who had spent nearly a year in prison previously for refusing to contribute to the king's forced loan. In 1637, Hampden, whose annual income is estimated to have been in excess of £1,500, declined to pay the 20-shilling ship money levied on him. Such defiance instantly made him a popular hero. His trial in 1637–38 before the Court of Exchequer in the matter of ship money was a milestone in the constitutional evolution of England. The twelve judges who tried Hampden had all been appointed by the king and held their posts at his pleasure. Even so, justice under the Stuarts was by no means at royal mercy, especially if the defendant enjoyed popular support: the crown, as a rule, did not interfere with judiciary proceedings. The judges heard out the lawyers pleading the case for the royal plaintiff as well as the defendant. One of Hampden's attorneys, Oliver Saint John, delivered a vigorous defense of his client, arguing on the basis of historical precedents reaching back to Anglo-Saxon times that the king was acting unlawfully. He argued as follows:

> If his Majesty . . . may without Parliament lay xx [20] s[hillings] upon the Defendents Goods . . . why by the same Reason of Law it might not have been xx £, and so *ad infinitum*; whereby it could come to pass, that if the Subject had any thing at all, he is not beholding to the Law for it, but it is left interely in the Mercy and Goodness of the King.*

In the end, the king won with the barest majority, seven of the twelve judges rendering judgment in his favor. The majority argued that the king was the sole judge of what constituted a threat to the nation and had not only the right but the duty to require his subjects to contribute to the common defense.[115] Hampden had to pay the money demanded of him. Even so, the verdict was widely perceived as a moral defeat for Charles, both because he had won with such a narrow margin and because the most respected judges had sided with the defendant. Hampden's biographer speaks of him as "the first member of the House of Commons to be hailed as a popular leader by the nation at large."[116]

The trial of Hampden strikes the historian of Russia as a mind-boggling event, since in the entire history of that country, extending over seven centuries, not a single instance can be found of a subject defying his sovereign and being given his day in court.

In 1640, Charles, hoping to secure funds to suppress a rebellion which had broken out in Scotland in protest against his religious policies there, summoned another parliament, but when it refused to appro-

The Tryal of John Hambden, Esq. . . . in the Great Case of Ship-Money Between His Majesty K. Charles I. and That Gentleman (London, 1719), 31. St. John echoed the words which Sir Herbert Crofts had uttered in the Commons a quarter of a century earlier: "If the King may impose by his absolute Power, no one would be certain what he hath: for it shall be subject to the King's Pleasure." J. P. Sommerville, *Politics and Ideology in England, 1603–1640* (London and New York, 1986), 154. This suggests how widespread the idea was.

priate money for a campaign against the rebels (with whom it privately sympathized), he dissolved it. It has been known ever since as the Short Parliament.

Charles's financial situation was by now critical, for even London's private bankers refused to extend to him further loans. Later that year, desperate for money to pay the army that fought the Scottish invaders, the king consented to summon yet another parliament: it was destined to sit for thirteen years and to be known as the Long Parliament. This time the opponents of the king, in whose ranks were subjects who had been imprisoned for refusing to contribute to the forced loan or for other political offenses, outnumbered his supporters by a ratio of nearly two to one.[117] They were led by an accomplished parliamentary tactician, John Pym, who challenged the king head-on in the knowledge that the parliamentary majority could count on the country's support. Pym exploited Charles's financial distress to subject him more than any English monarch had ever been subjected to the power of the Commons.

In December 1640 the Commons declared the king's earlier resort to ship money unlawful and revoked the judgment against Hampden on the grounds that it was "contrary to and against the laws and statutes of this realm, the right of property, [and] the liberty of the subjects."[118] Next, it assumed control of the king's administrative staff by making its members accountable to itself; and as if this were not enough, it also instructed customs officials to supply the king with no more money than was required for the maintenance of his household.[119] The weakened and unpopular king had no choice but to submit to these humiliations.

In order to preclude a repetition of the eleven-year hiatus during which parliament was not convened, the Long Parliament passed in 1641, again with the king's reluctant consent, the Triennial Act, requiring parliaments to meet no less than once every three years with or without the crown's summons; they were to be allowed to sit in session for at least fifty days.[120] Next, the parliament declared it illegal for the king to adjourn, prorogue, or dissolve this parliament without its consent.[121] To this measure, too, the king had to acquiesce. Other revolutionary acts followed in rapid succession: one declaring it unlawful to levy tonnage and poundage without parliamentary authorization; another abolishing the so-called prerogative courts, including the detested Star Chamber and the Court of High Commission, administrative bodies that acted as courts; and a third declaring null and void the legal proceedings against those who had refused to pay ship money.

Despite the king's concessions, hostility between parliament and court escalated, aggravated by religious issues and the king's tactless behavior. For the king, the last straw was the move by Pym and his party in 1641 to deny him the power to appoint the country's chief officials and to control the armed forces. In early 1642, in an atmosphere charged with violence, Charles withdrew from London. His departure marked the onset of the Civil War, which would divide the country into pro- and anti-royalist parties. The Cavaliers, enriched by the crown, backed Charles, while the Roundheads, merchants, yeomen, and other middle-class groups, including the Puritans, supported parliament.

The Civil War, which lasted from 1642 to 1648, ended with a decisive victory of the New Model army commanded by Oliver Cromwell, and culminated in the execution of the king in January 1649.

7. *The Commonwealth*

The Commonwealth confiscated all the royal estates (minus the forests). Most of this land was sold, hastily and often at prices below its true market value, because of the pressing need to pay the wages of the army which was the Commonwealth's mainstay.[122] The Long Parliament also declared subject to confiscation the landed properties of royalists, Catholic landlords, and the church. Recent researches have revealed, however, that in reality many of the royalist and Catholic landlords managed by one subterfuge or another to hold on to their properties, with the result that the composition of the landed gentry remained remarkably stable.[123]

The House of Commons settled on Cromwell an annual income of £1.3 million, which would provide the model for financing the crown after the Restoration.[124]

Because the Commonwealth rested on the army and the army cost a great deal of money, the tax burden imposed on the people of Britain increased enormously. And yet the nation bore this burden with minimum, if any, resistance—in sharp contrast to its defiance of taxes and other impositions not sanctioned by parliament.[125]

8. *The late Stuarts*

At one time historians believed that after the Restoration the crown retrieved only a fraction of its confiscated estates, because of the difficulty of reclaiming them from the new owners.[126] But recent scholarship has revealed that, in fact, Charles II, on his coronation, recovered "virtually the whole of the Crown lands."[127] Some of the dispossessed owners of royal lands were compensated for their loss, but others were left empty-handed.[128] The income from these restored royal estates, however, was by now so small that it barely sufficed to support the queen mother and the queen consort.[129]

After the Restoration, it became apparent that England's entire taxation system, still rooted in feudal conditions, had to be revamped. The new king, Charles II, relinquished the very unpopular feudal prerogatives, such as escheat and wardship (see above, p. 126), which had provided the crown with an important source of nonparliamentary revenue.[130] In return, he received a lifelong annuity of £1.2 million, a figure arrived at by estimating the income of Charles I as £900,000 and increasing it by one-third.* Charles II further received the lifelong right to collect tonnage and poundage.[131] Out of these appropriations he was expected to pay not only for his personal expenses and those of the court but also for the costs of the civil service. It was the last gasp of the medieval idea that the king should live on his own and turn to parliament for funds only in national emergencies.[132]

Just how greatly the ability of the British crown to live off its own income declined between 1558 and 1714 is evident from the following figures indicating what percentage crown income constituted of the national revenue:

1558–1603	28.83%
1604–25	20.41%
1625–40	12.24%
[1649–59	3.16%]
1661–85	5.41%
1686–88	6.97%
1689–1714	1.98%[133]

In addition to placing the king on an allowance, parliament introduced the novel principle (as it had attempted to do, without success, since the fourteenth century) that it was entitled to know how the mon-

*C. D. Chandaman, *The English Public Revenue, 1660–1688* (Oxford, 1975), 263–64. Parliament had first proposed to pay the king an allowance in place of his feudal prerogatives in 1610, but the attempt failed. Gordon Batho in Finberg, ed., *Agrarian History,* IV, 273.

eys which it appropriated were spent. To this end, it created a Public Accounts Committee composed of its members, whose responsibility it was to ensure that the king did not misuse the sums allocated for war or other specific purposes.[134] Such fiscal controls required parliament to meet regularly. The Triennial Act of 1664 repealed the 1641 act of the same name, replacing it with a milder version but still requiring parliaments to be summoned every three years.[135] In fact, between 1660–1 and 1676 (with one exception), parliaments were summoned annually, mainly because of the crown's need for money.[136] Such measures, ultimately grounded in fiscal controls, at long last made parliament an integral part of England's constitution.[137]

Despite the severity of the fiscal restraints imposed on the crown by parliament, in the early 1680s its power began to increase once again, in good measure because of its improved financial situation. By limiting expenditures and improving the collection of taxes as well as profiting from rising customs revenues, Charles II waxed rich.[138]

His brother and successor, James II, benefited from this new wealth to make himself independent of parliament. Parliament increased his annual allowance to £1.85 million, which, with the income he received as Duke of York, gave him an income of £2 million a year. [139] Parliament was then dissolved and did not meet even once in the next three years of James's reign.

Both Charles II and James II pledged never to "invade" their subjects' properties.[140] But the term "property" by now acquired a meaning that was synonymous with "liberty," embracing everything that an Englishman considered his birthright, and that very much included his religion.

James II lost the throne mainly for religious reasons. His own Catholicism and determination to suspend the discriminatory laws against Catholics in the hope of ensuring the triumph of Catholicism in England alarmed alike the Whigs and Tories, not only because of the threat to the established faith but also because many Englishmen identified Catholicism with royal absolutism. His improved financial condition further increased anxieties about the survival of parliament. The king's opponents entered into contact with William of Orange, stadholder of the Netherlands and grandson of Charles I, and his wife, Mary, the daughter of James II, both staunch Protestants. When William invaded England in November 1688 with the aim of claiming the throne and bringing England into a grand alliance against France, the hapless James had to flee, forfeiting the crown.

9. The Glorious Revolution

Unlike natural scientists who can demonstrate their findings in a conclusive manner by reproducing the experiments that had suggested them, historians operate in the world of impressions that may or may not convince their readers and can never be demonstrated beyond the shadow of a doubt. Hence, while the former broaden and deepen established truths, the latter keep on revising them. Each generation of historians establishes its claims to the originality on which modern reputations rest by casting doubt on the work of its predecessors, usually by stressing exceptions and nuances. Those who come at the end of the chain, unable to revise the revisionists, sometimes are desperate enough to commit the ultimate revision by declaring historical evidence to be immaterial and even denying that history exists. When this stage is reached—as it recently has been reached with the absurd movement known as "deconstructionism"—anything goes. It is for this reason that the last word on any given historical subject is often the first.

The Revolution of 1688 was not precipitated by social unrest or economic crisis and hence did not meet the conventional criteria of revolutions, which is why some revisionist historians deny it amounted to anything more than a palace coup. England was both tranquil and prosperous when it took place.[141] The events of 1688–89 were indeed a classic coup d'état carried out by politicians with the backing of a nation which did not want a Catholic ruler and took advantage of the Catholic king's unpopularity to be rid of him and put in his place two stalwart Protestants from whom they wrested critical political concessions as the price of the throne.

The flight of James II to France was treated as tantamount to abdication. The parliament which convened in 1688 was duly elected, but since it met without the king it was labeled the Convention Parliament. It was conservative in the sense that the revolution it carried out was meant to restore what it considered ancient traditions. In reality, its actions bore a rather radical character.

Before bestowing the crown on William and Mary, the Convention Parliament presented them with a Declaration of Rights. Hastily drawn up in February 1689 as a restatement of parliament's traditional demands, it was called "Act declaring the Rights and Liberties of the Subjects and Settling the Succession of the Crown." Because the Convention Parliament lacked constitutional standing, its leaders felt it important to transform the declaration into a statute. This took the form of the Bill of Rights, which William III signed into law in December 1689.[142] The Bill of Rights—called by one historian the "greatest constitutional document [in English history] since the Magna Carta"[143] —spelled out what the parliamentary majority considered to be ancient foundations of English liberties. The king pledged not to suspend laws* or to levy taxes without parliamentary sanction. Additional clauses called for parliamentary approval for maintaining a standing army in time of peace, the right of Protestant subjects to bear arms for their defense, guarantees of freedom of speech for members of parliament, and frequent convocations of parliament. William and Mary got tonnage and poundage for four years only because, in the words of the House of Commons, "it was the best security that the nation could have for frequent parliaments."[144] (It later relented and granted tonnage and poundage to the new monarchs for life.)

William III waged constant wars, which required him constantly to refer to parliament for funds. He summoned parliament annually, as was done in the Netherlands, whence he had come. This became constitutional practice: from that time on, English parliaments have convened every year.[145] The House of Commons now not only controlled the crown's budget but also supervised how the money was spent: beginning with 1690–1, the Commons frequently appropriated money for specific purposes and made certain that it was not diverted to other uses.[146] The establishment of the Bank of England and the introduction of the National Debt in 1693–94 further enhanced the financial powers of parliament because it became the norm that the House of Commons underwrote all loans taken out by the crown.[147] Excise taxes and land taxes were regulated; for the first time in English history, "taxation was accepted as a *normal* part of the crown's revenue."[148] Revenues doubled and the English henceforth were more heavily taxed than the French. The crown's total reliance on parliament for finances compelled it increasingly to consult parliament on matters of foreign policy and even to appoint ministers acceptable to it.

Another important principle established after 1688 which severely limited the power of the crown concerned justice. Under the Stuarts, judges served at the pleasure of the monarch and could be removed if

*In making this demand, the parliamentarians acted in the belief that laws, once passed, become "the joint property of those who made them" and hence could not be revoked and altered except by consent of all the "owners." Howard Nenner in J. R. Jones, ed., *Liberty Secured? Britain Before and After 1688* (Stanford, Calif., 1992), 93.

they displeased him for any reason. Now the rule was established that judges held office during good behavior and could not be dismissed unless either they were convicted of an offense or their removal was requested by both houses of parliament.[149] This custom established the independence of the judiciary.

Relations between the court and the House of Commons in the eighteenth century were not always amicable. But the settlement reached in 1688–89, crowning as it did the long struggle of parliament to assert its rights, left no doubt as to the outcome. Suffice it to say that when in 1810, in the midst of the war against Napoleonic France, King George III was pronounced incurably insane, his inability to perform his duties no longer made any difference to the functioning of the British government,[150] for power had shifted decisively and irrevocably to parliament.

10. Continental Europe

Although England led the world in the establishment of parliamentary democracy, it was far from being the only European country to develop parliamentary institutions. Parliaments (or Estates) were universal in medieval Europe. They could be found throughout the length and breadth of the continent: in Portugal as well as Denmark, Sicily as well as Poland, on both the national and the regional level.

The principal function of continental parliaments was the same as in England, namely to vote money to the crown for extraordinary expenses, principally connected with waging war. Their very prevalence demonstrates how widespread private property was in medieval Europe, for kings could not very well ask for taxes from people who owned nothing. Indeed, crowned heads who claimed to own all the land, as did the rulers of Russia, a country which was only partly in Europe, never bothered to appeal to their subjects for money and never convened parliaments until forced to do so by public opinion at the beginning of the twentieth century. As happened in England, the continental estates often took advantage of their kings' fiscal predicament to extract privileges for themselves. The originality of the English parliament, therefore, lies not in its antiquity and function but in its longevity, for it went from strength to strength, whereas its continental counterparts, with a few exceptions (notably Poland, Sweden, and the Netherlands), did not survive the era of royal absolutism.[151]

Parliaments were a by-product of feudalism. They emerged from gatherings of vassals whose obligation was to counsel and aid their lords: for the top feudatories, these lords were kings and princes. Attendance at such assemblies was mandatory; the participants represented no one but themselves. In time, however, kings and princes found it advantageous to assume that although not elected, the participants at such assemblies spoke for their estates and regions, and even the realm as a whole, since this presumption lent the counsel and aid they received from them greater weight. For this reason, gradually and imperceptibly, feudal assemblies in most of Europe turned into representative bodies. As such, they differed alike from primitive folkmoots, in which all freemen participated in person, and the royal councils, in which the participants represented only themselves.*

The earliest representative institutions in world history emerged in the late twelfth century (1188) in the Spanish kingdoms of Leon and Castile.† Before long, Spain developed representative assemblies (*cortes*) both regionally and nationally. England, Austria, Brandenburg, Sicily, Portugal, and the Holy Roman Empire followed suit in the thirteenth century; France, the Netherlands, Scotland, and Hungary in the fourteenth; Poland, Sweden, and Denmark in the fifteenth.[152] Representative legislatures were unique to Europe until either copied or transplanted to other continents by Europeans.

A striking feature of the history of parliaments is their uneven development. In the middle of the fourteenth century, the French Estates General claimed extraordinary powers, requiring the king, in return for urgently needed military appropriations, to make concessions that would have been unthinkable even in contemporary England, including frequent convocations of the Estates General with the authority to collect taxes and supervise their expenditure.[153] An observer at the time might well have concluded that the French were in advance of the English in bridling the authority of the crown. But that was not to be: French parliamentary opposition soon collapsed and the Estates General turned into a supine accessory of royal authority. From 1484 until 1560 the Estates General did not convene. They resumed sessions in the next half century, but the last met in 1614, and they did not reassemble until 1789.

In Spain, by the fourteenth century, the *cortes* of Castile, Aragon,

*As we shall see below, this process did not occur in Poland, where each deputy to the Diet represented his own region and was obliged to veto legislative proposals that violated his mandate.

†Some claim that the oldest parliament in the world is the Icelandic Althing, formed around 930 C.E. However, as its name indicates (*thing* or *ding* meaning "assembly"), it was a popular gathering and not a representative body.

Catalonia, and Valencia won the right to approve all extraordinary taxes as well as to participate in the drafting and implementation of laws. The Aragonese oath of allegiance to the king exceeded in boldness anything the British House of Commons would have dared to utter: "We who are as good as you swear to you who are no better than we, to accept you as our king and sovereign lord, provided you observe all our liberties and laws; but if not, not."[154] And yet the Spanish *cortes*, too, went into decline in the early sixteenth century and by the end of the seventeenth ceased to matter.

The German Reichstag or Imperial Diet also rose for a while and then waned. Emperor Leopold I convened one in 1663 and it sat in permanent session until 1806, when Napoleon dissolved the Holy Roman Empire.

Why this reversal of fortunes?

One factor that bolsters parliamentarism is territorial smallness. As a rule, the smaller the country and its population the easier it is to forge effective democratic institutions, because they represent manageable communities with shared interests and capable of concerted action: conversely, the larger a country the greater is the diversity of social and regional interests, which impedes unity. England was in a very advantageous position in this respect: the first national monarchy in Europe, it had as early as the thirteenth century a sense of the "community of the realm" (*communitas terrae*)[155] absent on the continent, which as yet knew no national states. At a time when travel was slow, expensive, and dangerous, large kingdoms like France and the Holy Roman Empire had difficulty persuading the provinces to send representatives to the Estates General; the latter often preferred to pay the taxes demanded of them rather than attend. For this reason, the provincial Estates on the continent fared better and lasted longer than the national ones. Both France and Spain had vigorous regional parliaments: France those of the Langue d'Oïl (North) and Langue d'Oc (South), as well as provincial ones (e.g., Burgundy, Touraine, and Brittany), some of which survived until the French Revolution, long after the Estates General had become a historical memory. Spain had them in Castile, Aragon, Valencia, Catalonia, etc. But these gatherings were preoccupied with local matters and did not challenge the crown. In this respect, too, England was fortunate, because being not much larger than a typical province, she never developed provincial parliaments.

Another factor promoting or inhibiting the power of parliaments was external and internal security: countries torn by foreign invasions and civil wars were prone to trade liberty for peace.[156] France can serve as a prime exemplar of this rule. The Hundred Years War (1337–1453), provoked by the English crown's claims to the French throne, was fought entirely on the soil of France and neighboring Flanders, both of which it ravaged. Toward the end of the war, in 1439, the French Estates General relinquished to the king the authority to impose and collect the country's most important tax, the *taille,* a general levy on commoners, which would form one of the bases of the French monarchy's revenues until 1790. The *taille,* combined with the even more profitable salt tax (*gabelle*), made the French crown fiscally independent of parliament and hence politically independent as well, allowing it to dispense with the Estates General. In the second half of the sixteenth century (1562–98), France was torn by religious wars between Catholics and Protestants. At their conclusion, the exhausted nation surrendered all power to the crown, which created an absolutist regime that served as the model for the rest of Europe.

Contributing to the growth of absolutism in France was the wealth of the crown: wealth derived from its taxatory powers but also from the incomes provided by the royal domain. The English monarchy, a good share of whose revenues was controlled by parliament, kept on selling its estates until it had almost no private income left. French kings, by contrast, were not allowed to alienate any part of the royal domain; on their accession they had to swear an oath to this effect. As a result, in the fourteenth and fifteenth centuries, a decisive period in the history of parliamentary institutions, the French crown was the richest royal house in Europe.[157]

The situation of Spain was exceedingly complicated, in good measure because throughout the medieval period it consisted of several sovereign kingdoms as well as a large area ruled by the Muslims. The union of the two most important of these kingdoms in the late fifteenth century through the marriage of Ferdinand of Aragon and Isabella of Castile laid the foundation of the future national state. The Cortes of Aragon and Castile met separately, although they were occasionally summoned to joint sessions known as Cortes Generales.

The basis of royal absolutism in early modern Spain, as in France, was the crown's financial independence. The principal tax, called *alcabala,* a levy on commercial transactions introduced in 1342 as a temporary measure to raise money to fight the Moors, became in time permanent: it required no consent of the *cortes*. The revenues from this source grew prodigiously and in time came to constitute 80–90 percent of the Spanish crown's income.[158] It is generally regarded as having had a blighting effect on Spain's economic development: Merriman called it a "cancer that was destined to eat away the very vitals of the Spanish Empire."* But it helped free the crown of dependence on parliament. Since both the nobility and clergy were exempt from taxes, neither developed an interest in attending the Cortes, with the result that the entire brunt of confronting the monarchy fell on representatives of the towns, who were prone to cave in.[159] In the sixteenth century, the Spanish crown secured still greater fiscal independence by drawing revenues from foreign possessions, namely the Low Countries, Italy, and (after 1550) the New World.[160] Fiscal self-sufficiency freed Spanish kings from the need to summon the Cortes Generales, except in times of national emergency. In the seventeenth century the Cortes was allowed to fall into oblivion.

A decisive factor in the decline of continental parliaments was the revolution in warfare which began in the late Middle Ages with the introduction of gunpowder and culminated in the seventeenth century with the creation of modern national armies. National armies required national governments with strong authority, and that spelled the doom of medieval estates which had given rise to parliaments.

For a thousand or so years following the fall of the Roman Empire, the dominant branch of the armed forces throughout Europe had been the cavalry. The mounted warriors were nobles while the foot soldiers accompanying them consisted of serfs and other commoners. The primacy of the cavalry started to decline with the introduction of the rapid-firing longbow and dropped precipitously when guns came into their own in the fourteenth century, first as artillery and then as firearms. Their respective roles now reversed as the infantry moved to the fore and the cavalry turned into an auxiliary force. In sixteenth-century France, Germany, Sweden, and several other countries, such transitional armies were raised privately and consisted mostly of mercenaries. A by-product of this development in the art of warfare was a decline of the nobility, the backbone of feudal armies as well as of parliaments.

After 1500, the development of new weapons and the changes in tactics which they made possible led to the emergence of modern armies. These were pioneered in Spain in the sixteenth century, followed by Sweden under Gustavus Adolphus and France under Louis XIV in the seventeenth, and ultimately emulated by most major European powers, with the notable exception of England. These countries produced stand-

*Roger Bigelow Merriman, *The Rise of the Spanish Empire*, IV (New York, 1962), 301. Prescott saw it as "one of the most successful means ever devised by a government for shackling the industry and enterprise of its subjects." William H. Prescott, *History of the Reign of Ferdinand and Isabella, the Catholic*, III (Boston, 1838), 438n.

ing armies manned sometimes with conscripts (Sweden, Russia) but mostly with volunteers drawn from the lower classes and officered by nobles. They were equipped by the state with standardized weapons and uniforms and subjected to incessant drill to improve their steadfastness under enemy fire as well as the effectiveness of their own firepower. Their emergence greatly enhanced the power of central government, because it alone could provide the organization and the wherewithal, and correspondingly weakened that of the nobility and its institutions:

> [A]bsolutism in its prime . . . proved itself superior to the other possible forms of government, by virtue of its ability to keep the peace at home and to mobilize men and money for national defence and aggrandizement. It also possessed potentialities . . . for increasing wealth, and thus for creating the economic conditions necessary for the waging of prolonged wars.[161]

To the extent that parliaments not only proved unable to provide the centralized organization and the funding which these new military formations required but were seen as obstructing them, they went into eclipse in most of continental Europe.

The English crown was unable to exploit the military revolution to assert absolute power. Britain fought her share of wars, but unlike the continental powers, she waged them outside her borders, on foreign shores; thus they never directly threatened her own population. She had no standing army (except briefly under the Commonwealth) and relied largely on her naval power and on subsidies paid to foreign governments. The Bill of Rights of 1689 explicitly forbade the crown to maintain a standing army in peacetime except with parliamentary approval. Hence, the English crown's subjects could take advantage of its need for funds for war to extract political concessions.

In three countries besides England—Sweden, the Netherlands, and Poland—parliaments did succeed in bridling the power of the crown.

The Swedish monarchy substantially whittled down the authority of the Rigsdag in the course of its great military triumphs of the seventeenth century. But following the disastrous defeat of its armies in Russia at the beginning of the eighteenth, the Swedish parliament reasserted its authority and by the middle of the eighteenth century reduced the crown to virtual impotence.

The Protestant United Provinces of the Netherlands, the richest region in Europe, with a wealthy bourgeoisie and impoverished nobility, rebelled against Spanish authority in the 1560s and in 1581 declared their independence. The Netherlands became a republic, whose chief executive, called the stadholder, was elected by the Estates of the seven united provinces. In matters affecting finance, foreign policy, the army, and the navy, he was subject to the authority of the States-General.

Poland's parliamentary experience was unique: here the nobility overwhelmed the monarchy and created a constitutional imbalance that ultimately destroyed the country. Because of a dynastic accident, Poland in the late fourteenth century adopted the principle of elective monarchy. Casimir the Great, the last king of the Piast dynasty, which had ruled since the tenth century, had no male issue. Since the Polish constitution barred women from the succession, Casimir designated as his heir Louis of Anjou, the king of Hungary. Louis, too, had no sons, and to secure the crown for one of his daughters he granted the Polish nobility, in the so-called Privilege of Koszyce (1374), virtual exemption from taxes. He also agreed that all extraordinary taxes would require the consent of the entire Polish nobility. For the next four centuries, aspirants to the Polish throne, who needed the unanimous approval of the nobles for their election, conceded to them further privileges.

Until the very end of her existence as a sovereign state, Poland failed to make the transition from an agglomeration of provincial estates to a true national parliament. The Diet (Sejm), in existence since 1493, was really an assembly of deputies, representing sovereign regional assemblies (*sejmiki*). They came bearing mandates, at first verbal, then written, which they had to follow to the letter and which the Diet was powerless to overrule. This meant that each item of legislation required unanimity: any one deputy, by exercising the infamous *liberum veto,* could kill a legislative proposal and even cause the Diet to dissolve. The principle was not unlike that adopted in the independent Netherlands[162]—but whereas the stolid Dutch burghers managed to make the system work, the undisciplined Polish nobles brought legislation to a standstill.

The result was an excess of liberty. The Diet, consisting exclusively of nobles—the cities were unrepresented—was an organization which thought not in national but exclusively in regional and estate terms. By the seventeenth century it had full authority to set taxes, paid mostly by the peasantry and burghers, each of which required the Diet's assent and was granted for no more than a year at a time; it also controlled the administration and foreign policy. Poland never made the transition to a modern army, relying on mercenaries. In the second half of the eighteenth century, neighboring Prussia, Austria, and Russia, all three governed by absolute monarchs who viewed with distaste the dominance of Polish nobles, had little difficulty in dividing Poland among themselves.

Russia went her own way. Geographically part of Europe, she nevertheless developed a system of government resembling the Oriental model which, until modern times, accorded private property no legitimate status. What effect this fact had on the liberties of its inhabitants will be the subject of the next chapter.

4

PATRIMONIAL RUSSIA*

> In our Moscow state of the Great Sovereign and in Siberia, the servitors of all ranks serve our Great Sovereign from the land, and the peasants till the tithe fields and pay quit-rent, and no one holds land for free.
>
> —Peter the Great[1]

Prior to 1991, Russians and the nations on which they imposed their rule enjoyed few civil rights and (with the exception of the single decade 1906–17) no political rights. In the age of absolutism, Russia's sovereigns exercised authority in a more absolute manner than their Western counterparts; in the age of democracy, Russia clung to absolutism longer than any other European country. And during the seven decades of Communist rule, she produced a regime that deprived her people of liberties to an extent previously unknown in world history. For two and a half centuries (c. 1600–1861) the vast majority of Russians lived as serfs of the state or of landlords, tied to the soil and without legal recourse to protect them from their masters and government officials.

Why this divergence from the pattern set by Western Europe, to which Russia belongs by virtue of her race and religion as well as geographic proximity?

The Russian propensity for authoritarian government cannot be

*For the historical background of this chapter, the reader is referred to the author's *Russia Under the Old Regime* (London and New York, 1974), from which some of the material in it is drawn.

attributed to genetic factors. As will be shown below, the city-state of Novgorod, which at its height in the fourteenth and fifteenth centuries encompassed most of northern Russia, granted its citizens rights which equaled and in some respects surpassed those enjoyed by contemporary Western Europeans. The causes of the phenomenon must, therefore, be sought elsewhere. It is the author's contention that the critical factor in the failure of Russia to develop rights and liberties was the liquidation of landed property in the Grand Duchy of Moscow, the principality which in time conquered all Russia and imposed on her a regime under which the monarch not only ruled the realm and its inhabitants but literally owned them. The fusion of sovereignty and ownership, a type of government known as "patrimonial," vested all titles to the land in the hands of the monarch and allowed him to claim unlimited services from his subjects, noble and commoner alike. In marked contrast to the rest of Western Europe, where the authority of kings stopped at the boundary of private property, in Russia (until the end of the eighteenth century, at any rate) such constraint on royal power was unknown and, indeed, unthinkable.* And when, toward the close of the eighteenth century, tsarism belatedly acknowledged private property in land, it encountered, for reasons which will be spelled out below, a great deal of hostility from both the educated elite and the mass of the peasantry.

The absence of property in land deprived Russians of all those levers by means of which the English succeeded in limiting the power of their kings. Since they required no taxes because all the land paid them rents and rendered them services, the tsars had no need to convene parliaments. Legal institutions which everywhere accompany property were rudimentary and served mainly as instruments of administration. The notion of individual rights was totally submerged by the notion of duties to the monarch. It was only in 1762 that the Russian crown exempted its upper class from compulsory state service, and as late as 1785 that it granted it title to its estates. It was only in 1861 that Russian peasants were freed from serfdom. And it was only in 1905–6 that Russian subjects received civil rights and a voice in legislation.

*In theory, some Western monarchs also enjoyed "patrimonial" authority. Thus, William I, on conquering England, claimed the entire realm as his property. Isabella of Castille was declared on her accession in 1474 *reina proprietaria*—the queen proprietress—of her kingdom. And as we have seen, Louis XIV instructed his son and heir as late as 1666 that the French king was "absolute seigneur" of the country's wealth. But these were empty formulas, as demonstrated by the fact that throughout Europe kings solicited taxes from their subjects through parliaments, which they would not have had to do were they truly patrimonial rulers.

Thus the history of Russia offers an excellent example of the role that property plays in the development of civil and political rights, demonstrating how its absence makes possible the maintenance of arbitrary and despotic government.

1. *Pre-Muscovite Russia*

As stated previously, an object of property claims must meet two criteria: it has to be desirable, and available only in limited supply. For people who support themselves primarily by agriculture, this object is arable land. The scarcer it is, the more likely it is to be contested and claimed as property. It so happened that the forests of Great Russia which the Eastern Slavs penetrated at the end of the first millennium offered the newcomers unlimited quantities of land.* Land, as such, therefore, was worthless; the thing of value was labor. This was the more the case in that the early Slavs did not practice sedentary agriculture but a nomadic variant known as "slash and burn." Peasants who employed this technique would make a clearing in the forest and set fire to the felled trees; after the flames had died down, they would scatter seed on the ash-enriched soil. As soon as the soil showed signs of exhaustion they moved on to another part of the boundless forest to repeat the procedure.

The surfeit of land in Russia prior to the nineteenth century had two important effects. In the first place, it led to the underdevelopment of all those institutions which in regions where land was in short supply produced civil societies: for where land is scarce, the local population is compelled to devise ways of resolving peacefully conflicts over it.

> We are led to a paradox: land is fought over when it is abundant, but when it becomes scarce (by population increase) institutions of land adjudication evolve and boundaries become precise. . . . [W]hen land is abundant, the need to work out institutions of adjudication—with all the negotiating, compromis-

*Initially, the Russians were confined to the northern forest zone or taiga because the southern black-earth steppe was under the control of nomadic, cattle-grazing Turkic tribes which tolerated no farmers on their territory. Russians infiltrated and colonized this area only after the middle of the sixteenth century, following their conquest of the Muslim khanates of Kazan and Astrakhan.

ing, and impartial trust that they imply—is not so sorely felt as when land is scarce.*

Secondly, the seemingly inexhaustible profusion of land prior to the nineteenth century impressed on the Russian peasant the conviction that the soil, like water and air, was *res nullius* which God had created for everyone's benefit and which, therefore, could not be owned. Everyone was free to use it, but no one could claim exclusive title to it. One could appropriate only that which one grew or made: since no one made the land, no one could own it. In the mind of the Russian peasant, the forest was common possession but lumber belonged to him who had cut it. This outlook, quite typical of primitive societies, in the case of Russia outlasted the era of abundance and retained its hold on the peasant's mind into the early twentieth century, when, owing to rapid population growth and the end of territorial expansion, arable soil became scarce.

The situation here was thus dramatically different from that prevailing in Western Europe, where sedentary farming had been practiced for millennia—in the case of England, at least since 2500 B.C.E.—and where already in classical antiquity, possession of land enjoyed social and sometimes legal protection.

Different, too, and tending toward the same end, which is the neglect of property, was the nature of the first Russian state, founded in the ninth century by Swedish Vikings. Unlike the Norwegian and Danish Vikings who descended on Western Europe, the Swedish invaders came to Russia not as landlords but as merchant adventurers. Russia did not offer the rich farmlands, vineyards, and olive groves of England, France, or Spain which attracted the Scandinavians to these countries, first as robbers and then as settlers. Her principal economic attraction lay in the transit route she provided to Byzantium and the Arab Middle East by means of a network of riverways linking the Baltic with the Black Sea and the Caspian. It was a lucrative commercial route, because the Muslim conquest of the Mediterranean in the seventh and eighth centuries had disrupted the Western European trade with the Middle East. One of the earliest surviving Russian documents is a commercial treaty between the Vikings, then known as "Russians," and Constantinople, drawn up in 912 C.E. Hoards of Byzantine and Arab coins dug up in northwestern Russia and Scandinavia attest to a vigorous trade

*John P. Powelson, *The Story of Land* (Cambridge, Mass., 1988), 308–9. According to the author, a situation similar to Russia's prevailed until the twentieth century in China, the Middle East, Southeast Asia, and India. Ibid., 309.

with the eastern Mediterranean carried out by the Vikings by way of Russia.

The Scandinavian conquerors of Russia did not settle down and turn into landlords. Commerce offered much greater rewards than agriculture in a country where the soil was of low fertility, the agricultural season short, and labor highly mobile. Instead, they built fortress-cities along the principal river routes to store the commodities which they collected as tribute from indigenous Slavs and Finns and shipped under heavy guard every spring to Constantinople. As in other parts of Europe, they married local women and, in time, assimilated: it is generally believed that by the middle of the eleventh century they were Slavicized.

The Russian Vikings devised a peculiar system of administration to support their military-commercial activities, a conspicuous feature of which was the rotation of princes, members of the ruling dynasty, from one fortified city to another in accord with the principle of seniority. The post of great prince entitled the bearer to rule Kiev, the city on the Dnieper which served as the final staging area for the annual expedition to Constantinople. Junior members of the clan governed the other fortresses. The Viking realm expanded rapidly across the Eurasian plain, meeting with little resistance from the scattered, primitive Slavic and Finnic tribes. The objective of this expansion, however, was not land but tribute, consisting mainly of slaves, furs, and wax. The vast territory ruled from Kiev was very lightly administered. The fortresses, staffed by armed men with small resident populations of artisans, tradesmen, clergy, and slaves, developed a rudimentary political life which allowed freemen to participate in popular assemblies, known as *veches*.[2] The essential fact to bear in mind is that being a military-commercial ruling caste, the early Vikings in Russia neither pursued agriculture nor acquired landed properties—this in striking contrast to England, where the Norman conquerors claimed title to all the land. One consequence of this fact was that the founders of the first Russian state developed no clear distinction between their public and private functions: they ruled their realm and disposed of its wealth without distinguishing the one activity from the other.

No evidence exists that during the so-called Kievan period of Russian history (tenth to mid-thirteenth century) and even the century that followed, anyone—prince, noble, or peasant—claimed ownership of land. The earliest Russian legal code, *Russkaia pravda*, compiled in the eleventh century, makes no reference to immovable property.[3] Virtually no land deeds have come to light from northeastern Russia prior to the first half of the fourteenth century, and very few from the second half.[4] Property in land, as distinct from ownership of territory, came to Russia only around 1400, when the country was ruled by the Mongols. This is a significant fact, given the highly developed system of land tenure in contemporary Europe. In England, individual ownership of landed property not only by the nobility but, according to recent studies, even by ordinary freemen and villeins can be traced as far back as 1200.[5] And throughout feudal Europe, fiefs were heritable and therefore *de facto* property.

Interest in land first emerged among Russia's rulers in consequence of the invasions of the Black Sea steppe by nomadic warriors from Asia. Around 1200, recurrent assaults by Turkic tribes known as Pechenegs or Polovtsy on the caravan routes traversing the Black Sea steppe disrupted and ultimately put an end to Kiev's trade with Constantinople. Deprived of commercial income, the princes began to settle down. This held especially true of those in the northern principalities, which were safe from nomad incursions: in the words of Kliuchevskii, "the prince-proprietor (*kniaz'-votchinnik*), a hereditary settled landlord, replaced his southern ancestor, the prince-relative (*kniaz'-rodich*), the mobile, successive co-ruler of the Russian land"—in his view, this new type of ruler provided the basis for the authority of Muscovite tsars.[6] Because they had as yet no private property in land to contend with, the princes became both sovereigns and owners, treating their principality as patrimony, disposable by testament.* The concept of sovereignty in Russia thus antedated that of private property—a fact that was to have momentous consequences for that country's historical evolution. It explains why to this day the same word—*vladetel'*—denotes in Russian both "possessor" and "sovereign."

The Kievan state, severely crippled by Pecheneg raids, was destroyed in the years 1237–42 by the Mongols. The new invaders demolished every city which offered them resistance, Kiev included, slaughtering many of the inhabitants. They advanced steadily into Europe and might well have conquered it—for they were never defeated in battle—when news of the death of their emperor Ogodei, Genghis Khan's successor, in 1241 made them turn around and head back for Mongolia.

*In neighboring Poland, the first royal dynasty, the Piasts, also regarded the realm as patrimony, which they divided among their heirs until 1139, when the principle was introduced that the nucleus of the state went to the great prince. Stanislaw Kutrzeba, *Historia ustroju Polski v zarysie*, I, 3rd ed. (Lwów, 1912), 19–20. In Poland the development of property in land put an early end to the idea of patrimonial rule.

Russia, weakly unified to begin with, now fell apart. The southern and southwestern regions of what had been the Kievan state (today's western Ukraine) fell under the domination of first the Lithuanians and then the Poles. The northern area, dominated by Novgorod, which the Mongols failed to conquer but compelled to pay tribute (*iasak*), became *de facto* a sovereign city-state. The central regions, the core of the future Russian state, disintegrated into numerous petty dynastic principalities. The Mongols turned them into a province of their empire, which they ruled from Sarai on the Volga, the capital of the Golden Horde, one of the successor states of Genghis Khan's domain. They left the principalities intact, allowing their ruling princes to divide the realm among their sons. On succeeding to his share, a Russian prince had to travel to Sarai to be invested with a charter assigning it to him as his patrimony (*otchina*).[7] It was a perilous journey from which some never returned.

The Mongols did not physically occupy their Russian realm, as they did China, Korea, and Iran, probably because it was both poor and difficult to access. As was the case with the Vikings, their principal interest was tribute. In the years 1257–59 they compiled a cadaster of the Volga-Oka region and Novgorod to serve as a basis for taxation. Initially, they entrusted the task of collecting the tribute to Muslim tax farmers, whom they backed with an armed force manned in good measure with Russians under the command of Mongol officers known as *basquaqs*. But these tax farmers proved so unpopular and were so often the target of assaults and lynchings that following a series of urban uprisings in the 1260s and 1270s, which they brutally suppressed, the Mongols entrusted the responsibility to the Russian princes themselves. At the beginning of the fourteenth century, the ruler of the city of Vladimir assumed charge of the collection and delivery of the *iasak* in all the principalities under Mongol rule, by virtue of which he became great prince.[8] The responsibility stayed in the hands of the great princes, first of Vladimir and then of Moscow, until the end of the fifteenth century, when the Golden Horde dissolved and Russia ceased to pay the tribute.

Even after the Kievan state fell apart, a certain notion of the unity of the Russian land survived. It was inspired by the Orthodox faith, which gave the Russians a sense of community by distinguishing them from the Mongols and Muslims in the East and the Catholics in the West. Collective responsibility for the payment of tribute to the Golden Horde also contributed to the sense of unity. So did the Mongols' willingness to maintain the post of great prince, now transplanted from Kiev to the northeast.

During Mongol rule, also known as the "appanage period" (from the medieval term "appanage," meaning land or other source of income set aside by the ruler for the upkeep of his children), Russian princes viewed their realms as private property, from which they made land grants to the clergy as well as to personal servitors. Boris Chicherin, a nineteenth-century historian, first called attention to the fact that the princely testaments and treaties from this era were couched in terms of civil law, exactly like private testaments. The rulers of Moscow, from Ivan I Kalita (1325–40) to Ivan III (1462–1505), disposed of their realms as if they were landed estates, dividing them among sons and widows as their fancy dictated. No distinction was drawn between the princes' private assets and those belonging to the state.* This attitude received reinforcement from the Mongols' practice of treating their immense empire as the property of the reigning emperor and the other descendants of Genghis Khan.[9] It is of utmost importance for the entire subsequent development of Russia that, as noted by another early historian, "the sovereign was the possessor of all Russia and private property derived from the sovereign"[10]—in other words, that the private sphere in Russia issued from the public. Private property in that country neither gave rise to the state (as in classical Athens and Rome) nor developed alongside the state (as in most of Western Europe) but emanated from it. It was the product of its benevolence.

The assumption by the Russian princes of responsibility for the maintenance of order and collection of the tribute on behalf of the Mongols had various consequences for the political future of the country, all of them unfavorable to the cause of self-rule. For one, these highly unpopular functions estranged the princes from their people, creating a gulf between rulers and ruled that became a permanent feature of Russian history. For another, it encouraged the princes to adopt autocratic methods. Before the Mongol conquest, the Russian principalities had been administered by the princes in consultation with the *veche*, an analogue of the Anglo-Saxon folkmoot.[11] German merchants who visited medieval Novgorod were struck by the similarity between the *veche* and the institutions which they knew from home, sometimes referred to as the *ghemeyne ding* or "common thing," "thing" being used in the old sense of assembly. All pre-Mongol Russian cities had *veches*, and the

*B[oris] Chicherin, *Opyty po istorii russkogo prava* (Moscow, 1858), 232–375. Sergei Soloviev had advanced even earlier the thesis that the appanage was the prince's private property: *Ob otnosheniiakh Novgoroda k velikim kniaz'iam* (Moscow, 1846), 17–22. The legal historian M. F. Vladimirskii-Budanov (*Obzor istorii russkogo prava*, 4th ed. [St. Petersburg and Kiev, 1905], 161–62), however, dissented from this view.

more powerful among them routinely expelled princes who lost a battle or otherwise failed to live up to expectations. It is not unreasonable to assume, therefore, that in the natural course of events, Russian cities might have evolved, like their Western counterparts, into centers of self-government and guarantors of civil rights for their residents.

The Mongols prevented such an evolution. They had no use for the *veche,* since it was the fulcrum of resistance to their exactions. Russian princes charged with collecting the Mongol tribute had no more reason to favor popular assemblies which hindered them in the execution of their duties on behalf of the Mongol overlords. As a consequence, in the second half of the thirteenth century these assemblies fell into disuse. Except in the north, notably in Pskov and Novgorod, the *veche* disappeared, leaving the princes in exclusive possession of authority. Whenever they encountered resistance from their subjects, the princes turned to their Mongol masters for help. Prince Alexander Nevskii, whom Sarai appointed great prince of Vladimir (1252–63) and who was later canonized by the Russian church, distinguished himself in brutally repressing all popular resistance to Mongol exactions. The same held true of Ivan I Kalita of Moscow.

Thus under Mongol rule, a process of natural selection was set in motion by virtue of which the most renegade and despotic princes acquired the greatest power. The Mongol manner of administering Russia through the agency of prince-collaborators led to the liquidation of democratic institutions and laid the foundations of her future autocracy. The issue of Mongol influence on Russian history—stressed by some historians and minimized by others—can be resolved by conceding that the Russians did not emulate the Mongol political system, since the *institutions* of a nomadic empire built by conquest and maintained by military power were not suitable for an agrarian population. But the Russians certainly did adopt Mongol political *attitudes*: for by serving as Mongol agents they became accustomed to treating their people as vanquished subjects, devoid of any rights. This mentality outlived Mongol rule.

One of the difficulties in dealing with property relations in medieval Russia is of a terminological nature. The common term for property was *votchina* (or *otchina*), a synonym of the Latin *patrimonium,* meaning an inheritance from one's father. The trouble is that since medieval Russians did not distinguish private from public law, everything obtained by inheritance, including political authority, was designated by this word. Thus the appanage princes referred to their principalities as *votchiny* and their servitors called their estates by the same name. Occasionally even peasants did so if they settled down and tilled the same soil as their fathers.[12] As in other societies where property titles are unknown, length of possession was proof of ownership, and inheritance the best way of demonstrating it. "This is mine because I have it from my father" was in premodern societies the main validation of ownership. From such practices it followed that if one inherited the right to govern, that right, too, could become patrimony.

During the latter stages of Mongol domination, in the fifteenth century, the appanage princes recognized four categories of land. There were (1) court (*dvortsovye*) lands (princely demesne), incomes from which went to support the prince's household; these were managed by the court's household staff. The rest of the realm was divided into "white" and "black" land. The "white" lands were the possessions of the (2) clergy and the (3) nobles, which the princes granted them in perpetuity. Their holders paid no taxes (which is what the adjective "white" meant) but were expected to perform services, which in the case of clergy meant praying and in the case of the nobles manning the armed forces. (4) The rest of the land, covering the bulk of the principality, was designated "black." It rendered a variety of obligations to the prince subsumed under the name *tiaglo*, which involved payments of money or the performance of menial labor or both.[13] The princes regarded the "black" lands, cultivated by free peasants, as a store from which to make donations to churches, monasteries, and nobles. The effect of such transfer was to transform "black" lands into "white." Owing to such "whiting," the quantity of "black" land kept on shrinking until by the seventeenth century it disappeared everywhere except in the far north.[14]

The earliest private properties in land in Russia—properties distinct from the supreme ownership of the patrimonial prince—were the "white" possessions of the monasteries and princely servitors known as boyars. The monasteries accumulated sizable holdings from princes and nobles who made them grants to ensure the monks would pray for the salvation of their souls. The nobles obtained their *votchiny* as grants from princes and exploited them by means of peasant-tenants and indentured slaves. *Votchina* land, whether donated by the prince for services rendered, inherited, or purchased, was allodial property: accords between the appanage princes commonly contained a formula guaranteeing every noble possession of his estate even if he did not serve the prince on whose territory it was located.[15] Such freedom and such unconditional property prevailed until the late fifteenth century, when Moscow put an end to both by enforcing the rule that all secular subjects who held land on its territory, no matter how acquired, owed service to its prince. As Moscow expanded, this rule was applied to areas which it conquered or procured by some other means such as marriage or purchase.

The process of transforming allodial property into tenure conditional on state service began in earnest in the reign of Ivan III at the end of the fifteenth century, by which time the Golden Horde had disintegrated and Russia had, for all practical purposes, become a sovereign state. During the next two hundred years, all *votchiny* on the territories of the great princes of Moscow were, to employ modern terminology, nationalized. (Clerical holdings suffered this fate only in the eighteenth century.) Private property in land disappeared.

How differently Russia might have developed were it not for the Mongol conquest can be seen from the example of Novgorod, a state which for a time rivaled Moscow in size and influence.

2. *Novgorod*

Swedish Vikings founded Novgorod in the ninth century as their principal fortress in northern Russia: from here they spread to other parts of the country.

The Russian north, notably Novgorod and nearby Pskov, both fortunate to escape Mongol devastation, succeeded in preserving and developing institutions of self-rule which the Mongols had suppressed in central Russia. While paying the Mongols tribute, Novgorod maintained a central *veche,* which served the entire city-state, as well as separate *veches* for each of the five boroughs ("ends") into which the city was divided. All freemen of Novgorod and its environs, regardless of social status, were entitled to participate in its deliberations: decisions were reached by acclamation. Similar arrangements existed in several other cities of the north, notably Pskov.

Neither the soil nor the climate of Novgorod favors agriculture. Much of the region consists of lakes and marshes: only some 10 percent of the land surface is suitable for cultivation. The soil, an inferior type called podzol, being acidic, clayey, and sandy, requires a great deal of lime and fertilizer. The agricultural season here lasts a mere four months in the year. As a result of such adverse conditions, Novgorod always had to import food from central Russia and, in times of emergency, from abroad. However, its geographic location lent it great commercial importance. At the beginning of the thirteenth century, when nomadic Turks were disrupting the "Greek route," Novgorod entered into commercial relations with the Hanseatic League, which was gaining a dominant position in Baltic commerce. The Hansa opened a depot in Novgorod, similar to the ones it had in London, Bruges, and Bergen. In time, the Russian city became the most important single outpost of Hanseatic trade—and it probably was no coincidence that when in 1494 Ivan III, having conquered Novgorod, suppressed its activities there, the Hansa went into rapid decline.[16] The Novgorodians sold the Germans raw materials—furs, wax and tallow, flax and hemp, walrus tusks, and leather—and bought from them textiles, salt, weapons, precious metals, and, in years of famine, bread.[17]

To secure merchandise for export, Novgorod expanded in all directions. At its height in the mid-fifteenth century, it controlled extensive territories from Karelia and Lithuania in the west to the Urals in the east. Its southern possessions came within two hundred kilometers of Moscow. The city-state flourished. Its boyars formed an independent class of landowners and merchants.

The dominant political institution in Novgorod continued to be the *veche,* which elsewhere in Russia had gone into eclipse.* Novgorodian princes were outsiders with no patrimonial claim either to their title or to the state's wealth. Their main function was to command the city's armed forces. Although prior to the Mongol invasion the princes of Novgorod were appointed by the great prince of Kiev, there are grounds for believing that as early as 1125, if not earlier, they were invested as well as removed by the *veche.*[18] By the middle of the twelfth century, all political and clerical offices in Novgorod were elective: besides the prince himself, also the supreme executive officer, called *posadnik*, who on occasion replaced the prince (originally he had been appointed by the prince), as well as the bishop (previously installed by the metropolitan of Kiev). To assume his post, the prince had to swear an oath ("kiss the cross") to uphold a charter which set precise limits to his authority. Although nominally a principality, by the middle of the twelfth century Novgorod acquired a republican form of government in the sense that all its officials, from the prince down, were chosen by the citizens.

The princes of Novgorod never had much land of their own, because

*Marc Szeftel, *Russian Institutions and Culture up to Peter the Great* (London, 1975), Part IX, 624, credits the development of democratic institutions in Novgorod to contact with the free cities of the Hanseatic League. The explanation, however, is not convincing, given that the *veche* antedated relations with Hanseatic cities and that, as will be shown below, Novgorod kept the German traders in isolation. It seems rather that these institutions grew naturally, as in the contemporary West, as the by-product of an urban commercial culture.

their service here was generally of short duration, being treated as a stepping-stone to the post of great prince in Kiev.[19] Such land as they had managed to accumulate was taken away from them and turned over to the Cathedral of St. Sofia.[20] But even more important in shaping the Novgorodian constitution were provisions in the charters concerning princely landholding. Such charters, in essence contracts, were unique to Novgorod and Pskov, because elsewhere in Russia the princes ascended the throne either by virtue of appointment from Kiev (and later Sarai) or by hereditary right. The oldest of such surviving charters dates from 1264.[21] Its polished form has led some historians to view it as a relatively late example of contractual agreements dating to the close of the eleventh century.[22] In the 1264 contract between Novgorod and the prince and those that followed, the latter swore to observe faithfully several conditions. He pledged to respect the nation's customs. He was to make no decisions without the *posadnik*'s concurrence. He was not to deprive innocent persons of their land. Especially interesting for the present inquiry are provisions limiting his economic independence: they indicate that the elite of Novgorod realized the connection between the chief executive's wealth and his political authority. The charters forbade the princes as well as their spouses and retainers to acquire land on the territory of Novgorod by purchase or any other means. They were not to hand out to their followers Novgorod lands. They were not to deal directly with German traders but to do so only through Novgorod intermediaries.[23]

These provisions ensured that the princes of Novgorod had no private resources at their disposal and depended for their revenues entirely on the *veche,* which assigned them city land for temporary use from which to collect rents. They could earn additional moneys from the dispensation of justice. The princes served at the pleasure of the *veche,* which removed them at the slightest provocation, often following defeat in battle: between 1095 and 1304, Novgorod had fifty-eight princes, with an average tenure of 3.6 years.[24] Some Russian historians believe that by 1300, Novgorod no longer had any princes at all and had turned into a democratic republic in the full sense of the word—the only one in Russian history until the 1990s.[25]

Democracy and property went hand in hand. On the eve of Novgorod's conquest by Moscow at the end of the fifteenth century, some 60 percent of its land was privately owned.[26] Women owned land alongside men, an indication of an advanced concept of individual property.[27] Land not in private hands belonged to the church and the state. The bulk of the private land was the property of boyar families, from whose ranks came the majority of the city's elected officials. Their estates produced cereals and other foodstuffs, but their principal function was to furnish commodities for export.[28]

Like burghers of medieval Western Europe, the inhabitants of Novgorod enjoyed judiciary autonomy. The city's magistrates judged defendants without regard to their social status, on the implicit premise that citizenship bestowed equality before the law: the Novgorod Judicial Charter dating to the middle of the fifteenth century (*Novgorodskaia sudnaia gramota*) directed the court of the archbishop to "dispense equal justice to all, be he boyar, middle class burgher, or a lower rank burgher."[29]

In Pskov, which in 1347–48 split off from Novgorod and became an independent principality, a similar regime prevailed, the power of the prince being reduced to the point where he became "the principal servant of the *veche*"—in other words, a mercenary hired to lead the city's troops and retained only as long as he was successful in war. His only source of income came from the dispensation of justice, and not even all that was his.[30]

3. *Muscovy*

The principality of Moscow developed along very different lines. When, in the second half of the thirteenth century, the Mongols bestowed the rank of great prince on one of the Russian princes, the latter distinguished that rank and the territories that went with it from the title they held to their principalities; that is to say, they did not as yet treat the post of great prince as patrimonial property.[31] But once it became hereditary—first among the princes of Vladimir-Suzdal and ultimately among their successors, the princes of Moscow—they came to regard it as their property, since everything inherited was *votchina* and *votchina* was property.[32] The rank of great prince they interpreted to mean, in addition to granting them full possession of their own principalities, the right to claim sovereignty over all the lands that had once been part of the Kievan state. In this capacity, for example, they asserted—for the time being in theory only—sovereign authority over Novgorod.[33] Ivan I Kalita, the great prince of Vladimir from 1328 to 1340, who squeezed the Golden Horde's tribute from a defiant Novgorod, repeatedly sought to impose his rule on this city-state. When Pskov, with Moscow's backing, separated from Novgorod, it was required to acknowledge the ruler of Moscow as its *gosudar'*, that is, master. This patrimonial ideology would serve later to justify Moscow's claims to all Russia as both its realm and its property. It would also give Moscow's rulers grounds for denying their subjects all rights and freedoms, inasmuch as acknowledging them would have the effect of diluting their title to ownership.

As soon as the Golden Horde, torn by internal conflicts and routed by Tamerlane, dissolved—this occurred in the second half of the fifteenth century—Moscow's prince, Ivan III (ruled 1462–1505), viewing himself as successor to the Mongol khan, asserted his claim to sovereignty over all Russia. The main object of his attention was Novgorod, the largest and richest of the Russian principalities still outside his grasp.

The conquest of Novgorod proceeded in stages. In 1471, Ivan's troops dealt the armies defending the city-state a crushing defeat. For the time being, however, Ivan did not annex it, satisfied with Novgorod's willingness to acknowledge his suzerainty. Six years later, taking advantage of an inadvertent use of the appellation *gospodar* in reference to him by a Novgorodian diplomatic mission—a term which, like *gosudar'*, meant "master" and implied ownership—Ivan demanded complete submission. When Novgorod refused, his forces laid siege to the city. Facing certain defeat, the Novgorodians attempted to negotiate the terms of surrender by posing conditions as they had done with their own princes in the past. They offered to recognize the ruler of Moscow as their master (*gosudar'*) provided, among other conditions, that Novgorodians be subjected to neither deportations nor confiscations. They obviously knew well the fate that befell cities conquered by Moscow, most of which had to submit to such treatment.[34] Ivan indignantly rejected such stipulations:

> You have been told that we desire the same *gospodarstvo* in our patrimony (*otchina*) Novgorod that we have in the Low Country, on the Moscow [river]; and now you take it upon yourself to teach me how I should rule you? Is this government not mine?*

This language indicates that in Ivan's mind sovereignty was tantamount to property title to the conquered principality, that is, *dominium*—the right freely to dispose of its human and material resources.

Novgorod had no choice but to yield. What unconditional capitulation to the ruler of Moscow meant became apparent soon enough. One

***Patriarshaia ili Nikonovskaia Letopis'* in *Polnoe Sobranie Russkikh Letopisei,* XII (St. Petersburg, 1901), 181. Cf. Pipes, *Russia Under the Old Regime,* 80–2. *Gosudarstvo* (var. *gospodarstvo*), which in modern Russian means "state," is derived from *gosudar'*, or "master" and "owner."

of Ivan's first acts in conquered Novgorod was to abolish the *veche* and ship to Moscow the bell used to convene it. This action emulated Mongol behavior in central Russia two centuries earlier and symbolized the end of self-rule. Democratic institutions built up over centuries vanished in no time.

Ivan III's principal objective in Novgorod was to abolish private *votchina* holdings, the basis of the city's patrician wealth and power and the foundation of its democratic constitution. As long as the boyars held in absolute ownership the bulk of the city-state's productive assets, they could not be brought to heel. Aware how deeply rooted were democratic habits in the republic, Ivan carried out massive confiscations of landed estates, and to ensure that the seizures were irreversible, he deported the dispossessed owners to Muscovy.

The first victims were the leaders of the pro-Lithuanian faction, whom he ordered executed in 1475. They likely were Novgorod's most democratic elements, since neighboring Lithuania, by now united with Poland, had a far more liberal regime than Moscow. Further confiscations, accompanied by deportations, began on a small scale in the winter of 1475–76; the monasteries were among the first to lose their properties.* Then the process of expropriation got underway in earnest. In the winter of 1483–84, and then again that of 1487–89, several thousand of Novgorod's landowners along with their families were subjected to *vyvod*, or deportation. The boyars and merchants who suffered this treatment belonged alike to the pro- and anti-Moscow factions, which suggests that from Moscow's point of view what mattered was not the politics of its new subjects but their economic independence. By the time the *vyvod* was completed, all secular properties in Novgorod without exception had been confiscated, along with nearly all of the lands of the bishop and three-quarters of the remaining clerical holdings: titles to these properties were consigned to the great prince.[35] In 1494, Ivan shut down the Hansa depot in Novgorod, eliminating the city's last remaining source of independent income.

The seized lands were divided into two categories. The crown appropriated one-third for direct exploitation. Two-thirds went to its servitors—deposed appanage princes and boyars, as well as ordinary peasants and even slaves—who were transported to conquered Novgorod. These

*By contrast, in England half a century later, when Henry VIII confiscated monastic properties, title to them would be *granted* to him by an act of parliament. Furthermore, most of these lands were promptly either sold or handed out, with the result that they passed from hands of the crown to those of its subjects. In Russia, they were incorporated into the tsarist domain and remained there.

estates, however, were to be held not as *votchiny* but as conditional tenure called *pomestia*, the title to which remained vested in the Crown[36]—not as in feudal England, nominally, but in every legal and practical respect. In Russia, it must be stressed, conditional land tenure did not precede the creation of absolute monarchy but emanated from it.

Pomestie, or conditional tenure, which under one name or another would in time become the prevalent form of land tenure throughout Muscovy, originated in the appanage principalities. In addition to noble servitors whom they granted *votchiny,* the medieval princes also had domestic servants, called "princely slaves" (*kniazheskie kholopy*), who performed various household chores as scribes, artisans, gardeners, beekeepers, etc. Some of these servants they gave land allotments or other economic rewards (such as the right to fish or trap beavers on the prince's property) in compensation for work performed.[37] This land and these rights were not their property but temporary holdings which they exploited at their sovereign's pleasure, and as such they could not be alienated or even exchanged except with the authorization of the prince.[38] Unlike *votchiny,* which the owners retained no matter whom they served, *pomestia* reverted to the prince on the termination of the holder's services to him. The earliest instance of such an award has been traced to the fourteenth century, when an appanage prince is recorded as having made a land grant of this nature to the keeper of his kennels.[39]

From the reign of Ivan III onward, the rulers of Moscow increasingly resorted to *pomestia,* handing them out to their military and civil servitors, a class collectively known as *dvoriane*, or "men of the prince's household (*dvor*)." Title to these estates remained with the Great Prince.[40] *Pomestie* land came in part from confiscated *votchiny,* in part from conquests, and in part from the crown's storehouse of "black" properties.

The most extensive expropriations and deportations of *votchina* owners occurred in the reign of Ivan IV the Terrible (1533–1584), during the so-called *oprichnina.* Historians dispute to this day the purpose of this extraordinary measure, some arguing that the tsar wanted to eliminate the entire class of boyars, others that he struck selectively at families whom he suspected of sedition, yet others that he acted irrationally and without design in fits of madness. However, there is no disagreement that he separated from the realm large territories which he took under his personal command and called *oprichnina*, and in which he unleashed a reign of terror, not unlike that inflicted by Ivan III on conquered Novgorod half a century earlier. Its principal victims were powerful boyar families, especially those descended from the once independent appanage princes whose lands Moscow had absorbed. Having title to their properties registered in his name, Ivan IV proceeded to rid himself of their owners by execution and deportation.[41] Most of the nobles whose lives he chose to spare he exiled, together with their families, to Kazan, which he had recently conquered from the Tatars. There he gave them *pomestia* carved out of the lands taken from the natives.[42] The result of these policies was the destruction, sometimes physical, always economic, of much of the landed aristocracy in Russia. If Ivan III liquidated the independent nobility of Novgorod, Ivan IV completed the ruin of that class in the central regions of the country.

Ivan pursued similar policies in conquered Kazan, where he expropriated Muslim landowners. The seized properties he turned over as *pomestia* to Russian princes and boyars expelled by the *oprichnina*. He executed some Tatar princes and nobles, and the rest he ordered deported, along with some smaller landowners, to Moscow, Novgorod, and Pskov.[43]

By such means, the nobility of Russia was not only deprived of its hereditary estates but uprooted and scattered: displacement was designed to deprive it of a local power base and thereby render it politically impotent. This effect was noted shortly after the death of Ivan IV by Giles Fletcher, an English visitor to Moscow:

> Having thus pulled them and seased all their inheritaunce, landes, priviledges, &c. save some verie small part which he left to their name, [Ivan] gave them other landes of the tenour of *Pomestnoy* (as they call it) that are helde at the Emperour's pleasure, lying farre of in an other countrey, and so removed them into other of his Provinces, where they might have neyther favour, nor authoritie, not being native nor well knowen there.[44]

Such large-scale confiscations and expulsions were unknown in Western Europe at any time: they were applied only to the Jews, who were considered aliens. They resembled rather the actions of ancient Middle Eastern monarchies, like Assyria.

One interesting by-product of the Muscovite land policy was noted by the nineteenth-century historian Sergei Soloviev. He observed that whereas in Western Europe aristocrats identified themselves with reference to their estates by using such prefixes as "of," "de," and "von," followed by the name of their domains, which had since the early Middle Ages been their heritable possession or property, Russian nobles identified themselves by their Christian names and patronymics. This practice indicates that they attached greater importance to their family descent than to their estates, which they did not own.[45]

In Muscovite Russia the bulk of the state revenues derived from indirect taxes. The tsars collected tolls on the transport of goods and imposed sales taxes. An important source of income was the excise tax on alcohol consumption (after the art of distilling alcohol had been learned from the Tatars in the sixteenth century). There were also customs revenues and tributes in the form of furs and other commodities. In the middle of the sixteenth century, taxes were imposed on commoners, assessed either on land acreage or on the household.

An essential feature of the patrimonial system was that all privately held land, *votchina* as well as *pomestie,* had to render service. Moscow's rulers took the first steps in this direction in the middle of the fifteenth century; the process was completed a century later in the reign of Ivan IV.[46]

It had always been customary for *votchina* owners to serve, although they were free to choose their prince. When the appanage principalities, one by one, were incorporated into Muscovy, they lost that freedom. By the reign of Ivan III, Moscow was powerful enough to extradite any *votchina* owner who deserted its service.* The only alternative to serving Moscow was to enroll in the ranks of the grand duke of Lithuania—but inasmuch as the ruler of Lithuania had since 1386 been a Catholic, such action automatically incurred the charge of apostasy and high treason, leading to the confiscation of estates.

As so often in Russian history, where the most momentous innovations are introduced piecemeal and made law by precedent rather than legislation, no edict was ever issued making the holding of *votchina* land contingent on service. The principle was established by custom.[47] The earliest-known edict making *votchina* ownership conditional on service to the Moscow princes dates from 1556,[48] but the rule was certainly in place a century earlier. In the 1556 edict, which took compul-

*There is evidence, however, that this practice was much older and that as early as the beginning of the thirteenth century, the great princes of Moscow, while theoretically upholding the principle of boyar free departure in order to attract boyars of other princes into their service, in their own realm confiscated *votchiny* of nobles who dared to abandon them. Nikolai Zagoskin, *Ocherki organizatsii i proiskhozhdeniia slushilogo sosloviia v do-Petrovskoi Rusi* (Kazan, 1876), 69; M. Diakonov, *Ocherki obshchestvennogo i gosudarstvennogo stroia drevnei Rusi,* 4th ed. (St. Petersburg, 1912), 249–50. This set a precedent for the policies they implemented as rulers of all Russia.

sory service for granted, the government established identical norms of service from both *votchina* land and *pomestia:* so many armed men—the holder included—from an estate of such-and-such size. *Ukazy* of 1589 and 1590 prescribed that the estates—again, regardless of whether held as *votchina* or *pomestie*—of those who failed to turn up for service were to be confiscated on behalf of the crown, which would turn it over to more reliable servitors.[49] The estates of *dvoriane* lacking male issue also reverted to the government. No limits were placed on the duration of service: it was lifelong and in practice involved six months of the year, from April to October.* As a result of such measures, it became an unalterable rule that "one could not hold *votchina* land in the state of Moscow without serving its prince; one could not leave his service without forfeiting one's *votchina*": "the land must not leave the service."[50] However, even those servitors who punctiliously fulfilled their obligations to the state were not secure in their possession, as evidenced by complaints of *dvoriane,* preserved in the archives, that the government seized their estates arbitrarily (*bez viny*, i.e., "without cause").[51]

The equalization of status between the two forms of landholding explains why *votchina* tenure did not disappear. In fact, at the beginning of the seventeenth century in Muscovy, 39.1 percent of the land in private possession was held as *votchina.*[52] From the tsar's point of view it made no difference whether their servitors owned *pomestia* or *votchiny;* from the servitor's point of view, however, *votchiny* were preferable. *Votchiny* could be bequeathed to heirs and alienated (with some limitations) as well as mortgaged, whereas *pomestia* could not. Even so, from the sixteenth century onward, *votchina* sales had to be reported to a special office, whose responsibility it was to ensure that all the land rendered proper service.[53]

But even this difference between the two forms of land tenure began to narrow. As in the feudal West, the Russian equivalent of fiefs tended to become hereditary, because other things being equal, it suited the owners (in Russia's case, the tsars) to leave them in the possession of the same family. The practice was established in Russia by the middle of the seventeenth century that as long as he was capable of performing service, the son of a servitor living on a *pomestie* (i.e., a *pomeshchik*) inherited his father's estate.[54]

Russian servitors had no guarantees of personal rights, which is why

*In feudal England, by contrast, service to the king had been limited to forty days a year. Stephen Dowell, *A History of Taxation and Taxes in England,* 2nd ed., I (London, 1888), 20.

they cannot properly be called nobles: their landed estates, indeed their ranks and very lives, were dependent on the goodwill of the tsar and his officials. No charters were issued to them before the modern era (1785) of the kind that were familiar in medieval Poland, Hungary, England, and Spain. From this point of view, the status of a Russian "noble" was no different from that of the lowest commoner, and so it comes as no surprise that in addressing the tsar the highest dignitaries of the realm referred to themselves as his "slaves." Land tenure entailed not so much rights as obligations, and there were even cases—heavily punishable under a law of 1642—of *dvoriane* trying to evade state service by bonding themselves as slaves to other landlords.[55]

How extreme was the hostility of the Russian monarchy to private property can be seen from the fact that it refused to acknowledge as inviolate property even personal belongings, recognized as such by the most primitive societies. Russians had no certainty that government agents would not seize any object of value in their possession and forbid trade in any commodity by declaring it a state monopoly. Fletcher thus describes the anxiety he encountered among Russian merchants:

> The great oppression over the poore Commons, maketh them to have no courage in following their trades: for that the more they have, the more daunger they are in, not onely of their goods, but of their lives also. And if they have any thing, they conceale it all they can, sometimes conueying it into Monasteries, sometimes hiding it under the ground, and in woods, as men are woont to doo where they are in feare of forreine invasion. In so much that many times you shall see them afraide to be knowen to any *Boiuren* or Gentleman of such commodities as they have to sell. I have seene them sometimes when they have layed open their commodities for a liking [approval] (as their principall furres & such like) to looke still behind them, and towards every doore: as men in some feare, that looked to be set upon, & surprised by some enimie. Whereof asking the cause, I found it to be this, that they have doubted lest some Nobleman or *Sinaboiarskey* of the Emperour had bene in companie, & so layed a traine for them to pray upon their comodities perforce.[56]

An important consequence of the appropriation of all land by the tsars and their ability to confiscate any and all commodities in trade was that they could tax the population at will. We have seen what critical role in the development of parliamentary power—and ultimately, parliamentary democracy—in England was played by the crown's need to secure parliamentary approval of taxes and customs revenues. In Russia, by contrast, the tsars needed no one's authorization to impose or raise taxes, regalia, and customs duties. And this, in turn, meant that they had no need of parliaments.

Tsarist Russia did have two advisory bodies. One, the Boyar Council (Duma), resembled the *witena gemot* of Anglo-Saxon kings and other Germanic tribes: it rendered advice but did not legislate. This institution disappeared in the reign of Peter the Great. The other, the Assembly (Sobor, also known as the Zemskii Sobor), met now and then—the first probably around 1550, the last in 1653—usually when the state sought the country's sanction for some major undertaking, such as installing a new dynasty, ratifying a new law code, or concluding a foreign treaty. Representation was haphazard; delegates received pay, because they were considered to be performing state service. It resembled the typical pre-parliamentary assembly of Western Europe, but it never evolved into a parliament and never became part of the country's constitution.

Under the patrimonial regime, there was no place for law as an independent institution, superior to human will. It was merely a branch of administration which served to enhance rather than limit the monarch's authority. Specific ordinances were issued as *ukazy*, whereas more general rulings were issued as codes, or *sudebniki*. It was simply unthinkable that a subject could challenge the sovereign or the sovereign's officials in court, as happened in England.

As can be seen, the evolution in Russia of property in land ran in the diametrically opposite direction from the rest of Europe. At the time when Western Europe knew mainly conditional land tenure in the form of fiefs, Russia knew only allodial property. By the time conditional tenure in Western Europe yielded to outright ownership, in Russia allodial holdings turned into royal fiefs and their onetime owners became the ruler's tenants in chief. No single factor in Russia's history explains better the divergence of her political and economic evolution from that of the rest of Europe, because it meant that in the age of absolutism in Russia, unlike most of Western Europe, property presented no barrier to royal power.*

*In a bold revisionist article, the American scholar George G. Weickhardt challenges this thesis, espoused by virtually all Russian historians, arguing that Muscovite Russia "gradually developed a concept of private property for land which more or less approached that of the English 'fee simple.' . . ." *Slavic Review* 52, No. 4 (1993), 665. (In English law, "fee simple" referred to estates held in absolute ownership without any restrictions on the right of bequeathal or disposal by transfer of title.) The problem with

4. *The Russian city*

The absence in tsarist Russia of property in land would have had fewer consequences for her political evolution had that country developed self-governing urban communities. The Western European city gave rise to three institutions: (1) absolute private property in the form of capital and urban real estate at a time when the principal productive asset, land, was held conditionally; (2) self-government and judiciary autonomy; and (3) common citizenship in the sense that all urban inhabitants were freemen who shared civil rights by virtue of residence in the city rather than their social status. It is, therefore, of considerable importance that in Russia—with the notable exception of Novgorod and Pskov, neither of which survived into the modern era—cities of this kind failed to emerge.

As noted previously, at the dawn of her history (tenth and eleventh centuries) Russia had numerous urban centers which did not significantly differ in either appearance or function from those of Western Europe two centuries earlier. They were citadels built to protect the Viking ruling elite and its goods, outside whose walls artisans set up their workshops and traders their stalls. Typically, the early Russian city consisted of two parts: the fortress or *kreml,* near which stood the cathedral, both structures protected by a palisade of wood or stone; and the commercial settlement outside the walls, called *posad.*

In Western Europe during the eleventh and twelfth centuries, such primitive fortress-towns began to evolve into something quite different. Benefiting from the revival of trade, the cities of Italy, Germany, and the Low Countries organized into communes, which acquired the right to govern themselves and to dispense justice to their citizens. Again, with the exception of Novgorod and Pskov, nothing comparable occurred in Russia. The reasons were both economic and political. At the very time

---

this argument is twofold. One is that the author deliberately limits himself to "proclaimed legal principles" rather than "practice" (666). Secondly, by concentrating on laws dealing with inheritance and transfer of estates he not only ignores the fact that they required state approval (see above, p. 178) but also and above all that the state could and did confiscate private estates for reasons of its own (mainly nonfulfillment of service obligations) or for no reason at all. His analogy with Western practices under absolutism is invalid because as he himself concedes, the absolutist regimes in France, Prussia, Sweden, and Spain obtained the services of nobles "but not on a compulsory basis" (678). "Compulsion," of course, made all the difference. See my response in *Slavic Review* 53, No. 2 (1994), 524–30.

when trade revived in Western Europe, it declined in central and southern Russia: the disruption of the "Greek Route" and the resultant concentration on agriculture significantly reduced the commercial role of the cities. Secondly, the Mongols, viewing cities as centers of resistance, eliminated their organs of self-rule. The princes of Moscow, first as agents of the Mongols and then as sovereigns in their own right, would not tolerate autonomous enclaves exempt from tribute, service, and *tiaglo*. The patrimonial principle applied to the entire realm, without exception. Thus, the cities of central Russia turned into military-administrative outposts distinguished neither by a different economic structure nor by special rights. They were not oases of freedom in an unfree society but microcosms of the unfree society at large. Their population consisted of nobles bearing service and commoners bearing *tiaglo*. The city was militarized in that in the middle of the seventeenth century nearly two-thirds of Russian urban inhabitants consisted of military personnel.[57] These residents had no common bond other than physical proximity: they were defined by their social status and the obligations they owed the state, not by common citizenship. They enjoyed neither self-government nor independent courts. Nothing resembling the Western European class of "burghers" had a chance to emerge. Novgorod and Pskov, which did develop genuine urban institutions, after their conquest by Moscow were reduced to the same status as the rest of Muscovite cities.

The destruction of their self-government was only one aspect of Moscow's determination to bring all cities to heel. Moscow's expansion was everywhere accompanied by the physical destruction of cities and the expropriation of the owners of urban real estate, who were either deported or reclassified as servitors and commoners.[58] According to the chronicles, virtually every acquisition of a city by Moscow during the fourteenth and fifteenth centuries was followed by the confiscations of its privately held real estate on behalf of the great prince. This, for example, was the procedure adopted by Ivan I Kalita in the 1330s in Rostov.[59] Basil III, emulating his father, Ivan III, carried out mass expulsions from Pskov (1509), shutting down the *veche* and replacing the expellees with his own servitors. These were not impulsive acts but a system: a cadaster of nineteen Russian cities compiled in 1503 for the khan of the Golden Horde listed most of them as burned down, with their "bad" people banished and replaced with the great prince's loyal servants.[60]

Just as all private real estate was liquidated, so was every institution or practice faintly reminiscent of urban autonomy. In Russia, the juridical separation of the city from the land, a fundamental feature of European history since classical antiquity,[61] never occurred. The Muscovite city, like cities in most regions of the world untouched by Western culture, was a mirror image of the countryside. The resemblance even extended to appearance. Writing in the latter part of the nineteenth century, Russia's most prominent historian of the time thus described the Russian city:

> Europe consists of two regions: the western, constructed of *stone*, and the eastern, made of *wood*. . . . [Russian] cities consist of a heap of wooden huts: the first spark, and instead [of a city] there is a heap of ashes. No great loss, however: there is so little personal property that it is easy to carry it out, and building material is so cheap that to erect a new home costs next to nothing. For this reason, the ancient Russian so readily abandoned his home, his native town or village. . . .[62]

Muscovite cities were considered "black" land and as such subject to taxation. Their status as cities (*goroda*) was determined by the presence of a government official called the *voevoda*. The commoners inhabiting them were tied to their place of residence, like serfs, and forbidden to move out without permission. Whereas in the West, according to the German adage, "city air makes free," in the sense that a serf who had succeeded in residing in the city for a year and a day automatically gained his freedom, Russia recognized no statute of limitations on the retrieval of escaped serfs: serfdom was eternal. [63]

Like agricultural land, possession of urban real estate entailed service to the crown: "there was no form of urban property that private citizens [rather: subjects] might hold in right of full ownership."[64] For the ground on which buildings stood was held either as *votchina* or as *pomestie* and in either case was liable to be confiscated for the inability or unwillingness of the residents to render service. It could neither be bequeathed nor sold without government authorization.[65] Even the market sites on Moscow's Red Square belonged to the tsar.[66]

Lacking in both economic and legal privileges and subjected to heavy burdens, Russian cities developed slowly. The average Muscovite city in the mid-seventeenth century consisted of 430 households, each with five members, thus numbering slightly over two thousand inhabitants.[67] Whereas in much of Western Europe by 1700 urban inhabitants accounted for 25 percent of the total population, and in England for as much as 50 percent, in Russia in the middle of the eighteenth century they constituted a mere 3.2 percent of the country's male inhabitants subject to the soul tax (see below, p. 188), or approximately 7 percent of the population.[68] Moscow, where resided one-third of all of Russia's urban inhabitants, was as late as 1700 a large wooden village working mainly for the Kremlin.

5. *Rural Russia*

In sum, premodern Russia knew outright property neither in agricultural land nor in urban real estate: both assets were held conditionally. The landed aristocracy and the burghers—classes which in the West acquired in the late Middle Ages titles to their properties and all the rights that went with them—were in Russia servants of the state. As such, they had no guarantees of civil rights and no economic security. Their fortunes and social status were determined by their place in the government hierarchy and dependent on the crown's favor. Anyone who denies that medieval and early modern Russia differed fundamentally from Western Europe has to deal with these realities.

Given these facts, it is hardly surprising that the peasantry of Muscovite Russia, which accounted for nine-tenths of the population, also had neither property nor legal rights of any kind.

The "black" lands which medieval Russian peasants cultivated belonged to the prince and hence could not be sold or bequeathed. In practice, once the peasants abandoned "slash and burn" and went over to sedentary agriculture, their fields, by customary right, descended to their sons, who divided them among themselves in equal shares. However, even this practice was restricted by the institution of the peasant commune, which regarded the village arable as common rather than individual property.

The origins of the Russian peasant commune (*mir* or *obshchina*) have long been disputed by historians. Evolutionary sociologists, who dominated the field in the latter part of the nineteenth century, saw in the Russian peasant commune a relic of "primitive communism." Others attributed it to the fiscal needs of the Muscovite government, which, they believed, used the communal organization to ensure that the peasants met their obligations to the state. Field studies carried out at the turn of the twentieth century of communes in the process of formation (notably in Siberia) showed that they sprang up spontaneously in response to land shortages, which induced peasants to pool and periodically redistribute the arable. These findings demonstrated that in Russia, at any rate, land tenure progressed from household (family) farming to communal farming—a development directly contrary to that postulated by evolutionary sociologists.[69]

Whatever its origin, the commune indisputably helped the government administer its vast domain with the inadequate resources at its disposal. *Tiaglo* (see above, p. 168) was levied on communes, both rural and urban. To ensure its fulfillment, the state made the communes collectively responsible for the taxes and services of their members. The communes, in turn, distributed the burden among the households in proportion to the number of adult males. But inasmuch as households both grew and shrank in size over time, the communes carried out periodic redistributions so as to adjust to the number of its members the number of land strips allotted to each household. This was the principal feature of the institution which along with patrimonial autocracy, compulsory state service for the landowning class, and peasant serfdom shaped tsarist Russia.

Thus, from the late Middle Ages until the middle of the nineteenth century, the peasants of Great Russia owned no land: the soil they tilled belonged to the crown either directly or indirectly. And it was controlled, in most regions, by the commune.

From the end of the sixteenth century until the middle of the nineteenth, the majority of Russian peasants were serfs either of landlords or of the state, bound to the soil and increasingly subject to the unrestrained authority of their masters and crown officials. Russian serfdom was a very complicated institution which had some features in common with slavery but also significantly differed from it.* For one, strictly speaking, the serfs were the property not of the landlords but of the state, and hence, they could not be freed without government permission. Secondly, the serfs did not work on plantations under the supervision of overseers but lived in their own cottages and tilled their communal allotments, subject to the authority of the village assembly. They met their obligations to the landlord either by rendering services (*corvée* or *barshchina*), which typically entailed tilling three days a week the soil which the landlord had set aside for himself, or else by paying quitrent (*obrok*) partly in money, partly in kind, partly in services. Most important, that which the serf grew and that which he produced was his to consume or sell—if not *de jure*, since everything the serf possessed was in the eyes of the law the property of his landlord,

*On this subject, see my *Russia Under the Old Regime,* 144–57. Russian serfdom closely resembled villenage, which disappeared in England in the late Middle Ages at the very time that it made its appearance in Russia. J. H. Baker in R. W. Davis, ed., *The Origins of Modern Freedom in the West* (Stanford, Calif., 1995), 184–91.

then *de facto*, because such was custom, which a landlord could violate only at great risk to himself.

At the same time, like the slave, the serf was entirely at the mercy of the landlord as far as his obligations were concerned. The powers of landlords over serfs grew steadily until by the eighteenth century they did not differ appreciably from those of slave owners.

Serfdom came to Russia during the latter part of the sixteenth century and was firmly in place in 1649, when it received legal recognition in the law code (*Ulozhenie*). It came into being as an inescapable corollary of compulsory state service imposed on the landowning class. As we have noted, the object of value in Muscovite Russia was not land, which was available in unlimited quantities, but the labor to cultivate it. The farming population, however, was highly mobile. It would have been a futile gesture to reward servitors with *votchiny* and *pomestia* if they had no labor force to work their estates: a common complaint of Muscovite *dvoriane* was that large stretches of their land lay fallow for lack of labor. In response, the crown gradually restricted the movement of peasants and ultimately outlawed it altogether. In the words of a Russian legal historian, "peasants were bonded to the estates of *dvoriane* because *dvoriane* were bonded to obligatory state service."[70]

Thus, in respect to the farming population, as in respect to landed property, the evolution of Russia also proceeded in a direction opposite to that of the West. There, at the close of the Middle Ages, serfs became freemen; here, freemen turned into serfs.

6. *Peter the Great*

Peter the Great is commonly viewed as the monarch who did the most to Westernize Russia. The reputation is justified to the extent that he did profoundly alter the culture and manners of Russia's upper class—a class that at the onset of his reign numbered perhaps thirty thousand in a nation of five to seven million.[71] This he accomplished by compelling *dvoriane* to undergo a Western education and to adopt Western manners and garments. When, however, one scrutinizes his political and social policies one is driven to the conclusion that he not only kept intact the practices of Muscovy but by making them more efficient drew Russia still further away from Western Europe. In most respects, the reign of Peter marked the apogee of tsarist patrimonialism. Compulsory state service, land tenure conditional on state service, and serfdom to make such service possible were all rationalized to yield greater returns to the patrimonial autocracy. The power of the crown grew more, not less, arbitrary.

Peter abolished what remained of the legal distinction between *votchiny* and *pomestia,* transforming all land tenure into "immovable property" (*nedvizhimoe imushchestvo*), for which *pomestie* became in time the common designation. This action did little more than formalize a process underway during the seventeenth century. With *pomestia* becoming in effect hereditary and *votchina* owners obligated to bear service, the distinction between the two forms of land tenure blurred. In 1714, Peter abolished what was left of this distinction by making *pomestia* formally hereditary possessions. This he did in an *ukaz* which regulated how landed estates were bequeathed. Concerned that the custom of dividing estates in equal shares among male heirs impoverished both the service class and the peasantry, Peter ordered that the entire landed estate be bequeathed to one son (not necessarily the eldest). Neither *votchiny* nor *pomestia* could be sold except in emergencies and upon the payment of a special tax.[72] This attempt at introducing entail imposed a limitation on the testatory disposal of one's estate previously unknown in Russia and quite contrary to tradition, for which reason it was repealed in 1730.* Although some *dvoriane* interpreted the *ukaz* to mean that the tsar had given them their estates in outright property, since they were now free to designate their heir, in reality the law extended still further the authority of the crown over them by forcing them to choose a single heir.[73]

During the reigns of Peter and his immediate successors, Russian landlords enjoyed no more legal or economic security than before. In the first half of the eighteenth century the crown seized many estates for such offenses as the landlord's failure to show up for service (which Peter extended to sons of servitors ten years old, the age at which they were required to enroll in school), negligence in the performance of duties, embezzlement of state property, political dissent, or simply falling into disfavor. In fact, during this period (c. 1700–c. 1750) many more estates were confiscated than distributed: of the 171,000 peasant "souls" handed out to nobles during this half-century, only 23,700 came from crown lands; the remainder lived on private estates seized by the government

PSZ, Vol. viii, No. 5,653, December 9, 1730, pp. 345–47. This *ukaz* stated that the 1714 law was not only unjust but unworkable because some *dvoriane* sold their estates in order to provide equally for all their children, which was possible because money and other movable assets were exempt from the provisions of the 1714 law. The practice suggests that reality differed from theory, i.e., that it was possible to circumvent the prohibitions on the sale of real estate even in the early eighteenth century.

and transferred to another servitor.* So common were such requisitions that in 1729 St. Petersburg set up a Chancery of Confiscations, an office that may well be unique in the annals of government institutions.

Peter the Great immensely increased the tax burden of the population. In 1718 he introduced the "soul tax" on all adult male commoners; it became a major source of state revenues until abolished at the end of the nineteenth century. The amount of this tax was initially determined by calculating the amount of money required for the upkeep of the army and navy and dividing it by the number of adult male commoners. No one was consulted in the matter.

In the eighteenth century there still was no centralized treasury, and many government offices collected taxes for their own needs. The office of state treasurer was first created by Paul I at the very end of the eighteenth century.

Under Peter I, the state laid claim to assets whose status in Muscovite times had been vague. Virtually all commodities in commerce were declared a state monopoly. In 1703, to ensure the navy an adequate supply of timber, Peter ruled that forests belonged not to the persons on whose land they happened to grow but to the state. Landlords who cut certain specified kinds of trees were subject to fines; the cutting of even a single oak incurred the death penalty.† In 1704, the treasury asserted a monopoly on fishing, apiaries, and wild beehives. In the same year, all flour mills were declared state property.[74] The contents of the subsoil (metals and other minerals) of private estates were also claimed by the state.‡ Bathhouses and coach inns turned into regalia as well.[75]

The state also asserted a monopoly over what modern language calls intellectual property and modern law covers by copyrights and patents.

*V. Iakushkin, *Ocherki po istorii russkoi pozemel'noi politiki v XVIII i XIX v.*, I (Moscow, 1890), 5; Indova in Pavlenko, ed., *Dvorianstvo*, 279–80. A "soul" was a male commoner subject to the "soul" or capitation tax.

†*PSZ*, Vol. iv, No. 1,950, November 19, 1703, p. 228. V. Iakushkin, *Ocherki po istorii russkoi pozemel'noi politiki v XVIII i XIX v.*, I (Moscow, 1890), 16–37. This ordinance, repealed by Catherine II in 1782 (see below, p. 191), emulated a law of Queen Elizabeth of 1559 which forbade, with an exception made for the iron industry, the use of oak and other timber growing within fourteen miles of navigable rivers. James A. Williamson, *The Tudor Age* (London and New York, 1979), 274.

‡Iakushkin, *Ocherki*, I, 38–44. In English law, the principle prevailed that "possession of the land extends upwards to infinity and downwards to the centre of the earth." F. H. Lawson and Bernard Rudden, *The Law of Property*, 2nd ed. (Oxford, 1982), 21. But only in 1688–89 did England recognize as the property of the landlord minerals, other than gold and silver, found on their land. P. S. Atiyah, *The Rise and Fall of the Freedom of Contract* (Oxford, 1979), 87.

Until 1783, in Russia the government and the church held the exclusive right to print books:

> In contrast to Western countries where, from the moment of the emergence of bookprinting, typographies were in private hands and the publication of books was a matter of private initiative, in Russia the printing of books was from the outset a monopoly of the state, which determined the directions of publishing activity. . . .[76]

But even after privatizing printing, the tsarist government exercised tight censorship on all publications, requiring state approval before any work was submitted to the printer: such preventive censorship, unique to Russia in modern times (and restored by the Communists soon after coming to power), was replaced in 1864 by much milder "punitive" censorship applied after publication. The first Russian copyright law (1828) came into existence in connection with the censorship law of that year, which granted authors exclusive right to their works provided they abided by censorship rules. Two years later, the government recognized published works as private property of the creators.[77] The first patent laws in Russia were issued in 1833, two hundred years after England and half a century after France and the United States.

Peter's treatment of commoners not engaged in agriculture—merchants (*kuptsy*), burghers (*meshchane*), and the new class of industrial workers—also did nothing to enhance either their civil or property rights.

Peter's efforts to industrialize Russia were driven by the same patrimonial mentality that inspired his treatment of the landed service class. He forbade private persons to build factories without the permission of the College of Manufactures, which enjoyed a monopoly on industrial enterprises; violators of this ban risked having their enterprises confiscated.[78] Prominent merchants were conscripted to set up and run the fledgling state industries. A good example of Peter's service-oriented approach to industry is the Moscow Woolen Manufacture. A state factory founded in 1684 by Dutchmen to supply cloth to the army, it did not meet Peter's expectations and was turned over to private interests, a "Commercial Company," the first chartered business enterprise in Russia. The company's board was made up of the country's leading merchants, who were drafted by imperial *ukaz*. Conveyed to Moscow under military guard, they were furnished with capital from the treasury and ordered to deliver to the state, at cost, such cloth as it required; the surplus they were free to sell at a profit. Provided they operated it to the government's satisfaction, the factory was their "hereditary property"; should they fail, the state reserved itself the right to reclaim it and punish them.[79] This example indicates that Peter's government treated manufactures exactly as it did *pomestia*, and that its industrial policies contributed nothing to the development of property laws in Russia. All this was very different from the practices of England, where already in the thirteenth century there existed chartered companies, working for private profit.[80]

The same state interests dictated Peter's policies toward industrial labor. During his reign, the workers employed in manufactures and mines consisted partly of social outcasts (convicts, illegitimate children, vagabonds, prostitutes, etc.), and partly of state peasants conscripted for the purpose. A decree of 1721 authorized *dvoriane* and merchants to purchase populated estates and to attach the inhabitants in perpetuity to their factories.[81] Until 1816, when this decree was rescinded, workers and miners, known as "possessional serfs," were permanently bonded to their places of employment, exactly as peasants were tied to the soil.

The status of the rural population deteriorated considerably during Peter's reign. Several lower-class groups which in Muscovy had managed to elude serfdom were now amalgamated with the serf population. The new "soul tax" became the hallmark of inferior social status. Serfs were made liable to compulsory military service in the standing army, another of Peter's innovations.

In 1721, the state took over lands belonging to the church and monasteries.

7. *Catherine the Great*

Private property in land and in other productive assets, along with civil rights for a privileged minority, appeared in Russia in the second half of the eighteenth century.

The first measure to sound the death knell of the patrimonial regime was a 1762 manifesto issued by Peter III which exempted Russian *dvoriane* in perpetuity from obligatory state service.[82] With one stroke of the pen, and apparently in a quite casual manner, the new emperor annulled the work of his predecessors of the preceding three hundred years. The ruling did not immediately alter the country's political and social structure, because the great majority of *dvoriane* were too poor to take advantage of it. Most had neither land nor serfs; of those fortunate enough to possess both, 59 percent had fewer than twenty serfs and only 16 percent more than a hundred, the number considered the minimum to afford the life of a country squire.[83] The majority of *dvoriane*, therefore, had no choice but to remain in state service and draw a salary. An important principle, however, had been introduced: henceforth, Russia had a class of free subjects, independent of the state.

The Manifesto of 1762 left undefined the status of the land and the serfs working on it. It could have been interpreted to mean that the crown turned estates over to *dvoriane* as their outright property, since it did not require nobles who left the service to surrender their estates. For all practical purposes—though not as yet legally—they now held the land unconditionally. In 1752 the empress Elizabeth ordered a general land survey to determine the boundaries of towns, villages, and estates, a measure which would have led to the landlords being recognized as *de facto* owners of their land. The undertaking was not commenced, however, until 1765. Landlords in possession of estates were recognized as *de jure* owners without having to present documentary proof of ownership.[84] In 1769 the government laid it down, using rather clumsy terminology, in response to one landlord's petition, that "all private (*vladelcheskie*) lands . . . belong in property (*sobstvenno*) to the possessors."[85] Two edicts issued in 1782 ruled that the "property rights" of the owners of estates were not confined to the surface of the land but extended to the subsoil, bodies of water, and forests.[86] These *ukazy* seemed to take it for granted that the land belonged to the nobles, and they provide evidence that in Russia land was being transformed from possession into property.

The property rights of *dvoriane* to the land were formally confirmed in 1785 by Catherine the Great in the Charter of Rights, Freedoms, and Prerogatives of the Noble Russian Dvorianstvo, one of the most consequential legislative acts in Russian history.[87] The charter recognized that the *dvoriane* owned outright their landed estates and enjoyed, in addition, guarantees of civil rights. The recognition came some six hundred years after the English monarchy had granted similar rights to its subjects. The reason for this drastic change in attitude toward an institution in which until then the Russian monarchy had seen nothing but a threat to its authority was both political and ideological.

Catherine, who gained the crown in a coup that cost the life of her husband, Peter III, being both a usurper and a foreigner, felt highly insecure. She consciously—and successfully—sought to consolidate her authority by winning the loyalty of the *dvoriane* at the expense of the other social groups. To bolster the throne, she took the landed gentry into something like a partnership. The need for such an alliance became especially urgent after the peasant rebellion of 1773–75 under the leadership of the Cossack Emelian Pugachev. This uprising made Catherine aware how weak was the hold of her government on its far-flung realm, and persuaded her to rely on the *dvoriane* as an auxiliary administrative staff, with virtually unlimited authority over its peasantry.

As she knew from the *cahiers* which *dvoriane* had submitted to the Legislative Assembly convened in 1767 to give Russia a new code of laws, a major source of their dissatisfaction was the legally precarious status of their estates. The Moscow gentry, for example, requested that "the right of ownership (*sobstvennost'*) for both inherited and purchased estates be clearly defined." Other petitions sought confirmation that *dvoriane* owned their immovable properties as unconditionally as their personal belongings.[88] A commission was set up to deal with these questions. It proposed that nobles, and they alone, be recognized as having absolute property rights to their estates, while commoners' rights were restricted.[89] These recommendations were incorporated into the 1785 charter.

Considerations of *raison d'état* and personal self-interest of the empress received reinforcement from contemporary intellectual currents in the West, familiar to Catherine from her wide reading, which saw in private property the foundation of prosperity. Like Peter the Great, Catherine was well aware of the importance of the national economy for the country's power and prestige; but unlike Peter, who adopted mercantilism with its emphasis on the directing role of the state, she fell under the influence of the Physiocrats and their doctrines of economic liberalism. The theories of the Physiocrats, who regarded private property as the most fundamental of the laws of nature and agriculture as the principal source of wealth, played a part in influencing her to introduce to Russia ownership of land.

Sobstvennost', the Russian word for property, entered the vocabulary of official documents during Catherine's reign, being a translation of the German *Eigentum* (*Egindum*), which had come into usage in Germany as early as 1230.[90] *Sobstvennost'* appeared in the 1767 Instruction (Nakaz) to the procurator-general laying down the principles that were to guide preparations of the new Code of Laws: here Catherine defined the purpose of civil law as "protecting and making secure the property of every citizen."[91] Articles 295 and 296 of the 1767 Nakaz read as follows:

> Agriculture cannot flourish where neither the cultivator nor the laborer has anything of his own. This rests on a very simple

> principle: "Every man is more concerned with what belongs to him, than with what is another's and does not take care of that which he fears someone may take away from him."[92]

The key article (No. 22) of the Charter of Rights (Noble Charter) read:

> The noble who is the first legally to acquire an estate is granted the full power and freedom to make a gift of it, or to bequeath it, or to confer it as a dowry or a living, or to transfer it, or to sell it to whomsoever he chooses. Inherited estates, however, cannot be disposed of otherwise than as provided by law.*

An important and innovative clause in the charter decreed that the inherited estate of a noble convicted of a grave crime was not to be confiscated but turned over to his legitimate heirs (Article 23). Henceforth, noble properties could not be seized without court judgment.† Nobles were entitled to found factories and markets in their villages (Articles 28–29) and to acquire urban real estate (Article 30). Their exemption from personal taxes was confirmed (Article 36), and they were freed of the obligation of billeting soldiers in their rural residences (Article 35).

Although Catherine applied the teachings of the Physiocrats only to the upper class, it did not escape her, and some of her more thoughtful contemporaries, that they were germane to peasants as well. From the middle of the eighteenth century voices were heard arguing that peasants would be more productive and tranquil if given freedom along with title to the land they cultivated.[93] An international contest launched in 1766 by the St. Petersburg Free Economic Society on her initiative for the best response to the question whether the peasant should own the land which he cultivated awarded the first prize to a Frenchman, Béarde

*The last clause makes obeisance to the ancient tradition which accorded the relatives of the owner of hereditary *votchiny* the right over forty years to repurchase properties sold to outsiders. The limitations mentioned in Article 22 were not legally defined until 1823. V. N. Latkin, *Uchebnik istorii russkogo prava perioda imperii*, 2nd ed. (St. Petersburg, 1909), 538–39. The complicated rules concerning the disposal rights by testament of inherited (or patrimonial) land in the eighteenth and nineteenth centuries and Russian jurists' attempts to revise them in favor of outright individual property are discussed in William G. Wagner, *Marriage, Property, and Law in Late Imperial Russia* (Oxford, 1994), 227–377.

†And yet, respect for law was so weakly developed in Russia that in the reign of Catherine's grandson, Alexander I, when the government took over large areas to settle military colonists—soldiers on active duty who in peacetime supported themselves by agriculture—landlords with estates in these areas were summarily evicted and given land elsewhere. Richard Pipes, *Russia Observed* (Boulder, Colo., 1989), 88.

de l'Abbaye, who answered affirmatively on the grounds that one hundred peasant-proprietors would outproduce two thousand serfs.[94] In the Legislative Assembly, opponents of peasant land ownership did not deny the advantages of ownership but maintained that if peasants were given title to their land they would soon lose it and find themselves destitute.[95]

In her Instruction (Nakaz) (Article 261) Catherine hinted that it would be beneficial to grant property rights to serfs (whom she called "slaves"—*raby*). In her notes was found a proposal that all Russian subjects born during and after 1785, the year of the Noble Charter, be treated as freemen. She also drafted a proposal—never acted on—that would allow state peasants to acquire as property unpopulated land.[96]

The effect of such debates and proposals was to raise in Russia for the first time the issue of serfdom and, as a corollary, the question of private property for the common people. The initiative in both instances came from the crown. If, despite influential opinion favoring such a course, serfs were neither freed nor given land it was because considerations of state security, which demanded the support of the gentry, outweighed those of economic progress. It was only a century later, when serfdom came to be seen as a threat to state security, that tsarism ventured on emancipation.

With property rights came personal rights.

According to the 1785 Noble Charter, nobles were not to be deprived of life, title, or property except by the judgment of their peers (Articles 2, 5, 8, 10–12). They were exempt from corporal punishment (Article 15) and permitted to travel abroad as well as to enroll in the service of friendly foreign powers (Article 19).* The charter reaffirmed that nobles did not have to serve the state except in times of national emergency (Article 20). The thirty-six articles of the first part of the Noble Charter were a veritable Bill of Rights which created, for the first time in Russia, a class of persons whose life, personal liberty, and properties were guaranteed.

It was a revolutionary measure in the fullest and most constructive sense of the word, and it set the direction of Russia's development for the next 130 years. In their totality, its provisions proved far more innovative than the superficial efforts at Westernization of Peter the Great,

*Catherine's son and successor, Paul I, suspended during his reign this provision of the charter by making nobles convicted of crimes subject to corporal punishment. They were divested of their noble status, which automatically exempted them from the privileges embodied in the Noble Charter.

which copied Western techniques and manners while ignoring the spirit of Western civilization. True, Catherine's Noble Charter bestowed rights and freedoms on a small minority only; but as Western history demonstrates, general freedoms and rights usually originate in minority privileges. It has proved to be the most reliable way of implanting freedom and rights, because it gives rise to social groups interested in protecting their advantages. Thus ancient Athens, the home of modern democratic ideas and institutions, granted liberties to a minority of landowners and denied them to slaves and foreign-born freemen, who constituted the bulk of the city-state's professionals, businessmen, and artisans. The Magna Carta, the foundation stone of English liberties, was a feudal charter benefiting England's barons, not the nation at large. It was demonstrably exclusive:

> Liberties were always attached to particular persons or places; there was nothing general or national about them. They were definite concrete privileges, which some people enjoyed, but most did not. . . . [I]t was because they were rare privileges and not common rights that the framers of Magna Carta set so much store upon liberties.[97]

The same held true of the burghers of Western European cities, who extracted for themselves immunities and other rights from kings and lords, rights which in many ways provided the foundation of modern freedoms, but these, too, originated in exclusive privileges.[98] Freedom of speech had its origin in the exclusive rights granted by the English crown around the fifteenth century to members of the House of Commons.[99] The prerogatives of the fortunate few provide a model for the rest of the population. Once the principle of absolute private property had been established in Russia, therefore, it was only a matter of time before it would be extended to the population at large.

This said, it must be noted that the introduction of landed property into Russia was a mixed blessing, because it was purchased at the expense of the serfs. Although the 1785 charter referred only to land and made no reference to serfs, it had the effect of turning the latter—tied as they were to the land—into the private property of their landlords. Proprietary serfs constituted at the time approximately one-third of the country's population. Since the tsarist authorities neither laid down any rules governing the powers of the landlords over their serfs nor intervened on the serfs' behalf, they effectively surrendered sovereignty over one-third of the population to private interests. Not surprisingly, in conversation with the French *philosophe* Denis Diderot, Catherine referred to serfs as the "subjects" of their masters.[100]

Private property in Russia, therefore, spelled, besides freedom and rights for the few, intensified serfdom for the many. For the serfs, private property became anything but a liberating force, and this historic fact had a negative effect on property's reception in Russia. In the words of Richard Wortman:

> From its inception, the right of property [in Russia] became associated with the consolidation of the nobility's power over the peasants and the abuses of the serf system. . . . The property rights bestowed by the tsarist regime became identified with its despotic authority.[101]

Indeed, as we shall see, the bestowal of property rights on the gentry would prove to be a major obstacle to the abolition of serfdom. For both in practice and in law, the serfs were considered since 1785 to belong to their landlords: Michael Speransky, the chief minister of Alexander I in drafting his constitutional project of 1809, thought so;[102] and so did Sergei Lanskoi, the minister of the interior at the beginning of Alexander II's reign, when discussions of serf emancipation got seriously underway.[103]

In the eighteenth century, landlords acquired virtually unlimited power over their serfs. They had toward them only one obligation, and that was to feed them in time of crop failures. Their authority over them precluded only three actions: depriving them of life, beating them with the knout (a form of punishment often tantamount to execution), and torturing them. Their powers included:[104]

1. The right to exploit serf labor at will. Several attempts were made to persuade landlords to define the labor obligations of their serfs, but these were never formally enacted.

2. The right to sell serfs. This was somewhat ambiguous. Although Peter I criticized the practice of selling serfs without land ("like cattle"), he passed no law forbidding it and in fact encouraged it himself by authorizing *dvoriane* to sell peasants to other *dvoriane* to serve as recruits.[105] Thus, until 1843, when the practice was outlawed, serfs were commonly bought and sold, with their families but sometimes also individually. Landlords also had the right (with government or court permission) to shift serfs from one estate to another, no matter how distant, which the rich ones did by the thousands.

3. The right to force serfs to marry against their will.

4. The right to punish serfs in any way they saw fit short of depriving them of life. But since no means existed of supervising the many estates scattered throughout the empire, this limitation was unenforceable.

5. Since 1760, the right to exile serfs to Siberia for settlement,[106] and from 1765 to 1807 for hard labor (*katorga*).[107] Landlords could also turn serfs over to the army for lifelong military service.

6. Legal ownership of all the assets of their serfs. A serf could purchase property but only with the landlord's permission and in his name.

If, nevertheless, Russian serfs even at the nadir of their condition, in the reign of Catherine the Great, did not sink to the status of black slaves in the Americas, the reason is to be found in the backwardness of the Russian economy and in the constraints of custom.

Unlike the slave plantations of the West Indies and the southern United States, which worked for the market, Russian landed estates were largely self-sufficient household economies which consumed most of what they produced. They were, therefore, managed in a less demanding manner. The Russian landlord did not care to squeeze the utmost from his laborers by rationalizing agriculture and subjecting his serfs to close supervision. If his serfs paid quitrent, he knew that he would profit most by relying on their own enterprise. If they owed him services (*corvée*), then he faced a natural limit on what he could demand, because unless the serf was allowed to tend to his own fields he would have to be fed. There was no particular interest in obtaining a surplus, since there was no market for it. As a rule, Russian serf owners were more interested in securing reliable returns than in maximizing them, for which reason they were quite willing to let the peasants run their own affairs. The serfs' personal belongings and the fruits of their labor were with few exceptions treated as their own.* Indeed, some landlords are known to have helped their serfs circumvent the law by allowing them to buy, in their own name, land, even land populated by other serfs; the serfs of one of Russia's richest magnates, Count

*Commenting on Catherine's Instruction, in which she spoke of the desirability of the peasants' owning the land they tilled (Article 295), Prince M. M. Shcherbatov, a leader of the conservative nobility, wrote: "Although the Russian peasants are slaves of their masters, although the land they cultivate belongs to their landlords, who also have the right to their personal belongings, no one concerned for his own self-interest would take the personal property and land of the peasants, and the peasants to this day do not feel that these [objects] are not their property. The assertion [*vterzhenie*] of such ideas has been the cause of various rebellions, including the present one of Pugachev, and the killing of many landlords by their peasants. . . ." M. M. Shcherbatov, *Neizdannye proizvedeniia* (Moscow, 1935), 55–56.

Sheremetev, owned over six hundred serfs.[108] Finally, serfs were "liable to taxation and military service: not benefits, to be sure, but not characteristic of slavery either." [109]

The other factor restraining the landlord's authority over his serfs was the peasant commune. It was in the interest of the landlord to maintain the authority of the commune, since it ensured, by the device of collective responsibility, the collection of the soul tax, for which the state held him liable, and rents. The commune, for its part, up to a point could protect the peasant household from landlord interference. A certain equilibrium thus came into being between the theoretically boundless authority of the landlord and the *de facto* restraints imposed on it by economic realities, custom, and the commune, none of which played any part on slave plantations.

Perceived as self-serving license for the few rather than a basic human right, and moreover acquired at the expense of millions of human chattel, private property in tsarist Russia found few champions, even among conservatives and liberals. It was widely viewed as an enemy of both freedom and social justice. Russian liberals and liberal-conservatives throughout the last century of tsarism stressed law as the foundation of liberty and failed to perceive a connection between law and private property. It is difficult to find among the theorists and publicists of the late imperial era anyone prepared to defend private property as a natural right and basis of political liberty.* Nor has any Russian historian seen it worthwhile up to now to investigate the history of private property in his country.

Russian peasants did not acknowledge that the land was anyone's property but the state's, i.e., the tsar's, and for that reason they never reconciled themselves to the provisions of the 1785 Noble Charter, which gave *dvoriane* land while exempting them from compulsory state service.[110] As far as the peasants were concerned, the charter robbed serfdom of its rationale, inasmuch as their ancestors had been bonded in order to enable the nobles to fulfill their obligations to the tsar. Indeed, in their view, *tiaglo* "was not a rent they paid the supreme owner of the

*A notable exception was the liberal Boris Chicherin: see his *Sobstvennost' i gosudarstvo*, 2 vols. (Moscow, 1882–83). But Chicherin, an immensely learned man given to writing turgid prose, had little influence on public opinion, in good measure probably because of this unpopular position. On Russian thinkers' attitude to property, see K. Isupov and I. Savkin, eds., *Russkaia filosofiia sobstvennosti XVIII–XX vv.* (St. Petersburg, 1993).

land [i.e., the tsar] but the means of serving the government which it was their lot to perform."[111] Why should they continue serving, therefore, when their masters were no longer required to do so?

Catherine also introduced private property in urban real estate. In the "Charter of the Rights and Benefits of the Cities of the Russian Empire,"[112] issued concurrently with the Noble Charter, all Russians living in cities were formed into a corporation, subject to the same duties and responsible to the same administrative and judiciary authorities. The office of mayor became elective (Article 31). The urban population was divided into two estates, that of *kuptsy,* or merchants, and that of *meshchane*, artisans and tradesmen. The status of the latter resembled that of state peasants in that they bore, collectively, the same obligations, but they were able, by accumulating enough money, to move into the ranks of the merchant class. The merchants, whose status was determined by their capital, received various commercial privileges. The city charter established that urban inhabitants of both categories could own and enjoy undisturbed both movable and immovable properties (Article 4). Nobles who owned real estate in the cities were, from the administrative point of view, treated analogously with commoners, but they did not pay taxes or render *tiaglo* services (Article 13). The cities were formally self-governing but in fact remained under government supervision.[113] The very first article of the City Charter declared that new cities could be built only in accordance with plans approved by Her Majesty.

It soon turned out that one could not create an urban culture by government fiat. Russian cities developed slowly, for trade was meager: as late as the middle of the nineteenth century, of the approximately 1,000 localities designated as towns, 878 had fewer than 10,000 inhabitants and only two had more than 150,000.* In the final decades of the old regime, the majority of Russia's urban residents consisted of peasant peddlers and unemployed, looking for work. Russian cities were swamped by rural migrants who had neither legal urban status nor steady employment: around 1900, in the empire's two largest cities, St.

*Peter [*sic*] Miljukoff in *Vierteljahreschrift für Sozial- und Wirtschaftsgeschichte* XIV, No. 1 (1916), 135. In the words of Max Weber, "[U]ntil the abolition of serfdom, a city like Moscow resembled a large Oriental city from approximately the age of Diocletian: spent there were rents of the owners of land and serfs and incomes from offices." *Grundriss der Sozialökonomik: III, Wirtschaft und Gesellschaft,* 3rd ed., Vol. 2 (Tübingen, 1947), 585.

Petersburg and Moscow, nearly two-thirds of the inhabitants were peasants on temporary residence permits.[114]

Private property in assets other than real estate was encouraged by laws passed in the middle of the eighteenth century under the inspiration of Physiocratic theories. They resulted in the abolition of the numerous state monopolies on manufacture and trade in force since Peter I. In 1762, Peter III removed most restrictions on trade, including commerce in cereals, which had been a royal prerogative. In 1762 and again in 1775, Catherine II annulled prohibitions on unlicensed manufacture by allowing Russians of all estates to found factories. The main beneficiaries of these measures were *dvoriane,* who took advantage of their tax-free status and access to serf labor (now their exclusive privilege) to pursue manufacture and commerce. Before long, most of the industries in Russia were located in the countryside, on or near noble estates. Serfs also benefited from the new economic liberties, because landlords, hoping for higher rents, encouraged them to branch out to occupations other than agriculture. In the first half of the nineteenth century, certain sectors of Russian industry as well as retail commerce fell into the hands of serfs. Some of them became millionaires. In the eyes of the law, bonded entrepreneurs had no property guarantees: their landlords could, and occasionally did, appropriate their assets.[115] But such actions were exceptional. The net effect of the laws privatizing industry and commerce was to stimulate and enhance private property in Russia, although the main beneficiary was not the middle, urban class as much as the landlord and the peasant.

A further step in the dismantling of the patrimonial regime was the long-overdue separation of crown properties from those of the state. Traditionally in Russia, the two had been treated as one: revenues from taxes and incomes from state properties were pooled together and spent as needed, whether for the armed forces or the upkeep of the court. This system, characteristic of medieval government, had been abandoned in England between 1530 and 1542, in the reign of Henry VIII, when household management gave way to national bureaucratic management.[116] In neighboring Poland, the incomes of the king and the kingdom were separated in 1590.[117] In Russia, such a separation occurred only two centuries later. In 1797, Paul I decreed that crown estates came under the jurisdiction of a special office—the Department of Appanages (*Udely*). Members of the imperial family who stood in line of succession to the throne received revenues from state properties; all others drew them from crown lands.[118]

8. *The emancipation of serfs*

Until the middle of the nineteenth century, the Russian peasantry consisted of two major groups: state peasants and proprietary serfs. Both paid the soul tax and both furnished recruits for the army. Both were also required to provide the state with transport and fodder, carry mail, billet troops, and maintain roads and bridges.[119] Neither category owned the land which it tilled: the state peasants cultivated soil belonging to either the government or the crown, the serfs that of their landlords. The two groups were roughly equal in size.

While subject to many of the same obligations, the state and crown peasants were somewhat better off, because, although in effect serfs of the government and its officialdom, they did not have to live and work under the watchful eyes of landlords and their stewards. They further benefited from the crown's preferential treatment. After 1800, under the influence of abolitionist sentiments then gaining ground in the West, Russia's elite began to regard serfdom as an evil whose days were numbered. But the same circles also agreed that such a drastic step as abolishing serfdom was better taken later than sooner. Serfdom was regarded as essential to the security and stability of the country in that it supported the gentry, the mainstay of the monarchy. Nor were the serfs regarded as ready for freedom. Hence the crown postponed to the indefinite future the issue of abolition and concentrated on improving the lot of state and crown peasants. Step by step, in the first half of the nineteenth century, the tsarist regime expanded the civil and economic rights of these two groups. In 1837, Nicholas created a Ministry of State Properties under Count Paul Kiselev, for the purpose of improving the status of the 7.5 million state peasants and setting an example for serf owners. By 1850, state peasants could purchase and inherit property and enter into contractual relations. They could be deprived of their belongings only by court judgment.[120] These measures would provide a model for the 1861 edict emancipating proprietary serfs. The communal lands which state and crown peasants tilled, however, did not belong to them until 1886, when their rents were converted into purchase installments: until that time, they were, in the words of one scholar, "perpetual tenants of state-owned land."[121]

The first half of the nineteenth century marked a shift in tsarism's attitude toward the serfs of nobles. Alexander I and Nicholas I alike took steps to improve their legal as well as economic status. These were modest measures, for anything bolder was believed to threaten the country's social and political stability. Still, the trend was unmistakable, pointing toward ultimate emancipation.

Shortly after his accession, Alexander I stopped handing out state peasants to nobles, which his father, Paul I, and grandmother, Catherine II, had done on a lavish scale. As a consequence, the proportion of serfs in the population, which had already begun to fall in the middle of the eighteenth century, declined at an accelerated rate.[122] The law of free agriculturalists, passed in 1803, permitted landlords to manumit serfs with the proviso that they give them title to their land allotments. Few landlords took advantage of this law, but it introduced two important principles: that serfs had to be emancipated with land and that after they had compensated the landlord for it this land became theirs.* As a consequence of these two measures, in 1858 Russia had over 268,000 peasant-proprietors, owning 1.1 million hectares.[123]

In 1802, Alexander forbade landlords to exile serfs to Siberia except by court judgment, and in 1807 to condemn them to hard labor. In 1808, he outlawed serf auctions. Two further laws led to an improvement in the economic situation of serfs. In 1812, they were allowed to trade in every kind of merchandise, not only that which they themselves grew or manufactured, and in 1818 they received permission to build (with government license) factories. The latter provision led to a remarkable burgeoning of peasant industrial activity, especially textile manufacture.

Nicholas I expanded the serfs' economic rights by allowing them in 1848 to purchase unpopulated rural and urban real estates with their masters' permission but in their own name. Such immovable assets became the peasant's individual property as distinct from the rest of the household belongings, which were the joint property of its members.[124] Nicholas also restricted further the landlord's powers to inflict punishment on his serfs.

In private conversation, Nicholas expressed himself more than once in favor of abolishing serfdom: in 1834 he told one of his ministers that not a single one of his officials favored serfdom, and that some members of the imperial family totally opposed it.[125] Still, he did not dare to do away with it. There was the opposition from both landlords and bureaucrats, but that was not the only obstacle he faced. The difficulty

Sbornik Imperatorskogo Russkogo Istoricheskogo Obshchestva, LXXIV (1891), 199. In November 1827, a commission appointed by Nicholas I discussed a project which called for liberating the serfs also without land. Ibid., 198–201.

ran deeper. Catherine's Noble Charter of 1785 created a major impediment to the abolition of serfdom in that it recognized the land which the serfs tilled as landlord property. Positive as this measure was in the long run in promoting the cause of liberty, in the short run it had the contrary effect. Nicholas frequently reaffirmed that the landlords' land belonged to them.[126] Such was the law. At the same time, it was recognized in government circles that it would be both unjust and socially dangerous to liberate the serfs without land. Count Kiselev, the statesman responsible for reforming the status of state peasants under Nicholas I, argued in 1842 that it was as risky to transfer landlord property to the peasants as to liberate them without land.[127]

The edict emancipating serfs, issued in February 1861 after lengthy deliberations in which landlord representatives participated, was inspired by political as well as moral considerations. Russia's humiliating defeat in the Crimean War, in which she was beaten on her own soil by the armies of the allegedly "decadent" West, brought home to the country's ruling circles that Russia could not remain a great power as long as the bulk of her population remained in bondage, devoid of any legal and economic rights. In an oft-quoted remark, the new tsar, Alexander II, told his nobles that it was better to solve the issue of serfdom peacefully, from above, than have it solved violently from below.

The Emancipation Edict immediately deprived *dvoriane* of personal authority over their peasants. The ex-serf now became a legal person, able to sue and be sued, to amass every kind of property, and (after 1864) to participate in elections to newly created local self-government boards. Even so, his civil rights were circumscribed. The commune now acquired many of the powers over the peasants previously enjoyed by their masters, including the authority to restrict their movement and to punish them in accord with local customary law. This was done mainly to ensure that the peasants met their fiscal obligations to the state—both Peter the Great's soul tax and the new "redemption payments," mortgage premiums owed the government for reimbursing the landlord for the land he had been compelled to turn over to his ex-serfs. In this manner, the commune was officially recognized as an agent of the state in place of the landlord.

The land which the ex-serfs received (roughly that portion of the landlord's estate which under serfdom they had tilled for themselves) was given not to the individual households but to the communes, which acquired the status of juridical persons. The authorities were ambivalent on the issue of private property, some officials advocating that the land be sold to the emancipated serfs outright. The majority of the members of the commissions drafting the Emancipation Edict favored such a course as more conducive to efficient production, but they were overruled, partly for ideological reasons (the influence of Slavophile intellectuals who admired the commune) and partly for practical ones.[128] In the end, it was the commune that received title to the land, because such was considered the safer course. But it was assumed that once the emancipated serfs had paid up their mortgage debt to the government, the land would become their private property.

The Emancipation Edict made provisions allowing the peasant to withdraw from the commune and set up a family farm, but they were hedged with so many formalities that very few took advantage of them and in 1893 they were, for all practical purposes, eliminated. The peasants, of course, could and did purchase, sometimes individually but more often in partnerships, freehold land, mostly from the impoverished gentry. But the bulk of their holdings was communal land and not private property, which they could neither bequeath nor sell. This meant that the vast majority of Russians neither then nor later knew private property in their country's most important productive asset, arable soil.

The nation's antiproprietary culture received reinforcement from the fact that within the basic peasant social unit, the household, the family's assets were jointly owned. A peasant family did not think in terms of "I" or "we" in regard to the land, livestock, or implements. Since to the peasant land was not a commodity but the material basis of life, he did not distinguish between the subject and the object of land ownership: between him or them who own and that which they own. This was not a peculiar Russian attitude but one common to peasants everywhere; it is what differentiates the peasant from the farmer.* Although the head of the Russian household—the *khoiziain* or *bol'shak*—was the nominal owner of its assets (tools, purchased land, etc.), custom viewed them as the common property of the family. The household head was in effect not the owner but the manager of family property, for which reason he could be removed for incompetence or wastefulness: this practice was recognized by Russian courts.[129]

The entire economic environment in which he lived made the Russian peasant a *social* radical and a *political* conservative. He was socially revolutionary because he wanted all private land to be confiscated and distributed among the communes.† But he was politically

*See the remarks concerning the attitude to land of the Canadian Eskimos in Chapter II above (p. 83).

†It may appear contradictory that the peasant bought private land and, at the same time, denied that land could be privately owned. The contradiction can be resolved by

conservative because, acknowledging the tsar as the ultimate proprietor of Russia, he expected him to do the confiscating and distributing. Receptive to Socialist Revolutionary and Bolshevik propaganda, which promised him what he wanted, politically he was antidemocratic, wanting a "strong hand" at the helm of the government. He treated with suspicion liberals and democrats because he thought they opposed a national repartition. In the final analysis, he presented a great obstacle to the democratization of Russia.

9. *The rise of a moneyed economy*

If private property in land came to Russia in the latter part of the eighteenth century, industrial and commercial capital became a serious factor only a century later. Although nonagricultural fortunes had existed even in Muscovy, there was no institutionalized credit and therefore no true capitalism.[130] Prior to the 1860s, Russia lacked private banks. Except for small-scale lending, usually against landed collateral, and a few banking establishments run by foreigners, credit operations were a monopoly of state institutions, such as the Noble Bank, which extended mortgages to *dvoriane,* and the Commercial Bank, which provided government credit to merchants. The tsarist government, especially under Nicholas I, discouraged industrial development and railroad transport, from fear that they would have unsettling social effects.

The Crimean War changed the attitude to capital as it changed perceptions of serfdom. The governments of Alexander II and, even more, of his successor, Alexander III, aware that under modern conditions great-power status required economic development, vigorously promoted banking, industry, and railroad construction. After 1864, commercial banks experienced impressive growth. The adoption of the Gold Standard in 1897, which made the ruble convertible into bullion, stimulated foreign investment in Russian industries, mines, and financial enterprises. The 1890s were a decade of unprecedented industrial growth: Russia's rate is estimated to have been the most rapid in the world at the time. Between 1892 and 1914, approximately one-half of

---

allowing that the peasant recognized titles to land which the owner cultivated in person. He did not recognize it as an abstract right which entitled the owner to do with property as he wished.

all the capital invested in Russian enterprises came from abroad, principally France.[131]

Sergei Witte, who served first as minister of finance and then as prime minister, was the driving force behind these developments. He believed that a country which failed to attain economic independence could not aspire to great-power status, and that economic independence in the modern world required intensive industrialization. The monarchy adopted this view, but not without misgivings, because, from its vantage point, capitalist development had undesirable side effects. Foreign and domestic investors, interested primarily in profit and the security of their investments, increasingly made decisions affecting the lives of Russians at the expense of the autocratic government and its bureaucracy. They wanted stability, and stability, from their experience, meant representative government, civil rights, and the rule of law. The modern economy confronted the tsarist regime with the choice of diminished world influence or diminished domestic authority. Tsarism reluctantly opted for the second alternative.

By the beginning of the twentieth century the tsarist government was resolutely committed to the principle of private property. Where it had once feared private property as a threat to its power and the social order, the rise of the revolutionary movement in the second half of the nineteenth century made it appear a guarantor of stability.

Ivan Goremykin, a bureaucrat of the old school, a convinced monarchist, addressing in 1906 the State Duma, Russia's first parliament, made the case for private property by rejecting the land reform bill introduced by the liberal Constitutional Democratic Party, which called for compulsory expropriation of large estates. "The government," Goremykin said,

> cannot acknowledge the right of property to land for some and, at the same time, deny it to others. Nor can the government repudiate the right of private property in land without, at the same time, repudiating it for all other forms of property. The principle of the inalienability and inviolability of property is in the entire world and on all levels of social development the cornerstone of a people's welfare and society's progress. It is the foundation of statehood, without which its very existence is unthinkable.[132]

Goremykin was merely echoing the sentiments of his sovereign, Nicholas II, who also rejected proposals popular even among his ministers calling for the compulsory transfer of land from private owners to peasants, on the grounds that "[p]rivate property must remain inviolable."[133]

Peter Stolypin, Goremykin's successor and Russia's prime minister from 1906 to 1911, saw with particular clarity how privatizing peasant land could create a conservative rural class and, at the same time, take the wind out of the sails of radical agitation. In 1907, he passed as an emergency measure a law that enabled peasants to claim title to their communal allotment and withdraw from the commune. His hope of creating a large class of independent farmers was rather disappointed, however, because the majority of the peasants who availed themselves of the new law, living in smaller and poorer households, had a hard time making ends meet: they took title only to sell the land. The farmsteads that emerged from the Stolypin legislation were viewed by the communal peasants—eight-tenths of Russia's rural inhabitants—as thieves of common property. In 1917–18 they compelled the farmstead owners to surrender their land and rejoin the communes. At the same time, the peasants seized estates held by private persons and associations, placing them in the communal pool. By 1928, the eve of "collectivization," 99 percent of arable land in Russia was communally held. Thus private property in land had a short and tenuous existence in Russia and then disappeared once again.

Political democracy, of a limited kind, came to Russia in 1905–6 as the result of pressures on the tsarist regime brought about by defeat in the war with Japan, the growing restlessness of the peasantry, and a campaign for constitutional government launched by the liberal elite. The government made political concessions with the greatest reluctance, not only because it was loath to yield power but also because it believed that in Russia democracy would result in the breakdown of law and order. In October 1905, confronted with the threat of a general strike organized by the liberals, it finally yielded, granting the country a constitution and parliament, and the population basic civil rights. The surrender did not truly pacify Russia, because the intelligentsia, liberal as well as radical, wanted much more power, while the monarchy, regretting its concessions as soon as order was reestablished, did its best to sabotage the new constitutional order. The hostility intensified during World War I, fueled by military disasters and incompetent management of the home front, hampering the war effort as in no other belligerent country and ultimately bringing the entire tsarist regime down.

10. *Concluding remarks*

The historical record of Russia demonstrates that private property is a necessary but not sufficient basis of liberty. In the last century and a half of its existence, the tsarist regime scrupulously observed the rights of property first in respect to land and then capital. Thus the Decembrists, nobles of some of Russia's most prestigious aristocratic families, who in 1825 mutinied against the tsar, were punished with execution or exile, but their estates were not touched, as they would have been a century earlier. Alexander Herzen, who, having emigrated to Western Europe, in his publications relentlessly castigated tsarism, had no difficulty drawing a handsome income from his Russian estates transmitted through European banks. And Lenin's mother, one of whose sons had been executed for an attempt on the tsar's life and other children imprisoned and exiled, received until death the pension due her as the widow of a government official.

And yet, while respecting their property rights, the tsarist government in the nineteenth and early twentieth centuries showed little respect for its subjects' civil rights and none for their political rights. Until their liberation in 1861, serfs were chattel whose landlords could have them whipped, sent for hard labor to Siberia, or inducted for life into the army. Others, including nobles, could be arrested and deprived of freedom (in violation of the 1785 Noble Charter) for suspected political crimes by administrative procedures. Society could not translate its growing economic power into safeguards of personal liberty because all the political and administrative levers were in the hands of the autocracy.

Political freedom and civil rights came to Russia in 1905–6 not as a natural outgrowth of people's power exercised through ownership and law, but as a desperate attempt on the part of the monarchy to thwart a looming revolution. As soon as the revolution broke out anyway a decade later, all the freedoms and rights, along with property, disappeared into thin air, because they had the shallowest of foundations. Russia's experience indicates that freedom cannot be legislated: it has to grow gradually, in close association with property and law. For while acquisitiveness is natural, respect for the property—and the liberty—of others is not. It has to be inculcated until it sinks such deep roots in the people's consciousness that it is able to withstand all efforts to crush it.

5

PROPERTY IN THE TWENTIETH CENTURY

> Private property once may have been conceived as a barrier to government power, but today that barrier is easily overcome, almost for the asking. . . . Under the present law the institution of private property places scant limitation upon the size and direction of the government activities that are characteristic of the modern welfare state.
>
> —Richard A. Epstein[1]

> We need a Constitution for the Welfare State.
>
> —Charles A. Reich[2]

Of all ages in history, the twentieth century has been the least favorable to the institution of private property, and this for both economic and political reasons.

The broad conception of property as encompassing the rights to life and freedom as well as goods arose in seventeenth-century England and became common wisdom in the English-speaking world in the eighteenth century. At the time, the majority of English-speakers were economically independent individuals and families, earning their livelihood either from freehold farming, retail trade, or artisanship. Locke's vindication of property as reward for the application of personal labor to ownerless objects described accurately the situation that prevailed in his time in England. Similarly, Jefferson's ideal of a republic resting on the labor and loyalty of a class of landowning, self-reliant farmers reflected the American reality of his time, when perhaps as many as 80 percent or more of white Americans lived on their own farms. But this situation did not last: it began to change in the course of the nineteenth century and receded into memory in the twentieth. Large-scale, capitalist agriculture together with the growth of manufacture and corporate enterprise led to a steady shrinking of self-employment and a corresponding expansion of wage-earning. A wage earner has no access to productive assets; his wages are not property because his job is not assured. The immense wealth created by the capitalist mode of production, combined with fear of social unrest, has induced modern democracies to institute welfare policies in the form of unemployment insurance, old-age pensions, and numerous other "entitlements." In the opinion of some scholars, these benefits offset the decline in private ownership—they are, in effect, rights and as such represent "property."* But even if this point is conceded, they resemble the conditional possession of the feudal era rather than genuine property inasmuch as they are not disposable assets.

The modern world has witnessed restrictions not only of property rights but also of liberties historically associated with them. Exploiting the social turmoil caused by two world wars and the intervening Great Depression, demagogues in many parts of the world, but especially in Europe, have resorted to socialist slogans to justify the expropriation or subordination of private property to the state. Where they have succeeded, the population became to a high degree dependent for economic survival on the goodwill of its rulers. This occurred in Communist Russia and China, as well as in National Socialist Germany, and their various emulators around the globe. The result was loss of freedom as well as slaughter on a scale never before known. The massacres were legitimized by political doctrines of a new kind demanding the physical "liquidation" of whole categories of people designated as belonging to the "wrong" social class, race, or ethnic group.

The simultaneous violation of property rights and destruction of human lives was not mere coincidence, for, as we have stressed, what a man is, what he does, and what he owns are of a piece, so that the assault on his belongings is an assault also on his individuality and his right to life.

But the well-intentioned measures of democratic social welfare have also encroached on both property and freedom—more elusively, and certainly less violently, but in the long run perhaps no less dangerously.

*Charles A. Reich in *Yale Law Journal* 73, No. 5 (1964), 785–87; C. B. Macpherson in *Dissent*, No. 24 (Winter 1977), 72–77. Indeed, the Supreme Court in the *Goldberg v. Kelly* case ruled that welfare was an "entitlement" and as such could not be denied to the recipient without due process. Michael Tanner, *The End of Welfare* (Washington, D.C., 1996), 54.

1. *Communism*

Totalitarianism, like democracy, is an ideal—an evil and destructive one, but still an ideal in the sense of being an objective so ambitious that it can never be fully attained. Democracy calls for government ruled by the people and subject to laws: in reality, however, democratic regimes are dominated by elites who devise ways of shaping and bending the law in their favor. Totalitarianism aspires to be the very opposite of democracy: it strives to atomize society and establish complete control over it, paying no heed to its wishes and acknowledging no law superior to the government's will. And yet, in practice, even the most extreme totalitarian regime, that of Stalin, did not succeed in altogether ignoring popular opinion and controlling every aspect of its citizens' lives.

The ultimate objective of totalitarianism is the concentration of all public authority in the hands of a self-appointed and self-perpetuating corps of the elect who call themselves a "party" but resemble rather an order, members of which owe loyalty only to their leaders and each other. This objective presupposes control, direct or indirect, depending on the circumstances, over the country's economic resources. Property which by its very nature sets limits to state authority is either abolished or transformed into possession contingent on satisfactory service to the ruling party.

Of all the totalitarian regimes, the Soviet Union came closest to realizing the Communist ideal of a propertyless society. On taking power in October 1917, Lenin and his associates had no clue of the function that property and law perform in economic life: all they knew from reading socialist literature was that they provided the basis of political power and social exploitation. Inspired by utopian literature and the doctrines of Marx and Engels, impressed by the successes of the quasi-socialized economies of wartime Europe, especially imperial Germany, the Bolsheviks proceeded at once to expropriate the private wealth of the citizenry—the nobility, church, and "bourgeoisie" to begin with, and ultimately the entire population.[3] A decree passed by the Second Congress of Soviets in October 1917, handpicked by the Bolsheviks to give their coup d'état the facade of legitimacy, abolished private property in land. Drafted by Lenin, the decree "socialized" all land, although for the time being it made an exception for the communal holdings of peasants, whom the insecure new regime did not wish to antagonize. Even so, the assault on private property in land got underway in earnest in the summer of 1918 when unrestrained force was employed to seize from communal peasants such grain as the government designated "surplus." In the case of "kulaks"—formally defined as peasants who hired labor but, as applied in practice, meaning all rural inhabitants who actively defied the Bolsheviks—their entire grain crop was to be expropriated, and some were ordered by Lenin to be publicly hanged by the hundreds as an example to the rest of the peasantry. Commerce in cereals and other agricultural produce was outlawed. Such actions, unthinkable even under serfdom, embroiled Soviet Russia in the most ferocious civil war in the country's history, in which hundreds of thousands of Red Army soldiers fought pitched battles against hundreds of thousands of peasants.[4]

Lenin pursued the expropriation of private property with fanatical zeal and unhesitating brutality, because he had been persuaded by Marx's analyses of the Paris Commune that all previous attempts at social revolution had failed by stopping halfway. Between 1917 and 1920, all forms of private property, except for communal land and modest personal effects, were nationalized. Trade, both retail and wholesale, became a state monopoly. Urban real estate was expropriated on behalf of the state. Lenin gave instructions that notarized deeds of ownership of land, real estate, factories, etc. be pulped.[5] In June 1918, large industrial establishments became national property; in the next two years, medium-sized and small manufacturing enterprises, including artisan workshops, suffered the same fate. This entire network of manufacturing establishments came under the supervision of the Supreme Council of the National Economy, whose responsibility it was to impose on Russia's nonagricultural sector a single economic plan. By 1920, private banks were liquidated and replaced by a single state-owned and state-run "People's Bank." Money was effectually abolished by the device of printing unlimited quantities of banknotes. In 1923, prices had risen 100 million times compared to tsarist times, and paper money lost nearly all value. This deliberate inflation liquidated accumulated savings, the ruble equivalent of billions of dollars which Russians had held in banks or at home.

There is ample evidence that this whole ambitious effort to introduce into Soviet Russia a Communist economy failed dismally. In 1920, industrial production, compared to 1913, fell by 82 percent. Grain production declined by some 40 percent, bringing the country to the edge of famine. Notwithstanding savage harassment by the political police, a black market in produce and manufactured goods flourished. Indeed, it is estimated that had it not been for the black market in food, Russia's cities in the years 1918–20 would have starved, for the official rations, often no more than a couple of ounces of bread a day, satisfied but a fraction of the population's needs.

Nevertheless, the new rulers persisted in such disastrous economic policies, later labeled "War Communism," even after their bankruptcy had become evident to all but the most fanatical. This they did for two reasons. They genuinely believed that the capitalist system, driven by personal profit, was inherently inefficient, and that a centrally run, planned economy would prove incomparably more productive. Secondly, they associated private property with political power. They feared that leaving intact even pockets of private wealth would allow enough citizens to escape state control to organize an opposition. Then, as later, monopoly on political power loomed more important in their eyes than economic productivity, the more so that, being complete masters of the country's resources, they could always divert such resources where they were most needed to shore up their authority.

In early 1921, however, the Communist leadership was finally forced to retreat. By that time, the countrywide peasant rebellion was joined by mutinies in the Red Navy and strikes in Petrograd factories. Production of consumer goods had reached a nadir. The country was seething; the methods of economic management put in place to ensure the Bolshevik dictatorship now threatened to undermine it. Realist that he was, Lenin decided on a temporary and limited withdrawal. The New Economic Policy (NEP), inaugurated in 1921, affected mainly agriculture. The peasants were acknowledged as owners of their produce and required to pay a set tax in lieu of the unlimited contributions of alleged "surplus." Any produce they had left over after meeting their obligations to the state they were free to sell on the open market. These measures promptly pacified the countryside. Assured that their crops would not be arbitrarily seized, peasants expanded the sown acreage, and by 1928, Russia's cereal production almost attained its pre-1914 levels. Even so, the turnabout in agrarian policy came too late to save the country from the worst famine in its history. It struck in 1921–22, following a severe drought. Coming on top of self-restricted production and shortages of seed grain, it claimed over five million lives.

The NEP also eased the state's hold on commerce and manufacture. The government retained the monopoly on wholesale trade and exports, on heavy industry, banking, and transport—the so-called "commanding heights" of the economy. But it did make concessions in the field of consumer goods. Unprofitable enterprises were leased; it was permissible to hire labor. The idea of a moneyless economy was abandoned and a new, stable ruble, based on gold, was put in circulation.

These measures aroused hopes among many in Russia and abroad that the country's rulers had abandoned communism. Drawing analogies with the history of the French Revolution, such optimists talked of a Communist "Thermidor," referring to the month of the French revolutionary calendar (July–August 1794) which saw the Jacobins overthrown and France launched on her slow evolution toward "bourgeois" stability. But such historical analogies proved false and the hopes they aroused illusory. Whereas in France the Jacobins had been toppled from power and guillotined, their Russian counterparts remained fully in control. They regarded the concessions to capitalism as temporary measures which they would revoke as soon as conditions permitted.

The "socialist offensive" resumed in 1928, following Stalin's decisive victory over his political rivals. Its linchpin was agrarian collectivization. The prosperity of the village gave the Communist authorities cause for anxiety, for it meant that their authority in the countryside, where lived 75–80 percent of the Soviet population, never strong to begin with, could slip from their hands altogether. The process of collectivization, originally projected by Lenin, nationalized all agricultural land: the communal strips, previously cultivated by households, were consolidated and placed under state management. Peasants turned into wage earners, paid in money and produce, and the entire harvest became state property. The only property in land allowed to the collective farm peasants was small garden plots adjoining their cottages, where they could grow fruits and vegetables and raise chickens and even some livestock for personal consumption or sale at (state-regulated) collective-farm markets. Peasants deemed politically unreliable as well as those who actively resisted the expropriation of their lands and livestock were sent by the millions to hard-labor camps, where most of them perished. It was a catastrophe without parallel in previous world history: no government had ever inflicted such destruction of lives and resources on its own people—a fact hardly assimilated by the outside world to this day. Concurrently, all private shops and manufacturing facilities of the NEP era were nationalized and many of their owners sent to hard-labor camps.

When the massive expropriation was completed, the state sector of the USSR was officially reported to account for 99.3 percent of the country's national income.[6] The government's control of resources made possible gigantic crash programs centered on military hardware, and ultimately defense allocations absorbed some 25 percent of the gross domestic product and the bulk of Russia's industries came to work directly or indirectly for the armed forces.

The elimination of private property ensured the security of the one-party apparatus. Essentially, the entire population of the Soviet Union—as well as that of those other countries which, after World War II, either were forced to adopt or on their own followed its example—worked for the government. This meant that any suspicion of antigovernment activity or even questionable loyalty could lead to dismissal or at least demotion of the suspect and his immediate family by the state, the country's sole employer. To survive, one had to collaborate. Along with the political police, endowed with unlimited powers over the lives of Soviet citizens, the monopoly on resources and employment was what made possible the totalitarian system. It also made possible prodigious military efforts which enabled the Soviet Union first to crush the German invaders and then to blackmail its own wartime allies.

But all this was achieved at enormous cost, which in the end proved self-defeating. The regime managed, with relative ease, to neutralize overt political resistance: apart from a relatively small body of heroic dissidents, the population conformed, at any rate outwardly. The price was a decay of national vitality. Except for criminal activity, individual efforts did not yield commensurate rewards, with the result that the population at large sank into the kind of collective apathy which William James anticipated when he wrote that "in every case [of the loss of possessions] there remains . . . a sense of the shrinkage of our personality, a partial conversion of ourselves to nothingness. . . ." After a temporary surge immediately following World War II, economic productivity kept on declining. The only sector of the economy which showed vigor was private farming: the 33 million private plots belonging to collective farm households, averaging 0.6 acre and constituting 1.5 percent of the country's cultivated area, furnished the postwar Soviet Union with nearly one-third of its foodstuffs. In 1979, they provided 30 percent of the meat, vegetables, and milk, 33 percent of the eggs, and 59 percent of the potatoes.[7] Various experiments were tried after Stalin's death to combine private initiative with state ownership in agriculture, but they came to naught because of the opposition of rural bureaucrats whose privileged status they threatened.

The central planning system also proved incapable of keeping up with the progress of technology, most strikingly in the field of computers, which in the free world revolutionized the storage, analysis, and flow of information. The Soviet leadership was slow to realize the impact of this technological revolution on warfare; they did so only after repeated setbacks of the weaponry in the hands of their own troops as well as those of their allies. In the 1980s, the prospect of the USSR's keeping up with its potential adversaries in the quality and use of weaponry began to look hopeless. Given the overriding importance attached by Moscow to military might for both domestic and international reasons, such a situation could not be tolerated. Hence, some of the most reactionary elements in the country, among them the generals, agreed on a program of economic reform. When it transpired that economic reform was not feasible without some degree of political reform, they ventured on this course as well. And it soon turned out that the Communist system was of a piece, that it could not be partially reformed. It unraveled at a speed that arouses astonishment to this day.

There obviously were many reasons for the collapse of the Soviet Union in late 1991, an event unparalleled in world history—an empire under peacetime conditions, disintegrating in a matter of weeks. But if, as there are good grounds to believe, the prime reason for this collapse was the faltering economy, then it is not unreasonable to conclude that the absence of private property was a major and possibly the decisive factor. It affected economic performance in two ways. The citizenry lacked incentives to produce beyond the minimum, since its basic needs were guaranteed whereas doing more brought no significant rewards and could even bring penalties in the form of higher production quotas. But even if, in disregard of such discouragement, a Soviet citizen displayed enterprise, he ran afoul of the bureaucratic apparatus whose self-interest required the stifling of every independent initiative. Thus the concentration of all economic resources in the hands of the state undermined the nation's work ethic and inhibited innovation. Far from making the communist economy the world's most efficient, as the Bolsheviks had once expected, the state monopoly on productive resources made it hidebound and lethargic. The regime died of anemia: the elimination of private ownership, pursued with a fanatical zeal and buttressed by the ruling elite's self-interest, led to the withering of personality, the prime mover of progress. The inevitability of such an outcome had been foreseen long before communism was tried. David Hume, writing in the late eighteenth century, predicted the result of attempts to impose "perfect equality":

> Render possessions ever so equal, men's different degrees of art, care, and industry, will immediately break that equality. Or

if you check these virtues, you reduce society to the most extreme indigence; and, instead of preventing want and beggary in a few, render it unavoidable to the whole community.[8]

Once the power of the bureaucratic behemoth was broken—and this happened in the second half of 1991 following the abortive putsch of the Communist diehards—the new leadership of Russia proceeded to privatize the economy. The same happened in the liberated countries of Eastern Europe. The transition from a command to a market economy proved immensely difficult, because the population had no experience in running private enterprises and because the old Communist elite lost no time in appropriating state assets. To make matters worse, the collapse of the Communist system caused the complete breakdown of a welfare structure that had guaranteed 100 percent of the population's elementary needs, leaving the citizenry to fend for itself in a bewildering world of competitive interests. Approximately one-third of the population, including many of the elderly, the unskilled, and the uneducated, suffered extreme hardship.* Still, privatization continued at a rapid pace, and in the mid-1990s, between two-thirds and three-quarters of Russia's gross domestic product came from the private sector. Like so much that happens in Russia, it was a process unparalleled in its scope. The results of the 1996 presidential elections indicated that the majority of Russians reject communism and the denial of private property associated with it. Indeed, the suppression for so many years of normal possessive instincts has led in formerly Communist countries to the eruption of acquisitiveness in particularly unattractive forms.

Thus, the most audacious attempt in human history to abolish private property has ended in disaster. It is unlikely to be repeated as long as the memory of that calamity remains fresh.

2. *Fascism and National Socialism*

In an effort to differentiate themselves from the nationalist, anti-Communist totalitarian regimes that sprang up in interwar Europe, regimes with which their own regime had embarrassingly much in common and often competed for the same constituencies, Communist propagandists redefined the term "fascism" to designate any government

*As we will note below, a similar proportion of U.S. citizens with similar characteristics depends almost entirely or largely on government largesse dispensed through welfare programs. Present-day Russia lacks the means to provide such services.

opposed to communism—specifically, Mussolini's Italy and Hitler's Germany, but, when the occasion called for it, also the United States and the other democracies. In this usage, any individual, group, or government that was not Communist or sympathetic to communism was actually or potentially "fascist." Such a Manichean definition was entirely inappropriate: there were vast differences between Fascist Italy and National Socialist Germany, not to speak of the unbridgeable chasm separating both from the United States.

The central argument of those who reject the concept of totalitarianism as a generic term for the USSR, Fascist Italy, and Nazi Germany holds that in contrast to the Soviet Union the latter two regimes allowed private property. This feature, in their eyes, means that they qualify as "conservative" and "bourgeois" regimes more like the "capitalist" ones than like "proletarian" Russia. The usage was sanctioned by the Communist International, which in the early 1920s defined "fascism" as the highest and final phase of "finance capitalism"—capitalism in its death throes.[9] Moscow's insistence that "fascism" was the polar opposite of "communism" found wide acceptance in socialist and liberal circles in the West.

Both Fascist Italy and Nazi Germany did indeed allow—or, more accurately, tolerated—private property. However, it was "property" in a peculiar and very restricted sense—not the virtually untrammeled private ownership of Roman law and nineteenth-century Europe, but rather conditional possession, under which the state, the owner of last resort, reserved to itself the right to interfere with and even confiscate assets which, in its judgment, were unsatisfactorily used. The economic policies of Mussolini's Italy and Hitler's Germany resembled the "state socialism" which Lenin wanted to institute in Soviet Russia upon coming to power, under which private enterprise would work for the government—an idea Lenin was forced to abandon under the pressure of the "Left Communists."[10] This system was successfully introduced in Italy and Germany because corporate business proved itself in these countries, as it did elsewhere (including the United States), to be accommodating, willing to submit to any kind of control and regulation as long as it could salvage its profits.

In dealing with Fascist Italy, it must be borne in mind that Benito Mussolini, its founder and leader, rose to political prominence before World War I as a socialist of the most radical kind, a close analogue of Lenin. Like Lenin, he doubted the revolutionary commitment of the working class and believed in a social revolution directed by an intellectual elite. Like Lenin, too, he despised nonrevolutionary, reform-minded socialists. His teacher and inspirer was Marx. In 1912 he succeeded in expelling from the Italian Socialist Party its moderate elements, which earned him the praise of Lenin; at this time he became editor of the party's official organ, the newspaper *Avanti!* In other words, the ideology of the founder of the Fascist Party was rooted in revolutionary socialism, equally antagonistic to conservatism and liberalism.

Before August 1914, Mussolini had opposed Italy's involvement in the looming world war, threatening civil violence if the government joined the belligerents. However, the spectacle of patriotic frenzy that seized Europe in the summer of 1914 convinced him that nationalism was a more potent force than class allegiance. In November 1914, to the surprise and dismay of his comrades, he came out in favor of Italy's intervention and enlisted in the army. This about-face resulted in Mussolini's expulsion from the Italian Socialist Party, but he continued to think of himself as a socialist until the middle of 1919, when, unable to regain the favor of his onetime associates, he founded the Fascist Party. This party initially adopted a revolutionary stance, agitating for industrial strikes and other forms of violence, seeking to outbid the socialists in exploiting the unrest that followed the advent of peace. The original program of the Fascists (1919) was radical and revolutionary. Mussolini's failure by these tactics to recapture leadership of the socialist movement, which adopted a pro-Communist stance, forced him to formulate a program of his own that blended socialism and nationalism. From 1920 onward, he depicted Italy as a "proletarian" nation exploited by hostile "plutocratic" countries determined to deny her her rightful place under the sun.[11] The true class struggle, according to Fascist doctrine, was the struggle between nations. Fascism strove to surmount narrow class allegiances: all classes had to subordinate their private interests to those of the nation and collaborate against the external enemy.

The propertied were no exception to this rule. Mussolini acknowledged the principle of private property, although not as a sacrosanct right but as a privilege bestowed by the state. Consonant with this philosophy, he applied heavy pressure on private enterprise. In the 1920s, he arrogated to himself the authority to interfere with the market, "correcting" profits and compelling business firms to recognize trade unions as an equal partner. On some occasions, the Fascist government replaced the management of private corporations. The self-serving Communist notion of "fascism" as an expression of "high capitalism" is therefore widely off the mark: it was a movement which placed national interest above private interest, and regulated business as much as it did labor. Indeed, in a speech in May 1934 Mussolini informed the Chamber of Deputies that three-quarters of Italy's industrial and agricultural economy were in the hands of the state which, he added, created conditions that would enable him to introduce into Italy either "State Capitalism" or "State Socialism" whenever he thought it necessary.[12]

Hitler did not have Mussolini's revolutionary socialist background. He admitted to learning much from the "Marxists," but this was mainly in the realm of crowd manipulation; of their theories he knew next to nothing. Nevertheless, he shared the socialist hatred of and contempt for the "bourgeoisie" and "capitalism" and exploited for his purposes the powerful socialist traditions of Germany. The adjectives "socialist" and "worker" in the official name of Hitler's party ("The Nationalist-Socialist German Workers' Party") had not merely propagandistic value. According to a leading authority on the history of Nazism, its ideology in the early years "contained a thoroughly revolutionary kernel within an irrational, violence-oriented political ideology. It was in no sense a mere expression of reactionary tendencies: it grew out of the world of workers and trade unionists."[13] On the eve of its coming to power, industrial workers composed nearly one-third of the Nazi Party membership and constituted its largest occupational group.[14] The party adopted the Red Flag, declared May 1 a paid national holiday, and required its members to address one another as *Genossen* or "comrades." On one occasion, in the midst of World War II, Hitler even declared that "basically National Socialism and Marxism are the same."[15] "Capitalism" was identified with "world Jewry" and contrasted with Nazi Germany, which allegedly had a "folkish" (*völkische*) character.[16] Hitler's ultimate social objective was a hierarchical society in which "aristocratic" status would be acquired by personal "heroism" demonstrated in battle.[17] It was this radical element in Nazi doctrine and practice which, contrary to the widespread myth that big business financed Hitler's climb to power, caused corporate executives to be suspicious of Hitler and withhold from him significant support.[18] The party's Twenty-five-Point Program, adopted in 1920, anticipated the ideas of the "welfare state" which would be formulated during World War II in the Beveridge Report (see below) and adopted by the British Labour Party in 1945. It called on the state to ensure full employment, nationalize trusts, take care of the aged, provide every citizen with an opportunity to acquire a higher education, offer support for the schooling of children from poor families, improve public health, and in all spheres of life place the interests of the "community" above those of the individual.[19]

Given their identification with the ideal of an ethnic community and the supreme value assigned to the nation (or race), it is not surprising that the Nazis refused to acknowledge fundamental rights of any kind, private property included. Law was for them—as for the Communists and Fascists—a tool of state power: lawful was that and only that which benefited the "people," by which term they understood the Nazi Party, its embodiment.[20] The economy's mission was to serve the state: specifically, as in the case of the Soviet Union after 1928, to prepare the country for the coming world war, which was to solve Germany's most urgent problems by securing her "living space." This overriding objective was to be achieved by blending public and private interests in a way that gave the state the ultimate say in the partnership. A 1935 official statement, behind the fuzzy language meant to reassure private interests, suggested how this was to be achieved:

> The power economy will not be run by the state, but by (private) entrepreneurs acting under their own free and unrestricted responsibility. . . . The *state* limits itself to the function of *control*, which is, of course, *all-inclusive*. It further reserves [itself] the right of intervention . . . in order to enforce the supremacy of considerations of public interest.*

Within a month of taking control of the German government, the Nazis suspended constitutional guarantees of the inviolability of private property.[21] Property was to be respected, but only as long as the owner used it for the benefit of the nation and state: in the words of a Nazi theorist, "[P]roperty was . . . no longer a private affair but a kind of State concession, limited by the condition that it be put to 'correct' use."[22] Hitler put the matter as follows in an off-the-record conversation with a newspaper editor two years before assuming dictatorial powers:

> I want everyone to keep the property he has acquired for himself according to the principle: common good takes precedence over self-interest. But the state must retain control and each property

*Johannes Darge in *Der deutsche Volkswirt* 10 (December 20, 1935), 537, cited in Samuel Lurie, *Private Investment in a Controlled Economy: Germany, 1933–1939* (New York, 1947), 5n. Emphasis added. "Power economy" probably is a clumsy translation of the untranslatable because meaningless *Machtwirtschaft*.

> owner should consider himself an agent of the state. . . . The Third Reich will always retain its right to control the owners of property.[23]

On these grounds, the German dictator claimed the authority to "limit or expropriate property at will where this limitation or expropriation was consonant with the 'tasks of the community.' "[24] In a programmatic statement on the future of the German economy drafted in 1931, private ownership was even defined as the right of "usufruct," that is, the right to enjoy and profit from assets belonging to another, in this case, the state.*

The first victims of this policy were Jewish citizens whose assets were expropriated piecemeal until they had nothing left, following which they were expelled from the country or sent to their death.[25] A 1934 law allowed the state also to expropriate the belongings of Communists. There was no need to take such drastic measures in regard to "Aryan" entrepreneurs, because German businessmen collaborated, loyally if not always enthusiastically, in the rearmament drive that was Hitler's foremost concern. This explains why the Nazis never found it necessary to nationalize their economy. Similarly, large landed estates were left intact, in part to gain the support of the Junkers, and in part because they were considered more efficient than small farms.

Still, the economic freedom of private enterprise was severely curtailed. Inspired by Mussolini's corporate ideal, the Nazi state intervened on all levels of economic activity, regulating prices, wages, dividends, and investments, limiting competition, and settling labor disputes.[26] The overriding purpose of the whole structure of controls imposed on the German economy was harnessing it for the aggressive war which was Hitler's immediate objective. Like the Soviet Union, Nazi Germany turned into a society organized for the coming war in which private property could not be permitted to interfere with efficient

*Avraham Barkai, *Nazi Economics* (New Haven and London, 1990), 37. A legal theoretician of National Socialism provided the following discrepant gloss on this policy: "Property is another essential stance of the national (*völkisch*) regimen. For Marxist and Bolshevik doctrine property was theft, for which reason it was to be eliminated by the 'transfer of the means of production to society.' German socialism, the basis of the new constitution, in contrast to Marxist-Bolshevik theory, acknowledges property as a necessary component of the national arrangement of the community. But it rejects no less sharply the corrupt liberal concept of private property. . . . For German socialism . . . all property is common property (*Gemeingut*)." Ernst Huber, *Verfassungsrecht des Grossdeutschen Reiches*, 2nd ed. (Hamburg, 1939), 372–73.

economic mobilization.* On a number of occasions Hitler warned private enterprise in Germany, with reference to the Soviet planned economy, that it would either render to the state the services required or the state would take over.[27]

In 1933 the government issued the "Law on Compulsory Cartels," by virtue of which it assumed the right to consolidate enterprises as a means of regulating the market for their products and reducing competition. In time, Berlin forged hundreds of such compulsory cartels, which determined, under state guidance, what their member firms could produce and what prices they could charge: the normal practice until the end of 1941 was for enterprises to operate on a cost-plus basis, presenting government agencies with evidence of costs and then being allowed to add 3–6 percent profit.[28] In 1936, the office of the Reich's Commissar for Price Formation was created to ensure "economically just prices." The operations of the price mechanism of the open market were thus suspended.[29] The cartel law made new investment conditional on state approval.[30] State authorities also regulated dividend payments: a law issued in 1934 decreed that the profits to be distributed to stockholders were not to exceed 6 percent of the paid-in capital; another law of that year provided that any excess was to be invested in state bonds for future distribution.[31] Holders of municipal and other bonds were compelled to convert them into new issues carrying lower interest rates.[32] Private enterprise was constantly whipped into shape by complaints of "economic egoism" and tireless reminders that the interests of the community took precedence over those of the individual.†

By degrees, the Nazi government also introduced controls over the labor market, eventually (1939) forbidding the movement of workers from one employer to another.[33] Collective bargaining was abolished: wages, as well as hours and conditions of work, were set by the enterprises under the supervision of government officials ("labor trustees").

*It is estimated that on the eve of World II, in 1938–39, German military expenditures absorbed 61 percent of government outlays and 19.7 percent of the gross domestic product. Wolfram Fischer, *Deutsche Wirtschaftspolitik, 1918–1945*, 3rd ed. (Opladen, 1968), 68. This is nearly as great a percentage as in the Soviet Union at the time of its collapse in 1991.

†R. J. Overy, *War and Economy in the Third Reich* (Oxford, 1994), 99 and *passim*. Hermann Göring's state-owned Reichswerke, originally an iron and steel trust, became in time the largest economic enterprise in Europe, involved in iron, steel, coal, and ore mining, as well as machine building and shipping. It was an exception to the policy of controlling rather than replacing private business.

On the eve of World War II (1938), wages were frozen at the depression levels of 1932–33.[34]

An illustration of the Nazi attitude toward property can be found in legislation regulating the use and disposal of farmland. Although agriculture was a declining factor in the German economy, it had for the Nazis great symbolic value because of their mystique of the land (*Blut und Boden*) and the cult of ancient Germanic tribes.[35] It further figured prominently in their preparations for war, in which an assured supply of food was a matter of great importance. The right of owners of small and medium-sized farms to dispose of their property by testament was severely curtailed through the introduction in 1933 of entail in favor of a single heir designated by the father. Such farms could not be sold without court permission. A decree of 1937 stipulated that the owner of a farm that was not efficiently cultivated could be required to follow state orders and, if he failed to do so, compelled to turn his farm over to a trustee or lease it to a more competent farmer; in extreme situations, he could be deprived of his property. Land could be expropriated for "community" use with compensation, the latter term being interpreted in a very arbitrary fashion, without much regard for market prices. Last but not least, the government determined what crops the farmer could grow and how much of his cereal crop he had to deliver to state agencies.[36] In many ways, landownership in Nazi Germany came to resemble a public trust by virtue of which the titular owner had many duties but few rights.

> It was expedience, not ideological bias, that left property in the hands of its owners. . . . Investment was controlled, occupational freedom was dead, prices were fixed, every sector of the economy was, at worst, a victim, at best an accomplice of the [Nazi] regime. . . .
>
> A generation of Marxist and neo-Marxist mythology notwithstanding, probably never in peacetime has an ostensibly capitalist economy been directed as non- and even anti-capitalistically as the German economy between 1933 and 1939.[37]

The encroachments on property in the Third Reich in the 1930s were only a pale version of what was intended after ultimate victory.

The curtailment to the point of abolition of personal rights and freedoms in totalitarian states thus went hand in hand with the curtailment, to the point of abolition, of private property. The process progressed furthest in the Communist states, somewhat less far in Nazi Germany, and least so in Fascist Italy; but in all three countries the striving for total political power was accompanied by determined assaults on the rights of private ownership. The totalitarian experience confirms that just as freedom requires guarantees of property rights, so the striving for unlimited personal power over citizens demands the subversion of the citizen's authority over things, because the latter enables him to elude the state's all-encompassing grasp.

3. *The welfare state*

In contrast to totalitarian and other despotic regimes, democracies proclaim unqualified commitment to the principle of private property: never before have so many of the world's constitutions declared its inviolability. Reality, however, is different. The rights to property and the liberties associated with them are subverted by a variety of devices, some open and seemingly constitutional, others oblique and of dubious legality: the state, it turns out, takes even as it gives. (Since, in Plato's words, "Of whatever thing a man is a smart guardian of that he is also a smart thief.") The assault on property rights is not always apparent, because it is carried out in the name of "common good," an elastic concept, defined by those whose interests it serves.

This development was not generally anticipated. In the 1920s, Morris Cohen, a professor of philosophy at Columbia University, a scholar with broad interests, felt confident that under modern conditions the traditional distinction between sovereignty and property, between *imperium* and *dominium*, had largely lost relevance. The great capitalists, he believed, had acquired so much power over so great a part of the population that they had turned into *de facto* sovereigns: "There can be no doubt," he wrote, using a formula that invariably serves as a warning that there are grounds for doubt, "that our property laws do confer sovereign power on our captains of industry and even more so on our captains of finance."[38] This belief was quite prevalent in the first half of the twentieth century.

But, as so often happens, at the very instant when trends appear unstoppable they are already in retreat, having set in motion countervailing forces. In the twentieth century, a sea change has occurred in the way democratic governments view their responsibilities, a change which has removed any possibility of private interests overriding public ones and entrepreneurs assuming the role of "sovereigns."

In the eighteenth and nineteenth centuries, it was generally assumed that poverty was the consequence of human failings and hence outside the scope of legislative action. Thus the Report of the English Poor Law Commissioners of 1834, which led to the drastic curtailment of the traditional relief given to the poor in their own homes, asserted that the existing Poor Laws could not succeed in their purpose because they sought to repeal "that law of nature by which the effects of each man's improvidence or misconduct are borne by himself and his family."[39] An article in an influential English periodical of the mid-Victorian era scoffed at the idea then advanced by some liberals that "property has its duties as well as its rights" by countering: "Property has no intrinsic duties of charity. It is the poor who have duties, not the rich; and it is the first duty of the industrious poor not to be poor."[40] A century ago, a Democratic president, Grover Cleveland, would refuse to sign a bill offering emergency relief to Texan farmers struck by drought, on the grounds that such help was best left to private charity lest citizens become overdependent on the government's "paternal care." "I do not believe," he wrote in justifying his veto,

> that the power and duty of the general government ought to be extended to the relief of individual suffering which is in no manner properly related to the public service or benefit. . . . [T]he lesson should be constantly enforced that, though the people support the government, the government should not support the people.[41]

Such sentiments, bluntly stated and difficult to understand today, reflected not so much moral callousness as the conviction that poverty was self-inflicted, being nature's punishment for such vices as sloth, profligacy, and alcoholism, a conviction inherited from an era when unemployment was a marginal phenomenon, inflation was virtually unknown, and the victims of sickness and other misfortunes were expected to be taken care of by private charity. But ignorance of the facts also played a role, for statistical information on the nature and extent of poverty was not then available.[42]

In the 1880s, attitudes began to change. Governments came gradually to acknowledge that much poverty stemmed from causes beyond the control of its victims and that untrammeled property rights enabled the rich to oppress the poor. But politics also played a role, namely the desire to win electoral support of the newly enfranchised lower-class voters combined with fear of socialism. The result was a shift of stress in social policy: freedom and property came to carry less weight than social justice and equality.

The ground for the new approach to social problems was prepared by a profound change in the way the people in the West came to regard law and legislation. As previously noted, the European tradition dating from the Middle Ages held that the function of law and legislation was not to innovate but to uphold custom: the great English statesman of the mid-eighteenth century, William Pitt the Elder, the Earl of Chatham, who served as prime minister for eight years, is said to have carried through parliament not a single legislative act.[43] Law was seen as immutable because it was anchored in nature as well as the will of the community: legislators and jurists had merely to ascertain what it was and how to apply it to concrete situations. The emergence in the late eighteenth century of "historicism," which taught that human institutions were forever evolving, changed this traditional view of law. It came to be acknowledged that inasmuch as everything in human affairs was the result of human volition, everything in human affairs was capable of being altered—and improved upon—by means of education and legislation. In England, which led the world in these matters, it was Jeremy Bentham who headed the assault on the traditional ways of thinking. A disciple of Helvétius, he criticized Blackstone for maintaining that the past provided a guide to the present. In contrast to Blackstone, who taught law as it was, Bentham undertook to teach law "as it should be."[44] It was Bentham, more than any other thinker, who popularized the notion that laws are capable of resolving every social evil. By the second quarter of the nineteenth century it became accepted wisdom that the principal function of parliament was to legislate. In the middle of the century, England created a professional civil service to monitor the nation's social problems and suggest measures to deal with them. Parliament often followed its recommendations, a good deal of which required "manifold and direct interference with freedom of contract" and carried "subtle implications for the whole ideal of a contract-based society."[45] Thus were laid the philosophical foundations of the welfare state.

Its political foundations were laid in Germany during the 1880s. Alarmed by the inroads which the outlawed Social Democratic Party was making among German workers, Bismarck enacted social insurance programs against sickness, work injuries, and the handicaps of old age. These measures were followed by laws requiring Sunday rest for labor. Industrial courts were set up to settle wage disputes. Similar legislation was passed in Great Britain in the early years of the twentieth century on the initiative of the Liberal Party: the Unemployed Workmen Act (1905); the Workmen's Compensation Acts (1897, 1906), which made employers financially liable for accidents at work; and the Old Age Pensions Act (1912), which ensured every low-income Briton seventy years of age or older a pension. This legislation culminated in the National Insurance Act of 1911, which provided protection against sickness and unemployment, financed by contributions from employers, employees, and the state. In 1912, Britain adopted a minimum-wage law.

Pre–World War I social legislation mainly provided coverage against the misfortunes of accidental injury or unemployment and the hardships of aging. In time, however, especially during the Great Depression with its unprecedented unemployment, the notion of what constituted basic human needs and what responsibility society had for meeting them expanded considerably. Imperceptibly, but with enormous consequences for property and liberty, social welfare legislation progressed from insurance to assurance: from insurance against calamity to assurance of what Franklin Roosevelt called "a comfortable living."* Expanded state responsibilities, in turn, inevitably led to expanded state involvement and interference in the life of society, and thus to infringement of liberty. For as Frederick Hayek has pointed out, every expansion of the scope of state authority, in and of itself, threatens liberty, because

> (1) people can usually agree on no more than a very few common tasks; (2) to be democratic, government must be consensual; (3) democratic government is therefore possible only when the state confines its activities to the few on which people can agree; (4) hence, when the state aspires to undertake important additional functions, it will find that it can do so only by coercion, and both liberty and democracy will be destroyed.[46]

The welfare programs introduced in some countries in the 1930s required immense monetary outlays, and these could be obtained only through taxation. They have transformed the modern democratic government into a giant mechanism for the redistribution of private assets: through income taxes, government appropriates a high percentage of the earnings of corporations and individual citizens, some of which it retains to pay for the costs of administering welfare programs and the

*During the 1932 presidential campaign, Roosevelt, in a glaring non sequitur, asserted: "Every man has a right to life and this means that he has also a right to make a comfortable living. . . ." Carl N. Degler, *Out of Our Past* (New York, 1959), 413.

rest of which it redistributes among welfare's beneficiaries. The philosophical justification of this operation is the socialist notion that government has the duty not only to alleviate the lot of the poor but to "abolish" poverty itself.* In pursuit of this objective, the government undertakes to guarantee not so much equality of opportunity, the fundamental aspiration of liberalism, as equality of reward—a notion that comes close to the Communist ideal of "from each according to his ability, to each according to his needs."[47] The goal was defined by President Lyndon Johnson, the principal architect of the postwar welfare state in the United States, in an address to Howard University in June 1965: "Freedom is not enough. . . . We seek not just freedom but opportunity . . . not just equality as a right and a theory but equality as a fact and as a *result*."†

It is doubtful that either Johnson and his speechwriters or the public at large had any inkling what a break with the Western tradition these words represented. Social equality can be attained, if at all, only by coercion, that is, at the expense of liberty. It necessarily requires the violation of the property rights of those citizens who possess more wealth or enjoy higher social status than the majority. Once the elimination of poverty becomes a state objective, the state is bound to treat property not as a fundamental right, which it is its supreme obligation to protect, but as an obstacle to social justice. It is, therefore, essential to all egalitarian doctrines to insist—very much in the manner of the proponents of royal absolutism like Hobbes—that property is not a natural right but a social institution, for which reason society, through the agency of the state, is entitled to regulate it.[48] In such arguments, by a sleight of hand, the fact that the state protects private property is construed to mean that the state holds ultimate title to it.

In premodern times such encroachments on property were effectively resisted in the name of freedom and personal "birthrights." But then the threat to property and everything associated with it came from hereditary kings: parliament, as representative of the people, could oppose arbitrary taxation on the grounds that the government (i.e., the

*Clint Bollick, *The Affirmative Action Fraud* (Washington, D.C., 1996), 43–45, sees the source of this idea in the United States in the writings of Michael Harrington (*The Other America* [New York, 1962]), and Christopher Jencks (*Inequality* [New York and London, 1972]). But, of course, it is grounded in the whole ideology of socialism.

†Hugh Davis Graham, *The Civil Rights Era* (New York, 1990), 174. Emphasis added. The speech, suggested by Bill Moyers, was written by Daniel Patrick Moynihan and Richard Goodwin. Ibid. The notion was already implicit in some of President Roosevelt's speeches. Richard A. Epstein in *Social Philosophy and Policy* 15, No. 2 (Summer 1998), 420.

crown) had no right to appropriate its subjects' assets without the latter's consent. But the situation changed radically once governments came to be elected, for whatever they legislate implies popular consent. In a democracy, property does not effectively limit political power, because the proprietors, as it were, sit on both sides of the bargaining table and tax themselves through their representatives.[49] These representatives, dependent as they are on an electorate which has more poor than rich voters, "foster electoral support by concentrating the benefits and dispersing the costs of specific policy initiatives."* Such practices, adopted by nearly all industrial democracies in the course of the twentieth century, have significantly altered the status of private property:

> One of the most important developments in the United States during the past decade has been the emergence of government as a major source of wealth. Government is a gigantic syphon. It draws in revenue and power, and pours forth wealth: money, benefits, services, contracts, franchises, and licenses. Government has always had this function. But while in early times it was minor, today's function of largess is on a vast, imperial scale.
>
> The valuables dispensed by the government take many forms, but they all share one characteristic. They are steadily taking the place of traditional forms of wealth—forms which are held as private property. Social insurance substitutes for savings; a government contract replaces a businessman's customers and goodwill. The wealth of more and more Americans depends on a relationship to government. Increasingly, Americans live on government largess—allocated by government on its own terms, and held by recipients subject to conditions which express "the public interest."
>
> The growth of government largess, accompanied by a distinctive system of law, is having profound consequences. It affects the underpinnings of individualism and independence. It influences the workings of the Bill of Rights.[50]

*Charles K. Rowley, Introduction to Charles K. Rowley, ed., *Property Rights and the Limits of Democracy* (Aldershot, England, and Brookfield, Vt., 1993), 20. Hayek questioned the ethics of a system "in which it is not a majority of givers who determine what should be given to the unfortunate few, but a majority of takers who decide what they will take from a wealthier minority." F. A. Hayek, *The Constitution of Liberty* (Chicago, 1960), 289.

Inasmuch as poor voters always and everywhere outnumber rich ones, in theory there are no limits to the democratic state's ability to ride roughshod over the rights of private property. Some observers fear that this process will inevitably lead to the destruction of democracy, but they ignore the inevitable reaction which has been gathering momentum since the 1980s as the costs of ever-expanding welfare programs threaten budgetary ruin. Another explanation why the encroachments on private property do not advance relentlessly to their logical conclusion, which is its abolition, is the fact that the most affluent are twice as likely to vote as the neediest.[51] Furthermore, the owners of property show greater resolve in defending their assets than do those who want to take it away for distribution: as a rule, private interests outsmart the custodians of the "common good" because they stand to lose more than the latter stand to gain. Even so, there is a steady, often imperceptible diminution of property rights and the various civil rights that emanate from it as a result of the modern welfare state's pursuit of social equality.

Thus the modern government* not only "redistributes" the possessions of its citizens, it also regulates their use. It invokes environmental laws to limit the use of land and housing. It interferes with the freedom of contract by legislating minimum wages and enforcing "affirmative action" hiring practices. It imposes rent controls. It interferes with virtually every aspect of business, punishing any action that looks like price-fixing, setting rates for public utilities, preventing the formation of trusts, regulating communications and transport, pressuring banks to lend to designated neighborhoods, and so on. The Task Force on Reinventing Government appointed by President Clinton and chaired by Vice President Gore estimated in 1993 that the "cost to the private sector of complying with [external] regulations is at least $430 billion annually—9 percent of our gross domestic product!"[52] As a result, private property today scarcely resembles what it was in the past several hundred years and increasingly approximates conditional tenure.

These measures are enforced by a regulatory bureaucracy which operates largely outside public control, arrogating to itself powers that the framers of the Constitution meant to keep separate:

*Unless otherwise specified, in the case of the United States by "government" is meant the federal government as well as state and local governments.

> Administrative agencies combine all the features of the legislative, executive and judiciary branches in one body. . . . Agencies promulgate regulations (a legislative function), interpreting statutes in the process (a judicial function). They enforce statutes and their own regulations (an executive function), determine whether regulations have been violated, and assess sanctions against the purportedly offending party (judicial functions). . . . If, as is now often the case, the courts abandon their constitutional role as guardians of rights and defer to the judgment of regulatory agencies in all their various functions, then the constitutional system as originally devised is radically altered.[53]

The difficulty of dealing with this unusual and dangerous situation resides in the fact that under modern conditions, government interference is unavoidable and in many respects beneficial, which may not have been the case when private property was threatened by royal absolutism. The concept of "public good," even if it lends itself to gross abuse, is nevertheless a genuine consideration. Pollution makes it imperative that the government monitor industrial and automotive emissions. Someone must see to it that citizens are not discriminated against by public institutions because of their race, religion, or sex, and that someone can only be public authority. Air safety has to be ensured. Physicians have to be licensed, and medical care provided for the elderly and the poor. All these services require state intervention. State intervention limits freedom, but it also protects it: it has been rightly said that "democracy is strengthened if certain types of economic freedom are curtailed."[54] We thus confront a novel and paradoxical situation: in the modern world, private property, traditionally the most effective bulwark of freedom, must be restricted for the benefit of society, which has the effect of enhancing the power of the state to the point where it limits and threatens society's freedom. And yet one is handicapped in resisting the state in the name of freedom because its actions reflect the free will of free citizens. This may mean that property no longer can serve as a guarantor of freedom and that its very survival is problematic. But it may also mean that a way must be found to ensure the preservation of property as a fundamental human right that society cannot properly violate while, at the same time, ensuring fundamental social justice. As we will suggest later, these twin objectives are achieved not so much by laws and institutions as by attitudes which determine how laws and institutions are employed.

Before proceeding further, we need to deal with the argument that private property in the traditional sense has been rendered obsolete by the operations of the modern economy—which, if true, would make further discussion pointless.

4. *Modern corporations and property*

The vast majority of mankind earns its livelihood today much as it always has, that is, growing food and fishing, practicing artisanship, trading, and selling its labor. Property for this majority continues to be associated with physical objects, especially land and commodities of every kind. But for the inhabitants of the advanced industrial societies the situation has changed drastically during the past two centuries. For them, wealth has come to be embodied in money, knowledge, and other nontangible assets; the productive sector shrinks in importance in proportion as the service and financial sectors expand. Increasingly, because of lower labor costs, the production of commodities is shifted to the poorer countries. While sizable fortunes are still made in real estate, land, until the nineteenth century the main form of private property, has been reduced to a minor factor in the economy.

> As a matter of fact, the total value under our law today of proprietary rights which have no material object is probably enormously greater than the value of such rights in all land and tangible objects. This modern incorporeal property includes, particularly, promissory notes, bills of exchange, patent rights, and shares of corporate stock.[55]

No less important a factor in the changing nature of property has been the growth of state intervention in the national economy, which in some countries has led to the nationalization of many productive assets and in others to the emergence of giant corporations which control most of such assets. These developments have led some scholars to question whether the traditional notion of private property retains any validity.

In 1932, Adolf A. Berle and Gardiner C. Means published an influential book titled *The Modern Corporation and Private Property*. Its central thesis was stated in its preface:

> The translation of perhaps two-thirds of the industrial wealth of the country from individual ownership to ownership by the large, publicly financed corporations vitally changes the lives

of property owners, the lives of workers, and the methods of property tenure.

The authors went on to claim that a divorce had occurred between what they called "the two attributes of ownership—risking collective wealth in profit seeking enterprise and ultimate management of responsibility for that enterprise." For this reason, in their opinion, one could no longer speak of "property in the old sense."[56] In the revised edition of the book, published in 1968, Berle argued that the process of concentration of productive wealth in the hands of public corporations has progressed without letup since its original publication. According to his calculations, in the 1960s, six or seven hundred large corporations accounted for 70 percent of nonagricultural commercial operations in the United States. The property in private hands came to consist predominantly of nonproductive assets in the form of owner-occupied homes, consumer durables, and securities.[57] Thus, because of a "massive collectivization of property devoted to production," corporations have established control over productive wealth while individuals have been left holding consumption assets: they have become "passive" owners. This theory served as the premise of the predictions, popular during the Cold War, that communism and capitalism were destined to "converge."*

The Berle-Means argument essentially rephrased the Marxist thesis of the rupture, under capitalism, between labor and the ownership of the means of production. It suffered from even more serious flaws than the source of its inspiration.[58] The facts to which it called attention are not in dispute; questionable are the conclusions it drew from them. The notion that corporate managers operate free of control of the shareholders is obviously false: by virtue of owning huge blocks of corporate stocks, pension funds and mutual funds enjoy considerable leverage over corporate management. Shareholders can express their dissatisfaction with management by dumping their stock and thus depressing their price. Managers who perform poorly are, sooner or later, replaced. In the words of Harold Demsetz, "In a world in which self-interest plays a significant role in economic behavior, it is foolish to believe that owners

*In an essay published in France on the eve of World War II, *L'homme et la propriété* (Paris, 1939), Berle argued in favor of a system much like Mussolini's "corporate state," urging that society be "organized around a central idea," that this idea be productivity, involving every able-bodied citizen "whose submission to social duties must be an affirmation of his liberty, and not a sign of his servitude" (56). It is striking how readily demoralized liberals of the 1930s adopted the ideas and even the language of both fascism and communism.

of valuable resources systematically relinquish control to managers who are not guided to serve their interests."[59]

Furthermore, the concept of "property" has never entailed personal management by the owners. In the classical definition, property meant the right to use and dispose of assets. Ownership has always been compatible with the practice of entrusting the management of one's belongings to others, on the understanding that the proprietor retained the title. As early as the fifteenth century, European merchants consigned their capital to chartered trading companies, franchised corporations, and joint-stock companies, run by professionals. Joint-stock companies, which made their appearance in sixteenth-century England, were managed not by the stock owners but by their agents. The corporate law in France provided for a type of business association known as *société commandité par actions* which required the stockholders to cede all control over their investment to the management; these made their appearance as early as the sixteenth century.[60] The modern holder of one hundred shares in a billion-dollar corporation is part owner of that corporation, even if to an infinitesimal degree, because he can at a moment's notice sell the shares on the open market. The notion that ownership requires personal management is as erroneous as would be the notion that democracy demands of each citizen personally to participate in legislation, as was the case with the ancient popular assemblies: the impossibility of multimillion populations doing so was recognized centuries ago and resolved through the institution of parliamentary representation. The modern corporation has not rendered private property obsolete. Indeed, by greatly enhancing the wealth of industrial democracies, it has contributed to its flowering.

Another flaw of the Berle-Means thesis lay in its definition of property. Possibly under the influence of the Marxist theory dominant in the Soviet Union at the time of writing, the authors limited this concept to "rights in the instruments of production," whereas in the real world it applies to any asset that yields the owner material rewards. Money, stocks, bonds, and real estate, "passive" though they may be, cannot be arbitrarily excluded from the concept; the same, of course, applies to incorporeal assets such as copyrights and patents.

No more convincing is the argument made by some contemporary authors that because modern property is incomparably more complicated than it was in the heyday of liberalism, representing not a "right" but a "shadowy bundle of rights," and as such eluding precise definition, the concept has "disintegrated."[61] Emulating scientists who assume that whatever cannot be measured does not exist, some social theoreticians deny the existence of whatever it is that they cannot precisely define. The difficulty one may experience in defining a phenomenon, however, does not invalidate its existence. Hernando de Soto recalls:

> When I was growing up in Peru, I was told that the farms I visited belonged to farming communities and not to individual farmers. Yet as I walked from field to field, a different dog would bark. The dogs were ignorant of the prevailing law: all they knew was which land their masters controlled.[62]

It is for these reasons that the Berle-Means volume, for all its popular appeal, has had little influence on the profession of economics. "Our own statistical analyses, using only data and methods familiar to economists of the time," write two critics,

> yield no clear evidence that the management-dominated corporations differed much from owner-dominated companies in practices of executive compensation or in the utilization of assets to produce profits. The main tradition of economic theory was perhaps instinctively recognizing these facts when it continued to work in complete disregard of *The Modern Corporation*.[63]

5. *Taxation*

Although taxes have become so much part of modern existence that, as the saying goes, along with death they are the only certainties in life, regular direct taxation of the population's income is an innovation of the twentieth century.* Until the emergence of the democratic state, governments were expected to live off their own assets, supplemented by customs, excise receipts, and a variety of dues. Direct taxes, like the French *taille* or the Russian soul tax, were imposed only on the lower classes, i.e., the poorest elements, and regarded as a mark of inferior social status. The affluent were asked for money only in national emergencies, which usually meant war or the threat of war. Hence, over the centuries direct taxes, when required, were treated as voluntary "aids."[64] In England, direct taxes were viewed as "gifts" offered the

*"Direct" taxes tax persons; "indirect" ones tax things, services, and transactions. Thus, the income tax is a direct tax, whereas real estate taxes, customs duties, and excise levies are indirect taxes.

crown through the subjects' representatives; this attitude prevailed also in colonial America.[65] In early modern France, taxes voted by the provincial estates were deemed "free gifts" (*dons gratuits*).[66]

In ancient Athens, taxes were considered a hallmark of tyranny: Athenian citizens were exempt from them. The city-state financed itself from incomes of public properties (including the silver mines of Laurion), court fees and fines, and indirect levies such as a sales tax and a harbor tax. In emergencies, Athenians donated money for the city's defense according to their ability; but they made certain that such occasional levies did not become permanent.[67] By contrast, Dionysius (405–367 B.C.E.), the tyrant of Syracuse, taxed the city's citizens so heavily that, according to Aristotle, it amounted to confiscation of their entire property.[68] Similar practices prevailed in ancient Rome: Romans regarded direct taxes as a form of tribute and imposed them only on conquered nations and other noncitizens.[69] The state financed itself from fees for the use of lands (*ager publicus*) and other public facilities, tribute, and war booty. The bulk of the nation's productive wealth—*ager privatus*—was exempt from taxation.[70]

In the Middle Ages, the obligation to pay regular taxes was perceived as tantamount to the loss of personal freedom, inasmuch as it entailed a regular tribute: such, for example, was the view of the Franks.[71] Medieval French kings were expected to pay their own way, for which reason they were forbidden to alienate any part of the royal domain. Neither the Merovingian nor the Carolingian kings had a regular tax system, instead defraying the costs of administration and defense from rents on their estates, tribute levied on conquered peoples, and war booty.[72] There is some evidence of income taxation in medieval Italian towns, where trade and manufacture replaced agriculture as the main source of wealth.* However, as a rule, direct taxes in Europe, as in ancient Athens, were emergency wartime measures. Thus, in 1695 France imposed a capitation tax which all subjects were required to pay according to their means for the duration of the War of the League of Augsburg.[73] In 1799, Britain imposed a progressive income tax to help cover the costs of the war with France. Subjects earning less than £60 a year were exempt, but the others were subject to a progressive tax: incomes of £200 and higher were taxed at 10 percent. The unpopular levy was allowed to lapse on the termination of the Napoleonic Wars.[74]

*See, e.g., the critical remarks by the sixteenth-century historian Franceso Guicciardini about the use of the progressive tax by the Medicis in Florence. Hayek, *Constitution of Liberty*, 515–16.

Later in the century, an income tax was reintroduced, but it was moderate, averaging 5 percent for those who qualified.

In the United States direct taxation was also a by-product of war. The Revolutionary War was financed not by taxes—Congress lacked as yet the authority to assess them—but by loans.[75] Until the Civil War, the U.S. government met its expenses mainly from the proceeds of customs duties and sales of land, which most of the time more than covered expenditures.[76] During the Civil War, however, government expenses increased twentyfold and an income tax was instituted. It was imposed in 1861 and taxed all income over $800 at a rate of 3 percent, which rose progressively to 10 percent on incomes over $5,000. It was abolished in 1872. In 1895, the Supreme Court declared unconstitutional a bill to impose a regular income tax on the grounds that being a direct tax, it had to be apportioned among the states according to their population.[77] It was finally and permanently established by the Sixteenth Amendment, adopted in 1913.*

The inheritance tax was occasionally imposed in classical antiquity (especially in Rome) as well as in medieval Europe,[78] but its great development occurred in the nineteenth century, and especially during and immediately after World War I, Great Britain introduced the "death duty" in 1894. In the United States a regular federal inheritance tax made its appearance during World War I.[79]

Historical evidence thus indicates that, as a rule, in the Western world since classical antiquity and until the twentieth century, regular (as distinct from emergency) direct taxation was regarded as unlawful except for subject peoples; when imposed domestically, it carried the stigma of social inferiority. Governments were expected, in peacetime, to be self-supporting. This was possible because the premodern state assumed very limited responsibilities and none corresponding to today's social services; the bulk of its outlays went for warfare and the upkeep of the royal court. Direct taxes were mainly resorted to in times of war. When such levies were required, they had to be approved by those who paid them, usually through their representatives.† These were seen not as something the government was entitled to but as gifts.

*The United States is said to be the only country in the world which taxes its citizens residing abroad, where they do not enjoy the benefits that their taxes theoretically pay for. According to a recent ruling, a U.S. citizen who renounces his citizenship is required to pay federal income taxes for ten years following such renunciation.

†Such was the belief of colonial Americans. The slogan "No taxation without representation" did not mean that Americans would happily pay taxes as long as they were given a voice in politics but that "taxes imposed without consent were a type of confis-

The regular direct and progressive tax on income is a by-product of the welfare state: it came into being concurrently and has been justified as necessary to finance the large outlays which social services demand.*

Doubts have been raised as to the moral justification of the very principle of taxation. A German scholar has called it "the greatest curiosity":

> How is it that people place at the disposal of the tax-hungry treasury up to one half or more of their honestly earned income, without demanding in exchange some special equivalent, and that the tax authorities manage to shape the rates of this taxation in quite differential ways, secretly raising them time and again by the device of maintaining constant tax rates even as the value of money deteriorates?†

Another scholar declares the power to tax to be nothing but a form of "eminent domain without compensation" and therefore "confiscation without cause."[80] Richard Epstein concurs: "With a tax, the government takes property in the narrowest sense of the term, ending up with ownership and possession of that which was once in private hands. . . . [T]axation is prima facie a taking of private property."‡

We shall set aside the question whether regular taxation is indeed "confiscation without cause" or, on the contrary, as others maintain, justified compensation for the services rendered its citizens by the modern state, and turn to the subject directly germane to our inquiry, namely

---

cation that destroyed the rights of property ownership." James W. Ely, Jr., *The Guardian of Every Other Right*, 2nd ed. (New York and Oxford, 1998), 27.

*It has been suggested, however, that since increases in the rate of taxation on income yield either a small or no increase and sometimes actually cause a diminution of revenues, they are driven not so much by economic and social considerations as by social resentment. Helmut Schoeck, *Envy* (New York, 1966), 325–26. Hayek concurs with this assessment. *Constitution of Liberty*, 311–12.

†Günter Schmölders in Uwe Schultz, ed., *Mit dem Zehnten fing es an* (Munich, 1986), 245. The author means that as a result of inflation people in the lower tax brackets are lifted into higher ones without a corresponding improvement in their real income.

‡Richard Epstein, *Takings* (Cambridge, Mass., 1985), 100. This argument, as well as the rest of Epstein's criticism of the welfare state, is said to have been "largely dismissed by academics, primarily because it stated a conclusion that was unpalatable to the political left. . . ." Calvin R. Massey in *Harvard Journal of Law and Public Policy* 20, No. 1 (1996), 85–86. Massey believes that taxation in general is legitimate but not "progressive taxation," which "burdens the few for the benefit of the many," thereby violating the Fifth Amendment's "takings" clause, which requires "that public burdens must be shared by the entire polity rather than borne by a selected few." Ibid., 88.

what effect it has on the status of private property and the rights traditionally associated with it.

6. *The growing power of the state*

The United States, which will henceforth be the focus of our attention, lagged far behind Western Europe in the adoption of social welfare programs because of its traditional emphasis on self-reliance. Although from the Middle Ages on, the sanctity of private property was a fundamental principle of Western Europe's unwritten constitutions, and especially so in England, it was nowhere more venerated than in colonial North America. The country that became the United States was unique in world history in that it was founded by individuals in quest of private property. The middle class here did not "rise"—it was present at the creation. Eighteenth-century America has been described as a "middle-class world."[81] The vast majority of immigrants who settled in North America came to obtain land. Land was abundant, and the colonies, eager to attract settlers, gave them generous allotments. Thus a landowning middle-class society emerged by the middle of the eighteenth century, when "most of the colonists owned land, and 80 percent of the population derived their living from agriculture."[82] Not surprisingly, the conviction that protection of property was the main function of government, and its corollary that a government that did not fulfill this obligation forfeited its mandate, acquired the status of a self-evident truth in the minds of the American colonists. The American revolution was carried out for the protection of property, the bastion of liberty, because it was believed that by taxing the colonists without giving them the opportunity to assent to taxation amounted to confiscation. "At every stage in the controversy to 1776 and beyond, Americans claimed to be defending property rights."*

*P. J. Marshall in John Brewer and Susan Staves, eds., *Early Modern Conceptions of Property* (London and New York, 1995), 533. In view of the paramount importance attached to private property in colonial America, many scholars have wondered why neither the U.S. Constitution nor the Bill of Rights unequivocally affirms the sanctity of property. A possible explanation of this omission is that at the time, the term "happiness" conveyed "property": "[T]he acquisition of property and the pursuit of happiness were so closely connected with each other in the minds of the founding generation that naming only one of the two sufficed to evoke both." Willi Paul Adams, *The First American Constitutions* (Chapel Hill, N.C., 1980), 193. This connection the New Hampshire Constitution of 1784 made explicit: "All men have certain natural, essential, and inherent rights which are—the enjoying and defending life and liberty—acquiring, possessing and protecting property—and in a word, of seeking and obtaining happiness." Cited

Yet to say this is not to claim that colonial America and the nineteenth-century United States were a land of unrestrained ownership. The vision of a laissez-faire American past was long ago exposed as a myth. The principle of eminent domain—the forcible requisition of private property for public use—was much more developed in North America both before and after the Revolution than in England.[83] Americans shared a broad consensus, religious in impulse, that while every man had a right to property to sustain himself and his family, ultimately wealth was meant to serve the community and hence the community had the moral right to regulate it.[84] Throughout the eighteenth and nineteenth centuries, legislatures frequently intervened on both the national and state levels to regulate private enterprise.[85] Indeed, precisely because so many essential enterprises that in Europe tended to be publicly owned—e.g., utilities, transport, telephone, and telegraph—were in America in private hands, the government was prone to monitor them and subject them to regulation. But the apparatus of enforcement was poorly developed, and public sentiment strongly identified with the spirit of individualism. The Supreme Court tended to favor property rights over social justice, promoting personal self-reliance as a solution to all social and economic problems.

Hence it happened that when the Great Depression struck in the early 1930s, throwing twelve million Americans out of work, Washington had no mechanism to aid the unemployed. It was the achievement of Roosevelt's New Deal to provide such a mechanism. New Deal legislation enacted the Social Security Act of 1935 to support the aged, disabled, and unemployed and the Fair Labor Standards Act of 1938 to set minimum wages and maximum working hours in certain industries. These measures belatedly guaranteed Americans the kind of social benefits that the Germans and English had taken for granted for decades. They were certainly needed and saved the United States from potentially ruinous social disturbances.

But the legislation passed under the New Deal represents only a part of the picture. Inspired by profound skepticism about the future of capitalism, Roosevelt and his advisors encouraged a fundamental and long-lasting change in attitude toward private property: laws conceived and presented as emergency measures were subtly transformed into innovative principles which fundamentally altered first governmental and then judicial attitudes toward ownership. This was accomplished by extend-

---

in James W. Ely, Jr., *The Guardian of Every Other Right*, 2nd ed. (New York and Oxford, 1998), 30.

ing the principle of fundamental "rights" from the political to the economic sphere,[86] which had the effect of converting the concept of right from meaning "security from" to "claim to." In the process the word "security" was redefined, in Roosevelt's words, to mean "not only physical security . . . from attacks by aggressors . . . [but] also economic security, social security, moral security."[87]

When the Supreme Court, operating under the old principles, declared unconstitutional a number of New Deal laws, Roosevelt tried to alter its composition by adding new and more liberal justices. Although the infamous attempt to "pack the Court" in 1937 failed, the demoralized Court beat a retreat, and as old justices retired and appointees of Roosevelt replaced them, its philosophical complexion underwent substantial change:

> The lacerating struggle over the validity of the New Deal Program engendered lasting hostility to the judicial protection of property rights. . . . Once the Supreme Court accepted the New Deal, the justices abruptly withdrew from the field of economic regulation. This reflected a monumental change in the Court's attitude toward property rights and entrepreneurial liberty. From its inception, one scholar noted, "the Court deemed its mission to be the protection of property against depredations by the people and their legislatures. After 1937 it gave up this mission." A sharply limited concept of property rights thus operated for the next generation. . . . Consequently, the Court gave great latitude to Congress and state legislatures to fashion economic policy, while expressing only perfunctory concern for the rights of individual property owners.[88]

This change of attitude found reflection in ambitious schemes of social reform launched in both Great Britain and the United States on the outbreak of World War II, and in the perception of what constitutes society's responsibility toward its less fortunate citizens. Traditionally, the "rights" of a citizen were a negative concept: they were freedoms "from" (from religious persecution, arbitrary arrest, censorship, and the like). Now they acquired a positive meaning in the sense of "claims to" (to housing, health care, etc.) which, it was asserted, the government had a duty to satisfy. This redefinition, even though it occurred quietly and as if unconsciously, ushered in a new phase in the evolution of the welfare state. The source of the modern attitude can be traced to Thomas Paine's *The Rights of Man*, in its day an immensely popular treatise. In Part One of the book, published in 1791, Paine still defined "rights" negatively to mean "liberty, property, security, and the resistance to oppression." But in Part Two (Chapter 5), brought out the following year, he adopted a novel positive view, advocating a radical program of social welfare: financial relief to the 20 percent of the population which he estimated to be poor, child support, and support for children's education, along with relief for the old, the last "not as a matter of grace and favour, but of right." Such ideas were a good century ahead of their time and hence had no immediate impact.

Their day dawned in the 1940s. An early appeal for the creation of the welfare state in the United States was made by President Roosevelt in his State of the Union address to Congress in January 1941 in which he referred to the "Four Freedoms" as a peace objective. Two of these "freedoms" were traditional and guaranteed by the Constitution: freedom of speech and freedom of religion. But the other two—freedom from want and from fear—were novel and raised questions that Roosevelt did not address. Setting aside the nebulous and rather meaningless slogan "freedom from fear," "freedom from want" meant really not a freedom but a right—the right to the necessities of life at public expense, i.e., the right to something that was not one's own. It committed the government to assure every citizen of the satisfaction of his needs—a term which by its very nature cannot be precisely defined and hence is capable of infinite expansion as society grows richer and each particular need is satisfied, giving rise to fresh needs. Enforcing true freedoms—free speech, practice of the religion of one's choice, access to the ballot box—costs nothing or next to nothing. Enforcing special rights, by contrast, requires large outlays. Since the democratic government has no money of its own, any demand for government money, however justified, is in effect a demand for the money of one's fellow citizens, a process in which the government acts merely as a transfer agent. It entails the shift, by the device of taxation, of assets from the wealthier citizens to the poorer—a responsibility and a function which governments had never previously assumed.*

*John Hospers depicts the process of social leveling as follows: "[T]he State well knows that people . . . desire . . . benefits, specifically economic benefits. And these the State endeavors to supply, if for no other reason than to keep them peaceful, and, in the case of a democracy, to win their votes. But this presents a problem, for the State has no resources of its own with which to confer these benefits. It can give to one person only by first seizing it from another; if one person gets something for nothing, another must get nothing for something. But the citizen-voter's attention is so centered on the attractiveness of the things being promised that he forgets that the politician making the promises doesn't have any of these things to give—and that he will have none of them

Roosevelt's new program marked a fateful leap from the principles of the original New Deal: "Nothing in the New Deal provided help just because a person was poor or hampered by social disadvantages."[89] It is not clear whether Roosevelt was aware of all the implications of his slogan, for it seems to have been quite casually formulated at the suggestion of a journalist from the *Philadelphia Inquirer*.[90] It can be assumed that those who heard the promise of "freedom from want" and applauded it as a reasonable and humanitarian objective did not understand that it could only be realized at the expense of private property rights.

Roosevelt's vague promises were spelled out in Great Britain the following year in the so-called Beveridge Report, prepared at the request of the government, which called on the postwar state to destroy "five giant evils"—want (i.e., poverty), disease, ignorance, squalor, and idleness (unemployment).* William Beveridge, an academic economist, defined "Destruction of Want" as "ensuring that every citizen, in return for service, has income sufficient for his subsistence and that of his dependents both when he is working and when he cannot work."[91] This objective required national planning and using the powers of the state "to whatever extent may prove to be necessary in order to maintain employment after the war."[92] The funding for this ambitious program of welfare was to come partly from employees, partly from employers, and partly from the state. It entailed "redistributing national income, so as to put first things first, so as to ensure abolition of want before the enjoyment of comforts."[93]

It was a full-scale socialist program that the Labour Party would adopt as its platform in the election of 1945 and use as the blueprint of its administration. The Labour government carried out massive nationalization of private industry and transport to eliminate the insecurity which its leaders regarded as "corroding the soul." Although personally Beveridge had rather conservative notions of the role of women in society, his report stimulated a feminist movement in Britain which demanded that household duties be regarded as employment and that women be granted full economic equality with men.

The Beveridge Report represented a considerable innovation in that

---

after he gets into office; he will seize the earnings of one special interest group and distribute those earnings to another such group (minus the government's 40% handling fee, of course)." "The Nature of the State" in *The Personalist* 59, No. 4 (October 1978), 399.

*Sir William H. Beveridge, *The Pillars of Security and Other War-time Essays and Addresses* (New York, 1943), 49, 91–92. They were anticipated in the 1920 program of the Nazi Party; see above, pp. 220–1.

previous social welfare programs had been directed toward *individuals* who, for one reason or another, required society's help. The welfare agenda outlined by Beveridge, by contrast, addressed itself not to individuals but to *society* at large, and was meant not to help alleviate need but to prevent need from arising.

This agenda, supplemented with additional vague promises, received international recognition in the semilegal Universal Declaration of Human Rights adopted unanimously by the United Nations in 1948, which pledged everyone on earth the right to work and an "adequate standard of living."

Repercussions of the British Labour program could be heard in the United States in the administration of President Kennedy, who spoke of the need to shift the focus of social legislation "from the dole . . . toward escape from the dole" by helping the needy to attain self-sufficiency.[94] But this objective became policy only under his successor, Lyndon Johnson. Driven by the most pernicious of human aspirations, that of making his mark on history, Johnson declared in 1964 a "national war on poverty" with the objective of "total victory."* The historian is less impressed by the sweep of the pledge than by its confusion. For "war" by definition entails the use of violence, and it is hard to see how violence can alleviate poverty. Furthermore, in view of the fact that poverty is a relative term, "total victory" over it is unattainable, because as society grows richer or poorer, its criteria change. (Given that average incomes in recent decades have been rising, writes Melanie Phillips, "taking upwards those below the average to a higher standard of living, at what point do these people stop being poor?")[95] Michael Harrington, the writer who had the greatest influence in inspiring "the war on poverty" in the United States, had himself great difficulty in defining what constituted poverty beyond basic needs of health, housing, food, and education, dissolving the definition in vague generalities about the psychological sense of "exclusion" and unfulfilled potential.[96]

Thus, along with the traditional concept of negative "freedoms"—freedoms "from"—there has emerged in the West a vision of freedoms (or better, rights) *to*. Such usage was not entirely new, since, as noted

**Public Papers of the Presidents of the United States: Lyndon B. Johnson, 1963–64*, I (Washington, D.C., 1965), 376. Charles Murray asserts that the discovery of "structural poverty" as a national problem in the midst of general prosperity can be dated with some precision to the year 1963. Its major premise held that "it was not the fault of the poor that they were poor": it was the fault of the "system." *Losing Ground* (New York, 1984), 26–27, 39. A significant influence in shaping such thinking was the appearance, two years earlier, of Michael Harrington's *The Other America*.

above, it had been anticipated by Thomas Paine in the 1790s. But what had been then the radical proposal of a solitary radical now turned into government policy. Historically, "rights" had referred to guarantees given to individuals that neither the state nor society would infringe on their life, liberty, and possessions; later it came to mean also that they would be ruled by a government of their choice. Civil rights and political rights constituted liberty.

Social "rights" are an altogether different matter. For when one promises the citizen "freedom from want" one accords him a guarantee which assures him not just protection of his own property but access to the property of others gained with the help of the state. This pledge opens the floodgates to a proliferation of spurious rights claimed by various groups formed for the purpose: "rights" of consumers, of renters, of nonsmokers, of patients, of the disabled, of immigrants, of homosexuals, and so on, all of which require the intervention of the state to enforce them and thereby lead to the enhancement of its authority. There is no limit to such "rights," since they are purchased at someone else's expense. The notion that every need creates a "right" has acquired a quasi-religious status in modern America, inhibiting rational discussion.[97]

The following are a couple of illustrations in support of this contention. An advertisement for a book on racial problems shows the photograph of a middle-aged black man, in a crowd, holding aloft a sign that reads: "Housing is a Human Right." This slogan can be interpreted in two ways. If it means that everyone has a right to buy, rent, or build a roof over his head, it is so self-evident and indisputable as to require no publicity. Hence, it is unlikely that this is what the man in the picture has in mind. He is apparently saying that everyone, himself included, has a "right" to be provided with housing by society—in other words, to have the federal, state, or local government, using taxpayers' money, buy, rent, or build him living accommodations. In this sense, the word "right" is entirely inappropriate, for no one has a "right" to anything at someone else's expense: one has no right to demand that a taxi driver, house painter, schoolteacher, bank teller, or gardener, all of whom pay taxes on their earnings, contribute the money their labor earns to provide someone else with housing. A conference sponsored by the United Nations in Istanbul in 1996 adopted resolutions on the "right to housing" as well as the "right to be fed," which the United States sensibly refused to endorse from fear of facing lawsuits by poorer nations[98] even though its refusal could be interpreted as indifference to homelessness and hunger.

Another example of the confusion which has come to prevail on the subject of "rights" is provided by debates in the United States about illegal immigrants. California has an estimated 800,000 such immigrants: the education of their children costs the state's taxpayers $1.8 billion a year. In 1993, the U.S. Congress discussed a bill that would allow states to deny public education to children of illegal immigrants. Commenting on this bill, a Mexican official stated that while his government did not favor illegal immigration, it was worried about the "rights" of such immigrants. Now common sense dictates that the only rights an illegal immigrant has are those shared by all mankind—to life, liberty, and property. He has no "right" to have his children educated at the expense of taxpayers of a country which he has entered unlawfully.

The obligations assumed by the welfare state require an army of civil servants to enforce its taxatory, regulatory, and distributive functions. This, in turn, means that the government (federal, state, and local) employs an ever larger proportion of its citizens and appropriates an ever larger share of the nation's wealth to pay their salaries. In 1900, the U.S. government owned 7 percent of the nation's capital assets (exclusive of public roads and streets and most military and naval equipment) and employed 4 percent of its labor force. During the next half century, these figures tripled: in 1950, the government owned 20 percent of the nation's assets and employed 12.5 percent of its labor force.[99] Its share of the gross domestic product grew exponentially: from 3.9 percent in 1870 to 27 percent in 1970.[100] This expansion occurred largely as the result of Roosevelt's New Deal and the welfare policies adopted during and immediately after World War II. But these figures grew still more dramatically in the second half of the twentieth century in the wake of vast increases in social services, especially those mandated by President Lyndon Johnson's "Great Society." In the 1990s, the share of government spending in the United States climbed to one-third of the GDP. (In Germany, it is over one-half of the GDP, and in Great Britain, 42 percent.)[101] Approximately one-half of that money goes for social welfare—nearly triple what it was in 1960.[102] By 1995, the number of American civilians directly employed by the government attained the figure of 19.5 million.[103] Thus, whereas the population of the United States between 1900 and 1992 increased 3.3 times (from 76 million to 250 million), the number of government employees grew 18.7 times, or nearly six times as fast.

Such immense concentration of citizens' wealth in the hands of the government carries with it obvious dangers to individual liberty, because the government, by dispensing or withholding its largesse, is able to influence the behavior (and secure the conformity) of a large segment of the population. It is not fortuitous that the foundations of Western liberty were laid when governments controlled but a small fraction of the nation's assets.*

7. *Environmental protection vs. private ownership*

Given the traditional role that private property has played in safeguarding individual liberty, the accumulation of wealth by the state and the assumption that it can tamper with property rights for social purposes raises the question whether social welfare in its contemporary guise does not jeopardize the country's freedoms.

In the West in general and the United States in particular, the courts do effectively protect the belongings of citizens from encroachments by other citizens. Direct, unambiguous seizures or "takings" by the government require justification and adequate compensation. However, in practice takings often come close to confiscation. For one, governments take a very liberal view of what constitutes "public good," and under this label seize land for questionable purposes, such as shopping malls and housing projects that benefit individuals or groups rather than society as a whole. Secondly, compensation is often rather arbitrarily established, sometimes below its value to the owner.

An additional threat to property rights today is of an indirect nature and entails measures that do not unambivalently fall under the protection of the Fifth and Fourteenth Amendments, the constitutional bases of an American citizen's property rights.† Since the 1930s the courts have tended to approve various government infringements on the rights of individuals to their assets in the name of "public interest." Without "taking" property in the strict sense of the word, government restricts the uses the owner can make of it through regulations that in the judgment of some legal authorities amount to "regulatory taking":

> Some regulations require owners to allow others to gain access and entry to their property. Land use regulation can limit land to

*"[I]n 1688 or 1685 in France and England the central government's expenditures accounted for seven percent of the national product." Frederick C. Lane in *Journal of Economic History* 35, No. 1 (March 1975), 16.

†The Fifth Amendment says: "No person shall . . . be deprived of life, liberty, or property, without due process of law; nor shall private property be taken for public use without just compensation." The Fourteenth Amendment enjoins individual states from violating this principle.

> residential, commercial or industrial uses; it can limit the densities of use upon such land; it can prohibit certain kinds of activities; it can specify the minimum lot size or minimum floor size or maximum heights, side yards, and setbacks for certain classes of improvements; it can designate certain structures as landmarks and insist that alteration or demolition, in whole or in part, be undertaken only with the approval of certain boards or commissions. Regulations limit the goods that can be sold in commerce and the prices charged for them. The difference among these various forms of regulation are sure to be important in any assessment of their economic consequences or their legal justification. Yet these protean forms of regulation all amount to partial takings of private property.*

Such encroachments on property rights do not encounter the kind of resistance that they might have provoked in the eighteenth or nineteenth century, in part because they do not affect most people, and in part because welfare programs have made citizens more concerned with what the state gives than with what it takes.

At the very height of laissez-faire in England and the United States, the state intervened in private enterprise. In the 1870s and 1880s, several American states enacted legislation designed to ensure that businesses whose activity affected public interest acted in the public interest even if such laws entailed restrictions on their property rights. This reasoning led to the imposition of price controls on utilities and transport. In 1877, in the *Munn v. Illinois* case, the Supreme Court upheld the right of the State of Illinois to regulate prices charged by the owners of Chicago grain elevators on the grounds that since such prices affected the public good they were subject to public control.[104] Subsequently, the Court approved of Pennsylvania's outlawing the manufacture of oleomargarine, an action justified on grounds that the product was injurious to health, although in reality it was taken in the interest of the state's dairy industry. The trouble with this logic was that although sound in principle it knew no limits in its application, since any industrial or commercial activity in one way or another affects the public interest.

Judge Stephen Field of the Supreme Court, who in these cases found

*Epstein, *Takings*, 101. Analyzing the restrictions on property rights in the contemporary United States, Epstein notes that whereas the government respects the ownership of land and generally compensates takings, "In contrast, the freedom of an individual to use or dispose of property is often sharply circumscribed." In *Social Philosophy and Policy* 15, No. 2 (Summer 1998), 424.

himself in a minority, made two forceful arguments. Unless an asset was given by the public, he argued, it was not subject to "public interest" restrictions. Secondly, "use" was an essential attribute of ownership and restrictions on it represented a "taking" which required compensation. The majority of the justices thought otherwise on the grounds that denying or limiting "use" did not represent a taking.[105] Thus began a drawn-out history of judiciary decisions concerning the nature of property rights in which, by and large, the Supreme Court came increasingly to favor public rights over private ones. In addition to permitting limited use, the Court came to interpret "taking" in such a way as to allow for partial taking not subject to compensation in the sense required by the Fifth Amendment. In an important decision in 1979, the Court decided that

> the denial of one traditional property right does not always amount to a taking. At least where an owner possesses a full "bundle" of property rights, the destruction of one "strand" of the bundle is not a taking because the aggregate must be viewed in its entirety.[106]

Citing this decision, Richard Epstein notes that it contradicts the oft-stated Supreme Court opinion that partial taking is covered by the eminent domain clause, because the criterion is not what the owner retains but what he loses.

The issue is especially sensitive in respect to environmental protection, a cause which has acquired since 1970 the intensity of a religious cult; indeed, some of its features recall pagan nature worship.* Environmental hysteria—the primeval fear that the planet is about to be destroyed, previously linked to nuclear weapons—provides a powerful emotional rationale for encroachments on property rights. For just as during the Cold War it was often said that any concession to the Soviet Union was justified if it prevented a putative nuclear holocaust, so today

*Dedicated environmentalists, among them Vice President Gore, like to cite a speech said to have been delivered by Chief Seattle, leader of the Duwamish Indians, in 1854, protesting white pressures on his people to sell their land. The speech contained the phrase "the earth does not belong to man, man belongs to the earth." Although such, indeed, is the common sentiment of primitive peoples (see above, pp. 82–83), this particular speech was invented in 1971 for a television play by an ABC screenwriter. Matt Ridley, *The Origins of Virtue* (New York, 1996), 213–14.

it is maintained—often by the same people—that property rights must be sacrificed for the sake of survival of life on earth. In both cases, the driving force is a deep-seated human propensity for doomsday scenarios.

The principal legislation affecting private use of land and other natural resources was the Clean Air Act (1970), the Federal Water Pollution Control Act (1972), and the Endangered Species Act (1973). These laws gave the federal bureaucracy broad regulatory authority—a fact not fully realized at a time of general enthusiasm for cleaning up the air and waterways. The laws were enforced by the Environmental Protection Agency (EPA), which President Nixon established in 1970.[107]

The environmental ordinances have unquestionably improved the quality of the air and water, but they have often been implemented in a manner that sometimes unreasonably limits the uses of natural resources by their owners, and they have done so without providing compensation.

An illustrative example is the application of environmental laws for the protection of the so-called wetlands. In 1989, President Bush redefined "wetlands" in the Water Act of 1972 to double the amount of land which the government controlled by designating an additional 100 million acres—75 percent of it privately owned—as falling within its definition. This land the owners had to maintain in pristine condition.[108] The enforcement of these laws was entrusted to the Army Corps of Engineers and the Environmental Protection Agency, both of which have been accused of acting in a very arbitrary fashion, in part for want of clear and authoritative definition of what constitutes a "wetland." Violators of the law, as interpreted by officials, have been sent to prison.

The Supreme Court over the years has lent support to these regulatory measures. Thus in 1972, it upheld a local statute which prohibited the use of landfill in designated wetlands on the grounds that

> [a]n owner of land has no absolute and unlimited right to change the essential natural character of his land so as to use it for a purpose for which it was unsuited in its natural state and which injures the rights of others.[109]

But, as Richard Epstein has persuasively argued, "The normal bundle of property rights contains no priority for land in its natural condition; it regards use, including development, as one of the standard incidents of ownership."[110]

In Great Britain the situation in respect to environmental protection has reached the point where a prominent authority on contracts asserts: "The idea of absolute ownership of land, of the absolute right of the owner to exploit and develop the land as he thinks best, has . . . entirely disappeared from English law."[111]

The wetlands legislation more than any other environmental measure contributed to spark a nationwide movement of protest against government encroachments on private uses of landed property.[112] It pits farmers, timber companies, and ordinary citizens who feel victims of uncompensated "takings" against government regulatory agencies as well as the environmental lobby and academic lawyers.[113] The feeling is gaining ground that all regulation of property use is a form of taking in the sense in which this term is used in the Fifth Amendment and if resorted to requires adequate indemnity. All over the country, private groups are organizing to resist governmental efforts to interfere with the free use of land.[114] One of the side effects of this resistance has been to force the government to abandon plans of elevating the official in charge of environmental protection to cabinet status.

It also seems to have had an effect on the Supreme Court, as evidenced by two landmark decisions in the case of *Dolan v. City of Tigard* (1994) and *Lucas v. South Carolina Coastal Council* (1992). The Dolan case involved the owner of a plumbing supply business in Oregon whom the city authorities had refused permission to enlarge it unless she set aside close to one-tenth of her land for use as a bicycle path and a greenway. The Lucas lawsuit involved two beachfront lots which the owner was unable to develop because of a beachfront protection statute: it rendered his property, for which he had paid nearly $1 million, virtually worthless.[115] The Supreme Court decided both suits in favor of the plaintiffs. In the Dolan case, it ruled that the town should have purchased the land rather than held it hostage. In the Lucas suit, the Coastal Council eventually paid the owner $1.5 million for his property. Both the Lucas and Dolan cases are seen as landmark decisions, reversing a trend prevalent since the 1930s, when the putative public interest usually prevailed over the actual interests of private owners: "For the first time in more than 50 years, [the Supreme Court] put property rights on a par with the individual rights protected by the First Amendment (speech, press, religion) and the Fourth Amendment (unlawful searches and seizures)."* Still, some authorities argue that property owners won

*Theodore J. Buotrous, Jr., in *Wall Street Journal*, June 29, 1994, p. A17. On the antiproprietary trends in Supreme Court decisions between 1937 and 1985, see Charles

only a partial victory, since the Court requires compensation only when government regulations prevent the owner from preserving or improving the property.[116]

Resistance to the abuses of environmental protection has also found reflection in legislative proposals. The Republican "Contract with America" of 1994, which, judging by the sweeping endorsement of Republican candidates in the congressional elections of that year, enjoyed wide popular support, contained a clause calling for compensation of property owners whenever government regulations reduced (rather than nullified) their value. The Private Property Rights Bill, passed by the House of Representatives in March 1995, called for compensation if government actions caused a property's worth to decline by 10 percent or more.[117] Neither proposal has as yet been enacted into law.

The government is not the only entity restricting property rights to real estate. Guilty also are private associations of homeowners which arrogate to themselves quasi-governmental functions. Such associations, set up by developers to administer condominia, cooperative apartments, and single-family planned units, have grown from fewer than 500 in 1964 to 150,000 in 1992; their rules and regulations affect an estimated 32 million people.[118] The objective of these associations is to protect property values of a community by imposing strict guidelines concerning the appearance and use of real estate. Paradoxically, by protecting the *values* of the community's housing they infringe on the property *rights* of the owners. Many of the restrictions are proper and sensible. But some communities go to extremes: they may forbid the growing of vegetables or the installation of air conditioners, limit visits by grandchildren, regulate the color of curtains, prohibit the home delivery of newspapers or the display of the American flag, etc., etc.[119] Failure to abide by the community's rules and regulations can lead to the imposition of fines. Although in theory membership in such regulated communities is voluntary, many families have no choice but to buy into them because of price, location, or some other compelling factor.[120] And once they do so, they lose a great deal of freedom and even privacy.

K. Rowley in Nicholas Mercuro, *Taking Property and Just Compensation* (Boston etc., 1992), 79–124. Rowley attributes earlier trends to the inferior caliber of the justices appointed to the Court and the pressure of special interests. The Court, in his judgment, "has established a politically charged double standard that has offered, ostensibly at least, a high place to personal and civil rights, while ignoring—indeed overriding—economic rights that are at least as well grounded in the Constitution" (95).

8. *Forfeitures*

Perhaps the crassest means of violating property rights in the contemporary United States occurs through the legal device of forfeiture, that is, the confiscation, on the government's behalf, of assets that are either deemed involved in a crime or belong to a person charged with one. In the former case, an inanimate object is treated as if it were an accomplice: its owner receives no compensation for the loss.[121] The practice of forfeiture is ancient: in classical Greece it was customary to punish inanimate objects that caused injury, and medieval Europeans tried and executed animals that had killed a human being. English common law called for the forfeiture of carts and boats responsible for damage.[122] This practice has received unprecedented impetus in recent years under the guise of combating traffic in illegal narcotics. It largely escapes public outrage because forfeitures are carried out for the laudable purpose of fighting the spread of drugs. The legal basis for such seizures was provided by the Supreme Court in 1974 in a decision that authorized the confiscation from a charter company of a yacht worth several hundred thousand dollars after government agents had found aboard it the remains of a single marijuana cigarette.[123] There are other instances of such seizures of properties of parties not personally involved in criminal activity which have received the blessing of the Supreme Court.*

Given such license, government agents have been pursuing with singular zeal the war against properties which had been used, even without their owners' knowledge or approval, for illegal purposes.

> [U]nder most civil asset forfeiture statutes, as opposed to criminal statutes, law enforcement officials can seize a person's property, real or chattel, without notice or hearing, upon an *ex parte* showing of mere probable cause to believe that the prop-

*"In any civil forfeiture case, the Court will not seriously scrutinize the injury to property rights, because it does not regard such rights as worthy of the same respect as the rights of an accused felon, a member of a minority race, or a First Amendment dissident. The rights of property rank far lower than civil rights or civil liberties in the Court's scale of constitutional values." Leonard W. Levy, *A License to Steal* (Chapel Hill, N.C., and London, 1996), 88.

> erty has somehow been involved in a crime. Proceeding thus *in rem*—against the property, not the person—the government need not charge the owner or anyone else with a crime, for the action is against "the property." The allegation of "involvement" may range from belief that the property is contraband to a belief that it represents the proceeds of crime (even if the property is in the hands of someone not suspected of a crime), that it is an instrumentality of crime, that it somehow "facilitates" crime. . . . Once the property is seized, the burden is upon the owner, if he wants to try to get his property back, to prove his "innocence." . . . Until recently, that proof has been all but impossible because the thing is considered to be the offender. Imbued with personality, the thing is said to be "tainted" by its unlawful use.[124]

Thus, by way of illustration, in a recent decision, the Supreme Court has ruled that an automobile, jointly owned by a married couple, whose male spouse used it to solicit a prostitute, may be forfeited. The wife protested that she neither knew about nor condoned her husband's behavior and therefore was entitled to compensation from the government for the confiscation of the car. Chief Justice William H. Rehnquist, referring to precedents dating to the early nineteenth century, ruled, however, that "an owner's interest in property may be forfeited by reason of the use to which the property is put even though the owner did not know that it was put to such use."[125]

The magnitude of such acquisitions by public institutions of private assets can be statistically demonstrated. Between 1985 and 1993, the Department of Justice carried out 170,000 seizures and turned over $2 billion realized from them to state and local law enforcement agencies and to other officials dealing with organized crime. In addition, possibly as much as $2 billion was obtained from state and local forfeiture proceedings.[126] In 1993, the Assets Forfeiture Fund of the Department of Justice held over $500 million in cash as well as over 27,000 properties with a combined value of more than $1.9 billion.[127] The statute requires the proceeds of such forfeitures to be used exclusively for law enforcement purposes; hence, much of the money acquired in this manner is transferred to local police authorities, which have been known to appropriate it for personal uses, such as Christmas parties and banquets.[128] To raise such funds, some have set up "sting operations" for drugs in valuable buildings or on land which they coveted. Blacks and Hispanics are singled out in such arbitrary proceedings: if found with large amounts of cash on their persons, they are presumed to have obtained it from drug sales and are likely to have it confiscated.

In 1993, Representative Henry Hyde introduced a bill, the Civil Asset Forfeiture Reform Act, intended to curb such violations of property rights. It has yet to be enacted into law.

9. *Entitlements*

The cases of infringement of property that we have discussed so far—taxes, environmental regulations, forfeitures—fall under the category of "takings." To the extent that property rights are an essential aspect of freedom, such actions represent violations of freedom. But, paradoxically, a case can be made that liberty in the modern welfare state is also jeopardized by "givings," that is, by the dependence created when individuals, business enterprises, and educational institutions come to rely heavily or even exclusively on government subsidies, contracts, and other favors which, for all the benefits they may bring, are not property in the true sense. For if freedom means independence, dependence spells its opposite.

In 1964, Charles A. Reich, a professor of law at Yale, published an influential essay called "The New Property," in which he drew attention to the appearance in the contemporary United States (and, by implication, the other industrial democracies) of a form of property that bore the characteristics of conditional or "feudal" ownership. This phenomenon, in his view, endangered individual liberty.

In support of this claim, Reich listed eight distinct ways in which government established economic influence over the population.[129] A comparison of the figures he provided with those of the early 1990s indicates that the dependence of U.S. citizens on government largesse has considerably increased in the intervening thirty-five years.

1. *Income and benefits*. These are government outlays to citizens who hold no public job; they take the form of Social Security payments, unemployment compensation, and social welfare benefits in money and kind of a great variety. Between 1950 and 1980, civilian social welfare costs increased, in constant dollars, twenty times, while the population only doubled.[130] A large item of expenditure until recently was Aid to Families with Dependent Children ($25 billion given to thirteen million families, over four million headed by single mothers, half of them never

married).* Then there is Medicaid, veterans' support, Supplemental Security Income, Food Stamps and other food benefits, low-income housing assistance, low-rent public housing, education aid, training for disadvantaged adults and youth, summer youth employment programs, and low-income energy assistance. Just how dependent a large segment of the U.S. population is on government handouts is demonstrated by statistics which indicate that in 1976, the poorest 20 percent of the populace received nearly its entire income from government payments: its own earnings amounted to only $3.3 billion, a sum augmented by "transfer payments" of $75.8 billion. The second-lowest quintile in terms of earnings had its income increased by the government from $76.3 billion to $119.7 billion, or by more than one-half.[131] These figures indicate that recently one-fifth of the U.S. population was almost wholly and another fifth heavily dependent on government handouts. They demonstrate that 60 percent of the U.S. population, its most productive element, fully or partly supported the other 40 percent.

2. *Public jobs*. In 1961, over nine million Americans were directly employed by the government. Adding to this figure the three to four million persons then working for defense industries which rely mainly on government funding, Reich estimated that between 15 and 20 percent of the U.S. labor force drew the bulk of its income from government funds. As noted previously, in 1995, the number of civilian government employees doubled to 10.5 million, of which number nearly three million worked for the federal government.[132] In some parts of the country, the majority of the inhabitants hold government jobs: thus in Alaska, one-third of the population is on the government payroll, while in Juneau, that state's capital, between one-half and two-thirds of the inhabitants work for the federal, state, or city government.[133]

These segments of the population, consisting of the poor, public employees, and a good portion of the aged compose what has been called the "high tax coalition," a pressure group with a vested interest in raising taxes as high as possible. In 1975, they were estimated to account for 44.8 percent of the electorate.[134]

3. *Occupational licenses,* i.e., permits to engage in various professions and occupations, from physicians to pawnbrokers to funeral direc-

**New York Times*, August 9, 1996, p. A27. The program, which was part of the Social Security Act of 1935, was originally designed to help widows with small children but in time was extended to single mothers. Under the welfare reform of 1996, this program is being phased out.

tors. (These, it has been argued, although ostensibly introduced to protect the public, in fact serve the interests of those engaged in the occupations as a means of restricting access and competition.)*

4. *Franchises,* a modern version of sixteenth-to-eighteenth-century monopolies, entitling the holder to certain specified economic privileges. Contemporary examples are television and radio channels, air routes, and liquor licenses. Government today acknowledges licenses as private property of the licensee, since he can sell them.

5. *Government contracts.* These play an especially prominent role in defense industries. In 1996, outlays for national defense amounted to 265.7 billion or 17 percent of the federal budget, 48.9 billion of which was allocated for procurement.[135]

6. *Subsidies* to agriculture, shipping, local airlines, and housing.

7. *Use of public resources.* The government owns a fair share of the American economy: hundreds of millions of acres of public lands which have valuable mining, grazing, lumbering, and recreational facilities, transport and communication routes, radio and television channels, and so on. Some of these assets are turned over to private interests free of charge or at subsidized rates.[136]

8. *Services,* many of them of commercial value, such as postal deliveries of privately owned publications and insurance for home builders.

To this list may be added new forms of entitlement introduced since Reich wrote his article, such as Medicare and Medicaid.

Reich asked how important the governmentally dispensed wealth was in relation to the national economy and came up with the following answer:

> In 1961, when personal income totaled [$]416,432,000,000, governmental expenditures on all levels amounted to [$]164,875,000,000. The governmental payroll alone approached forty-five billion dollars. And these figures do not take account of the vast intangible wealth represented by licenses, franchises, services, and resources. Moreover the *proportion* of governmental wealth is increasing. Hardly any citi-

*Paul T. Heyne, *Private Keepers of the Public Interest* (New York etc., 1968), 82–84. The licensing of medical doctors dates back to 1519, when Henry VIII granted the physicians of London a charter, confirmed by the House of Commons, empowering them to pass upon qualifications of other physicians in the city and suburbs. John R. Commons, *Legal Foundations of Capitalism* (New York, 1924), 227–28. In the seventeenth century, English courts annulled these restrictions. Ibid., 228.

> zen leads his life without at least partial dependence on wealth flowing through the giant governmental syphon.[137]

Now, on the face of it, the growing role of the government in the national economy does not adversely affect the basic rights and liberties of U.S. citizens. Their freedom of speech and their liberty to choose who governs them and where to work, live, and travel are guaranteed by the Constitution and protected by courts. Government does not confiscate private property (except in criminal cases) as was done in Communist Russia or Nazi Germany. So to all appearances, the principles articulated in the Bill of Rights remain intact. This suggests that the traditional relationship between private property and freedom may have been rendered obsolete: government apparently can legitimately appropriate and dispense at its discretion a sizable share of a citizen's wealth and yet refrain from encroaching on his liberties. The modern American citizen appears to enjoy the best of all worlds in that he keeps his rights and freedoms while benefiting from various forms of government bounty.

However, appearances in this respect are deceptive. Modern democratic governments establish a high degree of control over its citizenry by the device of wealth transfer, limiting in a variety of ways of dubious constitutional validity the rights of citizens to enjoy their assets and, at the same time, creating a dangerous degree of dependence among the beneficiaries of its largesse. Referring to the situation in Great Britain, which in many respects parallels that of the United States, the legal historian P. S. Atiyah says:

> Those who benefit from subsidized housing, free school meals, half-price bus fares, concessionary electricity, and the like, are equally deprived [as the rich] of their freedom of choice as to how they will spend their subsidies. The State provides but does not allow the individual to choose the form of the provision, or to sell his benefits.[138]

By accepting what the government dispenses through the means enumerated above, individuals and organizations leave themselves no choice but to submit to government's conditions whose objective is not private but public welfare as the government chooses to define it. When the exercise of a right is dependent on an external authority, it turns into a conditional privilege, which effectively divests the owner of his proprietary title, inasmuch as unconditionality is one of the essential attributes of ownership. These facts have led Reich to argue that government "givings" in the United States have created a modern feudalism.* His solution was to declare government "largesse" a "new property," and its benefits a "right" rather than a privilege; revocations should be subject to due process and compensated.†

10. *Contracts*

The right of private parties to enter into binding contracts is one of the defining attributes of property rights. This is especially true of modern industrial societies, in which most property consists not of physical objects but of credit and other intangibles.

> [W]hile the agricultural economy is an economy of "property" in the precise meaning of the word, based on the direct ownership of tangible goods, the industrial economy, by contrast, is an economy of "contracts," based on the division of labor among a large number of individuals who engage either their persons or their resources in the pursuit of a common objective, in the hope of future gain which is not directly linked to their own performance. The "circuits of production" stretch out. It is necessary to finance the purchase of machines, of raw materials, of stocks of finished products, the salaries paid to workers, before dreaming of pocketing the profits derived from the sale of what one has manufactured. Resort to credit is generalized. The industrial economy is, at one and the same time, an "economy of anticipations" and an "economy of debts." Wealth is no longer tied to a tangible and indestructible good which is land, but to that new "property" which is immaterial and fungible and called credit: the industrial economy is *one of credit.*[139]‡

*Reich in *Yale Law Journal* 73, No. 5 (April 1964), 770. "The characteristics of the public interest state are varied, but there is an underlying philosophy that unites them. This is the doctrine that the wealth that flows from government is held by its recipients conditionally, subject to confiscation in the interest of the paramount state." Ibid., 768.

†Ibid., 785–87. Also ibid. 75, No. 8 (July 1966), 1266. However, Robert H. Nelson in *Public Lands and Private Rights* (Lanham, Md., 1995) asserts that the process of "privatization" is already altering much of Reich's "new property," as in the late Middle Ages conditional tenure evolved into outright ownership (pp. 334–37).

‡In the words of Roscoe Pound, in the commercial world "wealth is made up largely of promises": *Introduction to the Philosophy of Law* (New Haven, Conn., 1922/1954), 133.

In the nineteenth century and the beginning of the twentieth, the U.S. Supreme Court more than once affirmed freedom of contract to be "part of the rights of personal liberty and private property"[140] and on these grounds declared unconstitutional attempts to interfere with it. But in the course of the twentieth century, attitudes toward contractual freedom have changed, because government has arrogated to itself the right to intervene on behalf of what it considers the weaker of the contracting parties. This practice is a reversion to medieval conditions when urban authorities and sometimes even national governments set "just" prices and "just" wages.* The government of the modern welfare state intrudes on the freedom of contractual parties at all levels of social and economic life: it sets minimum wages to be paid by private employers to private employees; it tells landlords to whom to rent and sometimes even what rents to charge; it sets racial and sex quotas for the hiring of personnel by private enterprises and admissions to private institutions of higher learning; it pressures private banks to lend money to certain neighborhoods and disadvantaged groups. As a consequence, the principle of private contractual freedom is in jeopardy, and along with it the institution of property.

a. MINIMUM WAGES

In the United States, the practice of legislative interference with employer-employee arrangements goes back to a Supreme Court decision of 1898 validating a law of the Utah legislature limiting to eight hours a day work in underground mines. Although in previous cases such limitations were judged to violate the freedom of contract, the Court now ruled, in recognition of the unequal powers of employers and employees, that such laws conformed to the Constitution. In 1912, Massachusetts was the first state to introduce a minimum-wage law, but its application was voluntary. This was not the case with mandatory minimum-wage laws adopted subsequently by other states. Such statutes were primarily directed against the practice of "sweating," common in the employment of women and children, a term which was defined to mean paying wages that did not enable an employee to afford the necessities of life.

In 1923, the Supreme Court nullified these state laws when it upheld the decision of a District of Columbia court in the case of *Children's Hospital v. Adkins* that minimum-wage laws represented "an unconsti-

*Local justices fixed wages in England in Tudor times. Keith Feiling, *History of England*, 509–13; Atiyah, *Rise and Fall*, 74.

tutional interference with the freedom of contract included within the guarantees of the due process clause of the Fifth Amendment."[141] But soon conditions changed, and so did the Court's notion of constitutionality. In 1937, at the height of the Depression, the Court, asked to rule on a state of Washington minimum-wage law for women, declared minimum-wage legislation consonant with the Constitution.[142] The following year, Congress passed the Fair Labor Standards Act, which has served as the basis for minimum-wage legislation ever since.

We shall refrain from addressing the controversial question whether minimum-wage laws bring wage earners the material benefits which is their purpose, except to note evidence that it outprices the labor of persons with little education, especially black youths, making some of them unemployable, and thus, unintentionally, discriminating against them.[143] But it is a striking fact that even the proponents of such legislation find little to say in its favor other than that it does no harm since it appears that very few workers not covered by it receive less than the statutory minimum wage. Hence, it is to be treated as a political rather than an economic "statement" and presumably to be judged as such.[144]

Thus contractual freedom is violated apparently for no purpose other than to deal another blow at proprietary rights.

b. RENT CONTROL

If the benefits of wage controls are in dispute, there is no disagreement about rent control, which virtually all economists, whatever their politics, regard as an unmitigated disaster and oppose except as a temporary emergency measure.[145] Nevertheless, it is zealously advocated by some radical ideologues who see in it a means of "raising the consciousness" of the poor: "The hope is that tenants will move from rent enactments to regulation of financial and corporate institutions, and to a radical reordering of priorities in society."*

Rent control was first introduced in France at the outbreak of World War I, to prevent landlords from taking advantage of the families of soldiers and defense workers. England and the United States followed suit, and so did most of the belligerent countries and even some that stayed

*Ted Dienstfrey in Walter Block and Edgar Olsen, eds., *Rent Control: Myths and Realities* (Vancouver, B.C., 1981), 7. This tactic emulates that adopted by Russian radicals in the 1890s who, determined to arouse the politically apathetic workers, supported their demands for higher wages and shorter hours, in the hope that the realization these demands could not be satisfied under the existing political and economic regime would radicalize them. The effort failed. See Richard Pipes, *Social Democracy and the St. Petersburg Labor Movement, 1885–1897* (Cambridge, Mass., 1963), 57–75.

neutral. The controls were kept in place for a time after the restoration of peace and in a few cases into the 1930s. They were resurrected during World War II.

In most American cities, rent controls were abolished after World War II (although not in New York City), but here and there—notably in several major university towns, such as Berkeley, California, and Cambridge, Massachusetts—they were reinstated in the 1970s under the pressure of radical activists. In New York City, which has been called "the rent control capital of the world," they have brought urban decay of unprecedented proportions as many landlords, unable to make any profit on their properties, either neglected or abandoned them. The hope that the victims of such neglect would turn to a "radical reordering in society" was not realized, because, as it turned out, the main beneficiaries of rent controls were not the poor, who lived in public housing and renovated apartments, but middle-aged, middle-class tenants able to enjoy the amenities of the city at subsidized cost, among them the mayor of New York City and the president of the American Stock Exchange.* At the time of writing, over two million persons, or one-quarter of New York City's population, live in rent-controlled or "rent-stabilized" apartments. Supporters of rent control have now shifted the basis of their argument: rather than claim that it helps the poor, which it visibly fails to do, they contend that it makes New York City a more "diverse" place. A professor of urban planning at Columbia University says that rent control "is a major factor in making New York the kind of city that's attractive to live in. It keeps neighborhoods stable and preserves diversity."[146]

Under this rubric one can also list government prohibitions on discrimination in renting or selling dwellings in accord with the 1968 Fair Housing Act (as amended in 1988).[147] The provisions of this act are difficult to enforce, because a high proportion of the renters and sellers are small owners. However, when the authorities chance on a major corporation engaging in discriminatory activity, denying housing on grounds of race, it imposes very stiff fines. Thus, in May 1997, a federal jury in Manhattan awarded $640,000 to a racially mixed couple who had been denied the right to sublet an apartment in a cooperative building on what were judged racial grounds.[148]

*Lawrence M. Friedman, *Government and Slum Housing* (Chicago, 1968), 128. This is a classic illustration of the contention, advanced by a number of critics of the welfare state, that welfare benefits the middle class at the expense of both the rich and the poor. See Albert O. Hirschman, *The Rhetoric of Reaction* (Cambridge, Mass., 1991), 60–9.

Now, the right to exclude has always been an essential attribute of ownership. When owners, in this case the owners of a cooperative apartment, cannot bar anyone from renting, for whatever reasons, they may be said no longer to possess it. Such antidiscrimination legislation, therefore, strikes at the very foundation of property rights. It has also proved counterproductive: evidence indicates that segregation by race between core cities and suburbs has increased since it has gone into effect.[149]

C. BANK REGULATIONS AND "SET-ASIDES"

A good example of the harm done by laws which seek to impose social obligations on private enterprise is regulation of banks.[150] Banks serve the community—as well as their owners—by making prudent loans: loans of moneys which belong to others who have entrusted them with their care. Unless evidence to the contrary is produced, there is no reason to believe that in extending loans they are influenced by any other consideration than the recipients' creditworthiness, that is, their willingness as well as ability to pay interest and repay the principal. *Pecunia non olet*—money has no smell, in the words attributed to the Roman emperor Vespasian. Thus Swiss bankers felt no compunctions about collaborating with Nazi Germany in handling assets stolen from Jews; nor have European or American bankers shied away from doing business with Communist regimes. One must assume, therefore, that profit made on blacks and women is every bit as welcome as that made on white males. If, therefore, banks show a reluctance to lend to certain neighborhoods or to certain groups of the population, the reasonable assumption is that experience has taught them that they pose an unacceptable risk. Historically, higher risks have been compensated for by higher interest rates. Such a solution, however, is no longer available, since it would constitute discrimination and be subject to legal prosecution. The result is that certain localities and certain groups find it more difficult to obtain mortgage money and other forms of credit.

This reality the government interprets as *prima facie* evidence of discrimination and seeks to remedy by monitoring the performance of banks in lending to minority groups and the communities in which the banks are located. The legal basis for this interference with private enterprise is three laws: the 1974 Equal Credit Opportunity Act, which outlawed discrimination in lending on the basis of race, religion, and sex; the 1975 Home Mortgage Disclosure Act, which required banks to provide the government with detailed information on the race, sex, and income of every mortgagee; and the 1977 Community Reinvestment Act, which required banks to lend within their own communities.[151] Because the Department of Justice does not provide clear criteria under which a bank can legitimately refuse credit, potentially any such refusal can be interpreted as discrimination.[152]

Each year Federal Reserve Board regulators rate banks from "poor" to "excellent" on the basis of their record in meeting the standards of this legislation. These ratings have monetary value, because they influence the decisions of regulators authorizing bank mergers, expansions, and acquisitions.[153] While compelling banks to assume special risks by requiring them to loan money to persons with a low credit rating, the federal government shows no inclination to compensate them for the losses they may suffer as a result of defaults.

Another form of government control imposed on business for the ostensible purpose of obtaining a greater racial balance is the so-called "set-aside," by virtue of which minority firms are given preference in the awarding of federal contracts. Such contracts amount to some $200 billion annually paid to 60,000 companies employing over one-fifth of the nation's labor force.* Under this practice, firms owned by blacks and women may be awarded federal contracts even if they do not submit the lowest bids. Such set-asides are inequitable in two ways: they discriminate against nonblack, male bidders, and they waste citizens' tax money by paying more than necessary for goods and services. In 1995, the Supreme Court ruled one such case unconstitutional, a case in which a Colorado company owned by a white person lost a federal highway contract to a firm owned by a Hispanic person, even though it had submitted a lower bid. According to a newspaper account, the Court ruled: "There is no across-the-board entitlement, among all members of a minority group, to Government preference based solely on historic discrimination." However, the Court left the door open to the continuance of such practices by allowing "race-based preference programs . . . in response to quantifiable evidence of discrimination against an affected party."[154]

In order to satisfy "important Democratic constituencies: blacks and other minorities, as well as women" and still meet Supreme Court standards, the Clinton administration has decided to preserve set-aside pro-

*Associated Press, September 2, 1996. In 1995–96, these set-asides amounted to $6.4 billion awarded to over six thousand companies, almost all owned by members of ethnic or racial minorities. *New York Times*, August 15, 1997, p. A1.

grams by ruling that discrimination occurs whenever "minority" businesses do not receive their share of contracts or are not "utilized" in proportion to their "capacity."[155] The possibility that minority businesses are "underutilized" because they are less efficient or more costly apparently does not enter into consideration. And so the practice continues. In February 1998, the Clinton administration, which requires manufacturers of automobiles who sell vehicles to the government to present their "goals for procurement from minority companies," pressured the Big Three to increase by the year 2001 their procurement from such companies to 5 percent or $8.8 billion a year.[156]

11. *Affirmative action in employment*

Far and away the most egregious form of government interference with the contractual rights of private persons and organizations is carried out in the name of affirmative action—the laws and regulations enacted since 1964 under the capacious category of "civil rights." Introduced by President Johnson, affirmative action has been broadened in application by subsequent administrations, Democratic and Republican alike. Initially conceived as a long-overdue means of enforcing the principle of nondiscrimination in regard to black citizens mandated by the Fourteenth and Fifteenth Amendments, it was soon extended to other groups, including women and the disabled, and ultimately turned into a vehicle for "reverse discrimination" against whites and males. This was inevitable, because ideals, however noble, when ordained by legislation, are enforced by bureaucrats who, by the nature of their responsibilities, are prone to concentrate on the means and neglect the objectives. And bureaucrats are the key factor, for "while presidents and congresses come and go, the federal agencies abide. . . ."[157]

> It is the fate of any social reform in the United States—perhaps anywhere—that, instituted by enthusiasts, men of vision, politicians, statesmen, it is soon put into the keeping of full-time professionals. This has two consequences. On the one hand, the job is done well. The enthusiasts move on to new causes while the professionals continue working in the area of reform left behind by public attention. But there is a second consequence. The professionals, concentrating exclusively on the area of reform, may become more and more remote from public opinion and, indeed, from common sense. They end up at a point

> that seems perfectly logical and necessary to them—but which seems perfectly outrageous to almost everyone else.[158]

The legislative basis of affirmative action is provided by the Civil Rights Act of 1964 and several executive orders by President Johnson, the enforcement of which was entrusted to the Equal Employment Opportunity Commission and other federal agencies. The 1964 Act was the most radical law affecting civil rights ever passed by any nation.* The act contained a number of laudable provisions, designed to prevent discrimination in voting and access to public facilities as well as segregation in public schools. Its main target was the South, but its most important provisions had far broader ramifications. Title VI provided: "No person in the United States shall, on the ground of race, color, or national origin, be excluded from participation in, be denied the benefits of, or be subjected to discrimination under any program or activity *receiving Federal financial assistance,*"[159] which term, as we shall see, applies to a great deal of private business and many private institutions of higher learning. Two years later, this prohibition was extended to discrimination on grounds of sex, and in 1973 on grounds of physical disability.

The antidiscrimination provisions of Title VI, applying as they did only to institutions in receipt of federal financial aid, included almost all public schools and universities and a large proportion of medical facilities.[160] Title VII, however, extended this provision by banning discrimination on the basis of race, color, religion, sex, or national origin in trade unions, employment agencies, and all enterprises with more than fifteen employees engaged in interstate commerce or doing business with the federal government but excluding (until 1972) 10.1 million employees of state and local government and 4.3 million employees of educational institutions.[161] The officials charged with implementing these rulings required every contractor who fell within the purview of this legislation to develop "an acceptable affirmative action program," which would include

> an analysis of the areas within which the contractor is deficient in the utilization of minority groups and women, and further,

*The term "affirmative action" was first employed rather casually in an executive order by President Kennedy in March 1961. It was promoted by Vice President Johnson, who revived an ambiguous phrase from the National Labor Relations (Wagner) Act of 1935. Graham, *Civil Rights Era,* 27–28, 33–36.

goals and timetables to which the contractor's good faith efforts must be directed to correct the deficiencies.[162]

In 1965 and again in 1967, President Johnson signed executive orders to implement the provisions of the act by specifically prohibiting discrimination on the basis of "race, creed, color, or national origin" (to which sex was added later). These provisions required massive record-keeping by both the government and private institutions concerning the racial, religious, ethnic, and sexual composition of their workforce. The scope of this legislation becomes apparent when one considers that today it applies to nearly 200,000 firms employing some 26 million people or almost one-quarter of the country's labor force.[163] In 1972 the ruling was extended to educational institutions as well as to state and local governments.

Title VII was a revolutionary measure which provided the basis for numerous antidiscriminatory laws and regulations, the enforcement of which immensely increased the power of the state and reduced correspondingly the contractual freedom of individuals and enterprises. Extended first to women, then to the aged, and finally to the physically handicapped, it handed the government unheard-of powers to interfere in relations between and among private citizens. It was undemocratic as well by virtue of the fact that it was opposed by a solid majority of citizens, including those whom it was intended to benefit. A Gallup Poll survey in 1977 found that Americans as a whole opposed minority preferences by a margin of eight to one; nonwhites did so by a margin of better than two to one. The poll-takers concluded: "Rarely is public opinion, on such a controversial issue, as united as over this question. Not a single population group supports affirmative action."[164]

It may be noted in this connection that the verb "to discriminate" has been politicized to the point where its original meaning—to distinguish, to discern—has been all but lost. In the customary sense, of course, it is an essential ingredient of freedom. To prevent citizens—in contrast to governments—from discriminating is to deprive them of a fundamental right.

Title VII exempted employers from granting "preferential treatment to any individual or group": it promoted equality of opportunity, a negative objective. This qualification helped passage of the Civil Rights Act in Congress, where it had run into stiff resistance. But as we know, President Johnson had something much more positive in mind when he said, the year after the passage of the Civil Rights Act, that he wanted "not just equality as a right and a theory but equality as a fact and as a *result*." With this objective in mind, the federal government undertook an ambitious campaign of social engineering.

The Civil Rights Act of 1964, as implemented, stood in stark contrast with its 1866 namesake, which stressed citizens' rights to property and equality before the law.[165] It resembled rather the 1875 Civil Rights Act, which prohibited discrimination in private enterprises (public accommodations, public conveyances, and places of amusement). This act the Supreme Court had ruled unconstitutional in 1883, on the grounds—startling and repugnant to us today—that it encroached on the rights of private persons and enterprises:

> It would be running the slavery argument into the ground to make it apply to every act of discrimination which a person may see fit to make as to the guests he will entertain, or as to the people he will take into his coach or cab or car, or admit to his concert or theater, or deal with in other matters of intercourse or business.[166]

One difficulty with administering antidiscriminatory legislation is that it does not—and, indeed, cannot—establish unambiguous criteria for determining when it is violated. Officials enforcing laws cannot act on nebulous impressions of intent: they must have clear, unequivocal standards, and these can only be statistics of results. Soon after the passage of the Civil Rights Act, therefore, it became the practice of government agencies to *infer* discrimination from significant disparities in employment of white males and minorities (by race or sex).[167] As early as 1968, the Office of Federal Contract Compliance of the Department of Labor, avoiding the term "quotas," issued guidelines in which it spoke of "goals and timetables." In December 1971 these terms were defined to mean increasing "materially the utilization of minorities and women," "underutilization" being defined as "having fewer minorities or women in a particular job classification than would reasonably be expected by their availability."[168] With the assistance of lawyers working for the Equal Employment Opportunity Commission, a body of case law was established in the lower courts to replace "the traditional intent test with an effects test":

> This in turn would allow the agency to construct prima facie cases based on statistical data irrespective of intent, and

> through this device to throw upon employers a burden of proof that, in light of the damaging statistics, would be difficult to sustain.[169]

Such "tests" consist of numerical quotas specifying what proportion of persons employed and promoted as well as students admitted were to be nonwhite and female. Quotas, however, were from the beginning judged to be of dubious constitutional validity: Title VII of the Civil Rights Act prohibited them, and in 1978 the Supreme Court declared them unconstitutional. The Court nevertheless permitted "flexible" affirmative action norms. In practice, therefore, bureaucracies charged with implementing the program tended toward quotas euphemistically labeled "goals." In 1970, the Department of Labor issued a ruling to employers requiring that the "rate of minority applicants recruited should approximate or equal the rate of minorities in the population in each location."[170]

One problem with the enforcement of this objective is that employers use tests for hiring, admission, and promotion, and that in taking these tests such minority groups as blacks and Hispanics as well as women generally perform less well than do white males and Asians. To overcome this hurdle, courts have ruled that the application of criteria that have no direct bearing on the duties required (such as possession of a high school diploma) violates civil rights. The same is said to hold of the administration of identical examinations to all applicants. Thus in the precedent-setting *Griggs v. Duke Power Co.* case heard in 1971, the Supreme Court unanimously ruled that an employer cannot impose minimum qualifications as a condition of employment unless he is able to prove they are essential to the performance of a given job. (In this case, the company required for all promotions a high school diploma and the passing of an aptitude test.)[171] The Court further ruled that discrimination occurred when identical standards were set for all applicants. A black man who had been refused employment by Motorola in 1963 because he had performed poorly on a multiple-choice test filed a grievance with the Illinois Fair Employment Commission. The commission held the test unfair to "culturally deprived and disadvantaged groups" because "it failed to account for differences in the environment," and it ordered Motorola to hire the black applicant and to stop administering the test.[172]

In the words of Chief Justice Burger: "Congress directed the thrust of the [Civil Rights] Act to the *consequences* of employment practices, not simply the motivation." This was a manifest misinterpretation of the 1964 act.[173] According to this criterion, any general requirement and any qualifying test which blacks and whites passed with different rates could serve as *prima facie* evidence of discrimination.[174] It meant that nondiscrimination in the application of standards represented discrimination—a classic example of Orwellian Newspeak.

Businesses now came under pressure to devise devious ways of "improving" the qualifications of minority employees in order to obtain the desired mix of races and sexes and avoid legal action. Thus, the original striving for color-blindness gave way to racial quotas and timetables. Businesses are required regularly to submit to government agencies bulky records containing information on how many members of each minority group they employ at each occupational level. Litigation over discrimination, real or imagined, is a flourishing business.

The trouble with quotas, however labeled, is that they are inherently discriminatory because they make the attainment of something desirable dependent not on a person's personal qualifications and attainments but on membership in a racial, ethnic, or sex group. This was not the intent of those who framed the legislation, but it inevitably evolved this way because otherwise the legislation would have been unenforceable.

A kind of ultimate absurdity in the application of civil rights legislation occurs in the enforcement of the Americans with Disabilities Act of 1990. In 1997, the act was interpreted to apply to employees suffering "mental illness" as manifested in chronic lateness, poor judgment, and hostility toward coworkers and supervisors. Under the 1997 "guidance," employers are forbidden to take disciplinary action against employees who behave rudely or come to work disheveled. Instead, they must do all in their power to make such employees feel "comfortable."[175]

The entire body of antidiscriminatory laws and regulations, as it has evolved since 1964, not only discriminates against individuals who do not happen to belong to the groups which it singles out for preferential treatment but also subverts the organizations and institutions affected by it. It rests on the faulty premise that private institutions—whether business enterprises or universities—are microcosms of society at large and that their purpose is the satisfaction of the members' personal needs and wants rather than the attainment of their own objectives, whether improving production and profitability or providing a superior education. "Distributive justice" cannot be properly applied to appointments to businesses or institutions of higher learning because "considerations of distributive justice have a bearing only with respect to social practices that exist to confer benefits or opportunities upon their participants."[176] These considerations have no bearing on faculty appointments:

> [T]he common belief that they do have a bearing is based on a defective model of a college or university faculty—namely, that it is to be considered as a miniature civil society. . . . University faculties exist not to confer benefits and opportunities on the actual or possible members of those faculties but rather to serve the external goals of excellence in teaching and research. Thus the only relevant question for faculty appointment . . . is this: Is the college or university hiring the person best able . . . to attain these goals. All other considerations are either irrelevant or secondary.*

The same argument, of course, applies to business hiring and promotion practices.

Nor is there merit in self-serving arguments in favor of quotas which claim that they enhance the "diversity" of the university. There are various kinds of "diversity" besides those based on criteria of race and sex. A 1989 survey by the Carnegie Foundation for the Advancement of Teaching found that a mere 4 percent of university faculty teaching the humanities and 2.2 percent of those teaching the social sciences identify themselves as "conservative," whereas over 40 percent of the faculties in the same fields say they are "liberals." Yet the American Association of University Professors, which actively promotes "diversity" in respect to race and gender, "has never suggested remedying this situation by setting 'goals and timetables' for hiring conservatives or the proponents of other under-represented perspectives," on the grounds that "with respect to political views [it] would not endorse the right of faculty to make judgments based on diversity criteria."[177]

Affirmative action procedures have shifted in a very dangerous way

*Jeffrie G. Murphy in Steven M. Cahn, ed., *Affirmative Action and the University* (Philadelphia, 1993), 165, 168. The absurdity of the requirement that each profession or organization reflect, in terms of race and gender, the structure of society at large is brought into relief by the following tongue-in-cheek demand on behalf of the Jewish minority: "Jews come from athletically deprived backgrounds. Irving is kept off the sandlot by too much homework and too many music lessons. He is now 25 and still can't play ball but 'he has the desire to learn.' Therefore, the Jewish Defense League is demanding that New York City, which has a 24 percent Jewish population, fill the city's ball teams with 24 percent Jews." Cited in George C. Roche, *The Balancing Act* (La Salle, Ill., 1974), 27–28.

the prerogative to admit and to employ from private institutions to the state, i.e., the government bureaucracy:

> An antidiscrimination law is the antithesis of the freedom of contract, a principle that allows all persons to do business with whomever they please for good reason, bad reason, or no reason at all. Under the contractual regime, the chief job of the state is to ensure that all persons enjoy the civil capacity to own property, to contract, to sue and be sued, and to give evidence. The rights that the state thereby recognizes and protects are easily made universal, and can be held simultaneously by all persons. . . . The state secures for all persons a zone of freedom against aggression and fraud. . . . The antidiscrimination principle operates as a powerful brake against this view of freedom of contract and the concomitant but limited role of the state.[178]

Title VII of the 1964 Civil Rights Act has been further subverted to interfere with freedom of speech in the workplace. Although its original wording made no allusion to such matters, as interpreted by government agencies and courts it prohibits expression of "racist," "sexist," or even religious opinions that one's fellow workers may find offensive. Thus in 1988, a U.S. Circuit Court of Appeals declared as follows:

> While Title VII does not require an employer to fire all "Archie Bunkers" in its employ [!], the law does require that an employer take prompt action to prevent such bigots from expressing their opinions in a way that abuses or offends their coworkers. By informing people that the expression of racist or sexist attitudes in public is unacceptable, people may eventually learn that such views are undesirable in private, as well. Thus Title VII may advance the goal of eliminating prejudices and biases in our society.[179]

This ruling is a classic example of how a law, in this case barring employment discrimination on grounds of race, religion, or sex, can be broadened far beyond its original intent to inhibit free speech and change social behavior.

12. *Affirmative action in higher education*

A persuasive illustration of how the newly acquired financial powers of the government enable it to violate the contractual rights of its citizens is provided by federal interference with higher education. Generous subsidies to colleges and universities in the form of research grants, student aid, and tax exemptions have permitted an extraordinary expansion of American higher education: in proportion to the population, the number of students graduating from college between 1870 and 1992 has increased tenfold, and for a number of years now, between 33 and 45 percent of high school graduates have earned college degrees. (In 1900, only 4 percent of American youths aged eighteen to twenty-one attended college.)[180] Although the federal government began to support higher education as early as 1862, when it launched the land-grant program to colleges, until World War II, Washington played a negligible role in financing either universities or their students. As late as the mid-1930s, federal support of colleges and universities accounted for less than 5 percent of the moneys spent on higher education in the United States.[181] This situation changed following World War II. The Serviceman's Readjustment Act, popularly known as the GI Bill, passed in 1944 and subsequently amended several times, provided veterans admitted to college with tuition and modest living expenses. The result was that enrollment in colleges and universities rose from 1.5 million in 1940 to 2.7 million in 1950.[182]

In 1957, when the Soviet Union surprised the world by launching Sputnik, the first artificial earth satellite, no country was more affected than the United States, which never before had felt itself physically threatened by a hostile power, for Sputnik demonstrated the capacity of the Soviet military to deliver nuclear-tipped missiles to any part of the globe. The United States, as it would prove before long, was perfectly capable of emulating this feat: if it had been beaten in the missile race it was because it had made a deliberate decision not to race. Having concluded, on the advice of its scientists, that ballistic missiles could not be made sufficiently accurate for military purposes, it had chosen instead to rely on intercontinental bombers as the principal means of delivery of the nuclear deterrent. Nevertheless, in the ensuing hysteria, the educational establishment managed to persuade the American public and Congress that Russia's technical achievement was made possible by superior education. The National Defense Education Act of 1958 allocated vast sums of federal aid for students, partly as outright grants, partly as loans. Billions of dollars were dispensed to universities to carry out defense-related research. Each subsequent decade made more federal money available for such purposes. The Higher Education Act of 1965, part of Johnson's Great Society program, exceeded all previous aspirations by proposing to enable every American to attend college. In 1977, federal expenditures on higher education amounted to nearly $14 billion a year.[183] More recently, 75 percent of student aid has come from federal sources.[184]

The effects—both positive and negative—of this lavish outpouring of federal money on the quality of American education and the financial condition of institutions of higher learning are outside the scope of this study.[185] Our concern is with the power which its largesse gives the government to interfere with higher education, especially with the admission of students and the hiring of faculty. From this vantage point, the effect has been consistently harmful.

Neither the 1964 Civil Rights Act nor any legislation related to it called for "affirmative action" in institutions of higher learning. Indeed, since the 1950s, the nation's basic educational statutes have barred "any department, agency, officer, or employee of the United States" from exercising "any direction, supervision or control" over the educational process of schools and colleges, for which reason one authority asserts flatly that "federal control [over educational establishments] is illegal."[186] And yet the Department of Health, Education, and Welfare established criteria for determining whether discrimination was being practiced at universities and colleges by setting for them what amounted to racial and sex quotas. All colleges and universities in receipt of government financing—there are over two thousand of them—are now required regularly to submit to the government statistics on the racial and sex composition of their students and faculties—statistics which previously they have not been in the habit of compiling. If judged "unsatisfactory," they must make strenuous and demonstrable efforts to rectify the sex and race balance or risk losing federal money. The legal justification for government interference with university admission and hiring derives from the fact that, being tax-exempt, educational institutions receive an indirect tax subsidy; in addition, both they and their students are beneficiaries of direct government grants.

Increasingly, institutions of higher learning find themselves under the watchful eye of the federal bureaucracy when hiring or promoting faculty. They have been complying with government demands because they cannot afford to risk losing federal money. In 1939–40, private institutions of higher learning received 0.7 percent of their current income from the federal government; by 1969–70, this figure had risen to 22.5 percent.[187] Columbia University at one time received half of its annual budget from Washington. Government subsidies for research and training accounted in 1968 for 38 percent of Harvard's budget.[188] Princeton, which has the third-largest university endowment in the country, obtained in 1991 32.4 percent of its revenues from governmental contracts and grants, about one-third more than earned by its endowment income.[189] Colleges simply cannot afford to lose federal money, not only for their own operating expenses but also for student aid, by insisting on their right to admit, hire, and promote according to their own standards and judgment. As far as can be determined, only two small schools, with a combined enrollment of five thousand, have had the courage to do so. In 1996 there were only three all-male colleges left in the United States. (There were, however, still eighty-four private colleges catering exclusively to women.)[190] Recently, the government and courts have compelled two venerable military academies, the Virginia Military Institute and the Citadel, to abandon their traditional policy of admitting exclusively male students. Following the decision of the Supreme Court that VMI had to admit women, Judge Antonin Scalia in his dissenting opinion observed that "under the constitutional principles announced and applied today, single-sex public education is unconstitutional."[191]

Affirmative action procedures inevitably entail "reverse discrimination," that is, the exclusion of white and/or male applicants to college or faculty candidates with equal or better qualifications for admission than black and/or female applicants or candidates. In the early 1970s, the president of Cornell University spelled out, with uncommon candor, a policy that many others have followed tacitly when he instructed his faculty to hire "additional minority persons and females" even if "in many instances it may be necessary to hire unqualified or marginally qualified people."[192] Much the same procedure was adopted in regard to student admissions by lowering standards for minority applicants. When the University of California in 1997 abandoned affirmative action procedures for black and Hispanic applicants, which led to a significant drop in the admission of applicants from these two groups, the Department of Justice advised the university that it was investigating whether it was not in violation of federal civil rights law on the grounds that the application of standard tests for admission favored white students. Should the department find that the university violated these laws—that is, discriminated by not discriminating—it stood to lose more than $1.1

billion in federal funds.[193] Mercifully, the federal government has not as yet demanded that universities abandon standardized course examinations, as would logically follow from its admission criteria. It may be noted that a high proportion of the black and other minority students admitted to American colleges on the basis of quota preferences are unable to complete their education: their dropout rate in 1993 amounted to 72 percent.*

The constitutional aspect of affirmative action policies in college admissions confronted the Supreme Court in the form of the question whether "a person who is not of a minority race may be disadvantaged by preference given by official action to others on the basis of race alone."[194] The most celebrated of the cases considered by the Court in this connection was *Regents of the University of California v. Bakke* (1978). The plaintiff, Allan Bakke, had been denied admission to the medical school of the University of California at Davis, although both his grade averages and performance on the Medical College Admission Test were higher than those of some black students admitted under the "set-aside" rules. He sued, charging that he had been discriminated against on grounds of race in violation of the Fourteenth Amendment, which guarantees equal protection. The case aroused unusual interest because of its implications for the entire affirmative action program. The Supreme Court split five to four in favor of Bakke, requiring the University of California to admit him, but the Court's decision, while outlawing rigid quotas, did not unequivocally forbid racial preferences, leaving the door open to further abuses. The four dissenting judges argued that Bakke would not have "outperformed" the minority applicants were it not for prior discrimination against the latter.[195]

One way in which universities and colleges discriminate against white male applicants is to tamper with admission tests by adjusting them to achieve the desired goal of "balance." White male applicants score considerably higher than female applicants in mathematical tests for college admission (the SAT) and better than black applicants in both verbal and mathematical tests: in 1993, males qualified at more than twice the rate of females in Preliminary SAT tests because they scored substantially higher in the mathematical portion. To give female appli-

*Clint Bolick, *The Affirmative Action Fraud* (Washington, D.C., 1996), 79. "A University of California study a decade ago found that while 65 percent to 75 percent of Berkeley's white and Asian students graduated in four years, the five-year graduation rate was 18 percent for black and 22 percent for Hispanic students. Thirty percent of all black and Hispanic students dropped out in their first year." William L. O'Neill in *New York Times*, April 7, 1998, p. A30.

cants a better chance, the weight assigned to the verbal score, in which they nearly matched the males, was doubled. This arbitrary procedure penalized male applicants in general and Asian males in particular because Asians (of either sex) perform outstandingly well on the mathematical portion and comparatively poorly on the verbal one.[196] But since such tampering still did not bring about the desired results, other methods have been resorted to. Thus the Office for Civil Rights, determined to increase the number of girls qualifying for National Merit Scholarships, had the College Board in October 1997 add a novel "writing skills section" to the test, "anticipating that girls' total scores would rise, since writing is one area where girls tend to outscore boys." This procedure improved the girls' performance somewhat but not sufficiently, and other changes in the test may be introduced to yield the desired results.[197]

To achieve the required "balance," some institutions of higher learning have engaged in blatant reverse discrimination against white male and Asian applicants: black and Hispanic students are admitted if they meet minimum admission requirements, whereas Asians and whites must produce near-perfect scores.[198]

13. *School busing*

No interference by the government in the life of society for the sake of racial equality has been more destructive of freedom as well as counterproductive than the practice of forcible busing of school children. As was the case with affirmative action programs, the practice was initially designed on a limited scale to rectify indisputable wrongs. However, driven by the quest for social justice, it was soon broadened in scope to other issues of public life. Federal moneys again played a major role in this process.

The 1964 Civil Rights Act was directed primarily at southern schools which practiced rigid racial segregation. The Elementary and Secondary Education Act of 1965 made large federal grants available to schools; these furnished the federal authorities with a club with which to enforce school desegregation in the south. The problem was different and more difficult to resolve in the north, where school segregation was not deliberate policy but the natural result of the fact that white, black, and Hispanic urban communities lived in separate neighborhoods, which led to public schools being segregated *de facto*.

To deal with the problem, resort was had to forcible busing. In the north, it began in Boston in 1974 and from there spread to other cities. Busing was instituted with the blessing of the Supreme Court and carried out with the mindless zeal of which social reformers are capable when they interpret failure of their endeavors as evidence that they have not been sufficiently determined. The majority of Americans, white and black alike, opposed forcible busing: in the 1970s, 70 percent of blacks, for whose benefit the effort had been launched, opposed federal intervention to integrate schools.[199] The attempt at enforced equality ended up with a flagrant violation of freedom: no child was allowed to "flee" the school to which it had been assigned on the basis of race or national origin.[200] It was a form of forcible conscription practiced on helpless children.

It also proved self-defeating, inasmuch as school busing increased school segregation in the northern cities, as white families, unwilling to have their children treated as chattels, either enrolled them in private schools or else moved to the suburbs. In 1972, before forced busing had gotten underway, some 60 percent of the pupils in the Boston public schools were white; in 1995, non-Latino whites were reduced to 18 percent of the city's school population.[201] A study by the Harvard Graduate School of Education, released in 1997, showed that these figures were not an aberration but the reflection of a nationwide trend: in the 1990s, largely because of the flight of whites from metropolitan areas to avoid busing, the school segregation of black and Latino students has been steadily increasing, and is likely to continue to do so.[202]

14. Summing up

The survey of property rights in the twentieth century indicates that the winds have not been favorable to the rights of ownership and all that accompanies them. The fact that in the contest between totalitarianism and democracy, democracy and the rights to property ultimately carried the day must not obscure the fact that even in democratic societies the concept of property has undergone substantial revision, transforming it from absolute dominion into something akin to conditional possession, and that, as a result, the rights of individuals to their assets have been and continue to be systematically violated. Democratic procedures in electing governments do not automatically ensure respect for the civil rights of citizens. If proof is required, one need only recall the reign of Napoleon III, the first French head of state elected by universal male franchise, who used his lawfully obtained mandate to suppress freedom of the press, to arrest and exile citizens without due process, and altogether to arrogate to himself dictatorial powers. Democracy, indeed, can be "illiberal."[203]

Now it may be argued that a certain sacrifice of personal freedom is acceptable if it purchases a significant improvement in the condition of the less fortunate elements of society. But the problem is that such improvement is not evident: indeed, it appears that welfare which aims at providing more than basic needs actually increases poverty.

We have shown that such measures as minimum wages, rent control, and forced school busing either do not solve the problems for the sake of which they have been enacted or aggravate them. But there are more troubling indications that the whole panoply of welfare measures intended to abolish poverty and to create equality has been counterproductive:

> Since the War on Poverty began in 1965, federal, state, and local governments have spent more than $5.4 trillion fighting poverty in this country. How much money is $5.4 trillion? It is 70 percent more than it cost to fight World War II. For $5.4 trillion you could purchase the assets of all the Fortune 500 corporations *and* all the farmland in the United States. Yet . . . the poverty rate is actually higher today [1996] than it was in 1965.[204]

Between the launching of the Great Society in 1965 and 1993, the percentage of the population living below the poverty line rose from about 12.5 percent to 15 percent. This has occurred during a period when welfare spending increased from under $50 billion annually to $324 billion.[205] The reason for this unexpected development is that welfare fosters dependency and dependency promotes poverty. This trend is most obvious in the case of the program of Aid to Families with Dependent Children. Originally conceived as a way of assisting widowed mothers, its main effect has been to encourage unmarried women to have children, who become government wards. Thus, whereas in 1960 only 5.3 percent of births occurred out of wedlock, in 1990 this figure rose to 28 percent; among blacks, it was 65.2 percent. Ninety-two percent of families on welfare have no father present.* Bountiful welfare, welfare which does not confine itself to meeting emergencies and

*Tanner, *End of Welfare*, 70, 63. In Germany, 500,000 children are supported not by their fathers but by the state. Vera Gaserow in *Die Zeit*, No. 51 (December 13, 1996), p. 67.

situations out of the recipients' control but attempts artificially to provide them (in Franklin Delano Roosevelt's words) with a "comfortable living," is not only injurious to the principle of property, an indispensable adjunct of freedom, but self-defeating.

The right to property in and of itself does not guarantee civil rights and liberties. But historically speaking, it has been the single most effective device for ensuring both, because it creates an autonomous sphere in which, by mutual consent, neither the state nor society can encroach: by drawing a line between the public and the private, it makes the owner co-sovereign, as it were. Hence, it is arguably more important than the right to vote.* The weakening of property rights by such devices as wealth distribution for purposes of social welfare and interference with contractual rights for the sake of "civil rights" undermines liberty in the most advanced democracies even as the peacetime accumulation of wealth and the observance of democratic procedures conveys the impression that all is well.

*"The State Department uses democracy as an important criterion of human rights. The department's survey of human rights in 1995 denounced China as an 'authoritarian state,' in which the Communist Party 'monopolizes decision-making authority.' This was inaccurate, inasmuch as considerable decision-making authority—the decisions that people make in earning a living: the decisions to sow, reap, harvest, barter and exchange—had been largely delegated to the people. Only if life is viewed as a life of politics is the State Department's view correct." Tom Bethell, *The Noblest Triumph* (New York, 1998), 335. I do not know that I would go that far, but the thrust of the argument is valid.

PORTENTS

> A world in which all men are free and equal would be heaven on earth. Such a world is difficult to realize; and when forced to choose, we ought to place freedom above equality. Because the absence of freedom necessarily leads to the crassest inequality and injustice: to despotism. But inequality need not lead to the absence of freedom.
>
> —Karl Popper[1]

We have traced the evolution of both the idea and the institution of property and then demonstrated, on the contrasting examples of England and Russia, how closely property and its offshoot, law, relate to liberty: that they are its necessary though not sufficient precondition. In the final chapter we have presented evidence of disturbing developments in the twentieth century that have enabled governments, in the name of social justice and the "common good," to abolish or infringe on property rights and, by so doing, sometimes abolish and often restrict individual freedoms.

As the twentieth century draws to a close, the traditional threats to liberty and property no longer loom large. The downfall of communism has eliminated the most direct and dangerous challenge to them, while the economic failures of socialism have discredited the notion that the abolition of private ownership in the means of production solves all social ills. Even though tyrannies which tolerate no private property still manage to hang on to power here and there, they are either isolated or else slowly yielding to the spirit of the times: the slogans of the day are democracy and privatization.*

*This holds true despite the fact that the ex-Communist countries which have recently adopted democracy and privatization, notably Russia, are experiencing

Yet these welcome changes by no means signify that liberty's future is secure: it is still at peril, although from a different and novel source. The main threat to freedom today comes not from tyranny but from equality—equality defined as identity of reward. Related to it is the quest for security.

Liberty is by its nature inegalitarian, because living creatures differ in strength, intelligence, ambition, courage, perseverance, and all else that makes for success. Equality of opportunity and equality before the law (in the sense laid down to the Israelites through Moses in Leviticus 24:22: "Ye shall have one manner of law, as well for the stranger, as for the home-born; for I am the Lord your God") are not only compatible with liberty but essential to it. Equality of reward is not. Since this kind of equality exists neither in the animal kingdom nor among primitive peoples, it must be regarded as unnatural, and hence attainable only by coercion, which is why all utopian schemes presuppose despotic authority and all despots insist on the equality of their subjects.* As Walter Bagehot observed over a century ago, "there is no method by which men can be both free and equal."[2]

Ironically, the enforcement of equality destroys not only liberty but equality as well, for as the experience of communism has demonstrated, those charged with ensuring social equality claim for themselves privileges that elevate them high above the common herd. It also results in pervasive corruption, inasmuch as the elite which monopolizes goods and services, as must be done if they are to be equitably distributed, expects, in return for distributing them, rewards for itself.

And yet the ideal of a Golden Age when all were equal because there was no "mine and thine" has never ceased to appeal to humanity: it is one of its persistent and seemingly indestructible myths. In the contest

immense difficulties in adopting the Western model. It must be borne in mind that even the Communist parties of these countries no longer talk of a return to the Soviet model. They want to blend democracy and the market with social welfare policies and a certain degree of government intervention in the economy, which is not an infeasible combination.

*Aware of this problem, some modern political theorists have tried to redefine "equality" so as to make it seem compatible with liberty. Thus Michael Walzer in *Spheres of Justice* (New York, 1983) distinguishes between "simple" equality—equality in the ordinary sense of the word—and "complex equality" in which people are unequal in different spheres of life and do not thereby acquire the power to dominate, the elimination of which he defines as the aim of political egalitarianism (xiii). The distinction, whatever its theoretical merit, has little bearing on everyday life where "simple" equality alone matters. Significantly, in advancing his program, Walzer disavows any intention of depicting "how we might go about creating such a society" (xiv).

between equality and liberty, the former holds the stronger hand, because the loss of liberty is felt only when it occurs, whereas the pain of inequality rankles every moment of the day.

The trend of modern times appears to indicate that citizens of democracies are willing heedlessly to surrender their freedoms to purchase social equality (along with economic security), apparently oblivious of the consequences. And the consequences are that their ability to hold on to and use what they earn and own, to hire and fire at will, to enter freely into contracts, and even to speak their mind is steadily being eroded by governments bent on redistributing private assets and subordinating individual rights to group rights. The entire concept of the welfare state as it has evolved in the second half of the twentieth century is incompatible with individual liberty, for it allows various groups with common needs to combine and claim the right to satisfy them at the expense of society at large, in the process steadily enhancing the power of the state which acts on their behalf.* This reality is currently masked by the immense wealth generated by the industrial economies, operating on a global scale in time of peace. It could become painfully apparent, however, should the economic situation drastically deteriorate and the controls established by the state in time of prosperity enable it to restore social stability at the cost of freedom.

Abolishing welfare with its sundry "entitlements" and spurious "rights" and returning the responsibilities for social assistance to the family or private charity, which shouldered them prior to the twentieth century, would go a long way toward resolving this predicament. But such a solution is not feasible. The libertarian ideal of a society in which the government runs nothing is as unrealistic as the utopian ideal of one in which it runs everything. Even at the height of laissez-faire, govern-

*Albert O. Hirschman, in his *Rhetoric of Reaction* (Cambridge, Mass., 1991), challenges the whole corpus of criticism of the democratic and welfare state from the French Revolution to the present, including Tocqueville's, by demonstrating that its principal themes—that "progressive" reforms accomplish the very opposite of what they intend or else accomplish nothing and yet always jeopardize liberty—recur with monotonous regularity whenever significant change is proposed. The author's apparent aim—to discredit opposition to "progressive" change (which he does not define)—fails in its purpose, because he deliberately refrains from asking himself whether or not the criticism is just: "[I]t is not my purpose," he writes, "to discuss the substance of the various arguments against social welfare policies" but rather to show how "the protagonists of this 'reactionary' episode" have been "powerfully attracted time and again by the same form of reasoning" (35). But, as he himself acknowledges (164, 166), the recurrence of the same "form of reasoning" proves nothing and certainly does not invalidate its conclusions; in fact, it can just as well prove its soundness.

ment everywhere intervened in some measure in economic and social affairs: the notion of a passive state is as much a myth as that of primitive communism.

But it should be possible to find a sensible alternative to the two extreme positions. In dealing with the scope of state power, the question is not either/or—either none or all-embracing—but more or less. When, in the nineteenth century, the Supreme Court found it necessary to intervene in private contractual engagements—and it did so with great reluctance—the interference was often accompanied by the cautionary adjective "reasonable." The state must regulate today more than ever, but it should do so reluctantly, to the minimum extent necessary, always bearing in mind that the economic rights of its citizens (rights to property) are as essential as their civil rights (rights to equal treatment), and that, indeed, the two are inseparable. And as for the "right" to equal reward, it is unattainable and, in any event, destructive of true, private rights.

It is imperative to abandon the idea, rooted in the Enlightenment and indispensable to the ideal of egalitarianism, that human beings are infinitely malleable creatures who, subjected to proper dressage by education, indoctrination, and legislation, are capable of attaining moral perfection. Anthropology and history alike indicate the persistence of a hard core of human nature immune to external pressure. The legislative frenzy of modern times which derives from the fallacious belief that human behavior can be fundamentally and permanently altered runs into the teeth of this knowledge, especially after the collapse of Soviet communism, the most determined effort ever undertaken to condition people's thoughts and behavior. If the premodern idea that law is eternal and immutable, requiring only to be interpreted, is not sustainable, then neither is the Benthamite notion that law is nothing but legislation and its function is social engineering. Common sense dictates that certain aspects of human behavior are immune to change, because they recur everywhere and at all times. As James Harrington put it three and a half centuries ago, "What was always so and no otherwise, and still is so and no otherwise, the same shall ever be so and no otherwise."* This means that there are limits to what legislation and instruction, even if accompanied by coercion, are capable of achieving: that of themselves they

*James Harrington, *Politicaster* (London, 1659), cited in Charles Blitzer, *An Immortal Commonwealth* (New Haven, Conn., 1960), 93. Apparently an echo of Ecclesiastes 1.9: "The thing that hath been, it is that which shall be."

cannot eliminate social envy, or racial antipathy, or hostility to homosexuals, and that attempts to use them for this end are likely to produce the contrary result.

One of the constants of human nature, impervious to legislative and pedagogic manipulation, is acquisitiveness. I trust that the reader will have been persuaded by my evidence that the desire to possess no more manifests greed than the appetite for food manifests gluttony, or love lechery. Acquisitiveness is common to all living things, being universal among animals and children as well as adults at every level of civilization, for which reason it is not a proper subject of moralizing. On the most elementary level, it is an expression of the instinct of survival. But beyond this, it constitutes a basic trait of the human personality, for which achievements and acquisitions are means of self-fulfillment. And inasmuch as fulfillment of the self is the essence of liberty, liberty cannot flourish when property and the inequality to which it gives rise are forcibly eliminated. In the words of a nineteenth-century English political theorist, "private property is the very essence of inequality" and, at the same time, acquiring property is the most important of liberties.[3]

Property is an indispensable ingredient of both prosperity and freedom.

The close relationship between property and prosperity is demonstrated by the course of history, which shows that one of the main reasons for the rise of the West to the position of global economic preeminence lies in the institution of property, which originated there and found there its fullest development. This fact has been convincingly presented in a number of scholarly works by such authors as North and Thomas, Landes, and Bethell.[4] It can be further demonstrated statistically for the contemporary world. Even if one allows that statistics of this kind do not meet the standards of the exact sciences because the categories employed are in some measure subjective in character, the results are, nevertheless, impressive in their consistency. Studies sponsored jointly by the Heritage Foundation and the *Wall Street Journal* indicate that countries that provide the firmest guarantees of economic independence, including private property rights, are virtually without exception the richest. They also enjoy the best civil services and judiciary institutions. This holds true not only of those populated by Europeans but also of Japan, South Korea, Hong Kong, Chile, and Taiwan. Conversely, countries that rate lowest in terms of property rights and market freedom (Cuba, Somalia, and North Korea, for instance) are at the bottom of the scale.[5]

The relationship of property to freedom is more complex, because unlike prosperity, "freedom" has more than one meaning (see "Definitions," p. xvi): thus it is possible to enjoy firm property (economic) rights without political rights, that is, the right to vote. In Western Europe, property rights were respected long before citizens were granted the franchise. Today some of the most prosperous countries (e.g., Singapore, Hong Kong, and Taiwan) with the firmest guarantees of property are run in an authoritarian fashion. It is a serious mistake, unfortunately often committed by the U.S. government in its foreign dealings, to define freedom to mean exclusively democracy, for, as noted above, ordinary citizens may enjoy a wide range of economic and legal freedoms along with personal rights without being able to choose their government.[6] It is probably due to the fact that Americans, as heirs and beneficiaries of English constitutional development, take such freedoms and rights so much for granted that they identify freedom with representative government. The historical evidence indicates that property can coexist with arbitrary and even oppressive political power, whereas democracy cannot do without it.

The symbiotic relationship between property and freedom does not preclude the state from imposing reasonable restraints on the uses made of objects owned, or ensuring the basic living standards of the neediest strata of the population. Clearly, one cannot allow property rights to serve as a license for ravaging the environment or ignoring the fundamental needs of the unemployed, sick, and aged. Hardly anyone contests this proposition today: even Frederick Hayek, an implacable foe of state intervention in the economy, agreed that the state has the duty to ensure for all citizens "a minimum of food, shelter, and clothing, sufficient to preserve health and the capacity to work."[7] But to say this is not to grant the state the authority to use the powers at its disposal to interfere with the freedom of contract, to redistribute wealth, or to compel one part of the population to bear the costs of the self-defined "rights" of special constituencies. Limitations on the use of property imposed for public good should surely be interpreted as "takings" and adequately compensated. As the Supreme Court pronounced in the Dolan case (see above, p. 252), "We can see no reason why the Takings Clause of the Fifth Amendment, as much a part of the Bill of Rights as the First Amendment or the Fourth Amendment, should be relegated to the status of a poor relation."[8] The rights of ownership need to be restored to their proper place in the scale of values instead of being sacrificed to the unattainable ideal of social equality and all-embracing economic security. This calls for a shift of attitude on the part of the highest organs of the judiciary, which since the late 1930s have assumed "that civil rights and property rights can be sharply distinguished, and that civil rights . . . merit greater judicial protection than property rights."*

The balance between "civil" and "property" rights has to be redressed if we care about freedom. Property rights, which increasingly have come to mean exclusive possession rather than unconstrained use, should be restored to the maximum degree possible to their original, comprehensive meaning. Similarly, the whole concept of civil rights requires reexamination. The Civil Rights Act of 1964 gave the government no license to set quotas for hiring personnel by private enterprise or admitting students to institutions of higher learning, and yet the federal bureaucracy acts as if it had. Even less did the act authorize interference with freedom of speech in the workplace. Just as property rights have been steadily narrowed in application, so the category of "civil rights" has been broadened to include the claims of any group to goods and services which fellow citizens must pay for either by sacrificing some of their own rights or else footing the bill. Citing a catalog of what she calls "printing-press rights" from the Democratic Party platform of 1960, Ayn Rand asks "at whose expense" are these "rights" to be secured? She answers that since jobs, food, clothing, recreation, homes, medical care, education, etc. "do not grow in nature," they can only be provided by others. This being the case, they are not "rights":

> If some men are entitled *by right* to the products of the work of others, it means that those others are deprived of rights and condemned to slave labor. Any alleged "right" of one man, which necessitates the violation of the rights of another, is not and cannot be a right. No man can have a right to impose an unchosen obligation, an unrewarded duty or an involuntary servitude on another man. . . . A right does not include the material implementation of that right by other men: it includes only the freedom to earn that implementation by one's own effort.†

*William H. Riker in Ellen Frankel Paul and Howard Dickman, eds., *Liberty, Property, and the Future of Constitutional Development* (Albany, N.Y., 1990), 49. The fictitious contrast between the "rights of property" and the "rights of men" was drawn as early as 1910 by Theodore Roosevelt and restated by Franklin Delano Roosevelt in 1936. Tom Bethell, *The Noblest Triumph* (New York, 1998), 174–76.

†Ayn Rand, *Capitalism: The Unknown Ideal* (New York, 1966), 290–1. "Observe, in this context," she adds, "the intellectual precision of the Founding Fathers: they spoke of the right to *the pursuit* of happiness—*not* of the right to happiness. It means that a man has the right to take the actions he deems necessary to achieve his happiness: it does *not* mean that others must make him happy" (291).

Such "class rights," therefore, are a phantom: "[T]here neither exist nor can exist rights other than the Rights of Man, that is to say, rights which concern that which is truly universal in each human being as an individual, and which apply to all without distinction of race, religion, color, profession, etc."*

Rights, in any meaningful sense, are natural rights, not those bestowed by legislative fiat.[9] The so-called "social rights" of today are not "rights" and certainly not "entitlements," since no one is entitled to anything at someone else's expense; they are rather claims on society which it may or may not grant. And yet in modern industrial democracies a large number of citizens are required to work for the support of others: in Sweden, the most retrograde state in this respect, for each citizen who earns his own living, 1.8 are fully or partially maintained by taxes which he is required to pay; in Germany and Great Britain the ratio is 1:1, and in the United States 1:0.76.[10] Because the population dependent on the state includes a heavy proportion of the elderly while the taxpayers are younger wage and salary earners, an unhealthy generational conflict may well develop in welfare societies as the population ages.

The modern habit of thinking in terms of group rights rather than individual rights carries an additional danger: just as it can be used to identify those who qualify for special benefits, so it can serve to single them out for special punishment. Stalin's program of "liquidating," i.e., murdering, "kulaks," for example, and Hitler's genocide of Jews and gypsies were justified by the notion that people are to be judged and treated on the basis not of their personal behavior but of their membership in a designated group, be it social, ethnic, or racial.

Unless the greatest care is exercised in protecting the rights to property, we may well end up with a regime which without being tyrannical in the customary sense of the word is nevertheless unfree. The framers of the American Constitution did not anticipate this possibility: "They intended to protect the people against their rulers, not against themselves."[11] That happened because they sought to defend liberty from the only threat which they knew, namely royal absolutism. But, as it has turned out, under conditions of modern, welfare-oriented democracy, the threat can also emanate from below, from one's fellow citizens who,

*Henri Lepage, *Pourquoi la propriété* (Paris,1985), 438. Cf. Rand, *Capitalism*, 292: "There are only *the Rights of Man*—rights possessed by every individual man and *all* men as individuals."

being increasingly dependent on government largesse, care more about their personal security than about general freedom. "Experience," wrote Justice Brandeis,

> should teach us, to be most on our guard to protect liberty when the Government's purposes are *beneficent*. Men born to freedom are naturally alert to repel invasion of their liberty by evil-minded rulers. The greatest dangers to liberty lurk in insidious encroachments by men of zeal, well-meaning but without understanding.[12]

The reason for this is that despotism appears in two distinct guises. There is the arbitrary rule of absolutist monarchs or dictators, elected by no one and subject neither to constitutional nor parliamentary restraints. And there is the tyranny in democratic societies of one part of the population over another: that of the majority over the minority, but also—where elections are won with narrow margins—of minorities over the majority. Tsarist Russia in its classical guise provided an extreme example of traditional despotism: the authorities could detain, imprison, or exile any subject without due process; they could confiscate his properties; they legislated as they saw fit. And yet in practice, the average Russian under the old regime had scarcely any contact with the government and felt little interference from it, because the scope of government activity was very narrow, being largely confined to the collection of taxes, the drafting of recruits, and the preservation of the established order. Today, the scope of government activity is immeasurably broader: the government is elected, to be sure, but its interference in the life of citizens is greater than it has ever been.

As Hayek pointed out, the broadening of the scope of government, in and of itself, carries seeds of a despotism at least as invidious as the traditional kind. Hayek's main concern was with protecting liberty from the seemingly unstoppable trend in Western democracies to subject the national economy to planning, which, he felt, would inevitably lead to tyranny. His fears in this respect proved unfounded. But his observations on the dangers implicit in the extension of the government's reach retain their validity:

> [T]he probability of agreement of a substantial portion of the population upon a particular course of action decreases as the scope of State activity expands. . . . Democratic government worked successfully so long as, by a widely accepted creed, the

> functions of the State were limited to fields where real agreement among a majority could be achieved. The price we have to pay for a democratic system is the restriction of State action to those fields where agreement can be obtained; and it is the great merit of a liberal society that it reduces the necessity of agreement to a minimum compatible with the diversity of opinions which in a free society will exist.[13]

This reasoning explains why government interference in the life of the citizenry even for benevolent purposes endangers liberty: it posits a consensus which does not exist and hence requires coercion. As we have pointed out, the modern welfare state indeed coerces in a variety of ways to attain its unattainable ends.

But well-meaning patriarchalism also enervates people by robbing them of the entrepreneurial spirit implicit in freedom. What harm long-term dependence on the welfare state can inflict became apparent after the collapse of the Soviet Union, when a substantial part of the population, suddenly deprived of comprehensive state support and unaccustomed to fending for itself, came to yearn for the restoration of the despotic yoke.

The trouble is that because schools fail to teach history, especially legal and constitutional history, the vast majority of today's citizens have no inkling to what they owe their liberty and prosperity, namely a long and successful struggle for rights of which the right to property is the most fundamental. They are therefore unaware what debilitating effect the restrictions on property rights will, over the long run, have on their lives.

The aristocrat Tocqueville, observing the democratic United States and his native bourgeois France a century and a half ago, had a premonition that the modern world faced dangers to liberty previously unknown. "I have no fear that they will meet with tyrants in their rulers," he wrote of future generations, "but rather with guardians."[14] Such "guardians" will deprive their peoples of liberty by gratifying their desires and then exploit their dependence on such generosity. He foresaw a kind of democratic despotism in which "an innumerable multitude of men, all equal and alike" incessantly strive to pursue "the petty and paltry pleasures with which they glut their lives."[15] The benign paternalistic government—the modern welfare state—hovers over them:

> For their happiness such a government willingly labors, but it chooses to be the sole and only arbiter of that happiness; it pro-

> vides for their security, foresees and supplies their necessities, facilitates their pleasures, manages their principal concerns, directs their industry, regulates the descent of property, and subdivides their inheritances: what remains, but to spare them all the care of thinking and all the trouble of living?

The "principle of equality has prepared men for these things" and "oftentimes to look on them as benefits."

> After having thus taken each member of the community in its powerful grasp, and fashioned him at will, the supreme power then extends its arms over the whole community. It covers the surface of society with a network of small complicated rules, minute and uniform, through which the most original minds and the most energetic characters cannot penetrate, to rise above the crowd. The will of man is not shattered, but softened, bent and guided; men are seldom forced by it to act, but they are constantly restrained from acting: such a power does not destroy, but it prevents existence; it does not tyrannize, but it compresses, enervates, extinguishes, and stupefies a people, till each nation is reduced to be nothing better than a flock of timid and industrious animals, of which the government is the shepherd.[16]

Is this what we want ?

REFERENCES

INTRODUCTION AND DEFINITIONS

1. William Blackstone, *Commentaries on the Laws of England,* II (London, 1809), 2.
2. A. N. Wilson, *Tolstoy* (London, 1988), 365.
3. Marcus Cunliffe, *The Right to Property: A Theme in American History* (Leicester University Press, 1974), 5.
4. *The Writings of James Madison,* ed. Gaillard Hunt, VI (New York and London, 1906).
5. Jacob Burckhardt, *Weltgeschichtliche Betrachtungen* (Munich, 1978), 16.
6. C. B. Macpherson, ed., *Property: Mainstream and Critical Positions* (Oxford, 1978), 3.
7. Stephen R. Munzer, *A Theory of Property* (Cambridge, 1990), 17.
8. Morris Cohen in *Cornell Law Quarterly* 13, No. 1 (December 1927), 12.
9. Isaiah Berlin, *Two Concepts of Liberty* (Oxford, 1958), 14.

CHAPTER I: THE IDEA OF PROPERTY

1. Lewis Mumford, *The Story of Utopias* (New York, 1922), 13–14.
2. Kenneth R. Minogue in *Nomos,* No. 22 (1980), 3.
3. Rigobert Günther and Reimar Müller, *Das Goldene Zeitalter* (Stuttgart, 1988), 19–20; Arnold Künzli, *Mein und Dein* (Köln, 1986), 65; Frank E. Manuel and Fritzie P. Manuel, *Utopian Thought in the Western World* (Cambridge, Mass., 1979), 66–70. Hesiod felt he had been robbed of his inheritance by his brother, Perses.
4. *The Dialogues of Plato,* ed. B. Jowett, III (Oxford, 1892), 156–57.
5. Ibid., 159.
6. *Plato's Republic,* ed. and trans. I. A. Richards (Cambridge, 1966), Book VIII, Nos. 550–51, p. 146.
7. *Dialogues of Plato,* V, 121–22.
8. Aristotle, *Politics,* 1266a and 1266b. *The Student's Oxford Aristotle,* ed. and trans. W. D. Ross, VI (London etc., 1942)
9. Richard McKeon in *Ethics* 18, No. 3 (April 1938), 304–12.
10. Aristotle, *Politics,* 1328a.
11. Ibid., 1263a/40.
12. Ibid., 1266b/29–30.
13. Ibid., 1263b/13.
14. Ibid., 1295b/35–36, 41.
15. Aristotle, *Nicomachean Ethics,* 1134–35; cf. Frederick Pollock, *Essays in the Law* (London, 1922), 32–33.
16. G. H. Sabine and Stanley B. Smith, Introduction to Cicero's *On the Commonwealth* (Columbus, Ohio, 1929), 22.
17. Richard Schlatter, *Private Property: The History of an Idea* (New Brunswick, N.J., 1951), 11.
18. Virgil, *Georgics,* I/126–29, trans. L. P. Wilkinson (Harmondsworth, 1982), 61.

19. Ovid, *Metamorphoses,* I/134–36, trans. David R. Slavitt (Baltimore and London, 1994), 4.
20. Seneca, *Ad Lucilium Epistulae Morales,* Loeb Classical Library, I (London and New York, 1917), 19; see also 111, 123, 145, etc.
21. Cited in Max Beer, *A History of British Socialism,* I (London, 1919), 4.
22. R. Besnier in *Annales d'histoire économique et sociale,* no. 46 (July 31, 1937), 328.
23. On this subject, see Vittorio Scialoja, *Teoria della proprietà nel diritto romano,* 2 vols. (Rome, 1928–31).
24. James Bryce, *Studies in History and Jurisprudence,* II (New York, 1901), 585.
25. Schlatter, *Private Property,* 26–32.
26. Cicero, *De Officiis,* Loeb Classical Library, II (New York, 1913), 20–23.
27. Mark 10:25. See further Matthew 10:9–10 and 19:21–24; Mark 6:8–9 and 10:21.
28. Martin Hengel, *Property and Riches in the Early Church* (London, 1974), 26–28; Otto Schilling, *Reichtum und Eigentum in der altkirchlichen Literatur* (Tübingen and Freiburg, 1908), 17–18.
29. R. W. and A. J. Carlyle, *A History of Medieval Political Theory in the West,* I (Edinburgh and London, 1927), 132; Hengel, *Property and Riches,* 84.
30. Ibid., I, 62.
31. Bede Jarrett, *Social Theories of the Middle Ages, 1200–1500* (Westminster, Md., 1942), 122.
32. Cited in Alfons Heilmann, ed., *Texte der Kirchenväter,* III (Munich, 1964), 208.
33. Edward L. Surtz in Sir Thomas More, *Utopia,* ed. Robert B. Adams (New York and London, 1992), 170–1.
34. Hengel, *Property and Riches,* 20–1.
35. Ibid., 17.
36. Deuteronomy 26:12.
37. B. W. Dempsey in St. Thomas Aquinas, *Summa theologica,* III (New York, 1948), p. 3357.
38. *Summa theologica,* II, Question 66, Articles 1 and 2 (New York, 1947), pp. 1476–77.
39. Ibid., Article 1.
40. Carlyle and Carlyle, *Medieval Political Theory,* V (Edinburgh and London, 1928), 145–46. On this subject, see also Schilling, *Reichtum und Eigentum, passim.*
41. Alexander Gray, *The Socialist Tradition: Moses to Lenin* (London, 1963), 42–60.
42. Gordon Leff, *Heresy in the Later Middle Ages,* I (Manchester and New York, 1967), 9.
43. Ibid., I, 51–166, esp. 164–66.
44. Henri Lepage, *Pourquoi la propriété* (Paris, 1985), 54–55.
45. O. S. Brandt, ed., *Der grosse Bauernkrieg* (Jena, 1925), 265.
46. Troeltsch, *Social Teaching,* II, 641–50.
47. Schlatter, *Private Property,* 64–65; McKeon in *Ethics,* 329–30.
48. Schlatter, *Private Property,* 65–67; McKeon in *Ethics,* 330–32; Carlyle and Carlyle, *Medieval Political Theory,* V, 420–25.
49. *Tractatus de potestate regia et papali,* written c. 1303, cited in McKeon in *Ethics,* 331.
50. Arturo Graf, *Miti, Leggende e Superstizioni del Medio Evo,* I (Bologna, 1965).
51. Manuel and Manuel, *Utopian Thought,* 59.
52. Cecil Jane, ed., *Select Documents Illustrating the Four Voyages of Columbus,* I (London, 1930), 8.
53. Ibid., 14.
54. Gilbert Chinard, *L'Amérique et la rêve exotique* (Paris, 1934), 431. Rousseau's likely sources are listed in Karl-Heinz Kohl, *Entzauberter Blick* (Berlin, 1981), 283, n. 233. On Rousseau, see below, pp. 41–42.
55. *The First Four Voyages of Amerigo Vespucci* (London, 1893), 7–11.

56. Edward Arber, ed., *The First Three English Books on America* (Birmingham, 1885), 78.
57. Lewis Hanke, *The Spanish Struggle for Justice in the Conquest of America* (Philadelphia, 1949), 122.
58. Tomas Ortiz, cited in Lewis Hanke, *The First Social Experiments in America* (Cambridge, Mass., 1935), 51–52.
59. Kohl, *Entzauberter Blick*, 48–50.
60. Manuel and Manuel, *Utopian Thought*, 427.
61. Howard Mumford Jones, *O Strange New World* (New York, 1964), 50–61.
62. Louis de Bougainville, *A Voyage Round the World* (Amsterdam and New York, 1967), 252–53.
63. *Supplément au voyage de Bougainville* (1796), ed. Gilbert Chinard (Paris etc., 1935).
64. Kohl, *Entzauberter Blick*, 224.
65. Robert B. Adams in Sir Thomas More, *Utopia*, ed. Robert B. Adams (New York and London, 1992), viii.
66. R. W. Chambers in ibid., 145.
67. Edward Surtz and J. H. Hexter, eds., *The Complete Works of St. Thomas More*, IV (New Haven and London, 1965), 241, 243.
68. "The City of the Sun," in *Ideal Empires and Republics* (New York and London, 1901), 273–317.
69. Richard Pipes, *Russia Under the Bolshevik Regime* (New York, 1994), 314.
70. Cited in Hans Baron, *In Search of Florentine Civic Humanism*, I (Princeton, 1988), 232. Baron's book (Vol. I) devotes much attention to the conflict between the ideals of wealth and poverty during the Renaissance.
71. Werner Sombart, *Der Bourgeois* (Munich and Leipzig, 1913), 283.
72. Spinoza, *Ethics*, Part iv, Proposition xx. "Of use" is sometimes translated "his own profit."
73. Bryce, *Studies*, II, 593–97; Pollock, *Essays*, 40.
74. Bryce, *Studies*, II, 597.
75. Renée Neu Watkins, *The Family in Renaissance Florence* (Columbia, S.C., 1969), 12–14.
76. Ibid., 148.
77. Jean Bodin, *The Six Bookes of a Commonweale*, English trans. of 1606, reprinted by Harvard University Press, Cambridge, Mass., in 1962.
78. Ibid., 85.
79. Ibid., 110. This phrase comes from Seneca's *On Benefits*, Book VII, Chapter iv: *"Ad reges potestas omnium pertinet, ad singulos proprietas."*
80. *Six Bookes*, 11.
81. McKeon in *Ethics*, 342.
82. *Six Bookes*, 653. Cf. Quentin Skinner, *The Foundations of Modern Political Thought*, II (Cambridge, 1978), 293–94.
83. The best English edition is J. Barbeyrac, *The Rights of War and Peace* (London, 1738).
84. Hugo Grotius, *The Jurisprudence of Holland*, 2 vols., ed. and trans. R. W. Lee (Oxford, 1926–1936).
85. Richard Tuck, *Natural Rights Theories* (Cambridge, 1979), 73.
86. Grotius, *Rights of War and Peace*, 136.
87. Grotius, *Jurisprudence of Holland*, I, 79.
88. Grotius, *Rights of War and Peace*, 11.
89. Roger Lockyer, ed., *The Trial of Charles I* (London, 1959), 135.
90. Karl Olivecrona in *Archiv für Rechts- und Sozialphilosophie* 61, No. 1 (1975), 109–15; *Journal of the History of Ideas* 35, No. 2 (1974), 211–30.
91. B. W. Dempsey in St. Thomas Aquinas, *Summa theologica*, iii (New York, 1948), p. 3357. On Plato's usage, see Antony Flew in Colin Kolbert, ed., *The Idea of*

Property (Glasgow, 1997), 124; on Cicero's, Giorgio del Vecchio, *Die Gerechtigkeit* (Basel, 1958), 79–80, n. 27.

92. *Hobbes's Leviathan* (Oxford, 1943), 110 (Part I, Chapter xv); cf. Karl Olivecrona in *Archiv für Rechts- und Sozialphilosophie* 61, No. 1 (1975), 113; Tuck, *Natural Rights,* 29 and *passim.*
93. Grotius, *Jurisprudence of Holland,* I, 71, 73.
94. J. W. Allen, *English Political Thought, 1603–1660,* I (London, 1938), 27.
95. Ibid., 18.
96. Thomas Edwards, cited in C. H. Firth, ed., *The Clarke Papers,* I (London, 1891), lx–lxii.
97. Tuck, *Natural Rights Theories,* 150; Howard Nenner in J. R. Jones, ed., *Liberty Secured? Britain Before and After 1688* (Stanford, Calif., 1992), 94–95.
98. *De Cive,* in Sir William Molesworth, ed., *The English Works of Thomas Hobbes,* II London, 1841), vi–vii.
99. Hobbes, *Leviathan,* 165 (Part II, Chapter xxi).
100. James Harrington, *The Commonwealth of Oceana; and A System of Politics,* ed. J. G. A. Pocock (Cambridge, 1992), Chapter II, Article 10.
101. Ibid., Chapter II, Article 8.
102. Ibid., 271–72.
103. C. B. Macpherson, *The Political Theory of Possessive Individualism: Hobbes to Locke* (Oxford, 1962), 165.
104. Paschal Larkin, *Property in the Eighteenth Century* (London, 1930), 56.
105. Edited by Caroline Robbins in *Two English Republican Tracts* (Cambridge, 1969).
106. *Diayr* [sic!] *of Thomas Burton, Esq.,* III (London, 1828), 133.
107. Robbins, *Two English Republican Tracts,* 89–90.
108. Ibid., 133–35.
109. Ibid. 130.
110. H. F. Russell Smith, *Harrington and His Oceana* (Cambridge, 1914), 141–68.
111. John Locke, *Two Treatises of Government,* ed. Peter Laslett (Cambridge, 1960), 401, 368.
112. Peter Laslett in Locke, *Two Treatises,* 99–100.
113. Locke, *Two Treatises,* 286.
114. Ibid., 368–69.
115. On the anticapitalist implications of Locke's theory of property, see M[ax] Beer, *A History of British Socialism,* I (London, 1953), 102–3, 107, and *passim*; and C. H. Driver in F. J. C. Hearnshaw, ed., *The Social and Political Ideas of Some English Thinkers of the Augustan Age, A.D. 1650–1750* (London, 1928), 91.
116. Jeremy Waldron, *The Right to Private Property* (Oxford, 1988), 137.
117. Beer, *British Socialism,* I, 65–71.
118. Manuel and Manuel, *Utopian Thought,* 349–55, 574.
119. Firth, ed., *Clarke Papers,* I, lxix–lxx.
120. Cited in H. T. Dickinson, *Liberty and Property* (New York, 1977), 88.
121. See Chapter 2.
122. David Hume, *Essays Moral, Political, and Literary,* II, "Concerning the Principles of Morals: iii. Of Justice," in *The Philosophical Works,* IV (London, 1882), 191.
123. Adam Smith, *The Wealth of Nations,* ed. Edwin Cannan, Modern Library (New York, 1994), 418 (Book III, Chapter ii).
124. On this subject, see two studies by Gilbert Chinard: *L'exotisme américain dans la littérature française au XVIe siècle* (Paris, 1911), and *L'Amérique.*
125. Chinard, *L'Amérique,* v.
126. *Boswell on the Grand Tour: Germany and Switzerland, 1764* (New York etc., 1953), 223–24.
127. Morelly, *Code de la Nature* (Paris, 1910), 15–16.
128. Ibid., 85.
129. Ibid., 9.

130. Jean-Jacques Rousseau, *Discourse on the Origin of Inequality* (Indianapolis, 1992), 17.
131. Jean-Jacques Rousseau, *On the Social Contract,* ed. Donald A. Cress (Indianapolis, 1983), 179.
132. Ibid., 29 (Book I, Chapter 9).
133. Edward L. Walter in Introduction to Jean-Jacques Rousseau, *The Social Contract* (New York, 1906), xlviii.
134. Franco Venturi, *Utopia and Reform in the Enlightenment* (Cambridge, 1971), 97–98.
135. Jean Touchard, *Histoire des idées politiques,* II (Paris, 1959), 411.
136. Charles Gide and Charles Rist, *Histoire de Doctrines Économiques,* I (Paris, 1947), 27.
137. Touchard, *Histoire,* II, 412.
138. Larkin, *Property,* 213.
139. Ibid., 216.
140. Code Civil, Articles 544 and 545.
141. Guido de Ruggiero, *The History of European Liberalism* (Boston, 1959), 27–28.
142. Pierre Joseph Proudhon, *What Is Property?* (New York, 1966), 66.
143. Beer, *British Socialism,* I, 100.
144. Larkin, *Property,* 217.
145. Pierre Gaxotte, *The French Revolution* (London and New York, 1932), Chapter XII.
146. Manuel and Manuel, *Utopian Thought,* 557.
147. Filippo Buonarroti, *Conspiration pour l'égalité dite de Babeuf* (Paris, 1957). In English: Bronterre, ed., *Buonarroti's History of Babeuf's Conspiracy for Equality* (London, 1836).
148. Gaxotte, *French Revolution,* 292.
149. *Babeuf's Conspiracy,* 314–15.
150. Locke, *Two Treatises,* 322.
151. In William Godwin, *Political and Philosophical Writings,* ed. Mark Philp, III (London, 1993).
152. Ibid., 464.
153. They are ably treated in Gray's *Socialist Tradition,* Chapters vi through x.
154. Pierre-Joseph Proudhon, *Qu'est-ce la propriété* (Paris, 1840).
155. Alan Macfarlane, *The Origins of English Individualism* (Cambridge, 1979), 39.
156. Georg Hanssen, *Agrarhistorische Abhandlungen,* I (Leipzig, 1880), 1–76.
157. August von Haxthausen, *Studien über die inneren Zustände, das Volksleben und insbesondere die ländlichen Einrichtungen Russlands,* 3 vols. (Hanover, 1847–52).
158. Karl Dickopf, *Georg Ludwig von Maurer* (Kallmünz, 1960), 160–6.
159. Sumner Maine, *Lectures on the Early History of Institutions* (London, 1875), 1–2.
160. Josef Kulischer, *Allgemeine Wirtschaftsgeschichte,* I (Munich and Berlin, 1928), 29–30.
161. Karl Marx and Frederick Engels, *Selected Works,* I (Moscow, 1962), 47.
162. Shlomo Avineri, *The Social and Political Thought of Karl Marx* (Cambridge, 1968), 109.
163. Karl Marx and Friedrich Engels, *The German Ideology* (New York, 1947), 9–11.
164. Ibid., 11–13.
165. K. Marx and F. Engels, *The Holy Family* (Moscow, 1956), 51 (Chapter 4).
166. Marx, *Capital,* I (Moscow, 1961), Chapter xv, section 9, "The Factory Acts."
167. Marx and Engels, *German Ideology,* 53.
168. Gray, *Socialist Tradition,* 327.
169. Boris Chicherin, *Opyty po istorii russkogo prava* (Moscow, 1858), 1–58.

170. Denman W. Ross, *The Early History of Land-holding Among the Germans* (Boston, 1883), 39.
171. Fustel de Coulanges, *The Origin of Property in Land* (London, 1891); originally published in the *Revue des Questions Historiques,* No. 45 (1889), 349–439.
172. Coulanges, *Origin of Property in Land,* 17.
173. Ibid., 150.
174. John Stuart Mill, *Principles of Political Economy,* ed. Sir William Ashley (London, 1909), Book II, Chapters I and II, pp. 199–237.
175. Ibid., 208.
176. Ibid., 227–28.
177. Ibid., 231, 233.
178. P. S. Atiyah, *The Rise and Fall of Freedom of Contract* (Oxford, 1979), 628–29.
179. Léon Duguit (1905), cited in Lepage, *Pourquoi la propriété,* 436.
180. Carl N. Degler, *In Search of Human Nature* (New York, 1991), 32–34. See Chapter 2 below.
181. Charles Letourneau, *Property: Its Origin and Development* (London, 1892), x, 365.
182. Margaret Mead and Ruth L. Bunzel, eds., *The Golden Age of American Anthropology* (New York, 1960), 8.
183. C. R. Carpenter, cited by Edmund Leach in *New York Review of Books* 11, No. 6 (October 10, 1968), 24.
184. Theodosius Dobzhansky, cited by Roger D. Masters in *Social Science Information* 14, No. 2 (1975), 14, 24.
185. A. Irving Hallowell in *Quarterly Review of Biology,* No. 31 (1956), 91.
186. John Rawls, *A Theory of Justice* (Cambridge, Mass., 1971).
187. Ibid., 3.
188. Ibid., 62.
189. Ibid., 305. G. Hardin in Garrett Hardin and John Baden, eds., *Managing the Commons* (San Francisco, 1977), 7, calls the book "one long footnote to Marx."
190. Ibid., 73–74.
191. Ibid., 84.
192. Ibid., 106–7.
193. Ibid., 107, 101, 530–41.
194. See, for example, John Christman, *The Myth of Property: Toward an Egalitarian Theory of Ownership* (New York and Oxford, 1994).
195. Erich Fromm, *To Have or to Be?* (New York, 1976).
196. Ibid., 16.
197. Ibid., 170.
198. Alfred Marshall, *Principles of Economics,* 8th ed. (New York, 1948), 48.
199. Manuel and Manuel, *Utopian Thought,* 159.
200. Alan Ryan, *Property* (Stony Stratford, England, 1987), 55.
201. Douglass North and R. P. Thomas, *The Rise of the Western World* (Cambridge, 1973), 1. The argument is theoretically developed in North's *Structure and Change in Economic History* (New York and London, 1981).
202. North and Thomas, *Rise of the Western World,* 2–3, 8.
203. North, *Structure and Change,* 158–66. On this subject see further Tom Bethell, *The Noblest Triumph* (New York, 1998).

CHAPTER 2: THE INSTITUTION OF PROPERTY

1. Émile de Laveleye, *De la propriété et ses formes primitives* (Paris, 1874). There is a good bibliography of this literature in Wilhelm Schmidt, *Das Eigentum auf den ältesten Stufen der Menschheit,* I (Münster in Westfalen, 1937), 4–17.

2. A notable exception is the recently published ambitious treatise by John P. Powelson, *The Story of Land: A World History of Land Tenure and Agrarian Reform* (Cambridge, Mass., 1988).
3. L. T. Hobhouse, *Property: Its Duties and Rights* (London, 1913), 3–4.
4. The term has been coined by Robert Ardrey in *The Territorial Imperative: A Personal Inquiry into the Animal Origins of Property and Nations* (New York, 1966).
5. P. Leyhausen in K. Lorenz and P. Leyhausen, eds., *Motivation of Human and Animal Behavior* (New York, 1973), 99.
6. Edward T. Hall, *The Hidden Dimension* (Garden City, N.Y., 1966), 10–14.
7. H. Eliot Howard, *Territory in Bird Life* (London, 1920), 15, 180–6.
8. Ibid., 74.
9. V. C. Wynne-Edwards, *Animal Dispersion in Relation to Social Behaviour* (New York, 1962).
10. Ernest Beaglehole, *Property: A Study in Social Psychology* (London, 1931), 31–63.
11. Richard S. Miller in *Advances in Ecological Research* 4 (1967), 1–74, cited by E. O. Wilson in J. F. Eisenberg and W. S. Dillon, eds., *Man and Beast: Comparative Social Behavior* (Washington, D.C., 1971), 194.
12. N. Tinbergen, *Social Behavior in Animals* (London, 1953), 8–14.
13. Ardrey, *Territorial Imperative*, 3.
14. C. B. Moffat in *Irish Naturalist* 12, No. 6 (1903), 152–57.
15. Heini P. Hediger in Sherwood L. Washburn, *Social Life of Early Man* (Chicago, 1961), 36–38.
16. Monika Meyer-Holzapfel, *Die Bedeutung des Besitzes bei Tier und Mensch* (Biel, 1952), 3.
17. Ibid., 18n. Cf. *The American Heritage Dictionary of the English Language* (New York, 1970), s.v. "nest."
18. Meyer-Holzapfel, *Die Bedeutung*, 3.
19. Edward W. Soja, *The Political Organization of Space*, Commission on College Geography, Resource Paper 8 (Washington, D.C., 1971), 23.
20. Edward O. Wilson, *Sociobiology: The New Synthesis* (Cambridge, Mass., 1975), 565. See the table of selected animal ranges in Nicolas Peterson in *American Anthropologist* 77 (1975), 54.
21. N. Tinbergen, *The Study of Instinct* (Oxford, 1951), 176.
22. Hall, *Hidden Dimension*, 16–19.
23. Wilson, *Sociobiology*, 256–57.
24. Beaglehole, *Property*, 56.
25. On this, see Konrad Lorenz's *On Aggression* (New York, 1966); also Tinbergen in *Science* 160, No. 3,835 (1968), 1411–18, and his *Study of Instinct*.
26. Ashley Montagu, *Man and Aggression* (New York, 1968), 9. Emphasis added.
27. *Academic Questions* 8, No. 3 (Summer 1995), 76–81.
28. Stephen Jay Gould, *The Mismeasure of Man* (New York, 1981), 28.
29. Carl N. Degler, *In Search of Human Nature* (New York, 1991), 318–19, 321.
30. Leonard Berkowitz in *American Scientist* 57, No. 3 (Autumn 1969), 383.
31. Herbert Croly, *The Promise of American Life* (Cambridge, Mass., 1965), 400. Originally published in 1909.
32. Soja, *Political Organization of Space*, 3.
33. Cited in Jeremy Waldron, *The Right to Private Property* (Oxford, 1988), 377–78.
34. Jean Baechler in *Nomos*, No. 22 (1980), 273.
35. Richard Pipes, *Russia Under the Bolshevik Regime* (New York, 1994), 290–1.
36. Richard H. Tawney, *The Acquisitive Society* (New York, 1920), 73–74.
37. *The International Journal of Psycho-Analysis* 34, part 2 (1953), 89–97; N. Laura Kemptner in *Journal of Social Behavior and Personality* 6, No. 6 (1991), 210.
38. Arnold Gesell and Frances I. Ilg, *Child Development* (New York, 1949), 417–21.
39. Helen C. Dawe in *Child Development* 5, No. 2 (June 1934), 139–57, esp. 150.

40. Melford E. Spiro, *Children of the Kibbutz* (Cambridge, Mass., 1958), 373–76.
41. Lita Furby in *Political Psychology* 2, No. 1 (Spring 1980), 30–42.
42. Ibid., 31, 35.
43. Ibid., 32–33.
44. Spiro, *Children of the Kibbutz*, 397–98.
45. Torsten Malmberg, *Human Territoriality* (The Hague, 1980), 59, 308.
46. Carol J. Guardo in *Child Development* 40, No. 1 (March 1969), 143–51.
47. Melville J. Herskovitz, *Economic Anthropology* (New York, 1952), 327.
48. E. Adamson Hoebel, *Man in the Primitive World*, 2nd ed. (New York etc., 1958), 431.
49. C. Daryl Forde, *Habitat, Economy and Society* (London and New York, 1934), 461.
50. Max Weber, *General Economic History* (New Brunswick, N.J., 1981), 38.
51. Robert Lowie in *Yale Law Journal* 37, no. 5 (March 1928), 551.
52. Summarized in Malmberg, *Human Territoriality*, 86, from P. A. Sorokin, C.C. Zimmerman, and C.J. Galpin, eds., *A Systematic Source Book in Rural Sociology*, I (Minneapolis, 1930), 574–75. The latter work has a good discussion of the various theories concerning original landowning practices, pp. 568–76.
53. Beaglehole, *Property*, 145–47.
54. L. T. Hobhouse, G. C. Wheeler, and M. Ginsberg, *The Material Culture and Social Institutions of the Simpler Peoples* (London, 1915), 243.
55. Beaglehole, *Property*, 134.
56. Bronislaw Malinowski, *Crime and Custom in Savage Society* (New York, 1951), 60.
57. Beaglehole, *Property*, 158–66.
58. Ibid., 215–16.
59. Ibid., 140–2.
60. Robert H. Lowie, *Primitive Society* (New York, 1920), 235–36. Cf. W[alter] Nippold, *Die Anfänge des Eigentums bei den Naturvölkern und die Entstehung des Privateigentums* (The Hague, 1954), 82; Beaglehole, *Property*, 140–2.
61. Herskovits, *Man and His Works*, 283.
62. Colin Clark and Margaret Haswell, *The Economics of Subsistence Agriculture*, 3rd ed. (New York, 1967), 28–29.
63. Robert McC. Netting in Steadman Upham, ed., *The Evolution of Political Systems* (Cambridge, 1990), 59.
64. Terry L. Anderson and P. J. Hill in *Journal of Law and Economics* 18, No. 1 (1975), 175–76.
65. Edwin N. Wilmsen in *Journal of Anthropological Research* 29, No. 1 (Spring 1973), 4.
66. Lowie, *Primitive Society*, 213; Raymond Firth, *Primitive Economics of the New Zealand Maori* (New York, 1929), 361.
67. Paul Guiraud, *La Propriété Foncière en Grèce* (Paris, 1893), 32. See further J. B. Bury, *A History of Greece*, 3rd ed. (London, 1956), 54.
68. Leyhausen in Lorenz and Leyhausen, *Motivation*, 104.
69. Jomo Kenyatta, *Facing Mount Kenya* (London, 1953), 21. On this subject see also Daniel Biebuyck, ed., *African Agrarian Systems* (London, 1963).
70. Peter J. Usher in Terry L. Anderson, ed., *Property Rights and Indian Economics* (Lanham, Md., 1992), 47.
71. Frank A. Pitelka in *Condor* 61, No. 4 (1959), 253.
72. The phenomenon of "homesickness" (which, however, inexplicably ignores the above instances) is the subject of Ina-Maria Greverus, *Der territoriale Mensch* (Frankfurt am Main, 1972).
73. Jules Isaac, *The Teaching of Contempt* (New York, 1964), 45. The citation comes from Augustine's *The City of God*, Book 18, Chapter 46.
74. Isaac, *Teaching of Contempt*, 39–73.
75. Samuel Hazzard Cross and Olgerd P. Sherbowitz-Wetzor, *The Russian Primary Chronicle: Laurentian Text* (Cambridge, Mass., 1953), 97.

76. Nippold, *Die Anfänge,* 84.
77. Ardrey, *Territorial Imperative,* 102.
78. Richard Pipes, *The Russian Revolution* (New York, 1990), 113.
79. John E. Pfeiffer, *The Emergence of Society* (New York, 1977), 28.
80. Richard B. Lee and Irven DeVore, eds., *Man the Hunter* (Chicago, 1968), 3.
81. Lowie, *Primitive Society,* 211–13.
82. Wilmsen in *Journal of Anthropological Research,* No. 29/1 (1973), 1–31.
83. Eleanor Leacock in *American Anthropologist* 56, No. 5, Part 2, Memoir 78 (1954), 1–59.
84. Schmidt, *Das Eigentum,* I, 290–1.
85. Harold Demsetz in *American Economic Review* 57, No. 2 (May 1967), 352–53.
86. Schmidt, *Das Eigentum,* I, 294–95, lists some such items.
87. Forde, *Habitat, Economy and Society,* 332–34, and W. Schmidt, *Das Eigentum,* II (Münster in Westfalen, 1940), 192–96, cited in Malmberg, *Human Territoriality,* 77.
88. Irven DeVore in Eisenberg and Dillon, eds., *Man and Beast* (Washington, D.C., 1971), 309.
89. E.g., Leacock, in *American Anthropologist,* 2–3.
90. Lowie, *Primitive Society,* 210.
91. Max Ebert, ed., *Reallexikon der Vorgeschichte,* II (Berlin, 1925), 391; Beaglehole, *Property,* 208–9; Hoebel, *Man in the Primitive World,* 435, 442–43; Carleton Coon, *Hunting Peoples* (London, 1972), 176–80.
92. Vernon L. Smith in *Journal of Political Economy* 83, No. 4 (1975), 741. See further Douglass C. North in *Structure and Change in Economic History* (New York and London, 1981), 80.
93. Edella Schlager and Elinor Ostrom in Terry L. Anderson and Randy T. Simmons, eds., *The Political Economy of Customs and Culture* (Lanham, Md., 1993), 13–41.
94. Robert C. Ellickson, *Order Without Law* (Cambridge, Mass., 1991), 191–206. Cf. Chapter 89 of Herman Melville's *Moby-Dick* ("Fast Fish and Loose Fish"), which summarizes these simple rules. I am indebted for this reference to Prof. Charles Fried of the Harvard Law School.
95. James A. Wilson in Garrett Hardin and John Baden, eds., *Managing the Commons* (San Francisco, 1977), 96–111.
96. John Umbeck in *Explorations in Economic History* 14, No. 3 (July 1977), 197–226.
97. Ibid., 214–15.
98. John Baden in Hardin and Baden, eds., *Managing the Commons,* 137.
99. Wilson, *Sociobiology,* 564.
100. Hugh Thomas, *A History of the World* (New York, 1979), 12–13.
101. Clark and Haswell, *Subsistence Agriculture,* 26–27.
102. Vernon L. Smith in *Journal of Political Economy* 83, no. 4 (1975), 727–55. For a dissenting opinion, see Robert J. Wenke, *Patterns in Prehistory* (New York and Oxford, 1984), 152, 154.
103. Charles E. Kay in *Human Nature* 5, No. 4 (1994), 359–98, and in *Western Journal of Applied Forestry,* October 1995, 121–26.
104. Matt Ridley, *The Origins of Virtue* (New York, 1996), 213–25.
105. Beaglehole, *Property,* 211; Schmidt, *Eigentum,* I, 292.
106. Hobhouse, Wheeler, and Ginsberg, *Material Culture,* Appendix I, 255–81.
107. Lowie, *Primitive Society,* 231–33.
108. Philip C. Salzman in *Proceedings of the American Philosophical Society* 111, No. 2 (April 1967), 115–31.
109. Robert H. Lowie, *The Origin of the State* (New York, 1927).
110. Sir Henry Maine, *Ancient Law* (New York, 1864), 124, 126.
111. Lewis Henry Morgan, *Ancient Society* (Tucson, Ariz., 1985), 6–7.

112. J.E.A. Jolliffe, *The Constitutional History of Medieval England,* 4th ed. (London, 1961), 59–60.
113. Ibid., 24.
114. Lowie, *Origin of the State,* 12–19.
115. Chester G. Starr, *Individual and Community* (New York and Oxford, 1986), 42–46.
116. North, *Structure and Change,* 23.
117. Douglass C. North and Robert Paul Thomas, *The Rise of the Western World: A New Economic History* (Cambridge, 1973), 8. Cf. Frederick C. Lane in *Journal of Economic History* 35, No. 1 (1975), 8–17.
118. Marc Bloch, *Feudal Society,* I (Chicago, 1964), 115.
119. Douglass North in Svetozar Pejovich, *The Codetermination Movement in the West* (Lexington, Mass., 1978), 128.
120. Max Weber, *Grundriss der Sozialökonomik: III Abt., Wirtschaft und Gesellschaft,* 3rd ed., II (Tübingen, 1947), 679.
121. L. Delaporte, *Mesopotamia* (New York, 1970), 101–12.
122. Christian Meier, *The Greek Discovery of Politics* (Cambridge, Mass., 1990), 13.
123. M. I. Finley, *Economy and Society in Ancient Greece* (London, 1981), 71–72; Starr, *Individual and Community,* 28.
124. E.g., Alfred Zimmern, *The Greek Commonwealth,* 4th ed. (Oxford, 1924), 287–88. Other examples are listed in Jules Toutain, *The Economic Life of the Ancient World* (New York, 1930), 12.
125. Toutain, *Economic Life,* 14. Cf. Gustave Glotz, *Ancient Greece at Work: An Economic History of Greece* (London and New York, 1926), 8–9.
126. Finley, *Economy and Society,* 217.
127. Ibid., 218.
128. M. Rostovtseff, *Social and Economic History of the Hellenistic World,* I (Oxford, 1941), 273.
129. Starr, *Individual and Community,* vii.
130. Victor Davis Hanson, *The Other Greeks* (New York, 1995), 3.
131. *Cambridge Ancient History,* VI (Cambridge, 1933), 529.
132. Rostovtseff, *Social and Economic History,* 207–12.
133. Stephen Hodkinson in *Classical Quarterly,* n. s., 36, No. 2 (1986), 404.
134. Toutain, *Economic Life,* 113.
135. A. Bouché-Leclercq, *Histoire des Lagides,* Vol. iii, Part 1 (Paris, 1906), 179.
136. Ibid., 191–92.
137. Rostovtseff, *Social and Economic History,* 300; Bouché-Leclercq, *Histoire des Lagides,* Vol. iii, Part 1, 237–71.
138. On this subject, see Reinold Noyes, *The Institution of Property* (New York, 1936), 27–220.
139. Tenney Frank, *An Economic History of Rome,* 2nd ed. (Baltimore, 1927), 14–15.
140. Noyes, *Institution of Property,* 44–49, 78–79.
141. P. S. Atiyah, *The Rise and Fall of the Freedom of Contract* (Oxford, 1979), 110.
142. Toutain, *Economic Life,* 272–74.
143. Henri Lepage, *Pourquoi la propriété* (Paris, 1985), 44.
144. Abbot Payson Usher, *A History of Mechanical Inventions,* rev. ed. (Cambridge, Mass., 1954), 32.
145. This subject is exhaustively treated in Maxime Kowalewsky, *Die Ökonomische Entwicklung Europas bis zum Beginn der kapitalistischen Wirtschaftsform,* I (Berlin, 1901).
146. Bloch, *Feudal Society,* I, 228.
147. Helen Cam, *England Before Elizabeth* (New York, 1952), 97.
148. Bloch, *Feudal Society,* I, 190–2.
149. Ibid., 196–98.
150. Ibid., 208–10.

151. Birgit Sawyer, *Property and Inheritance in Viking Scandinavia: The Runic Evidence* (Alingsas, Sweden, 1988), 16.
152. Henri Pirenne, *Medieval Cities* (Princeton, 1946), 131–32.
153. Cited by John Hine Mundy in R. W. Davis, ed., *The Origins of Modern Freedom in the West* (Stanford, Calif., 1995), 113.
154. Based on Robert von Keller, *Freiheitsgarantien für Person und Eigentum im Mittelalter* (Heidelberg, 1933), 86–238; see further Weber, *Wirtschaft und Gesellschaft,* II, 576–79.
155. John H. Mundy, Introduction to Henri Pirenne, *Early Democracies in the Low Countries* (New York, 1963), xxvi.
156. Weber, *General Economic History,* 318.
157. George H. Sabine, *A History of Political Theory,* rev. ed. (New York, 1955), 403–4.
158. J. H. Elliott, *Imperial Spain, 1469–1716* (London, 1963), 73.
159. Jean Bodin, *The Six Bookes of a Commonweale* (Cambridge, Mass., 1962), 651–53.
160. Reinhold Schmid, *Die Gesetze der Angelsachsen* (Leipzig, 1858), 506.
161. Barbara Suchy in Uwe Schultz, ed., *Mit dem Zehnten fing es an* (Munich, 1986), 116.
162. Ingvar Andersson, *Schwedische Geschichte* (Munich, 1950), 237.
163. J. P. Sommerville, *Politics and Ideology in England, 1603–1640* (London, 1986), 160–3. See below, Chapter 3.
164. J.L.M. de Gain-Montagnac, ed., *Mémoires de Louis XIV, écrits par lui-même,* I (Paris, 1806), 156.
165. Sir William Blackstone, *Commentaries on the Laws of England,* Book I, Chapter 2, 15th ed. (London, 1809), 170.
166. Kirk H. Porter, *A History of Suffrage in the United States* (Chicago, 1918), 2–3. See further Chilton Williamson, *American Suffrage* (Princeton, 1968).
167. Charles Seymour and Donald Paige Frary, *How the World Votes,* I (Springfield, Mass., 1918), 64–180.
168. Porter, *History of Suffrage,* 7–13.
169. Ibid., 109.
170. Jennifer Nedelsky, *Private Property and the Limits of American Constitutionalism* (Chicago and London, 1990), 18–19.
171. James A. Henretta, *The Evolution of American Society* (Lexington, Mass., 1973), 88–112; Williamson, *American Suffrage,* 20–61.
172. Guido de Ruggiero, *The History of European Liberalism* (Boston, 1961), 159, 177.
173. Karl Marx and Frederick Engels, "The Class Struggles in France, 1848–1850," Part I, in *Selected Works,* I (Moscow, 1962), 142.
174. Peter-Christian Witt in Schultz, ed., *Mit dem Zehnten,* 191–93; G. Schmölders in ibid., 248.
175. Thomas Erskine Holland, *The Elements of Jurisprudence,* 12th ed. (Oxford, 1916), 82.
176. Orlando Patterson, *Freedom,* I (New York, 1991), 48. According to the author, the first scholar to call attention to this supposed link was Max Pohlenz. Ibid., 79.
177. Herodotus, *Persian Wars,* Book V, Chapter 78.
178. Thucydides, *History of the Peloponnesian War,* II, xli, trans. Charles Forster Smith, Loeb Classical Library (Cambridge, Mass., 1991), I, 331.
179. Finley, *Ancient Economy,* 28–29. Emphasis added.

CHAPTER 3: ENGLAND AND THE BIRTH OF PARLIAMENTARY DEMOCRACY

1. Edmund Burke, speech, "Conciliation with the Colonies," in *The Works of . . . Edmund Burke,* III (London, 1823), 50.

2. A. F. Pollard, *The Evolution of Parliament,* 2nd ed. (London, 1926), 3–4.
3. J. Churton Collins, *Voltaire, Montesquieu and Rousseau in England* (London, 1908), 158.
4. Voltaire, *Letters Concerning the English Nation* (London, 1926), Letter viii, 41–42.
5. Frederic Milner, *Economic Evolution of England* (London, 1931), 248.
6. Hans W. Kopp, *Parlamente: Geschichte, Grösse, Grenzen* (Frankfurt am Main, 1966), 16.
7. Sidney J. Madge, *The Domesday of Crown Lands* (London, 1938), 14.
8. Ibid., 14–15, 19–20.
9. F. M. Stenton, *Anglo-Saxon England,* 3rd ed. (Oxford, 1971), 550–4.
10. F. W. Maitland, *The Constitutional History of England* (Cambridge, 1946), 60; J.E.A. Jolliffe, *The Constitutional History of Medieval England,* 4th ed. (London, 1961), 55.
11. Robert H. Lowie, *Primitive Society* (New York, 1920), 383–88.
12. Richard Thurnwald in *The Encyclopaedia of the Social Sciences,* XI (New York, 1944), 390–1.
13. Jacques Ellul, *Histoire des Institutions,* I (Paris, 1995), 649–50.
14. Helen Cam, *England Before Elizabeth* (New York, 1952), 47.
15. Marc Bloch, *Feudal Society,* I (Chicago, 1964), 111–12. See the citation from Henry Maine in Chapter 2, p. 95–96.
16. Jolliffe, *Constitutional History,* 57–58.
17. Ibid., 72–73.
18. Maitland, *Constitutional History,* 1.
19. Cam, *England Before Elizabeth,* 55–56.
20. Stephen Dowell, *A History of Taxation and Taxes in England,* I (London, 1888), 7.
21. Sally Harvey in Joan Thirsk, ed., *The Agrarian History of England and Wales,* II (Cambridge, 1988), 85. Cf. Charles H. Pearson, *History of England During the Early and Middle Ages,* I (London, 1867), 669.
22. C. W. Previté-Orton, *The Shorter Cambridge Medieval History,* I (Cambridge, 1953), 584, 586.
23. Dowell, *History of Taxation,* I, 7.
24. Madge, *Domesday,* 29.
25. Gordon Batho in H.P.R. Finberg, *The Agrarian History of England and Wales,* IV (Cambridge, 1967), 256.
26. Maitland, *Constitutional History,* 179; Cam, *England Before Elizabeth,* 123.
27. Maitland, *Constitutional History,* 180.
28. Cam, *England Before Elizabeth,* 104–5.
29. P. S. Atiyah, *The Rise and Fall of Freedom of Contract* (Oxford, 1979), 91.
30. Maitland, *Constitutional History,* 62.
31. Kopp, *Parlamente,* 12.
32. K. Smellie in *Encyclopaedia of the Social Sciences,* IX (New York, 1944), 369.
33. J. H. Baker, *An Introduction to English Legal History,* 3rd ed. (London, 1990), 296–317.
34. Cam, *England Before Elizabeth,* 89–90.
35. Alan Macfarlane, *The Origins of English Individualism* (Cambridge, 1979).
36. Alan Macfarlane, *The Culture of Capitalism* (Oxford, 1987), 192.
37. R.H. Tawney, *The Agrarian Problem in the Sixteenth Century* (London, 1912), 98–99.
38. Kopp, *Parlamente,* 14–15.
39. Cam, *England Before Elizabeth,* 125–26.
40. Maitland, *Constitutional History,* 185–87.
41. Ibid., 256–57; G. R. Elton, *Studies in Tudor and Stuart Politics and Government,* II (Cambridge, 1974), 29–30.
42. Maitland, *Constitutional History,* 195.

43. Sir John Fortescue, *De Laudibus Legum Angliae*, ed. and trans. S. B. Chrimes (Cambridge, 1949), 24–25.
44. On this subject, see William Holdsworth, *Some Makers of English Law* (Cambridge, 1938), Chapter iii.
45. Paul Brand, *The Origins of the English Legal Profession* (Oxford, 1992).
46. J. H. Baker in R. W. Davis, ed., *The Origins of Modern Freedom in the West* (Stanford, 1995), 191. Baker's essay deals with the contribution that common law made to the growth in England of personal liberty.
47. Frank Smith Fussner, ed., in *Proceedings of the American Philosophical Society* 101, No.2 (1957), 206.
48. Arthur R. Hogue, *Origins of the Common Law* (Bloomington, Ind., 1966), 107.
49. Ibid., 232.
50. P. S. Atiyah, *The Rise and Fall of Freedom of Contract*, 95. Cf. Roscoe Pound in *Encyclopaedia of the Social Sciences*, IV (New York, 1944), 53.
51. James A. Williamson, *The Tudor Age* (London and New York, 1979), 439.
52. John R. Commons, *Legal Foundations of Capitalism* (New York, 1924), 233. Cf. J. G. A. Pocock, *The Ancient Constitution and the Feudal Law* (New York, 1967), *passim*.
53. J. P. Sommerville, *Politics and Ideology in England, 1603–1640* (London and New York, 1986), 87–92.
54. See William S. Holdsworth, *Essays in Law and History* (Oxford, 1946), 49.
55. David Harris Sacks in Philip T. Hoffman and Kathryn Norberg, *Fiscal Crises, Liberty, and Representative Government, 1450–1789* (Stanford, Calif., 1994), 16, citing Charles Gray.
56. Commons, *Legal Foundations*, 50.
57. A. L. Rowse, *The England of Elizabeth* (New York, 1951), 333–36.
58. Michael J. Braddick, *The Nerves of State* (Manchester and New York, 1996), 91–95.
59. Dowell, *History of Taxation*, I, 194.
60. Williamson, *Tudor Age*, 1–3.
61. Batho in Finberg, *Agrarian History*, IV, 256.
62. Madge, *Domesday*, 29.
63. Williamson, *Tudor Age*, 140.
64. Joyce Yowings in Finberg, *Agrarian History*, IV, 332–33.
65. Dowell, *History of Taxation*, I, 135–36.
66. Williamson, *Tudor Age*, 157.
67. Ibid.
68. Sacks in Hoffman and Norberg, *Fiscal Crises*, 39.
69. Batho in Finberg, *Agrarian History*, IV, 265–66.
70. Sacks in Hoffman and Norberg, *Fiscal Crises*, 39.
71. Williamson, *Tudor England*, 344.
72. Ibid., 421.
73. Kenyon, *Stuart England*, 54.
74. Ivor Jennings in *Encyclopaedia Britannica* (Chicago, 1970), XVII, 378.
75. Kenyon, *Stuart England*, 31; Maitland, *Constitutional History*, 240.
76. Williamson, *Tudor England*, 438.
77. Maitland, *Constitutional History*, 248–49. Williamson, *Tudor Age*, 438, provides somewhat different figures.
78. Kenyon, *Stuart England*, 32.
79. Ibid., 34.
80. Williamson, *Tudor Age*, 101–5, 243.
81. Ibid., 439.
82. Elton, *Studies*, I, 283. Cf. Williamson, *Tudor Age*, 9, 437.
83. George H. Sabine, *A History of Political Theory* (New York, 1938), 395–97.
84. Feiling, *History of England*, 445.

85. Kenyon, *Stuart England,* 71.
86. Lawrence Stone, *The Crisis of the Aristocracy, 1568–1641* (London, 1965), 65–128.
87. Frederick C. Dietz, *English Public Finance, 1558–1641,* II (New York, 1964), 299; Madge, *Domesday,* 50.
88. Batho in Finberg, *Agrarian History,* IV, 273.
89. C. V. Wedgwood, *The King's Peace, 1637–1641* (New York, 1956), 153–54; Christopher Clay in Thirsk, ed., *Agrarian History,* V, Vol. 2, 154.
90. Sommerville, *Politics and Ideology,* 147.
91. Ibid., 151.
92. Robert Zaller in J. H. Hexter, ed., *Parliament and Liberty from the Reign of Elizabeth to the English Civil War* (Stanford, Calif., 1992), 202.
93. Barry Coward, *The Stuart Age,* 2nd ed. (London and New York, 1994), 110.
94. Wedgwood, *King's Peace,* 153–54; Coward, *Stuart Age,* 108.
95. Dietz, *English Public Finance,* II, 299.
96. Conrad Russell, *Parliaments and English Politics, 1621–1629* (Oxford, 1979), 19.
97. Perez Zagorin, *The Court and the Country: The Beginning of the English Revolution* (New York, 1971), 98–99.
98. Ibid., 90.
99. Coward, *Stuart Age,* 95; Sommerville, *Politics and Ideology,* 116.
100. Zagorin, *Court and the Country,* 120–31.
101. "The Form of Apology and Satisfaction" is reproduced in J. P. Kenyon, ed., *The Stuart Constitution, 1603–1688,* 2nd ed. (Cambridge, 1986), 29–35; on "The Humble Answer," see Jack Hexter in J. H. Hexter, ed., *Parliament and Liberty* (Stanford, Calif., 1992), 28–32.
102. J. H. Hexter in Hexter, ed., *Parliament and Liberty,* 11–12. The subject is dealt with at length by Johann P. Sommerville in ibid., 56–84.
103. J. W. Allen, *English Political Thought, 1603–1660,* I (London, 1938), 26.
104. Ibid., 32.
105. S. Reed Brett, *John Pym, 1583–1643* (London, 1940), 86.
106. Ibid., 81–82, 86.
107. S[amuel] R. Gardiner, ed., *The Constitutional Documents of the Puritan Revolution: 1625–1660,* 3rd ed. (Oxford, 1936), 69.
108. Ibid., 67.
109. Hexter in Hexter, ed., *Parliament and Liberty,* 1.
110. Brett, *Pym,* 82.
111. Dietz, *Public Finance,* II, 262–63.
112. Feiling, *History of England,* 457.
113. Zagorin, *Court and the Country,* 116.
114. Sommerville, *Politics and Ideology,* 159.
115. Clive Holmes in Hexter, ed., *Parliament and Liberty,* 135–36.
116. John Adair, *A Life of John Hampden* (London, 1976), 3.
117. Brett, *Pym,* 225–26.
118. Dowell, *History of Taxation,* I, 222.
119. Wedgwood, *King's Peace,* 383.
120. Kenyon, *Stuart England,* 125; Maitland, *Constitutional History,* 293.
121. Kenyon, *Stuart England,* 127; Maitland, *Constitutional History,* 294.
122. Madge, *Domesday,* 63–66.
123. Christopher Clay in Thirsk, ed., *Agrarian History,* V, vol. 2, 119–54.
124. Feiling, *History of England,* 507.
125. M. J. Braddick, *Parliamentary Taxation in Seventeenth-Century England* (Woodbridge, Suffolk, 1994), 292, 293n.
126. Madge, *Domesday,* 262–63; George Clark, *The Later Stuarts, 1660–1714,* 2nd ed. (Oxford, 1955), 5.
127. C. D. Chandaman, *The English Public Revenue, 1660–1688* (Oxford, 1975), 111.

128. Joan Thirsk in *Journal of Modern History* 26, no. 4 (December 1954), 315–28; Clay in Thirsk, ed., *Agrarian History,* V. vol. ii, 156.
129. Chandaman, *English Public Revenue,* 111.
130. Milner, *Economic Evolution,* 249; Clark, *Later Stuarts,* 6–7; Wedgwood, *King's Peace,* 155.
131. Dowell, *History of Taxation and Taxes,* II, 41–42.
132. Chandaman, *English Public Revenue,* 2, 138.
133. Braddick, *Nerves of State,* 10.
134. Jones in Hoffman, *Fiscal Crises,* 70–1.
135. Coward, *Stuart Age,* 290.
136. Chandaman, *English Public Revenue,* 277.
137. Ibid., 278.
138. Coward, *Stuart Age,* 333, 335.
139. Madge, *Domesday,* 275.
140. Howard Nenner in J. R. Jones, ed., *Liberty Secured? Britain Before and After 1688* (Stanford, Calif., 1992), 92.
141. Kenyon, *Stuart England,* 228.
142. On this see Lois G. Schwoerer, *The Declaration of Rights, 1689* (Baltimore and London, 1981).
143. David Ogg, *England in the Reigns of James II and William III* (Oxford, 1955), 242.
144. Dowell, *History of Taxation,* II, 42.
145. Clark, *Later Stuarts,* 56–57, 149; Coward, *Stuart Age,* 348–49.
146. Coward, *Stuart Age,* 375–76.
147. Ibid., 379, 454.
148. Ibid., 453.
149. Maitland, *Constitutional History,* 312–13.
150. Élie Halévy, *A History of the English People in the Nineteenth Century, I. England in 1815* (London, 1949), 6.
151. This point is vigorously argued by A. R. Myers in *Parliaments and Estates in Europe to 1789* (London, 1975), one of the few comparative studies of representative institutions.
152. Myers, *Parliaments,* 24.
153. Antonio Marongiu, *Medieval Parliaments: A Comparative Study* (London, 1968), 100.
154. J. H. Elliott, *Imperial Spain, 1469–1716* (London, 1963), 18.
155. Frederick Powicke, cited in *Relazioni* of the Tenth International Congress of the Historical Sciences, Rome, 1955, I (Florence, 1955), 18.
156. R. Jalliffier, *Histoire des États Généraux (1302–1614)* (Paris, [1885]), 84.
157. Maurice Rey, *Le Domaine du Roi . . . sous Charles VI, 1388–1413* (Paris, 1965), 35.
158. Elliott, *Imperial Spain,* 80–1, 193–94.
159. Ibid., 80–1.
160. Douglass C. North and Robert P. Thomas, *The Rise of the Western World* (Cambridge, 1973), 129–31.
161. C.B.A. Behrens, *The Ancien Régime* (London, 1972), 90.
162. George Edmundson, *History of Holland* (Cambridge, 1922), 112.

CHAPTER 4: PATRIMONIAL RUSSIA

1. *Polnoe Sobranie Zakonov Rossiiskoi Imperii, s 1649 goda,* 1st ed., 45 vols. (St. Petersburg, 1830), Vol. iv, No. 1,857, June 20, 1701, pp. 169–70. Henceforth referred to as *PSZ.*
2. M. N. Tikhomirov, *Drevnerusskie goroda,* 2nd ed. (Moscow, 1956).

3. M. F. Vladimirskii-Budanov, *Obzor istorii russkogo prava,* 4th ed. (St. Petersburg and Kiev, 1905), 524; G. F. Shershenevich, *Uchebnik russkogo grazhdanskogo prava,* 7th ed. (St. Petersburg, 1909), 242.
4. V. B. Kobrin, *Vlast' i sobstvennost' v srednevekovoi Rossii (XV–XVIvv)* (Moscow, 1985), 32–33. Cf. S. V. Veselovskii, *Feodal'noe zemlevladenie v severo-vostochnoi Rusi,* I (Moscow and Leningrad, 1947), which somehow concludes from the virtual absence of sources documenting the existence of private property in land before c. 1350 that such property was "very widespread" (p. 8).
5. Alan Macfarlane, *The Origins of English Individualism* (Cambridge, 1979), Chapter 5.
6. V. O. Kliuchevskii, *Kurs russkoi istorii,* I (Moscow, 1937), Lecture xviii, pp. 327–28; cf. A. E. Presniakov, *Obrazovanie velikorusskogo gosudarstva* (Petrograd, 1918), 26–27.
7. A. N. Nasonov, *Mongoly i Rus'* (Moscow and Leningrad, 1940), 10.
8. Ibid., 77–78.
9. Ibid., 28–29.
10. Aleksandr Lakier, *O votchinakh i pomesti'iakh* (St. Petersburg, 1848), 132.
11. On this subject, see Klaus Zernack, *Die burgstädtischen Volksversammlungen bei den Ost- und Westslaven,* in *Giessener Abhandlungen zur Agrar- und Wirtschaftsforschung des Europäischen Ostens,* Reihe I, Band 33 (Wiesbaden, 1967).
12. M. Bogoslovskii, *Zemskoe samoupravlenie na russkom severe v XVII v.,* I (Moscow, 1909), 56.
13. I. M. Kulisher, *Istoriia russkogo narodnogo khoziaistva,* II (Moscow, 1925), 46; Bogoslovskii, *Zemskoe samoupravlenie,* 48.
14. Ia. E. Vodarskii, *Dvorianskoe zemlevladenie v Rossii v xvii–pervoi polovine xix v.* (Moscow, 1988), 3.
15. M. Diakonov, *Ocherki obshchestvennogo i gosudarstvennogo stroia drevnei Rusi,* 4th ed. (St. Petersburg, 1912), 244–47.
16. Ivan Andreevskii, *O dogovore Novagoroda s nemetskimi gorodami i Gotlandom* (St. Petersburg, 1855), 4.
17. A. L. Khoroshkevich, *Torgovlia Velikogo Novgoroda v XIV-XV vekakh* (Moscow, 1963).
18. N. L. Podvigina, *Ocherki sotsial'no-ekonomicheskoi i politicheskoi istorii Novgoroda Velikogo v XII-XIII vv.* (Moscow, 1976), 106.
19. Ibid., 38.
20. *Istoriia SSSR,* I (Moscow, 1948), 126.
21. S. N. Valk, ed., *Gramoty Velikogo Novgoroda i Pskova* (Moscow and Leningrad, 1949), 9–10.
22. Podvigina, *Ocherki,* 12–13, 115–16.
23. S. V. Iushkov, *Istoriia gosudarstva i prava SSSR,* I (Moscow, 1940), 200–1.
24. Podvigina, *Ocherki,* 114.
25. A. V. Artsikhovskii in *Istoricheskie Zapiski,* No. 2 (1938), 122, 125–26; O.V. Martyshin, *Vol'nyi Novgorod* (Moscow, 1992), 87–88.
26. A. M. Gnevushev, *Ocherki ekonomicheskoi i sotsial'noi zhizni sel'skogo naseleniia novgorodskoi oblasti posle prisoedineniia Novgoroda k Moskve,* I (Kiev, 1915), 310.
27. Artsikhovskii in *Istoricheskie Zapiski,* No. 2 (1938), 114–16.
28. Zernack, *Die burgstädtischen Volksversammlungen,* 189.
29. *Pamiatniki russkogo prava,* II (Moscow, 1953), 212; George G. Weickhardt in *Russian Review* 51 (October 1992), 467–68.
30. A. Nikitskii, *Ocherk vnutrennei istorii Pskova* (St. Petersburg, 1873), 120–1, 126.
31. Nasonov, *Mongoly,* 94.
32. Ibid., 128.
33. Ibid., 114.

34. See below, p. 182.
35. V. N. Bernadskii, *Novgorod i novgorodskaia zemlia v XV veke* (Moscow-Leningrad, 1961), 321–24.
36. Kulisher, *Istoriia,* II, 50; Veselovskii, *Feodal'noe zemlevladenie,* 288–90.
37. Diakonov, *Ocherki,* 256–58; V. Sergeevich, *Lektsii i issledovaniia po drevnei istorii russkogo prava,* 4th ed. (St. Petersburg, 1910), 543.
38. *Pamiatniki russkogo prava,* VI, *Sobornoe ulozhenie tsaria Alekseia Mikhailovicha 1649 goda* (Moscow, 1957), 223.
39. S.V. Rozhdestvenskii, *Sluzhiloe zemlevladenie v moskovskom gosudarstve XVI veka* (St. Petersburg, 1897), 8–9. Veselovskii, however, disputes that *pomestia* antedated the reign of Ivan III. *Feodal'noe zemlevladenie,* 302.
40. Veselovskii, *Feodal'noe zemlevladenie,* 55.
41. On this subject, see A. A. Zimin, *Oprichnina Ivana Groznogo* (Moscow, 1964), 306–59; and R. G. Skrynnikov, *Tsarstvo terrora* (St. Petersburg, 1992).
42. R. G. Skrynnikov, *Nachalo Oprichniny* (Leningrad, 1966), 278–97.
43. G. Peretiatkovich, *Povolzhe v XV i XVI vekakh* (Moscow, 1877), 246–71.
44. Giles Fletcher, *Of the Russe Commonwealth* (1591) (Cambridge, Mass., 1966), 26–26v.
45. *Istoriia Rossii s drevneishikh vremen,* III (Moscow, 1960), 705–6. On the Western practice, see J. C. Holt in *Past and Present,* No. 57 (1972), 7–8.
46. The fullest account of this process is Rozhdestvenskii, *Sluzhiloe zemlevladenie.*
47. Diakonov, *Ocherki,* 255–56.
48. The law survives in only one version: *Polnoe sobranie russkikh letopisei,* XIII (St. Petersburg, 1904), 268–69; Rozhdestvenskii, *Sluzhiloe zemlevladenie,* 51–52.
49. Veselovskii, *Feodal'noe zemlevladenie,* 89.
50. Rozhdestvenskii, *Sluzhiloe zemlevladenie,* 59, iii.
51. E. D. Stashevskii, *Zemlevladenie moskovskogo dvorianstva v pervoi polovine XVII veka* (Moscow, 1911), 26–27.
52. Ibid., 17.
53. Shershenevich, *Uchebnik,* 201–2.
54. *Pamiatniki russko prava,* VI, *Sobornoe ulozhenie,* 228.
55. E. I. Indova in E. I. Pavlenko, ed., *Dvorianstvo i krepostnoi stroi Rossii XVI–XVIII vv.* (Moscow, 1975), 275n.
56. Fletcher, *Russe Commonwealth,* 46v–47.
57. Pavel Smirnov, *Goroda moskovskogo gosudarstva v pervoi polovine xvii veka,* Vol. I, Part 1 (Kiev, 1919), 352.
58. Ibid., 77.
59. Ibid., 12.
60. Ibid., 14–15.
61. Otto Brunner, *Neue Wege der Verfassungs- und Sozialgeschichte,* 2nd ed. (Göttingen, 1968), 235–36.
62. S. M. Soloviev, *Istoriia Rossii s drevneishikh vremen,* VII (Moscow, 1962), 46.
63. Heiko Haumann in *Jahrbücher für die Geschichte Osteuropas,* Neue Folge, Vol. 27, Heft 4 (1979), 486; Vladimirskii-Budanov, *Obzor,* 245.
64. J. Michael Hittle, *The Service City* (Cambridge, Mass., 1979), 34.
65. Smirnov, *Goroda,* I/1, 20.
66. V. O. Kliuchevskii, Letter to the Editor, *Russkie vedomosti,* No. 125 (May 9, 1887).
67. Smirnov, *Goroda,* I/2, 351–52; A. M. Sakharov, *Obrazovanie i razvitie rossiiskogo gosudarstva v XIV–XVII v.* (Moscow, 1969), 77.
68. Iu. R. Klokman, *Sotsial'no ekonomicheskaia istoriia russkogo goroda* (Moscow, 1967), 31; Brunner, *Neue Wege,* 226. Keith Feiling, *A History of England* (London, 1950), 509, says that in England of 1640 "probably" no more than 50 percent of the population derived its living from agriculture.
69. Alexander A. Tschuprow [Chuprov], *Die Feldgemeinschaft* (Strassburg, 1902), Chapter II.

70. V. N. Latkin, *Uchebnik istorii russkogo prava perioda imperii,* 2nd ed. (St. Petersburg, 1909), 205. Cf. S. F. Platonov, *Ocherki po istorii smuty v moskovskom gosudarstve XVI–XVII vv.,* 3rd ed. (St. Petersburg, 1910), 155.
71. Ia. E. Vodarskii in *Voprosy voennoi istorii Rossii* (Moscow, 1969), 237–38.
72. *PSZ,* Vol. v, No. 2,789, March 23, 1714, pp. 91–94.
73. A. Romanovich-Slavatinskii, *Dvorianstvo v Rossii* (St. Petersburg, 1870), 239.
74. N. N. Efremova in Rossiiskaia Akademiia Nauk, Institut Gosudarstva i Prava, *Sobstvennost': Pravo i Svoboda* (Moscow, 1992), 47.
75. *Entsiklopedicheskii Slovar' Obshchestva Brogkauz i Efron,* Vol. XXVIIA, 187.
76. S. P. Luppov, *Kniga v Rossii v xvii veke* (Leningrad, 1970), 28.
77. A. Sergeev in *Knizhnoe Obozrenie,* No. 18 (May 2, 1995), 21.
78. Efremova in *Sobstvennost',* 47.
79. Richard Pipes, *Russia Under the Old Regime* (London and New York, 1974), 210.
80. Helen Cam, *England Before Elizabeth* (New York, 1952), 119.
81. Latkin, *Uchebnik,* 201–2.
82. *PSZ,* Vol. xv, No. 11,444, February 18, 1762, pp. 912–15.
83. Pipes, *Russia Under the Old Regime,* 178.
84. O. A. Omelchenko, *"Zakonnaia monarkhiia" Ekateriny Vtoroi* (Moscow, 1993), 29, 211. According to A. Kizevetter in *Istoricheskie siluety: liudi i sobytiia* (Berlin, 1931), 47–48, Russian landlords were very pleased with these surveys.
85. *PSZ,* Vol. xviii, No. 13,235, January 19, 1769, p. 805.
86. *PSZ,* Vol. xxi, No. 15,447, June 28, 1782, pp. 613–15, and No. 15,518, September 22, 1782, p. 676.
87. *PSZ,* Vol. xxii, No. 16,187, April 21, 1785, pp. 344–58. A partial English translation is in Basil Dmytryshyn, ed., *Imperial Russia: A Source Book, 1700–1917,* 2nd ed. (Hinsdale, Ill., 1974), 108–11.
88. V. N. Latkin, *Zakonodatel'nye kommissii v Rossii v XVIII st.,* I (St. Petersburg, 1887), 303–4.
89. Omelchenko, *"Zakonnaia monarkhiia,"* 178–79.
90. Heinrich Altrichter, *Wandlungen des Eigentumsbegriffs und neuere Ausgestaltung des Eigentumsrechts* (Marburg and Lahn, 1930), 1–2.
91. *PSZ,* Vol. xviii, No.12,950, July 30, 1767, Art. 10, p. 282.
92. N. D. Chechulin, ed., *Nakaz Imperatritsy Ekateriny II* (St. Petersburg, 1907), 86.
93. See V. I. Semevskii, *Krest'ianskii vopros v Rossii v XVIII i pervoi polovine XIX veka,* I (St. Petersburg, 1888), 196–222 and *passim.*
94. P. A. Khromov, *Ekonomicheskoe razvitie Rossii* (Moscow, 1967), 77.
95. Iakushkin, *Ocherki,* 192.
96. Vladimirskii-Budanov, *Obzor,* 247; Omelchenko, *"Zakonnaia monarkhiia,"* 236–38.
97. A. F. Pollard, *The Evolution of Parliament,* 2nd ed. (London, 1926), 169, 171.
98. Robert von Keller, *Freiheitsgarantien für Person und Eigentum im Mittelalter* (Heidelberg, 1933), 68.
99. William H. Riker in Ellen Frankel Paul and Howard Dickman, eds., *Liberty, Property, and the Future of Constitutional Government* (Albany, N.Y., 1990), 51–52.
100. I. K. Luppol, *Deni Didro* (Moscow, 1960), 107.
101. Richard Wortman in Olga Crisp and Linda Edmondson, eds., *Civil Rights in Imperial Russia* (Oxford, 1989), 16.
102. *Plan gosudarstvennogo preobrazovaniia Grafa M. M. Speranskogo* (Moscow, 1905), 305.
103. S. S. Tatishchev, *Imperator Aleksandr II: ego zhizn' i tsarstvovanie,* I (St. Petersburg, 1903), 308.
104. The following information is based on Latkin, *Uchebnik,* 212–32, and Vladimirskii-Budanov, *Obzor,* 245–47.
105. *PSZ,* Vol. vi, No. 3,669, October 29, 1720, p. 252.

106. *PSZ*, Vol. xv, No. 11,166, December 13, 1760, pp. 582–84, and No. 11,216, March 15, 1761, pp. 665–66.
107. *PSZ*, Vol. xvii, No. 12,311, January 17, 1765, p. 10.
108. Khromov, *Ekonomicheskoe razvitie*, 69–70.
109. Geoffrey Hosking, *Russia: People and Empire, 1552–1917* (Cambridge, Mass., 1997), 200.
110. Victor Leontovitsch, *Geschichte des Liberalismus in Russland* (Frankfurt am Main, 1957), 165.
111. O. Iu. Iakhshiian in *Mentalitet i agrarnoe razvitie Rossiii (XIX–XX vv.)* (Moscow, 1966), 92.
112. *PSZ*, Vol. xxii, No. 16,188, April 21, 1785, pp. 358–84. (In this, the first edition of the *PSZ*, this edict was mistakenly assigned the number 16,187, the same as the Noble Charter.)
113. Klokman, *Sotsial'no-ekonomicheskaia istoriia*, 119.
114. Joseph Bradley in *Russian History*, VI, Pt. i (1979), 22.
115. Pipes, *Russia Under the Old Regime*, 212–15.
116. G. R. Elton, *The Tudor Revolution in Government* (Cambridge, 1953), 415.
117. Stanislaw Kutrzeba, *Historia ustroju Polski v zarysie*, 3rd ed., I (Lwow, 1912), 204.
118. *PSZ*, Vol. xxiv, No. 17,906, April 5, 1797, pp. 525–69.
119. Latkin, *Uchebnik*, 204–5.
120. N. M. Druzhinin, *Gosudarstvennye krest'iane i reforma P.D. Kiseleva*, II (Moscow, 1958), 76.
121. Olga Crisp in Crisp and Edmondson, *Civil Rights*, 44.
122. V. M. Kabuzan, *Izmeneniia v razmeshchenii naseleniia v Rossii* (Moscow, 1971), 12.
123. Khromov, *Ekonomicheskoe razvitie*, 77–78.
124. Olga Crisp in Crisp and Edmondson, *Civil Rights*, 37; A. A. Kizevetter, *Istoricheskie ocherki* (Moscow, 1912), 486.
125. M. Polievktov, *Nikolai I* (Moscow, 1918), 304.
126. Kizevetter, *Istoricheskie Ocherki*, 481–83; Polievktov, *Nikolai*, 313.
127. Kizevetter, *Istoricheskie Ocherki*, 480–2.
128. P. P. Semenov Tian-Shanskii, *Memuary*, III, *Epokha osvobozhdeniia krest'ian* (Petrograd, 1915), 230–1.
129. Teodor Shanin, *The Awkward Class* (Oxford, 1972), 30–1, 220n; cf. Macfarlane, *Origins*, 19–20.
130. I. F. Gindin, *Russkie kommercheskie banki* (Moscow, 1948), 63.
131. Richard Pipes, *The Russian Revolution* (New York, 1990), 78.
132. Gosudarstvennaia Duma, *Stenograficheskii Otchet* (1906), I, i, p. 2. Session of May 13, 1906.
133. Cited in Geoffrey A. Hosking, *The Russian Constitutional Experiment* (Cambridge, 1973), 61.

CHAPTER 5: PROPERTY IN THE TWENTIETH CENTURY

1. Richard A. Epstein, *Takings* (Cambridge, Mass., 1985), x.
2. Charles A. Reich in *Yale Law Journal* 75, No. 8 (July 1966), 1269.
3. The information which follows is documented in the author's *Russian Revolution* (New York, 1990), Chapters 15 and 16, pp. 671–744, and *Russia Under the Bolshevik Regime* (New York, 1994), Chapter 8, pp. 369–435.
4. On this see Vladimir Brovkin, *Beyond the Front Lines of the Civil War* (Princeton, 1994).
5. Richard Pipes, ed., *The Unknown Lenin* (New Haven, Conn., 1996), 60–1.
6. Data for 1938 from *Strany mira: Ezhegodnyi Spravochnik* (Moscow, 1946), 129.

7. D. E. Tagunov in *Sovetskoe gosudarstvo i pravo* vii (1981), 130.
8. David Hume, "Of Justice," in *The Philosophical Works,* IV (London, 1882), 453.
9. Leonid Luks, *Entstehung der kommunistischen Faschismustheorie* (Stuttgart, 1984).
10. Pipes, *Russian Revolution,* 674–79.
11. A. James Gregor, *The Fascist Persuasion in Radical Politics* (Princeton, 1974), 176–77.
12. *Opera Omnia di Benito Mussolini,* XXVI (Florence, 1958), 256; see further Erwin von Beckerath, *Wesen und Werden des faschistischen Staates* (Berlin, 1927), 143–44.
13. Karl Dietrich Bracher, *Die deutsche Diktatur,* 2nd ed. (Frankfurt, 1979), 59.
14. Ibid., 156.
15. Cited in F. A. Hayek, *The Road to Serfdom* (London, 1976), 22n.
16. G. Feder (1923), cited in Axel Kuhn, *Das faschistische Herrschaftssystem und die moderne Gesellschaft* (Hamburg, 1973), 80.
17. Hermann Rauschning, *Hitler Speaks* (London, 1939), 48–50.
18. H. A. Turner, Jr., *German Big Business and the Rise of Hitler* (New York, 1985), 345.
19. Walther Hofer, ed., *Der Nationalsozialismus: Dokumente 1933–1945* (Frankfurt am Main, 1957), 28–31.
20. Bracher, *Die deutsche Diktatur,* 235, 394; Pipes, *Russia Under the Bolshevik Regime,* 275.
21. Frieda Wunderlich in *Social Research* 12, No.1 (February 1945), 68.
22. Quoted in David Schoenbaum, *Hitler's Social Revolution* (Garden City, N.Y., 1967), 147. Chapter 4 in this book provides an authoritative account of "The Third Reich and Business."
23. Edouard Calic, *Ohne Maske* (Frankfurt am Main, 1968), 37.
24. Schoenbaum, *Hitler's Social Revolution,* 147.
25. On this, see Avraham Barkai, *From Boycott to Annihilation* (Hanover, N.H., and London, 1989).
26. Samuel Lurie, *Private Investment in a Controlled Economy: Germany 1933–1939* (New York, 1947), 47–73.
27. Wolfram Fischer, *Deutsche Wirtschaftspolitik, 1918–1945,* 3rd ed. (Opladen, 1968), 77.
28. Avraham Barkai, *Nazi Economics* (Oxford, 1990), 237.
29. Lurie, *Private Investment,* 51.
30. Ibid., 200–1.
31. Ibid., 131–36.
32. Barkai, *Nazi Economics,* 204.
33. Ibid., 230; Lurie, *Private Investment,* 54–56.
34. Barkai, *Nazi Economics,* 229; Lurie, *Private Investment,* 56–58.
35. Wunderlich in *Social Research* 12, No. 1 (February 1945), 60–76; J. E. Farquharson, *The Plough and the Swastika* (London, 1976).
36. Barkai, *Nazi Economics,* 231.
37. Schoenbaum, *Hitler's Social Revolution,* 150, 114. See further Élie Halévy, *Histoire du socialisme européen* (Paris, 1948), 279–81.
38. Morris Cohen in *Cornell Law Quarterly* 13, No. 1 (December 1927), 29.
39. P. S. Atiyah, *The Rise and Fall of Freedom of Contract* (Oxford, 1979), 239.
40. George Jacob Holyoake in *The Nineteenth Century,* June 1879, 1115. The views on poverty in eighteenth- and nineteenth-century England are discussed by Karl Polanyi in *The Great Transformation* (New York, 1944), 86–129.
41. *The Writings and Speeches of Grover Cleveland* (New York, 1892), 450.
42. Atiyah, *Rise and Fall,* 241–44.
43. Ibid., 91.
44. Élie Halévy, *The Growth of Philosophical Radicalism* (Boston, 1955), 35.
45. Atiyah, *Rise and Fall,* 254–55.

46. Hayek's views as summarized by Albert O. Hirschman, *The Rhetoric of Reaction* (Cambridge, Mass., 1991), 112.
47. Marx, "Critique of the Gotha Programme" (1875) in Karl Marx and Frederick Engels, *Selected Works in Two Volumes,* II (Moscow, 1962), 24.
48. See, e.g., Kent Greenawalt, *Discrimination and Reverse Discrimination* (New York, 1983), 34.
49. C. Reinold Noyes in *Journal of Legal and Political Sociology* 1, No. 3–4 (April 1943), 91.
50. Charles A. Reich in *Yale Law Journal* 73, No. 5 (April 1964), 733.
51. *New York Times,* August 11, 1996, Section 4, pp. 1, 14.
52. Cited in Vice President Al Gore, ed., *Creating a Government That Works Better and Costs Less* (New York, 1993), 32.
53. Mark L. Pollot, *Grand Theft and Petit Larceny* (San Francisco, 1993), xxvi. Cf. F. A. Hayek, *The Constitution of Liberty* (Chicago, 1960), 258.
54. Dan Usher, *The Economic Prerequisites to Democracy* (New York, 1981), 90.
55. Francis S. Philbrick in *University of Pennsylvania Law Review* 86, no. 7 (May 1938), 692.
56. Adolf A. Berle and Gardiner C. Means, *The Modern Corporation and Private Property,* rev. ed. (New York, 1968), vii–viii.
57. Ibid., viii–x.
58. For a critical discussion of the Berle-Means book, on the fiftieth anniversary of its publication, see *Journal of Law and Economics* 26, No. 2 (June 1983).
59. Ibid., 390.
60. Nathan Rosenberg and L. E. Birdzell, Jr., *How the West Grew Rich* (New York, 1986), 205; Henri Lepage, *Pourquoi la propriété* (Paris, 1985), 143.
61. See, e.g., Thomas C. Grey in *Nomos,* No. 22 (1980), 69–85.
62. *Economist,* September 11, 1993, 12.
63. George J. Stigler and Claire Friedland in *Journal of Law and Economics* 26, No. 2 (June 1983), 259.
64. Uwe Schultz in Uwe Schultz, ed., *Mit dem Zehnten fing es an* (Munich, 1986), 7–8.
65. Forrest McDonald, *Novus Ordo Seclorum: The Intellectual Origins of the Constitution* (Lawrence, Kans., 1985), 24–25.
66. A. R. Myers, *Parliaments and Estates in Europe to 1789* (London, 1975), 104.
67. M. I. Finley, *Economy and Society in Ancient Greece* (London, 1981), 90, and *The Ancient Economy* (Berkeley and Los Angeles, 1973), 95–96.
68. Aristotle, *Politics,* 1313b.
69. Dietwulf Baatz in Schultz, *Mit dem Zehnten,* 38–50.
70. Noyes in *Journal of Legal and Political Sociology,* 74.
71. Elsbet Orth in Schultz, ed., *Mit dem Zehnten,* 78.
72. Henri Pirenne, *Medieval Cities* (Princeton, 1946), 40, 42.
73. Arthur Tilley, ed., *Modern France* (Cambridge, 1922), 298, 303.
74. Élie Halévy, *A History of the English People in 1815* (London, 1924), 326–28.
75. Edward C. Kirkland, *A History of American Economic Life,* 3rd ed. (New York, 1951), 262–63. The U.S. government was first authorized to levy taxes by the Federal Constitution, adopted in 1787–88.
76. Ibid., 267.
77. U.S. Constitution, Article I, Section 9, No. 4.
78. William J. Shultz in *Encyclopedia of the Social Sciences,* VIII (New York, 1944), 43–44.
79. Ibid., 44.
80. Noyes in *Journal of Legal and Political Sociology,* 92.
81. Richard Hofstadter, *America at 1750* (New York, 1970), 131.
82. James W. Ely, Jr., *The Guardian of Every Other Right* (New York and Oxford, 1998), 16.

83. James W. Ely, Jr., in James W. Ely, Jr., ed., *Property Rights in American History* (New York and London, 1997), 67–84.
84. William B. Scott, *In Pursuit of Happiness* (Bloomington, Ind., 1977), 15–23.
85. See Ely, *Guardian of Every Other Right,* 59–100.
86. Ayn Rand, *Capitalism: The Unknown Ideal* (New York, 1966), 290.
87. Franklin D. Roosevelt, *Nothing to Fear* (Freeport, N.Y., 1946), 389. See Richard A. Epstein in *Social Philosophy and Policy* 15, No. 2 (Summer 1998), 412–36.
88. Ely, *Guardian of Every Other Right,* 132–33. The quotation within the quotation is from Leo Pfeffer, *This Honorable Court* (Boston, 1965), 322.
89. Charles Murray, *Losing Ground* (New York, 1984), 17.
90. Robert E. Sherwood, *Roosevelt and Hopkins* (New York, 1948), 231.
91. Sir William H. Beveridge, *The Pillars of Security and Other War-time Essays and Addresses* (New York, 1943), 49–50.
92. Ibid., 58.
93. Ibid., 65.
94. Murray, *Losing Ground,* 23.
95. Melanie Phillips in Frank Field, *Stakeholder Welfare* (London, 1996), 99.
96. Michael Harrington, *The Other America* (New York, 1962), 179.
97. Garrett Hardin and John Baden, eds., *Managing the Commons* (San Francisco, 1977), x. Cf. Rand, *Capitalism,* 162.
98. *New York Times,* November 18, 1996, p. A3.
99. Solomon Fabricant, *The Trend of Government Activity in the United States Since 1900* (New York, 1952), 3, 7.
100. William Petersen in *Commentary,* January 1998, 3.
101. *Financial Times,* June 19, 1996, p. 2.
102. *Welt am Sonntag* (Berlin), December 15, 1996, p. 65.
103. *Statistical Abstract* (1997), Table 506, p. 321. Of this number, 2.9 million worked for the federal government.
104. Scott, *Pursuit of Happiness,* 140.
105. Ibid., 140–1.
106. Epstein, *Takings,* 76.
107. Alfred Marcus in James Q. Wilson, ed., *Politics of Regulation* (New York, 1980), 267–68.
108. Nancie G. Marzulla in Bruce Yandle, ed., *Land Rights* (Lanham, Md., 1995), 17. See also Karol J. Ceplo in ibid., 103–49, and Tom Bethell, *The Noblest Triumph* (New York, 1998), 306.
109. Epstein, *Takings,* 122.
110. Ibid., 123.
111. Atiyah, *Rise and Fall,* 729.
112. Richard Miniter in *Policy Review,* No. 70 (Fall 1994), 40; Tom Bethell in *American Spectator,* August 1994, 16–17.
113. Ceplo in Yandle, ed., *Land Rights,* 103.
114. On this see William Perry Pendley, *It Takes a Hero* (Bellevue, Wash., 1994), and Yandle, ed., *Land Rights, passim.*
115. On the Lucas case see James R. Rinehart and Jeffrey J. Pompe in Yandle, ed., *Land Rights,* 67–101.
116. Erin O'Hara in Yandle, ed., *Land Rights,* 50–1. Cf. David L. Callies in David L. Callies, ed., *Takings* ([Chicago], 1996), 10–11.
117. *New York Times,* May 15, 1995, p. 1.
118. Evan McKenzie, *Privatopia* (New Haven and London, 1994), 11.
119. Ibid., 13–15. See also Mitchell Pacelle in *Wall Street Journal,* September 21, 1994, pp. A1 and A6.
120. McKenzie, *Privatopia,* 25.
121. The most authoritative study of this little-known subject is by Leonard W. Levy, *A License to Steal* (Chapel Hill, N.C., and London, 1996). See further Henry J.

Hyde, *Forfeiting Our Property Rights* (Washington, D.C., 1995). The author, a Republican congressman, is chairman of the House Judiciary Committee.

122. William A. Robson, *Civilisation and the Growth of Law* (New York, 1935), 84–87.
123. *Calero-Toledo v. Pearson Yacht Leasing Co.,* in Hyde, *Forfeiting Our Property Rights,* 71; Levy, *A License to Steal,* 82–85.
124. Roger Pilon in Hyde, *Forfeiting Our Property Rights,* viii.
125. *New York Times,* March 5, 1996, p. A21.
126. Levy, *License to Steal,* 139.
127. Hyde, *Forfeiting Our Property Rights,* 30.
128. Levy, *License,* 144–60, lists many examples of such abuses and the corrupting effect they have on the nation's law enforcement officials.
129. Reich in *Yale Law Journal* 73, No. 5, 734–37.
130. Murray, *Losing Ground,* 14.
131. Usher, *Economic Prerequisites,* 122, 154.
132. *New York Times,* November 18, 1996, p. A3.
133. Jim DuFresne, *Alaska,* 4th ed. (Hawthorn, Australia, 1994), 29, 179.
134. Usher, *Economic Prerequisites,* 155.
135. *Statistical Abstract* (1997), Table 518, p. 334, and Table 520, p. 336.
136. Robert H. Nelson, *Public Lands and Private Rights* (Lanham, Md., 1995), 340–5.
137. Reich in *Yale Law Journal* 73, No. 5, 737.
138. Atiyah, *Rise and Fall,* 580.
139. Lepage, *Pourquoi la proprieté,* 113–14.
140. F. S. Philbrick in *University of Pennsylvania Law Review,* 86, No. 7 (May 1938), 720.
141. Willis J. Nordlund, *The Quest for a Living Wage* (Westport, Conn., 1997), 21–22.
142. Ibid., 26.
143. *New York Times,* July 9, 1996, pp. D1 and D18; Alan Walters in *Financial Times,* April 25, 1997, p. 14.
144. Nordlund, *Quest,* 201–3.
145. Walter Block and Edgar Olsen, eds., *Rent Control: Myths and Realities* (Vancouver, B.C., 1981), xiv.
146. *Boston Globe,* April 28, 1997, p. A4.
147. Nathan Glazer, *Affirmative Discrimination* (New York, 1975), 133.
148. *New York Times,* May 14, 1997, p. A20; also September 24, 1996, p. A16.
149. Glazer, *Affirmative Discrimination,* 136.
150. On this subject, see Bob Zelnick, *Backfire* (Washington, D.C., 1996), 317–38.
151. *New York Times,* September 29, 1994, p. D2.
152. Zelnick, *Backfire,* 320.
153. Ibid., 320.
154. *New York Times,* May 6, 1997, pp. A1 and A27.
155. Ibid.
156. Ibid., February 19, 1998, p. A16.
157. Hugh Davis Graham, *The Civil Rights Era* (New York, 1990), 7.
158. Glazer, *Affirmative Discrimination,* 77.
159. Emphasis added.
160. Jeremy Rabkin in Wilson, ed., *Politics of Regulation,* 307.
161. Graham, *Civil Rights Era,* 421.
162. Steven M. Cahn, ed., *Affirmative Action and the University* (Philadelphia, 1993), 1.
163. Zelnick, *Backfire,* 29.
164. *The Gallup Poll: Public Opinion, 1972–1977,* II (Wilmington, Del., 1978), pp. 1057–59.
165. Greenwalt, *Discrimination,* 92.
166. Ibid., 102, 104.
167. Graham, *Civil Rights Era,* 244ff.
168. Glazer, *Affirmative Discrimination,* 49.

169. Graham, *Civil Rights Era,* 250.
170. David G. Savage in *Los Angeles Times,* February 22, 1995, pp. A1 and A8.
171. Murray, *Losing Ground,* 94; Graham, *Civil Rights Era,* 383–84.
172. Zelnick, *Backfire,* 74.
173. Graham, *Civil Rights Era,* 387.
174. Glazer, *Affirmative Discrimination,* 52.
175. *New York Times,* April 30, 1997, pp. A1 and A20.
176. Jeffrie G. Murphy in Steven M. Cahn, ed., *Affirmative Action and the University* (Philadelphia, 1993), 168.
177. Stephen H. Balch and Peter N. Warren in *Chronicle of Higher Education,* June 21, 1996, p. A44; also in National Association of Scholars, *Newsletter: Update 7,* No. 3 (1996), 2–3.
178. Richard A. Epstein, *Forbidden Grounds* (Cambridge, Mass., 1992), 3–4.
179. Cited by Jonathan Rauch in *New Republic,* June 23, 1997, 26.
180. John D. Millett, *Financing Higher Education in the United States* (New York, 1952), 38.
181. George Roche, *The Fall of the Ivory Tower* (Washington, D.C., 1994), 30.
182. Millet, *Financing Higher Education,* 38–39.
183. Chester E. Finn, Jr., *Scholars, Dollars, and Bureaucrats* (Washington, D.C., 1978), 10.
184. Roche, *Fall,* 50.
185. The subject is treated at length, and with very pessimistic conclusions, by Roche in his *Fall of the Ivory Tower.* See also Dinesh D'Souza, *Illiberal Education: The Politics of Race and Sex on the Campus* (New York, 1991).
186. Finn, *Scholars,* 140.
187. Ibid., 14.
188. Richard M. Freeland, *Academia's Golden Age* (New York and Oxford, 1992), 384.
189. Philip G. Altbach and D. Bruce Johnstone, *The Funding of Higher Education* (New York and London, 1993), 74.
190. *New York Times,* August 21, 1996, p. B7.
191. Ibid., July 3, 1996, p. A23.
192. Ibid., January 6, 1972, p. A36.
193. Ibid., July 16, 1997, p. A19; *Boston Sunday Globe,* July 27, 1997, p. A8.
194. Ralph A. Rossum, *Reverse Discrimination* (New York, 1980), 1.
195. Thomas Sowell, *Civil Rights: Rhetoric or Reality?* (New York, 1984), 23.
196. David W. Murray in *Academic Questions* 9, No. 3 (Summer 1996), 10–17.
197. *New York Times,* January 14, 1998, p. C27.
198. John H. Bunzell in *Wall Street Journal,* February 1, 1988, p. A26.
199. Glazer, *Affirmative Discrimination,* 84; Graham, *Civil Rights Era,* 565.
200. Glazer, *Affirmative Discrimination,* 109.
201. Alan Lupo, *Boston Sunday Globe,* September 10, 1995, "City Weekly," pp. 2, 4; David Warsh in ibid., September 8, 1996, p. E1.
202. *Harvard University Gazette,* April 10, 1997, 1 and 4.
203. Fareed Zakaria in *Foreign Affairs,* November–December 1997, 22–43.
204. Michael Tanner, *The End of Welfare* (Washington, D.C., 1996), 69.
205. Ibid., 70.

PORTENTS

1. *Frankfurter Allgemeine Zeitung,* December 24, 1976.
2. *The Collected Works of Walter Bagehot,* IV (Cambridge, Mass., 1968), 94.
3. James Fitzjames Stephen, *Liberty, Equality, Fraternity* (Cambridge, 1967), 174–75.

4. Douglass C. North and Robert Paul Thomas, *The Rise of the Western World* (Cambridge, 1973); David Landes, *The Wealth and Poverty of Nations* (New York, 1998); Tom Bethell, *The Noblest Triumph* (New York, 1998).
5. Bryan T. Johnson, Kim R. Holmes, and Melanie Kirkpatrick, eds., *1998 Index of Economic Freedom* (Washington, D.C., 1998).
6. See above, p. 281.
7. F. A. Hayek, *The Road to Serfdom* (London, 1976), 90.
8. Cited by Richard Miniter in *Policy Review,* No. 70 (1994), 45–46.
9. Roger E. Meiners in Bruce Yandle, ed., *Land Rights: The 1990's Property Rights Rebellion* (Lanham, Md., 1995), 272.
10. Jan Herin in *Financial Times,* February 7, 1997, p. 10.
11. Roscoe Pound in *Yale Law Journal* 18, No. 7 (1909), 467.
12. In a dissenting opinion of 1927, cited in F. A. Hayek, *The Constitution of Liberty* (Chicago, 1960), 253. Emphasis added.
13. F. A. Hayek in *Contemporary Review* 153 (April 1938), 437–38.
14. Alexis de Tocqueville, *Democracy in America,* II (Cambridge, 1862), 391 (Book Four, Chapter vi).
15. Ibid.
16. Ibid., 392–93.

INDEX